Airlift

For Ann

Airlift

A History of Military Air Transport

David W. Wragg

PRESIDIO ★ PRESS

Contents

Acknowledgements

I should like to thank those who assisted in the research
and preparation of material used in this book, and in
particular those who assisted in the collection of the
illustrations, including:
British Aerospace
British Airways
Central Office of Information
Dornier
Imperial War Museum
Lockheed
McDonnell Douglas
Messerschmitt-Bolkow-Blohm
Novosti
Royal Air Force Museum
Sikorsky

Chapter One
A New Dimension

The response to the first flights by the Wright brothers on 17th December, 1903, varied, regardless of whether one is considering the reactions of civilians or of military men. It did take some time before the achievements of the brothers became widely accepted, with the truth not being fully understood or appreciated in Europe until after the demonstration flights of 1908. In the United States, the War Department had refused to believe in the success of the Wright brothers, and no doubt its attitude was influenced by having, in that same year, 1903, had its fingers badly burnt through providing $50,000 financial support for the unsuccessful rival of the Wrights, Samuel Pierpoint Langley. Perhaps there was also something symbolic in this, since Langley failed for a variety of reasons, but mainly because he possessed what has become known as the "chauffeur mentality", that is, he failed to appreciate the three dimensional nature of flight, and this same inability, in rather different ways, would be the undoing of many military commanders in the decades ahead.

The British were, for once, far more open minded. A British Army officer, Colonel J. E. Capper, later Superintendent of what was to be first the Government Aircraft Factory and then the Royal Aircraft Factory, at Farnborough in Hampshire, was sufficiently impressed after meeting the brothers during 1905, when he was visiting the United States, to write to the War Office in London:

> "I wish to invite very special attention to the wonderful advance in aviation made by the brothers Wright. I have every confidence in their uprightness, and in the correctness of their statements. It is a fact that they have flown and operated personally a flying machine for a distance of over three miles, at a speed of 35 mph."

Unfortunately, negotiations with the War Office were unsuccessful. The British would not buy without first seeing a demonstration, and the Wrights, even at this time showing the first signs of their growing and ultimately obsessive concern for their patents, would not show their aircraft to other experts without first receiving an order.

Initially, the military viewed the aeroplane as an extension of their experience with the balloon and the man-lifting kite, as purely an instrument for reconnaissance. Nevertheless, from this cautious and uninspiring beginning, other developments flowed, and it was not long before the value of the aeroplane as a message carrier became apparent, while other more warlike experiments were also undertaken well before the outbreak of World War I, the 'Great War', which many like to believe was solely to blame for corrupting the innocence of the new invention. Perhaps the limited performance of the early flying machines was the main reason for such a limited perception of their possibilities, since the idea of the use of flying machines of one kind and another for transport had a long history. As early as 1670, a Jesuit priest, Father Francesco de Lana de Terzi, drew an aerial ship, to be kept aloft by four copper spheres "empty of air". Within a few years of the invention of the hot air balloon by the Montgolfier brothers in 1783, a print appeared depicting large hot air balloons, each capable of carrying 3,000 men, to carry Napoleon's armies, with their horses and field artillery, across the English Channel for an invasion of England. Balloons carried mail from Paris during 1870 and 1871, while the city was besieged by Prussian forces. On a different, but ultimately related area of development, the first parachute descent had been as early as 1797, by André Joseph Garnerin.

While many of these early predictions can be largely discounted because they preceded the invention of the aeroplane, ideas were not too long in coming during the years before World War I. A German military expert, Rudolf Martin, in 1908 suggested the construction of a fleet of 50,000 Wright 'B' biplanes to carry a force of 100,000 men for the invasion of England. The invasion force was to land in the south-east, in Kent. This was a year before the Frenchman, Louis Blériot, made the first flight across the English Channel.

In spite of such bright ideas, the Germans made little or no use of aircraft for transport purposes during World War I, except for the delivery of despatches.

One of the more forward-looking ideas did, nevertheless, come during the war years. An American officer, Colonel, later to be Brigadier-General, William "Billy" Mitchell, commanding officer of the Air Service, United States First Army in France, proposed that an infantry division should be parachuted to seize the city of Metz. The operation was proposed for 1919, and, of course, the collapse of German resistance and the Armistice intervened well before the plan could be put into action. Whether or not the parachuting of a brigade of infantry, suggesting a force of as many as 20,000 men, would have been practical in 1919 is open to question, but a limited operation might have had a chance of success, since the parachute was well known, but only in very limited service use, mainly for balloon or airship crews, since World War I commanders, with a complete lack of humanity and even less understanding of human nature, believed that the issue of parachutes would encourage pilots to abandon their aircraft! In fact, experience since, with parachutes and ejector seats, has indicated exactly the opposite, because such means of escape give confidence to the aircrew.

There were a few practical transport operations by military aircraft during World War I, and on two occasions, the Royal Flying Corps and its successor, the Royal Air Force, used aircraft to supply ground forces cut off by enemy forces. The operations were of limited success, hindered by the absence of specialised transport aircraft and the poor performance of the aircraft used.

During the Mesopotamian Campaign of 1916, nine small biplanes of the Royal Flying Corps made 140 sorties within six days to sustain a beleaguered British garrison, although success eluded them. Rather more successful was the air supply operation mounted to save Belgian and French troops, cut off in the Houthulst Forest during October, 1918. The Royal Air Force, just six months old at this time, was asked to drop supplies to the Allied troops, and two squadrons were assigned to the task; No.82 Army Co-operation Squadron with Armstrong-Whitworth FK.8 biplanes and No.218 Squadron with Airco D.H.9 bomber biplanes. This, the first successful aerial supply mission in history, was mounted in the face of considerable practical problems. Sandbags were filled with soil and rations, to provide a crude container weighing about 18 lbs, which would include eight small ration packs including such delicacies as 'bully' beef, stew, jam, and ships' biscuits or 'hard tack'. Starting on 1st October and flying until 4th October, the two squadrons mounted a total of almost 200 sorties, and dropped 1,220 sandbags plus sixty boxes of ammunition, all of which had to be manhandled over

Above: The brilliant Russian designer, Igor Sikorsky, experimented with large transport aircraft in the years immediately before World War I, although his famous "Ilya Mourametz," meaning 'The Giant', actually entered service as a bomber. This is the earlier "Bolshoi", or 'Grand'.

Right: Airborne assault by hot air balloon. An artist's idea of a means of airlifting Napoleon's Army across the English Channel.

the sides of the aircraft by the observers, and aircraft sometimes had to make as many as six runs over the dropping zone before a full load could be supplied. Surprisingly in view of what was to happen twenty-five years and more later, at Stalingrad and at Arnhem, only one aircraft, a D.H.9, was lost. This operation ensured that the Belgians and French could hold out until relieved by advancing ground forces.

The lack of suitable aircraft for transport work during World War I owes more to the lack of appreciation at higher levels of the varied uses to which an aircraft could be put, than to the technology of the day, although that was, of course, limited. In Russia, that talented designer, Igor Sikorsky, had built two outstanding aeroplanes before the outbreak of war. The aircraft were his *Bolschoi* or 'Grand' of 1913, and, even more impressive, the *Ilya Mourametz* or 'Giant' of 1914, a four-engined aeroplane intended as an airliner and actually described at the time of its first flights as an "airbus" by one commentator. The *Ilya Mourametz* incorporated such advanced features for the day as an enclosed flight deck, but the outbreak of war meant that this promising design entered production as a bomber, with an initial batch of sixty being ordered, and was one of the first bomber aircraft to be equipped with a tail-gun.

Using the new toy

If the small Airco bomber biplanes were unsatisfactory for air supply operations in wartime, they also had their limitations as transport aircraft. Yet, many of the first airline flights in Europe, and some of those in Australia and North America as well, were by war-surplus Airco D.H.4a and D.H.9 bombers, offering accommodation for just two passengers, or, if operating as an air ambulance, for a single stretcher case, while cruising at no more than 100 mph and possessing a range of under 400 miles. Even so, the potential of the aeroplane for transport use, whether civil or military, was recognised by many, and for the much reduced post-war armed forces of the democratic countries, the aeroplane offered the opportunity of reducing the numbers of troops required to effectively garrison the more troublesome and remote areas. The high cost of using aeroplanes was more than countered by the ability to move small numbers of troops around, sometimes being deployed on their own, on other occasions being used to reinforce native levies. In effect, the transport aeroplane became an early example of the "force multiplier", increasing the productivity of the troops available.

The first use of transport aircraft in what may be regarded as the colonial policing role, came in 1920, when British forces in the Somaliland Protectorate were facing Dervish terrorists led by Sayid Muhammed, and the local administrator asked for reinforcements. The British Government despatched thirteen Airco D.H.9 biplane bombers aboard the Royal Navy's seaplane carrier, HMS *Ark Royal,* and on arrival these Royal Air Force aircraft were used primarily as bombers, but one was kept in reserve as an air ambulance after its arrival in Berber from Egypt.

A far more suitable aircraft was not to be long in

Successor to the RAF's Vickers Vernon was the Vickers Victoria, of similar appearance. One of No. 70 Squadron's aircraft, 'Thunderer', poses with a group of admiring Arabs.

Refuelling from 50 gallon drums was a time-consuming and tiresome task; No. 70 Squadron's Victorias at Hinaidi, again.

coming, however, and a year or so after the Somaliland Campaign, the Royal Air Force received its first Vickers Vernon troop carriers. The Vernon was a transport version of the World War I Vickers Vimy heavy bomber, the aircraft used by Alcock and Brown for the first non-stop trans-Atlantic flight by aeroplane in 1919. A twin-engined biplane, the Vernon conversion of the Vimy was

A Victoria loading native troops for rapid deployment during the late 1920s.

far more extensive, and for its time, satisfactory, than many of the later conversions of World War II bombers, and like them, it was used by both commercial and military transport operators; although the former preferred to describe the aeroplane as the 'Vimy Commercial'. A new, and rather bulbous, fuselage provided accommodation for up to ten passengers or for four stretcher cases plus two attendants. Most of the Vernons were deployed in Iraq, in what were often described as 'bomber transport' squadrons. One of their routine tasks was the operation of a fortnightly airmail service across the deserts from Cairo to Baghdad, with the then main RAF base in the Middle East, at

Heliopolis, being the eastern terminal for this service. Heliopolis had the advantage of being situated conveniently for operations in Arabia, India and Africa, enabling the RAF to make the best use of relatively small numbers of aircraft. Before long, an up-rated version of the original Vernon, the Vernon II, was introduced, replacing the Rolls-Royce Eagle engines of the original with the more powerful Napier Lion, to provide improved performance, especially when operating out of hot and high airfields.

The Napier Lion was also used on the Vernon's successor, the Vickers Victoria, the transport development of the Vickers Virginia bomber. Two squadrons of Victorias were based in Iraq from 1926 onwards, but at the new RAF base at Hinaidi. Assigned to numbers 70 and 216 squadrons, the Victorias could carry up to twenty passengers apiece, marking a significant improvement in the RAF's airlift capability in the Middle East, even though the aircraft did not, to the casual observer, differ too much in appearance from the Vernons which they replaced! By way of a contrast, the main airlift capability in the United Kingdom consisted of four Avro Andovers, single-engined transport aircraft developed from the Avro Aldershot bomber and which had originally been conceived as airmail carriers, but in fact served primarily on air-ambulance duties.

The Royal Air Force's growing transport capability was not put to the test when Mustafa Kemel was active in Turkey and the Lebanon; this particular problem was handled by carrier-borne aircraft of the Fleet Air Arm, at that time part of the Royal Air Force. An opportunity to show just what could be done was not too long in coming, however, and during unrest in northern Iraq during 1922, the RAF evacuated Iraqi troops from Salaimanaya in September of that year. This was followed in early 1923

Just as the Vernon evolved from the Vimy, and the G-2 from the ANT-6, the Clive was a transport development of the Handley Page Hinaidi all-metal bomber. Most of these aircraft saw service with RAF units in India.

by the airlift of almost 500 troops in Vernon transports to Kirkuk, an exercise which had to be repeated a year later.

A more demanding role came in Afghanistan during 1928, after King Amanullah's efforts at Westernisation and secularisation had resulted in a tribal revolt by the Shinwari. The revolt became sufficiently serious by December, that the British ambassador in Kabul, Sir Francis Humphreys, asked for the evacuation of the embassy staff. The Royal Air Force in India could only offer D.H.9s or Westland Wapitis, a so-called general-purpose aircraft which was starting to replace the D.H.9s and which was also too small to be of any practical transport use. Eventually, eight Vickers Victorias were

Passengers and crew before take-off on one of the RAF's fortnightly airmail flights from Hinaidi to Egypt, 1926.

sent from Iraq to Afghanistan, and operated from 23rd December, 1928, until mid-February, 1929, carrying almost 600 men, women and children out of Afghanistan, most of whom were not British subjects but were other foreigners resident in Kabul who had sought places on the airlift, and finally the RAF evacuated King Amanullah himself! The operation required eighty-four flights or sorties, and while this may seem to be few, it should be borne in mind that the aircraft had first flown a 2,800 mile positioning flight from Hinaidi to India, and then operated over high mountains into Kabul itself, seldom carrying anything approaching a full load in what was, for the day, a demanding task for aircraft and aircrew alike.

It would seem that one positive result of this operation was the decision to strengthen the transport capability of the RAF in India, introducing the Handley Page Clive all-metal transport, serving with the RAF at Lahore. The Clive was another close relative of the bomber, being developed from the Handley Page Hinaidi all-metal bomber. In due course, the Victorias were also up-dated, being replaced by the Vickers Valentia, often known as the Victoria Mk IV, with Bristol Siddeley Pegasus engines. These aircraft were expected to possess genuine dual bomber-transport capability.

Given the nature of the RAF's operations between the two world wars, it was hardly surprising that the Royal Air Force Tournament, or display, at Hendon in 1927, had featured the mock evacuation of a beleaguered desert garrison!

Other, later instances of RAF and Army operations included combined British and Iraqi operations against Sheik Mahmud at Barzan, close to the borders with Turkey and Iran, in northern Iraq in 1932. Westland Wapiti general-purpose biplanes dropped leaflets, while Vickers Victorias from Hinaidi and Heliopolis operated first as ambulance aircraft and then later dropped supplies to Iraqi and British troops pursuing Mahmud's men in the mountains, which were still covered with snow during March, 1932, and in considerable need of the blankets and greatcoats dropped from the air. A supply service was also maintained between Hinaidi and the Army's advance base at Erbil, close to the rebel stronghold. During the campaign, in spite of difficult flying conditions and inhospitable terrain, just one aircraft, a Wapiti, was lost, but its crew were saved.

The RAF's involvement with airmail was limited, and eventually even the service in the Middle East was taken over by Imperial Airways as the airline pushed its routes eastwards, through Iraq, then on to India, and eventually

Vickers Victoria of No. 70 Squadron in the air over Iraq.

to Australia. The United States Army Air Corps, on the other hand, seems to have been regarded at first as the first choice for airmail services by the US Post Office, and then later as a back-up service in the event of any disagreement with the airlines. Many of the early domestic airmail services within the United States during the early 1920s were handled by the USAAC's aircraft, but these were eventually transferred to the new airlines following a decision in 1925 by Congress to put the services out to commercial tender, with the routes and the airmail contracts providing the basis for many of today's leading airlines, including TWA and United and, on overseas routes, Pan Am. A dispute between the US Post Office and the airlines in 1934 resulted in the United States Army Air Service, as it had become in its long fight to break away from Army control, having to resume airmail flights at short notice after the airmail contracts were cancelled. Operating without suitable aircraft and at night, as well as often in very poor weather, keeping to a rigorous schedule, the Army Air Service suffered nine fatal accidents during the first three weeks of airmail operations, which started on 19th February. Fortunately, the airlines resumed airmail operations before too long.

Such operations apart, the Royal Air Force and the United States Army Air Corps, did much during the inter-war years to prepare the way for subsequent commercial airline operations, while also proving the increasing ability of the aeroplane to sustain long flights, often over water or inhospitable terrain. For the British, there was the need to bring together a vast sprawling Empire; for the Americans, the priority was to cover first the continental United States, and then to reach Hawaii, at that time not one of the states of the union, but nevertheless, a major naval base with a large army garrison as well.

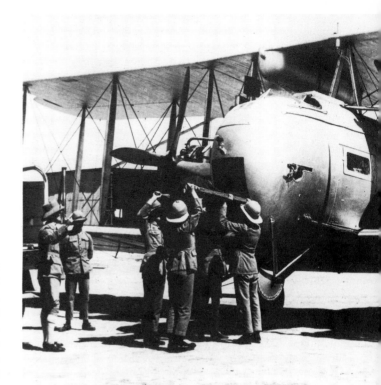

The Victorias also operated as flying ambulances, loading stretcher cases through the nose.

Russian success in their trials with paratroops soon led to demonstrations of their ability; paratroops jump from Tupolev G-2 transports at an air display in 1935.

The relative weakness of the American aircraft manufacturers at this time can be judged from the fact that a USAAC non-stop flight over the 2,500 mile distance between New York and San Diego, the Californian naval base, was accomplished using a Fokker T-2, as the USAAC designated the Fokker F.IV (although the aircraft had been built in the United States) which took twenty-six hours, fifty minutes. An endurance record of more than thirty-seven hours, using basic in-flight refuelling, used two D.H.4s! These flights were notable achievements, nevertheless, and took place during May and August, 1923, respectively. An indication of the growing capability of American designers and manufacturers was not too long in coming, with the USAAC using four Douglas World Cruiser biplanes for the first round-the-world flight, which took from 4th April, 1924, to 29th September, and meant that the aircraft covered 26,000 miles, from Seattle to Seattle, a city more usually associated with another major American aircraft manufacturer! Fokker tri-motors were used when, on 28th June, 1928, the USAAC flew more than 2,400 miles non-stop from Oakland, in California, to Hawaii, taking almost twenty-six hours, and again, in 1929, when, using in-flight refuelling, an endurance record of 151 hours was set between 1st and 7th January, with a crew of four men remaining airborne above San Francisco. Not to be left out, the United States Navy had already made some impressive long distance flights of its own. In 1919, the USN had made the first trans-Atlantic aeroplane flights using a Curtiss NC-4, although this had not flown non-stop and had taken the easier southern route through the Azores. On 31st August, 1925, a Naval Aircraft Factory PN-9 flying-boat left San Francisco to fly to Hawaii, covering 1,840 miles before landing in the sea after running out of fuel, and eventually reaching its destination with the wing fabric being used as a makeshift sail!

The Royal Air Force sent four Supermarine Southampton flying-boats on a twelve month tour of the Far East, with each aircraft covering some 27,000 miles from October, 1927, to December, 1928, while one of the RAF's new Short Singapore flying-boats was borrowed by Sir Alan Cobham for a flight around Africa, departing from England on 17th November, 1927, with the express intention of finding suitable landing places for the Royal Air Force and Imperial Airways, following an earlier flight to Australia in which he had used a variety of aircraft, although for most of the time he had used a de Havilland D.H.50 landplane fitted with floats.

Such flights had a serious purpose, since landing sites had to be found and surveyed, and then obstructions had to be cleared and arrangements made for fuel, and, if possible, spares, and even for hotels for passengers on long flights. Even if airfields could be found, operations could not be taken for granted, given the poor reliability of the aeroplane and the vulnerability of frail machines and their undercarriages to damage. Even the flying-boat was not always an answer, limiting flight to routes along the coast or to good inland lakes or rivers which would not be too fast flowing, nor too shallow. The flying-boat, in the words of one American pioneer carried "its airfield on its bottom", but had difficulty in "unsticking" if the water was too smooth, and problems, especially with porpoising, if the water was too rough. Smooth, clear,

water in the Mediterranean or parts of the Pacific could also be deceptive, leading pilots to level out too soon or too late, either was a recipe for disaster. Amphibians helped, and the RAF found these useful in the Middle East, but these were limited in size compared to the flying-boat as undercarriage designers struggled to keep pace with the ambitions of aircraft designers, and amphibians also tended to be slower than landplanes. Facilities which today would be taken for granted were lacking. Air traffic control was non-existent. Ground handling and support facilities were primitive in the extreme, and fuel often had to be poured from four gallon cans into aircraft tanks. Larger drums could be used, if hoists could be found and native labour was available, but it was not unknown for aircrew, including senior NCOs and officers, to have to do the job themselves when away from a main base and often working in desert or jungle heat. All this, for aircraft with a load of no more than twenty people! Concepts such as in-flight refuelling were a novelty, and in any case, from where would the tanker aircraft operate?

Transport aircraft designs, and especially those for commercial use, were starting to break away from the limitations imposed by the bomber. As early as 1913, the German Professor Hugo Junkers had built his F.13, a single-engined low-wing monoplane with a cantilever wing and corrugated all-metal construction, paving the way for the later development of his Ju.52, one of the first significant military transport aircraft. The F.13 offered little in the way of a step forward in speed or range, but it did offer the prospect in the aircraft which followed of better accommodation for the power available. The Fokker T-2 was a genuine transport aircraft, known to its manufacturer as the F.IV, and when Fokker started building its F.VII tri-motor, it was doing so in competition with companies such as Stout, which was soon acquired by Ford, and Stinson, as well as later from Junkers. American and European designers favoured either single-engined or tri-motor configurations, partly because the trimotor offered distinct advantages over the twin-engined aircraft, but without the extra strain on still primitive cantilever monoplane wing design of four engines. The British, who tended to stick to biplanes for transport operations, had greater flexibility in the number of engines used, although by chance, they too provided many tri-motors.

These difficulties, and those of money, meant that the transport aeroplane remained a luxury for many air forces and armies during the 1920s, and through into the 1930s for all but a few. Even the early years of World War II were not to bring a sudden expansion of air transport units to most air forces, although by this time there were other reasons for this. Nevertheless, there was a growing improvement in capability and a growing appreciation of what could be done, even if the attitudes of governments and defence planners were to lag behind.

Preparing for war

Credit for the pioneering work in the movement and supply or re-supply of troops by air belongs to the Royal Air Force and the British Army, but the distinction of conducting the pioneering work on the concept of the airborne assault belongs to the Soviet Union, which developed the technique and demonstrated its practicality during the 1930s. No doubt the freedom to undertake this work stemmed from the ability of a totalitarian state to ignore the economic and social consequences of massive arms expenditure, while the speed of redeployment of troops made possible by the use of airborne forces must have been attractive for a country of vast distances, poor roads and railways, and which was still anxious over the possibility of a counter-revolutionary uprising or invasion, so soon after the Revolution. As a totalitarian state, the Russians managed the incredible by obtaining many of the designs produced by Andrei Tupolev while he was a political prisoner! To be fair, Tupolev was able to do this because of the efforts of his assistant, Petlyakov. At the same time, one should not overlook the ability of Russian aviators and designers to develop new techniques, both during the Tzarist and Soviet periods, an ability which is the more surprising because of the general backwardness of much of Russian industry. Not only did the Russians prove that paratroops were more than just a possibility, they also developed the concept of the troop-carrying glider.

The first significant Soviet transport aircraft were developed, as were their British counterparts, from heavy bombers. This was the G-1, a transport version of Tupolev's ANT-4 twin-engined bomber, which entered service with the VVS, *Voenno-Vozdushnye Sily,* or Army Aviation Forces, during the late 1920s. The bombing and transport elements of the VVS were largely concerned with providing close support for the massive Red Army, as one would expect, but the role of the transport units was soon extended to include exercises in which paratroops were dropped, initially in battalion strength, but rising to brigade strength by 1932. The introduction of the ANT-4's successor, the massive ANT-6 four-engined bomber, during the early 1930s once again offered the chance of providing a transport variant, the G-2, which proved to offer a significant gain in performance compared to the earlier aircraft. While experiments and exercises with paratroops continued, the G-2 was frequently used to demonstrate the ability of the VVS to airlift large numbers of troops. During the summer of 1935, 2,500 men were airlifted during exercises near the Ukrainian city of Kiev, with light tanks and artillery actually carried between the long fixed undercarriage legs of the G-2 transports. Even more noteworthy was the movement, during February 1936, of a complete brigade from Moscow to Vladivostock, across Russia in the midst of winter. Russian pride in their achievement, and their confidence in their ability in making it work whenever it was required, even extended to providing a demonstration later in 1936 for the benefit of foreign observers, when a force of 1,500 men, with machine-guns and light artillery as well as other equipment, was parachuted. Amongst the British observers was General Wavell, who subsequently

Russian paratroops scramble out of a Tupolev G-2, 1936.

reported to the War Office in London that if "he had not witnessed it, he would not have believed such an operation possible". In spite of such a report by the man who was to become one of the great generals of World War II, no interest was taken in the concept of paratroop forces by the War Office, in complete contrast to the situation in Nazi Germany, where senior officers had acquired an understanding of the potential of airborne forces even before Hitler came to power, missing no opportunity to learn from the Russians.

Oleg Antonov had also found time to work on gliders, and as early as 1932, B. Borodin had flown an Antonov-designed glider for four hours whilst carrying two passengers.

The transport, assault or troop-carrying glider, differs substantially from the more familiar sports glider. One has to forget completely the image of the glider as a frail, lightweight, machine, and still less consider it to be a graceful and aero-dynamically near perfect form. The most significant difference between conventional gliders and those used for military purposes lies in the vastly higher wing-loading, which means that soaring flight is impossible and the glider cannot remain airborne for long after discarding its tow. It is essential that the troop-carrying glider is towed to its destination and that the tow is only released for the glider to make its landing descent. This may, at first, seem to be a disadvantage, but the advantages of the glider were many. Amongst the most obvious of the advantages, at least during the early days of World War II, was the sense of alarm conferred by the silent arrival of the glider, which, depending on size, could carry a force as large as company size, which was ready to fight as a unit as soon as it landed, rather than having to waste precious minutes in assembly as a paratroop force needed to do. Nor were glider-landed troops faced with the dangerous period of having to disentangle themselves from parachute harness and find weapons containers. Gliders were cheap to construct, often made little demand on strategic materials, and could easily double the number of men which a troop transport tug aircraft could carry, while also enabling

other aircraft, such as bombers, but even including some fighters, to play a part in transporting troops through acting as tugs, thus reducing the number of pure transport aircraft needed. Glider pilots, although well-trained, especially in the case of the British Army's Glider Pilot Regiment, were usually cheaper to train than the pilots of powered aircraft, and could also act as a reserve force for the assault troops after landing. Glider-landed troops, sometimes also known as air-landed troops, required less specialised training than did paratroops, Then too, given the technology of the day, gliders were often the only reliable, and even the only practical means of supplying an attacking force from the air with wheeled vehicles; the larger gliders often carried light tanks, small vehicles, artillery pieces, and even tractors or earth-moving equipment so that engineers could construct landing strips.

So impressed with the glider were the Russians, that many of their plans were extremely ambitious. In 1934, Lev Pavlovich Malinovski, who was in charge of the Scientific and Technical Administration of the Civilian Air Fleet, or *Grazhdanskiy Vozdushniy Flot*, the predecessor of *Aeroflot,* the Soviet airline, advocated the construction of cheap, powered gliders, easy to produce and cheap to operate, as a means of overcoming transport difficulties in remote areas of Russia. He estimated that a glider, once airborne, could carry a load of one ton using an engine of just 100 hp, and sustain flight over long distances with minimal fuel consumption. Such a machine would probably also have had to rely on favourable weather conditions as well!

On a more practical basis, a ten-seater, unpowered glider prototype led to an eighteen-seat glider, the G-31, which was available to the Soviet armed forces during the late 1930s. This so impressed the *Luftwaffe* Director General of Equipment, the former World War I fighter ace, General Ernst Udet, that it can only be regarded as having played a major part in influencing subsequent events. These were not the only gliders of the day, and others produced in Russia during the 1930s included the five-passenger Groshev G-4 of 1934, and in 1939,

The mainstay of the Italian aerial operations in North Africa and the Red Sea area during the late 1930s were the ubiquitous bomber-transport, including the Siai-Marchetti S.M.79, taxying-in after landing at an airfield in Abyssinia, or Ethiopia.

An early example of the Siai-Marchetti S.M.81, in 1935.

Antonov's eight-passenger A-7.

The other *Luftwaffe* general of particular significance to the story of the development of assault by paratroop and glider-borne forces was another former World War I ace, General Kurt Student. In fact the two senior officers viewed the glider in slightly different ways, with Udet seeing the glider as a "Trojan horse", simply as a silent means of transport, while Student favoured the concept of a fighting glider, and alone amongst all of the many air forces which used the glider in due course, the *Luftwaffe* fitted all gliders with machine guns. An enthusiastic admirer of Soviet work on paratroop and airborne forces, Student had observed and been aware of many of the Soviet exercises and experiments during the 1920s and 1930s, and he was a member of the *Luftwaffe* from its official creation in 1935. His first visits to the Soviet Union had been during the early 1920s as a captain in the Weimar Republic German Army. In contrast to British and American practice, German paratroops were part of the *Luftwaffe* rather than the German Army, and eventually there were no less than ten divisions of paratroops or *Fallschirmjäger,* in the *Luftwaffe,* with General Student as *Inspekteur der Fallschirm und Luftlandetroppen* — Inspector of Parachute and Air-landed troops — from 1st January, 1939.

In some respects, the German practice could be compared with that of the Royal Navy and the United States Navy in having the Royal Marines and the United States Marine Corps under overall naval control.

While these developments were leading directly to the strategies of World War II, the two most significant transport aircraft of the coming conflict had also appeared during the 1930s, the Junkers Ju.52/3m and the Douglas C-47. Although appearing within a few years of each other, the two aircraft were some distance apart in concept. The Junkers was a design in the mould of many aircraft of the late 1920s and early 1930s, perhaps more rugged than most, but with three engines and a fuselage and wings which imparted an air of utility, while the DC-3, the commercial version of the C-47, was far more in keeping with the concept of the modern airliner, with a sleek rounded fuselage, retractable undercarriage, and it generally set the classic appearance of all airliners until the advent of the jet aeroplane.

Usually considered as a trimotor, the Junkers design had first appeared as a single-engined aircraft. In common with many aircraft enjoying a long production period, the Ju.52/3m employed several different powerplants after it first flew in 1932. Early versions used 600 hp BMW radial engines, but later aircraft used 725 hp hp or 830 hp BMW engines, with others using 750 hp ENMASA Beta engines, 710 hp Wright Cyclones, or even the diesel Junkers Jumo 5 and 206. Most of the Wright-powered aircraft were built in France or Spain after the end of World War II, with some 400 aircraft being built in France under the designation of AAC-1, and many of these saw service in French Indo-China, while production of the aircraft in Spain by CASA continued into the 1970s, under the designation T.2b. Of course, most Ju.52/3ms were built in Germany, with Junkers producing 4,845 aircraft. The Ju.52/3m could carry up to eighteen passengers, although because of the equipment required by paratroops, in the paratrooping role it was usual to carry just thirteen parachutists at a time. At one stage, the Ju.52/3m accounted for 75 per cent of the fleet of the German airline, *Luft Hansa,* but half of the pre-1936 production were delivered as bombers, being the first heavy bomber of the new *Luftwaffe* with some remaining in service as bombers even after the outbreak of war in 1939, due to the failure of a planned successor, the Dornier Do.11.

Known to German paratroops during World War II as *Auntie Ju*, or the 'Iron Auntie', most of the wartime Ju.52/3ms were allocated to the training role, and major airborne operations or re-supply operations such as that at Stalingrad, could only be met at the cost of the bomber aircrew training programme. Losses, and with transport aircraft this often meant aircrew losses as well as aircraft losses, meant that invaluable qualified flying instructors were lost as well. The bomber origins of the *Luftwaffe's* Ju.52/3ms could be seen in the presence, even in transport versions, of a dorsal turret with a 13mm machine gun, although to be fair, and this was another way in which the aircraft showed its age, the "turret" was more of an open cockpit. Two 7.92mm MG15 machine guns were supposed to be fired by the occupants through the aft cabin windows if the aircraft came under attack by fighters. Yet in spite of its bomber origins, the Ju.52/3m had an excellent short take-off performance, aided by extensive flaps which effectively provided a double wing effect on the trailing edge, while the construction was robust, and the fixed undercarriage could be equipped with skis or floats. The maximum speed was 180 mph, but cruising speeds were more often in the region of 140 mph, and even slower if towing a glider.

By comparison, the C-47 was sleek, obviously a transport, and its design included a swept leading edge to the wing and a retractable undercarriage, although the bottom half of the wheels could still be seen after retraction! The C-47, or in civilian guise, the DC-3, was a development from two earlier designs, the DC-1, or 'Douglas Commercial 1', of which only one was built to a specification issued by Transcontinental and Western Air, the predecessor of today's Trans World Airlines. The DC-1 first flew in 1933, and a year later, a larger development, the DC-2, first flew. The DC-2 was powered by two 710 hp Wright Cyclone radial engines and was able to carry fourteen passengers at a maximum speed of 180 mph and over distances up to 350 miles. Although eclipsed by the success of the later DC-3, the DC-2 was a success in its own right, and included amongst its operators airlines such as KLM, Swissair and TWA, and after the outbreak of World War II, a small number even found their way into RAF service, while the

United States Army Air Service also had small numbers of this aircraft.

Just as often known by its USAAF designation of C-47 as by its civilian designation of DC-3, the DC-3 was an enlarged version of the DC-2, but retained the same basic shape. Military utility meant that the aircraft did not endear itself to all of the Allied servicemen who came into contact with it, although for the paratroops it was undoubtedly a marked improvement over the bombers which they had been using. Yet, when the DC-3 first flew in 1936, it was as the DST, or Douglas Sleeper Transport, for overnight services across the United States. The DST could carry fourteen passengers in curtained-off bunks, or twenty-one passengers as a reasonably comfortable day transport, although many post-World War II airlines used the aircraft with as many as thirty-two seats. Some 13,000 DC-3s and C-47s were built, more than 10,000 of them during the war years, and including 800 built after the war ended. The aircraft was also built in the Soviet Union as the Lisunov Li-2. Two 1,000 hp Wright Cyclone engines gave a maximum speed of 225 mph, although cruising speed was nearer 170 mph, and again less if towing a glider, while the range was usually up to 500 miles, although it could be extended to well over 1,000 miles if necessary. Later versions used 1,200 hp Pratt & Whitney R-1830-90C engines. Although never used as a bomber, the DC-2 itself had led to a bomber development, the B-18. With a cheapened structure and the engine nacelles faired over, additional C-47s were built as gliders during World War II. In USAAF service, the aircraft was known as the 'Skytrooper' if fitted out for paratroops, and the 'Skytrain' in the freight role, while the British Commonwealth air forces always referred to it by its RAF title of 'Dakota'.

Final preparations

The first major campaign to see transport aircraft employed as a significant element in the air power of one side, and only one side had air power in this instance, arose with Italy's invasion of Abyssinia, or Ethiopia, on 3rd October, 1935. As with British efforts elsewhere in Africa and the Middle East, the aeroplanes were the ubiquitous bomber-transports, reflecting the close links between the designs of these now distinct aircraft types, and the reluctance of the planners to allocate aircraft specifically for transport purposes. No less than 75 per cent of the aircraft deployed in Ethiopia by the Italian *Regia Aeronautica*, a total of 320 in all, were trimotor bomber-transports, including the Caproni Ca.101s, 111s and 133s, and Savoia-Marchetti S.M.79s and 81s. While paratroop operations were few and far between in this campaign, in spite of the Italian Army possessing two paratroop brigades, movement by air and the use of aircraft for supply drops were significant features; between October, 1935, and the following May, the *Regia Aeronautica* carried more than 2,000 tons of supplies, including food and ammunition, to Italian forces, flying over rough terrain, often unmapped, and using desert landing strips as well as parachuting and simply air-dropping supplies. It had earlier been realised that many supplies, including flour or grain, could be dropped with little damage to the contents if double bagged, and given

Vickers Virginia X drops packages by parachute as a demonstration of airborne supply capability at one of the Royal Air Force Displays at Hendon. Some 160 Virginia bombers were built for the Royal Air Force and once the type had been superseded as the Service's heavy bomber, it still remained in use until 1937, thirteen years after it first began squadron use.

suitable rubber or, later, plastic, containers, even motor and aircraft fuel could be quickly dropped in this way — far cheaper than using parachutes and with less chance of the supplies being caught by the wind and drifting off the dropping zone.

Just how much the Italian operations impressed Hitler, an admirer of the Italian dictator, Benito Mussolini, and how much of it was original thinking on the part of the *Führer* himself, but within two months of the end of the Abyssinian campaign, the *Luftwaffe* was mounting a major airlift of its own. Hitler was attending the Wagner Festival in Bayreuth when he was approached on 26th July, 1936, by General Franco, at that time a Spanish Army officer engaged in a struggle against a left-wing popular front government. Franco sought Hitler's help in moving the troops of the Spanish Foreign Legion and Moroccan troops from Morocco to Spain so that the balance of forces in Spain would be tilted in favour of the Nationalists. Hitler decided to send twenty *Luftwaffe* Junkers Ju.52/3m transports to aid Franco, and the following day, under the command of an experienced *Luft Hansa* pilot, Captain Jenke, the first aircraft left Berlin's Templehof aerodrome. The entire force of twenty aircraft was operating across the Straits of Gibraltar, between Tetuan and Seville, within a few days, carrying men and equipment on each flight, and occasionally aircraft would make as many as four flights a day. Altogether, some 13,500 troops and 300 tons of equipment were moved, enabling the future *Caudillo* to consolidate his position and establish an effective core force during the vital early days of the Spanish Civil War. There was no secrecy of the operation, the world soon knew what was happening, and indeed, Hitler even sent fighters to ensure the safety of the transports. The lessons were ignored, not least by the Germans themselves, for as the frantic struggle to build up Germany's armed forces during the late 1930s started to impose strains on the economy and Germany's industrial capacity, a shortage of steel and duralumin arose during 1937, and the Ju.52/3m was the worst affected of all types when production targets were reduced. Even so, when the *Luftwaffe's* 1st Special Duty Bomber Group was assigned to support the 7th Paratroop Division in October, 1937, it was soon split into two, in August, 1938, and both halves were brought up to full strength, but even this did not provide the airlift capacity needed by a full division. Nor did the German Ju.52/3m aircrew receive any special training for their demanding and specialised role, which the RAF, even while using bombers for paratroop drops, for supply dropping and for glider towing, did at least recognise.

By contrast, the Japanese did not make any significant use of paratroops during their war in China during the 1930s, although this should not be too surprising, since why use paratroops when other cheaper units can be used instead? Nor did the Germans, in spite of their enthusiasm for parachute or air-landed troops, use such forces when they occupied Austria and Czechoslovakia, or for the invasion of Poland on 1st September, 1939, which led directly to war with Britain and France on 3rd September. Both Germany and Russia did use aircraft for transport and communications duties during the respective occupations of Poland, but the assault was over the ground and not from the air.

Perhaps the most surprising point is that, during the Russo-Finnish War of 1939, the so-called "Winter War.", the only occasion in which Soviet paratroops were deployed resulted in the two brigades being so badly scattered that they failed to gain any of their objectives! This was from the pioneers and, one would have thought, the masters of the art, but the Germans did not become discouraged by the Soviet failure.

German understanding of the use of air transport had its limitations, but their understanding of the correct tactics for the deployment of airborne forces was far better. The use of airborne forces consists of rather more than delivering the right numbers of men and equipment to a given spot, although that in itself is by no means easy. There are severe limitations governing the effective deployment of airborne troops, be they from gliders or parachutes. They must be deployed in sufficient numbers to be effective, and close enough to their objectives to be able to make the most of surprise and neither have to fight their way there or suffer a long march when they should arrive fresh, but most important of all, there must be a good chance of their being joined either by additional forces and heavy weapons, or even better, by strong reinforcements moving over the ground, ideally with heavy armour, within a short period of being dropped or landed, otherwise relatively lightly-armed airborne forces are vulnerable to counter attack. That said, airborne forces can leapfrog over heavily defended positions, avoiding minefields and major artillery batteries, while seizing key positions and causing confusion as they surround an enemy or cut off his reinforcements by taking up a strong position at the rear. That these factors were fully appreciated by the Germans, and not always appreciated by the Allies, will become clear in the next two chapters.

Chapter Two
Put to the Test

On the outbreak of war in Europe, the use of transport aircraft was relatively limited. The German assault on Poland was a conventional armoured thrust in the wake of heavy bombing and strafing of Polish towns and cities, and while aircraft, in the form of the Junkers Ju.52/3m, were available for ambulance duties and to provide some transport and communications links, there was no concerted airborne assault or air supply operation. The same was true of the Russian advance into the regions of Poland assigned to them under their agreement with the Germans. The invasion of Poland was followed by a period of calm, aptly referred to by the British as the "phoney war", with relatively little activity in the air or on land, apart from the dispatch of a British Expeditionary Force to France to reinforce the French Army. Such activity as there was at first was at sea. None of this should be surprising, the onset of winter has never been a good time to mount a military campaign, and most of Germany's forces were occupied in central Europe, while those of Britain and France were moving onto a war footing. In truth, even the Germans were not really ready for a major war; the Munich Agreement of 1938 had given both sides precious extra time, and the first few quiet months of that first winter of war were to do much to improve matters, especially as far as the British were concerned, since they of all of the European nations, regardless of side, were the most successful at putting their industry onto a war footing. In the long run, Germany was to be defeated as much on the industrial front as on the battlefield or in the air, while nationalisation of the French aircraft industry had created chaos, and seriously delayed the delivery of what might otherwise have been some promising aircraft.

The calm could not last forever. Having confronted the United Kingdom, the main fear of the Germans was that of being blockaded in the Baltic, something which would not so much as affect supply routes, but instead would hinder the U-boat campaign against Britain's supplies, known to the Germans as the "trade war", which was seen as a major instrument in the defeat of the British. The U-boats were as significant a strategy to the Germans as the heavy bomber was to be to the British, both in their own ways represented the best means then available of taking the war to the enemy. With 75 per cent of the *Luftwaffe's* resources devoted to support of the Army, a major strategic bombing offensive was not an option seriously available to the Germans, even though they used the large numbers of light, medium and dive-bombing aircraft available to them as effectively as possible in the *Blitz* on English cities. German possession of oilfields in Rumania, meant that, as a continental power, Germany did not have the trade routes to disrupt

which would have justified a major British submarine campaign.

To ensure that the fleet had access to the open seas at all times, Germany had to secure Denmark and Norway. Denmark could also have provided another "front" for a British attack on Germany. Later, the fall of France would give the German fleet the access to the Atlantic that it required, but the conquest of the Scandinavian countries had a higher priority.

The invasion of Denmark and Norway on 9th April, 1940, provided a text book example of deploying airborne troops to the best advantage, in spite of adverse weather conditions over much of Norway on that day. Denmark was to surrender within hours rather than face ruin and bloodshed from the overwhelming German might which made defeat inevitable; the Norwegians, with the advantage of terrain on their side, and sufficient time to delay the Germans until British and French reinforcements could arrive, were to fight on for much longer, in spite of not having received the aircraft ordered at the last moment from the United States, and which could have made some difference to the outcome. Both countries were ideal for the use of paratroops; Denmark with its many islands and Norway with an exceptionally difficult terrain and a heavily and deeply indented coastline which made surface communications slow and difficult. Even so, Swedish neutrality was a factor which contributed to German success, along with the inability of the British and French to fly in substantial reinforcements, while also having to depend upon obsolete carrier-borne aircraft for air cover — earlier modernisation of the Fleet Air Arm, by now newly returned to the Royal Navy, could also have made a difference.

Even by the standards of post-World War II, with the acceptance of the importance of the transport aeroplane, the statistics of the invasion are impressive, with the *Luftwaffe* amassing a force of 500 transport aircraft. Most of the aircraft were, of course, the sturdy Ju.52/3ms, which comprised ten *Gruppe,* but an eleventh *Gruppe* included the more modern Junkers Ju.90 and Focke-Wulf Fw.200B Condor transports, graceful four-engined aircraft, although the Condor was not renowned for possessing great structural strength and, on occasion, could let its occupants down, badly! In addition, the *Luftwaffe's* strength was reinforced by a small number of ex-*Luft Hansa* aircraft, including the elegant Dornier Do.24 and Do.26 flying-boats, ideal for transport and communications duties in Norway.

While most of the early paratroop landings were in Norway, there were also early drops into Denmark by No.4 Company of the 1st Battalion, the 1st German Parachute Regiment, taking the airports at Aalborg East

Mainstay of the 'Luftwaffe's' medium-bomber, instrument flying school and transport units was the Junkers Ju.52/3m trimotor, which also flew with Luft Hansa, one of whose examples is seen landing here.

and Aalborg West, as well as a two-mile-long bridge near Copenhagen. Surprise was complete, and in some cases this very small force had taken its objectives with just pistols and sub-machine guns, not even having to remove rifles and machine guns from their containers: In contrast to British practice, at this time the German paratroops did not drop with their rifles strapped to their bodies.

Most of the *Luftwaffe's* air transport effort on the first day, and all of it in the days which followed, was directed at the Norwegian campaign, for which the transport squadrons were to move 30,000 men, 2,350 tons of dry supplies, including ammunition and 250,000 gallons of aircraft and motor vehicle fuel. Paratroops were assigned to capture the main Norwegian airfields, and then to make contact with the amphibious forces landing along the long Norwegian coastline.

There were problems, however, with stiff and prolonged resistance from the Norwegians, and the weather. At Sola airfield, near the strategically important town of Stavanger, the 1st Parachute Battalion's 3rd Company was dropped from 400 feet into a hail of machine gun fire, and the drop was only saved by the timely arrival of two long-range Messerschmitt Me.110 fighters over the airfield, which machine-gunned the defenders and enabled the paratroops to assemble and press home their attack. The lesson was as quickly learnt, and Kurt Student was to insist from this time on that all airborne invasions be supported by heavy ground attack and fighter cover, using Me.110s and Junkers Ju.87s. The situation also became confused at Fornebu, near Oslo. The remainder of the 1st Battalion was being flown in by twenty-nine Ju.52/3ms when the paratroops' aircraft ran into dense fog, and turned back. A follow-up wave of aircraft carrying the air-landed troops was ordered to press on by their commander, who was killed when his aircraft was shot down just before touchdown at Fornebu, and at this, many of the aircraft in the formation turned back. The situation was saved for the Germans by six Me.110s, circling to provide fighter cover, running short of fuel and landing at Fornebu, keeping the defenders covered with their machine guns and radioing for airborne reinforcements. Fornebu and the nearby Oslo-Kjelle airports were soon under German control, and Oslo itself was taken early in the afternoon.

The arrival in Norway of 13,000 British and French troops, supported by naval vessels at Narvik, forced the Germans to hastily assemble a parachute force which dropped onto Andalsnes, to stop the Allies and Norwegian forces teaming up. This was unsuccessful, with the Germans dropping too low and many men being killed before their parachutes could open, while the survivors were quickly captured by the Norwegians. German forces at Narvik, meanwhile, were soon cut off from the main German force, and could only be supplied from the air. Eventually reinforcements were dropped by parachute, and then Ju.52/3ms landed on a frozen lake to land artillery; the aircraft could not take off again on the ice, and were left there, sinking to the bottom of the lake as the spring thaw set in.

War in the West

Even before the Norwegian Campaign, the Germans had planned to advance to the North Sea and English Channel coasts, and some plans had even called for this operation to be mounted much earlier, before the invasion of Denmark and Norway, but for a variety of reasons this was delayed. The attack to the West was to show both the growing confidence of the Germans and further innovation in the use of air transport and of airborne troops, set against which, the Norwegian campaign had been conventional, except, of course, for the fact that no one had tried it, let alone made it work, before, apart from exercises of course!

The vehicle for much of the attack was to be the glider, and it was to be here that the Germans were to show just how much they had learned from the earlier Soviet experiments.

A larger, and more elegant glider, was the DFS.330, seen here.

Out of the many German glider designs, three were more significant than the others, the DFS.230, the Gotha Go.242 and the Messerschmitt Me.321, and these were all successful.

The DFS.230 was the first operational German glider, and the most numerous. It had been developed from an earlier design by the Rhoen-Rositten-Gesellschaft Research Institute in Munich, with a steel tube structure covered in fabric. It was one of the few, and perhaps the only, aircraft to have been test flown by a woman, Hanna Reisch, the diminutive aviatrix. Large scale production at the Gotha works accounted for most of more than 2,200 DFS.230s built during the war years. The aircraft could carry nine troops in addition to the pilot, or up to 2,800 lbs of supplies. Later versions had enlarged doors so that motor-cycles and anti-tank guns could be loaded and, even more important, unloaded quickly and easily, and these later versions also tended to use some form of

braking device, either rockets or parachutes, depending on the variant. It was the DFS.230 that carried troops to Eben Emael and the Rhine bridges, and accounted for much of the glider-borne force at Crete, for most of the re-supply of Rommel's hard-pressed *Afrika Korps,* and carried Mussolini's rescuers. A larger development the thirty-seat DFS.330, was built in relatively small numbers.

A larger glider, also built at the Gotha works, but designed there as well, was the Gotha Go.242, which was first delivered to operational units in 1941. The rather futuristic twin-boom fuselage could take twenty-two troops in addition to the pilot, but usually this glider was reserved for guns, light tanks and small vehicles, even though there was a paratroop-dropping version as well,

Germany's most numerous glider was the small DFS.230; this one was photographed before taking part in an operation.

Below: The Me.323, the powered development of the Me.321, was a successful aircraft in its own right, and pointed the way for much post-war transport aircraft development. In common with the rest of Germany's air transport fleet, it saw much of defeat, including CASEVAC operations here.

Above: Ugly but effective, the large Messerschmitt Me.321 'Gigant' glider flew well, but created difficulties for tug aircraft. One solution was to use two or three tugs, another was to use two Heinkel He.111s joined together as one aircraft and with a fifth engine, the HE.111Z, shown here.

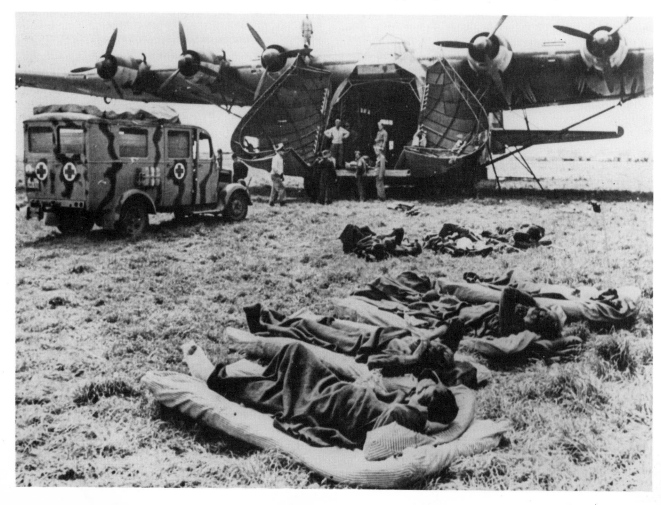

Above: A half-track personnel carrier and a field gun; all in the day's work for the Me.323.

Below: German paratroops jump from their Ju.52/3m over the Netherlands, April, 1940.

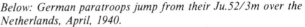

with the sound idea of using bomber aircraft as tugs for major operations. In some versions, additional take-off thrust for this heavy glider was provided by rockets, and in addition to the jettisonable undercarriage wheels, a fairly standard feature for most gliders, an unusual aspect was the incorporation of a plough for braking. More than 1500 were built, and the utility of this practical design was such that a powered derivative, the Go.244, was built, with more than a hundred of these being delivered to the *Luftwaffe*. The Go.242 saw more than its fair share of German defeat, being involved in many of the re-supply missions mounted on the Eastern Front, and especially at Kholm and Podolsk, and in the re-supply of the *Afrika Korps,* as well as in the evacuation of German forces from the Crimea.

Largest of all, and not just in comparison with German gliders, was the Messerschmitt Me.321, a glider which fully justified its name of *Gigant*, or 'Giant'. The large clamshell doors on the nose of the Me.321 could swallow a heavy tank or a tractor, or an 88mm anti-tank gun, or up to 200 troops on two decks. Designed for the invasion of England, the Me.321 was first flown on 25th February, 1941, with the powerful Junkers Ju.90 tug having great difficult in getting the glider airborne, even though on this flight no load was carried! Although the Me.321 did in fact fly very well, the unpowered controls were too heavy for one pilot and so two were needed. The major problem lay in getting such a large aircaft into the air once fully loaded, and often the solution had to be a 'troika' of three aircraft, usually Me.110s or Heinkel He.111s, to get the aircraft and its twenty-four ton load off the ground. A special version of the He.111, the He.111Z, was developed to overcome this problem, effectively matching up two He.111s, with a fifth engine at the place at which the port and starboard wings bonded to create a single aircraft! Take-off, not surprisingly on this large glider, was often assisted by rockets. More than 200 Me.321s were converted into powered aircraft, using six engines, and designated the Me.323, helping in the evacuation of German troops from North Africa, and on one such occasion 240 men were lifted on a single flight. Slightly smaller, and considerably less successful, was the Junkers Ju.322, sometimes known as the 'Goliath' but offically known as the *Mammot*, which was planned as an all-wood rival to the Me.321, which used steel. The Ju.322 also needed eight tons of steel to keep its large structure rigid. The flight test performance was poor, and the suitability of the glider was called into question when, early in the test programme, a tank fell through the wooden floor!

Before the outbreak of war, belated appreciation of the need to up-date the *Luftwaffe's* transport capability as well as providing a new transport for *Luft Hansa's* European services, had led to an improved version of the Ju.52/3m, the Ju.252 Hercules, a thirty-five passenger aircraft, a few of which did manage to enter *Luft Hansa* service during the last few months of peace in Europe. The same wartime pressure on raw materials, and the need to move non-metal working factories into aircraft production, led to the cancellation of this apparently useful and successful aircraft in favour of an all-wood version, the Ju.352, which was designed primarily for military use and had such advanced features as a rear loading ramp. This equally promising aircraft was cancelled in 1944, after two prototypes and more than forty production versions had been built, as manpower and materials shortages, including the demand for engines for bombers and fighters, meant that the *Luftwaffe* had become increasingly concerned with staving off defeat rather than supporting, or undertaking, ambitious assault missions.

Fall Gelbe, or 'Case Yellow', the German push in the West, called for 475 Junkers Ju.52/3ms and forty-five DFS.230 gliders, which were assigned to a *Luftflotte 2* staff known as the *Fliegerführer zur besonderen Verwendung,* or 'Air Command for Special Purposes'. The main attack was to be centred around massive air raids followed by a strong assault by *Panzer,* or tank, armies. The vital use of paratroops and air-landed troops was regarded as vital, however, in securing major objectives, including the bridges over the main rivers and canals in Belgium and the Netherlands, since these provided both strong lines of defence which could hinder the German advance if the bridges were demolished as Dutch and Belgian troops fell back before the German onslaught. Other objectives included securing airfields, both to speed up the advance by flying reinforcements in once paratroops had secured an airborne bridgehead, and to prevent these from being used to mount fighter and bomber counter-attacks. Important though these installations all were, the operation was most famous for the daring, and successful raid on the Belgian fort of Eben Emael.

Constructed between 1931 and 1935, Fort Eben Emael's sole purpose was to delay any invasion of Belgium for long enough for the Belgian Army to reassemble behind the Albert Canal and the Meuse, at the junction of which the fort stood, with one side rising sheer 120 feet above the canal, which was in a deep cutting at this point. Close to the fort were three major bridges, at Velchrezelt, Vroenhaven and Kanne, the last mentioned being under both the control of Eben Emael and within sight of the fort. The assault on the fort and the three bridges was carefully co-ordinated, since success in neutralising the fort would be wasted if the bridges were all blown, and *vice versa*. The strategy was more than simply a means of entering Belgium, but it was intended also to allow a by-passing of the French Maginot Line and of cutting off Dutch forces from French and British reinforcements by driving a wedge between France and the Netherlands.

Planning and preparation for the mission had started in Germany as early as November, 1939, with the formation of a special combat group under Hauptmann Walter Koch, with its members drawn from the 1st Parachute Regiment and the 7th Air Division of Engineers. The fort was impregnable to bombing attack, and in any event such an attack also ran an unacceptable risk of destroying or at the very least damaging the bridges. The plan was for a combination of gliders and transports to mount the attack, with the gliders being towed by Ju.52/3ms at 8,000 feet before being released to glide silently across the Maastricht "peninsula" avoiding Belgian anti-aircraft sound detectors. The special unit, or *Sturmabteilung,* was divided into four assault groups, 'Concrete', to take the Vroenhofen bridge; 'Steel' to take the Velchrezelt bridge, 'Iron' to take the Kanne bridge, and 'Granite' to take the fort itself. The gliders were to land alongside their objectives, except for those carrying the fort assault team, which were to land on the flat roof of the fort. Even if Dutch and Belgian air defences had been more closely integrated on something approaching the pattern established by NATO today, this daring raid would probably still have reached its objectives undetected, given the rudimentary nature of anti-aircraft precautions at the time.

On 10th May, 1940, before dawn, at 04.30 thirty-one Ju.52/3ms took off, each towing a single DFS.230 glider, and climbed to 8,000 feet, and flew towards the Dutch and Belgian borders. All went well on the fly-in, except for the tow line breaking on the glider carrying the leader of the Eben Emael assault team, who found himself and key demolition troops stranded well inside the Fatherland. Nevertheless, this still left nine gliders for the assault on Eben Emael, and at dawn these landed, discharging seventy assault troops and engineers, using hollow charges to blow holes in the six-foot-thick reinforced concrete walls of the fort, and neutralising the fort, keeping the garrison of 1,200 men entombed for twenty-four hours before they could be taken prisoner by units of the German Fourth *Panzer* Division, at a cost of six German dead and twenty wounded out of the landing force of seventy. Their commander, Oberleutnant Witzig, eventually arrived aboard a fresh glider at 08.30 to find the mission successfully accomplished.

Meanwhile, down on the bridges, those at Velchrezelt and Vroenhofen were taken intact, the gliders landing so close that the defenders had little time to react, and a last-minute plea by the troops at Velchrezelt for permission to demolish the bridge being refused by a disbelieving duty officer at head-quarters! The attack on Kanne was unsuccessful, the gliders not being able to land close enough to their objective due to the surrounding hills, and permission to demolish the bridge being granted by the officers at Eben Emael, within sight of the bridge and with belief enforced by the assault on the fort which was well underway!

In spite of many problems and setbacks, and strong resistance, nevertheless, the airborne assault on the Netherlands and Belgium was one of the best co-ordinated of World War II, and the Germans themselves were never again to manage an operation so well. While ground forces rolled forward and the bridges over the Albert Canal were saved from demolition, paratroops had started dropping in a long carpet to seize the bridges at Moerdijk and Dordrecht, and over the Nieuwe Maas at Rotterdam, as well as the airfield at Waalhaven, in an attempt to reinforce control of a thirty mile length of the route of the advancing armies across the Netherlands. The paratroops dropped in force from 05.00 onwards. Other paratroops were being dropped to seize the airfields at the Hague and Delft, so that infantry regiments could be air-landed to seize the Hague and to take the Dutch Royal Family into custody, along with the leaders of the main political parties.

The German parachutists found themselves with a

The dated lines of the Ju.52/3m are all the more obvious when compared with its successor, the streamlined Ju.252, which incorporated such features as a retractable undercarriage. Few were built due to a shortage of strategic materials. Although not in Luft Hansa colours, this example had a civilian registration.

major fight on their hands, and their eventual success was due more to Dutch reluctance to blow bridges, in the belief that a blown bridge is lost forever, while a lost bridge can be recaptured, than to any rapid attainment of their objectives. The early seizure of the bridge at Moerdijk was followed by strong Dutch counter-attacks, but the paratroops held on until relieved by *Panzers* early on 12th May. The bridge at Dordrecht was less easy to take, again because the troops could not land close enough to their objective to take it before the defences were alerted, and the bridge was only taken after considerable delay, heavy casualties and hard fighting. There were moments of brilliance and great daring in the German strategy, and perhaps the two best examples were in the taking of the bridge over the Nieuwe Maas and in the seizure of the airfield at Waalhaven. At Waalhaven, the 3rd Battalion, 1st Parachute Regiment, landed close to, but not actually on, the airfield, and while the defenders were engaged in heavy fighting, transport aircraft landed behind them and flew in two battalions of the 16th Infantry Regiment, with more than 250 aircraft landing during the day, despite attacks by RAF aircraft, to provide urgently needed reinforcements for the paratroops fighting at Dordrecht. The twin bridges over the Nieuwe Maas, on the outskirts of Rotterdam, were taken by just 120 men from the 16th Infantry Regiment, who were landed in twelve Heinkel He.59 seaplanes, which skimmed at speed along the waterway until they reached the bridges, with troops swarming ashore to cut the wires to the demolition

A DFS.230 after landing during the invasion of Crete; the most costly German airborne assault in terms of men and aircraft. Bodies of glider-landed troops are scattered around the aircraft.

charges and take the bridges intact. This small force was quickly reinforced by a group of fifty paratroops who dropped from their Ju.52/3ms into a sports stadium, seizing Dutch civilian vehicles to make their way to the bridges. Even so, the Germans were sooned pinned down on the bridges by the Dutch defenders until relieved by ground forces.

Not all of the operation was completely successful, and the 22nd Infantry Division's attempt to take three airfields and then the Hague, with the 47th and 65th Infantry Regiments and a reinforced parachute battalion, met with heavy losses. Time was wasted searching for the airfields as the aircraft flew across the flat and featureless Dutch countryside, and the first waves of aircraft were destroyed with, for example, eleven of the thirteen Ju.52/3ms assigned to take Ypenburg being shot down. In the end, only 2,000 out of the Division's 7,000 troops were landed or dropped, and the attack on the Hague was cancelled. The troops were redirected to the battle for Rotterdam, but this city had to be bombed and reduced to rubble before the Dutch Government finally agreed to surrender. Out of almost 500 Ju.52/3ms used on the invasion of the Low Countries, 170 were destroyed, mainly by anti-aircraft fire, while about the same number were damaged, and of the 2,000 men of the 22nd Division

who actually put foot on Dutch soil, about a third became casualties.

The implications of this action spread far beyond the battles for the Low Countries, with French troops being diverted from the Battle for France to be rushed north in a futile attempt to counter the German advance from the Netherlands. The distraction also aided the rapid advance of German troops through the Ardennes region of Belgium, where they might have found their armoured units trapped on the narrow roads through the forests.

The heavy losses in men and aircraft of the successful raid on the key objectives in Belgium and the Netherlands, meant that it was difficult to plan any further airborne assaults to support German forces advancing through France. Nor was there sufficient time to plan and implement such attacks, with major objectives falling before the need for paratroops or air-landed troops arose. Aircraft were used to fly in urgently needed supplies, and as air ambulances retrieving German wounded and returning them to base hospitals in Germany, not only performing a humanitarian mission as far as the wounded were concerned, but also relieving German commanders of the need to find and defend suitable hospital facilities. Given the circumstances of the push through France, it is understandable why paratroops were not used, since these would only have been worth the cost if the advance had, for some reason, been stalled.

As British forces withdrew to Dunkirk, ready for the evacuation from 26th May to 3rd June, the RAF produced a hastily assembled air supply operation, using obsolete Hector biplanes and some modified airliners, but this was a case of too little, too late, and supplies alone weren't going to save the day. Worse, although the aircraft used may have been expendable, their crews certainly weren't, and yet they ran a very real risk of becoming casualties to the fast moving Messerschmitt Bf.109 fighters: To no one's surprise, the operation was, of necessity, short-lived.

It was to be almost a year before German airborne troops were to be in action again, giving the paratroops and the transport squadrons time to re-equip and replace their manpower losses. This was not the end of air transport in the West, however. During June, 1940 British forces withdrew from the Channel Islands, which it was felt could not be defended, so close to the coast of France. On 1st July, after demanding the surrender of the islands and observing the required signs of compliance, the first of a large number of German troops arrived. The advance parties arrived aboard Ju.52/3ms, landing in Jersey and Guernsey. The main force came by sea.

A Pyrrhic Victory

Italian transport aircraft were used to support the Italian Army's ill-fated attempt to invade Greece late in 1940. The need to protect Germany's vital oil supplies in the Balkans from an attack through Greece, and the possibility of relieving an Italian humiliation, led to a German invasion of Yugoslavia and Greece during spring, 1941.

The operations in Yugoslavia and Greece, and, later, Crete, were to be the ultimate undoing of the German Army and of the *Luftwaffe,* delaying the planned invasion of Russia, *'Operation Barbarossa',* by a vital two months, and so ensuring that the German Army could not secure its main objectives before the onset of the severe Russian winter, for which it was so badly prepared.

There had been close co-operation between Italian and German Air Force units from as early as June, 1940, with the creation of a joint liaison staff known as *ItalLuft,* under the command of General Ritter von Pohl. While the *Luftwaffe* had assisted the Italian operations in Albania and Greece during late 1940, with Ju.52/3ms ferrying Italian troops to Albania, paratroops and airborne troops were not used by either country. Initially, German thoughts were elsewhere, with *Fliegerkorps X* arriving in Sicily and then building up its strength between December, 1940, and March, 1941, to 450 aircraft, of which no less than 200 were transport aircraft, as usual, mainly Ju.52/3ms, for a planned invasion of Malta, which would have given the Germans complete control of the central Mediterranean, and would have made British operations in the eastern Mediterranean and North Africa extremely difficult, if not impossible.

On 6th April, 1941, the German Army launched *Operation Marita,* the simultaneous invasion of Greece and Yugoslavia, using a straightforward assault across the frontiers and without any early paratroop involvement. Axis forces reached Zagreb on 10th April and Yugoslavia surrendered on 17th April, with Greek surrender following on 20th April. It was not until after Greek surrender that German paratroops were deployed in Greece! A substantial British Commonwealth force,

with troops from the UK, Australia and New Zealand, had been in Greece since the abortive Italian invasion attempt of the previous year, and these forces, still with Greek units fighting alongside them, fell back towards the Peloponnese during the Greek surrender. In an attempt to cut off the retreating British forces and prevent another Dunkirk-style rescue, German airborne forces were landed just outside the town of Corinth to prevent the bridge over the Corinth Canal from being blown. Three Junkers Ju.52/3m transports and three DFS.230 gliders were used to land a small force to seize the bridge, with a glider landing at each end of the bridge, with the defending forces rapidly overcome and engineers removing the demolition charges on the bridge. This advance force was quickly followed up by two parachute battalions, specially strengthened for the occasion by additional paratroops and a parachute artillery unit, with one strengthened parachute battalion to the north of the bridge and another to the south. While the taking of the bridge was successful, the objective of saving it was lost when a British artillery shell hit the explosives originally intended for demolition, which the German Army engineers had removed and placed in the centre of the roadway! However, a secondary purpose was achieved, with the capture of 10,000 out of the original 50,000 British and Commonwealth troops retreating through Greece.

Having taken Greece, the next German objective was to seize the island of Crete, to which most of the British, Australian, New Zealand and Greek troops evacuated from Greece had been taken. This was not the sole reason for taking the island, *Operation Merkur,* or 'Mercury', was planned because of the strategic position of Crete, centrally placed in the eastern Mediterranean, a stepping stone for a possible invasion of Cyprus, which would have given the Axis forces the prospect of aerial supremacy over the approaches to the Suez Canal and the opportunity of launching other attacks to help Rommel in his thrust towards Egypt and the Canal. The capture of Crete and Cyprus might also have persuaded Turkey to join the Axis powers, further tipping the balance of power in the Middle East and on the frontier with Russia — yet another consideration. Crete itself also offered the naval base at Suda Bay and three airfields, at Heraklion, Retima and Maleme.

Strangely, for such a significant operation as the invasion of Crete, the Army High Command was not consulted about the feasibility nor the desirability of the invasion. Possibly, this was because they might have preferred a seaborne attack, an amphibious assault, in spite of the Royal Navy having complete control of the seas following the successful raid on the Italian fleet at Taranto, and the battle at Cape Matapan. The *Luftwaffe* had aerial supremacy, and its own paratroops, giving it the opportunity to show off, to prove just how significant a force it had become. This all pre-supposes some degree of inter-service rivalry, and certainly such rivalries did flourish, and were made so much the worse under the 'Führer system' by the policy of keeping the service chiefs largely unaware of the problems and advantages encountered by their colleagues in other arms. Possibly, however, there was something more at stake. The *Luftwaffe* could use Crete, whether or not Cyprus was to be next on the list of stepping stones across the

Mediterranean. Having failed in the Battle of Britain, it needed a resounding success, so that Göering could have renewed precedence over the generals. Perhaps most important of all, since the German general staff knew that an invasion of the Soviet Union was next on the list, the *Luftwaffe* guessed that the Army would oppose such an exercise and insist on pressing ahead with 'Barbarossa', the invasion of Russia. Of course, there may have been yet another, more constructive, reason, the hope that an invasion of Crete would mean that the invasion of Russia would be postponed, perhaps indefinitely, for there were those amongst Germany's senior officers in all three services who rightly feared the consequences of a second front.

The acceptance of the operation by Hitler meant that a substantial number of German Army personnel were ordered to join the operation, but even so, this was the first major airborne assault in history, which had the main thrust of the invasion coming from paratroops and from troops flown into the airfields as soon as these were captured, or at least as soon as the fighting permitted loaded troop-carrying Ju.52/3m transports to land with a fair chance of success! Seaborne forces were to play a supporting role. *Operation Merkur* was the brainchild of General Kurt Student, who quickly assembled three airborne or paratroop regiments, each with its own support units and each of three battalions, from the 7th Airborne Division, for the invasion, which was to take 22,750 troops, of whom 750 were to land by glider, 10,000 by parachute, 5,000 were to be flown in by aircraft, and

The troops who rescued Mussolini from imprisonment on the Gran Sasso. Although glider-landed, they are in typical paratroop gear.

just 7,000 were to be landed from the sea. For the invasion, a force of 500 Junkers Ju.52/3m transports was assigned to *Fliegerkorps XI*, along with eighty DFS.230 gliders, while air cover and support was to be provided by 280 bombers, 150 dive-bombers and 180 fighter aircraft. Against this force would be very little in the way of British fighter aircraft, partly because the RAF had been extremely weak in the Eastern Mediterranean and partly because the exposed nature of the three airfields on Crete and German aerial superiority had forced the RAF to withdraw its squadrons for fear of their being wiped out while on the ground. The intelligence reports available to Student, nevertheless, did seriously mislead him by indicating that his force could expect just 15,000 British and Commonwealth troops, when in fact there were twice that number, plus 11,000 Greek troops. On the other hand, the defenders were extremely badly equipped, having lost their heavy equipment in the evacuation from Greece, and possessing little artillery and almost no radios at all, while ammunition was also in short supply. The poor roads and mountainous terrain were to make it difficult for the British and Greek forces to respond quickly to an attack, especially since the bulk of the available forces had been deployed along the coast expecting an amphibious assault; another instance of two dimensional military thinking a year after the fall of the Scandinavian countries, and the Netherlands and Belgium!

The invasion troops assembled in Athens, travelling there by road, rail and air, before being deployed to the departure airfields at Elevsis, Tatoi, Megara and Corinth. Transport difficulties, including poor road and rail communications within Greece, eventually forced Student to postpone the operation from 16th May to 20th

May. Although the transport force available had a theoretical airlift capability of 6,500 paratroops, the need to fly in equipment at an early stage meant that the numbers which could be lifted on any one lift would be 5,000 troops, and so it was decided that the airlift would have to be in two stages. The first airlift would drop the Western group, to seize Maleme, and half of the Central Group, which would take Canea; the second airlift would bring the remainder of the Central Group to take Retimo, while the remainder of the lift would be devoted to flying-in the Eastern Group to take Heraklion. The paratroops of the 7th Air Division would be joined by the 5th Mountain Division, with four regiments of three battalions each, plus its own parachute battalion. A weakness in the plan was that the two airlifts could not be less than eight hours apart, giving the defenders some time in which to respond, unless, of course, the defending forces did not expect a second lift?

On the morning of 20th May, 1941, the first lift took-off from its airfields in Greece at an early hour, with 493 Junkers Ju.52/3m transports and fifty-three gliders, including five gliders carrying headquarters units; one of these, carrying Sussman, the commander of the Central Group, breaking up in mid-air, possibly as a result of being overloaded. The heavy bombing and the poor state of the air defences on Crete meant that only seven of the first wave of Ju.52/3ms were lost, but the gliders, proportionately, were less lucky, and several of those in the Western Group crashed while others ran into heavy and well aimed machine-gun fire from the defending forces. Nor did the paratroops have it all their own way, with many being shot as they dropped, so that before the day was over, the olive trees which abound on the island were to be festooned with the bodies and harnesses of dead paratroops. Many more Germans were killed as they left their gliders, or as they struggled to reach weapons containers after disentangling themselves from their parachutes. Even at this time, German paratroops were still not strapping rifles and machine-guns to themselves, and only had small arms with which to defend themselves during the vulnerable first few moments of landing. Nevertheless, after landing in a light haze at Maleme at 08.00, the men of the Western Group were able to take the bridge over the Tavronitis River, neutralising the anti-aircraft batteries close to the mouth of the river, while another group attempted to seize Hill 107, which overlooked the airfield. Others took the airfield itself. The Central Group, including 270 glider-borne troops, and more than 2,000 paratroops, occupied the Akrotiri Peninsula and also landed astride the Canae-Akikianou road, but a well-organised counter-attack by British troops almost wiped out many units, and by nightfall the German force was badly scattered and fighting as small isolated groups.

Serious congestion back at the departure airfields in Greece meant that the second lift was slow and scattered. The remainder of the Central Group did not start to drop onto the airfield at Retimo until 16.15, only a little late, but the full drop was slow and the men widely scattered, while anti-aircraft fire, such as it was, had become more concentrated as the ground forces had been expecting the further drop. The Eastern Group also suffered, with the first aircraft appearing over Heraklion at 14.30, but the congestion at Greek airfields ensuring that the final

aircraft did not drop their paratroops until 19.30, by which time all element of surprise had long since been lost and casualties were extremely heavy. Perhaps the Ju.52/3m pilots were badly fatigued by this time, and the aircraft, lacking the reliability and ability to cope with high utilisation rates with which modern aircraft have to operate, may well have been showing a distinct need for attention.

Confusion amongst the defending forces helped the Germans, for without it they would have been lost, but fighting an enemy without much in the way of radio and in an island with extremely poor road communications in a difficult terrain, the attackers still had certain advantages. At nightfall, the German forces were pinned down everywhere. Unfortunately the defenders were often unaware of the true position even locally and as a result mistakes were made by the defending forces, including the decision to move off Hill 107 to regroup, a costly mistake, for in desperation, Student and General Meindl decided to gamble everything on seizing Maleme airfield, needing just one airfield to establish an air bridgehead and to fly in reinforcements. At 08.00 on 21st May, six Ju.52/3m transports landed on the beach near the mouth of the Tavronitis, while more paratroops dropped in the rear of the defenders, although many of these landed straight on top of defending troops and suffered heavy casualties, leaving just eighty paratroops ready to fight. An air-landing in the midst of the fighting onto Maleme airfield regardless of losses started at 17.00, enabling the airfield to be seized. The remainder of the air-landed troops were flown in during the following day.

Fighting continued for some days afterwards, so that all but 5,000 troops of the defending forces were lifted from Crete by the Royal Navy in a second, or perhaps one should say, third, 'Dunkirk'. Both sides had had their hardships, little equipment for the British, Australians, New Zealanders and Greeks, and no lightweight summer uniforms for the Germans.

While ultimately successful, the cost of the invasion to the Germans had been horrifying, especially by the standards of the war at that early date. More than 4,000 paratroops and air-landed troops were killed, excluding the sad total of 327 men known to have drowned as gliders or aircraft plunged into the sea. Some forty combat aircraft were lost, but even this pales into insignificance against the total of 170 Ju.52/3ms destroyed, while many more aircraft were seriously damaged. This was in spite of the advantage of surprise, although delay and confusion frittered this away, and total aerial supremacy. The costs were such that Hitler forbade any further major assaults from the air, and plans to invade Malta and Cyprus were abandoned. Eighteen months later, Rommel, by this time on the defensive in North Africa, was to rue the decision not to take Malta as aircraft from the island threatened his airborne supply lines, and even these were an answer to the success which the Royal Navy and the Royal Air Force had enjoyed even earlier in stopping his seaborne supplies. As the tide of war turned against the Germans elsewhere, the losses at Crete faded into insignificance in the face of other greater losses on later battlefields, especially in Russia.

There were few further German airborne assaults in the Mediterranean, although smaller scale operations

Loading a motorcycle and sidecar into a Ju.52/3m for the flight to North Africa from Italy could be time-consuming.

were mounted, or nearly, in one case, in which German paratroops were beaten to a North African airfield by the British! Although the *Luftwaffe* ferried German troops to seize Italian airfields following Italian capitulation on 8th September, 1943, just two operations are of significance in Italy and elsewhere.

Following the collapse of Italian power in the Mediterranean, the British seized a number of islands, of which one of the more important was Leros, one of the Dodecanese, which was taken by the 11th Parachute Battalion and the RAF-trained Iraqi Parachute Company, and later garrisoned by 3,000 British troops, supported by a number of Italian and Greek troops. On 12th November, 1943, German forces made a successful seaborne landing on the island, timed to coincide with a drop of the 2nd German Parachute Regiment over the mile wide neck of land between Gurna and Alinda Bay, effectively cutting the island in two and achieving the dual aim of isolating the British forces fighting the seaborne invaders, and distracting them from this latter task. The British defence was paralysed.

Before this, the Germans had made one of their few secret operations of the war. Following the capitulation of Italy, Benito Mussolini was deposed by the Fascist Grand Council, and a provisional Italian Government was established by Marshal Badoglio, which sought an armistice with the Allies. Mussolini was imprisoned in the disused Hotel *Camp d'Imperatore* on the Gran Sasso, a 9,000 feet high mountain in the Abruzzi range, where he was guarded by a force of several hundred *carabineri* in what was considered to be an impregnable stronghold. The only access to the hotel was by a funicular railway, which had been closed. Late in 1941, Student had raised a special battalion of paratroops, the *Parachute Lehr Battalion*, to develop special techniques, including the firing of weapons during descent, and it was to a company from this battalion, under the command of Major Mors', that the rescue of Mussolini, *Operation Eiche*, was given. Major Mors men were reinforced by a number of SS troops under the command of Hauptsturmführer Otto Skorzeny. The altitude of the Gran Sasso meant that a parachute assault was out of the question, although paratroops were used to seize the

lower end of the funicular, but instead on 12th September, 1943, twelve DFS.230 gliders were towed by Heinkel He.126s from Rome, and in poor weather landed successfully on a ledge by the hotel. Taken by surprise, the *carabineri* surrendered and Mussolini was freed by the German troops. A small Fieseler Storch army co-operation aeroplane landed to take off Mussolini, but to the pilot's certain dismay, Skorzeny insisted on flying with them as well! Troops held the aircraft back as the pilot revved up, and after being released, the small aeroplane trundled along the ledge, struck a rock and was damaged before diving off the ledge, only then gathering control speed and recovering, taking Mussolini to Rome. Skorzeny claimed the credit for leading the operation, while for the short time that remained, Mussolini became a German puppet, administering that part of Italy still under German control.

German defeat in the Mediterranean came slowly, with every Allied advance countered and every advantage opposed. As early as September, 1941, almost 40 per cent of all the supplies being shipped to Rommel's *Afrika Korps* in North Africa were being lost to British air and naval forces based on Malta and Alexandria. Earlier plans to launch a 1,000 glider invasion, *Operation Hercules,* of Malta had been shelved by this time. As the situation worsened, the Germans were forced to use the *Luftwaffe* and the *Regia Aeronautica* to conduct a supply operation across the Mediterranean. At first, a mix of shipping and air transport was used, and the supply situation had improved sufficiently by January, 1942, following the arrival of several convoys, for Rommel to return to the offensive once more. Yet, by summer, *Luftwaffe* operations in North Africa were being seriously curtailed by fuel shortages and as winter approached, the *Luftwaffe* was forced to provide an air bridge across the Mediterranean, losing seventy Ju.52/3ms to Allied fighters during November alone, and then reinforcing the battered Ju.52/3m force in December with twenty of the giant Messerschmitt Me.323 six-engined transports, a large number of gliders, including not only DFS.230s but also Gotha Go.242s, and small numbers of Junkers Ju.90s, Ju.290s and

British control of the sea lanes in the Mediterranean eventually forced the 'Afrika Korps' to be almost entirely dependant upon the 'Luftwaffe' for its supplies and reinforcements.

Focke-Wulf Fw.200s, which with 400 Ju.52/3ms managed to lift 9,000 men and almost 5,000 tons of supplies and equipment during December, 1942, and January, 1943. The smaller aircraft handled fuel, and the Ju.90s, Ju.290s and Fw.200s, with their greater speed and substantial carrying capacity were preferred for this, while the largest items were handled by the Me.323s. However, when even this didn't stave off eventual defeat, the *Luftwaffe* did what it could to evacuate as many of the *Afrika Korps* as possible to Sicily and Italy.

Staving off defeat

The debacle in the North African campaign and the role of the transport aeroplane was typical of the measures forced upon the *Luftwaffe* as Germany's ambitious plans came to nothing.

One of the worst planned of many ill-conceived operations was the German invasion of Russia, *Operation Barbarossa,* which as we have already noted was delayed while the Germans secured their position in the Balkans and in Greece and Crete. In spite of the late start, Hitler still expected the invasion to achieve its objectives before the onset of the severe Russian winter caught an Army criminally ill-prepared for it, and with its lines of communications fully stretched. The crack *Panzer* units were the image which the German Army liked to portray, the complete picture was of foot soldiers marching and, if they were lucky, riding in horse-drawn wagons or riding bicycles, with motor cycles occasionally. Artillery was often not mechanised. Even when the *Panzers* scored a success, often it could not be consolidated for want of infantry at the spearhead. For once, a transport force, five Wings with a total of 150 Ju.52/3ms, had been assigned as part of the *Luftwaffe* force of 2,000 aircraft for the invasion of Russia, but after Crete, there were no paratroops available for deployment, and no airborne operations as part of the invasion. Little regard had been given for the well-being of the soldiers once overtaken by winter, even though success would still have meant maintaining substantial garrisons throughout the Russian winter. *Luftwaffe* personnel were more fortunate, thanks to the managerial ability of Göering's number two, Erhard Milch, an ex-*Luft Hansa* director, who ordered winter clothing for *Luftwaffe* personnel as soon as he heard of the operation. He might have done better to have persuaded his masters to order additional transport aircraft, for the small force was still to require aircraft from the training squadrons to boost its strength as soon as demands for aerial supply operations became irresistible; and even then the force would still be inadequate for the task, even with conscripted Heinkel He.111 bombers operating in the transport role.

Retreating from Moscow during that first bitter winter on the Eastern Front, the German 2nd Corps found itself surrounded at Demyansk in February, 1942. With 100,000 men cut off, Hitler forbade a breakout to the rear, and demanded instead that the *Luftwaffe* supply the beleaguered force. Herman Göering, its Commander-in-

A return load for 'Luftwaffe' aircraft operating across the Mediterranean was inevitably the casualties of the North African campaign.

Chief, having failed to break the RAF and prevent increasingly heavy air raids on Germany, was in no position to argue against such an operation. In fact, and in view of what was to come, unfortunately the *Luftwaffe* succeeded on this occasion, but at the cost of 160 trainloads of none too plentiful aviation fuel, and no less than 262 Ju.52/3ms and many of their brave crews. Despite the appointment of a senior officer responsible for air transport in Smolensk in October, 1941, there was no one really senior enough to challenge a decision to conduct an air supply mission in circumstances where it might be unsuitable to attempt to supply troops from the air. Hitler did not, in any case, want to hear of retreat, even while it was still possible.

Part of the strain of maintaining the supply mission was borne by the still comparatively new Gotha Go.242 gliders, which were also in use at Kholm and Podolsk.

During summer, 1942, the second summer of the campaign, the German armies failed to isolate, let alone take, Stalingrad, whose defenders were always able to count on supplies being ferried across the Volga, and received little or nothing from the air, not least because three-quarters of Russia's air forces had been destroyed on the ground during the opening days of the 1941 invasion. In November, Russian forces which had earlier assembled East of the River Don broke through on 19th, and three days later, breaking through Rumanian positions, had completed a successful encirclement of General von Paulus's 6th Army, which was already short of food, ammunition and medical supplies. In spite of the Commander-in-Chief of Army Group B, Generalfeld-marschall von Weichs, suggesting a fight out of encirclement, effectively making a strategic withdrawal,

Elsewhere in North Africa, the undercarriage has collapsed on this Italian Siai-Marchetti S.M.79 at Addis Ababa in 1941. Even so, it is in better shape than the aircraft next to it!

Hitler demanded that the encircled troops dig in for the winter and that the *Luftwaffe* conduct another air supply mission. This time, 300,000 troops had to be sustained. The normal daily requirement of such a force amounted to a minimum of 1,500 tons of food and ammunition, and even that figure pre-supposed some difficulty, while precluding an advance or even a fighting retreat. A fleet of 500 aircraft — seemingly a magic number for the German transport units, largely due to the dual training role of these squadrons determining the number of units and aircraft available — but to make matters worse, little more than half of these were Ju.52/3ms, while there were a few of the other more modern Junkers and Focke-Wulf types, plus gliders, although in German service these were more or less condemned to a one-way trip in many cases. The remainder of the force consisted of bombers in which, in what can only be regarded as stupidity, the Germans assumed that their airlift capacity would be the same as their bomb-load, ignoring the lower density of supplies such as food and clothing, and the lack of suitable containers to make the most effective use of bomb-bay space. As the weather became colder, operations were not always possible, and aircraft were usually warmed before operations by having fires lit under the engines. The best daily tally was far short of the 1,500 tons needed; 289 tons on 19th December, and during the period from 22nd November, 1942, to 16th January, 1943, when the airlift finally ended as the Russians closed in around the Germans with the loss of the airfields at Pitomnik and Gumrak, the average daily tally was less than a hundred tons. Seldom were more than 30 per cent of the aircraft available and little attempt seems to have been made to air drop supplies, either by parachute or in a free drop, due to heavy Russian anti-aircraft fire and growing Soviet aerial superiority over the battlefield. It was not surprising that the Eastern Front was regarded as a punishment posting. On 2nd February,

1943, the Germans surrendered, with 94,000 Germans and Italians being taken prisoner, leaving more than twice that number dead.

Not surprisingly, Generalmajor Fritz Moritz, who was eventually to take over as Air Transport Chief, was appalled by the waste of resources at Stalingrad, and was to argue that before launching an airlift or air supply operation, "every possible effort must first have been made to obviate the necessity for one".

For all their brilliance in weaving the use of airborne troops into their overall strategy, and in evolving tactics which would make the best use of the highly-trained paratroops and glider-borne or air-landed formations, the Germans showed a persistent reluctance to establish a dedicated air transport force; worse, for while the British also lacked a transport force as such, at least the airmen engaged on paratroop, supply-dropping and glider towing missions receiving special training, including training with those Army units with whom they would be working. Instead, the *Luftwaffe* left all demands for transport aircraft to be met by the Instrument Training Schools, or 'C-Schools', under the nominal control of the Chief of Training, although he too was subjected to the whims of the air fleet commanders and almost as unable to devise a consistent and comprehensive training policy as his opposite numbers, when such existed, responsible for meeting the air transport requirements of the *Wehrmacht*. So, the situation arose in which the transport units were ill-prepared for their tasks, and during their absence, and as a result of the ravages of combat evident on their return, the training programme was badly disrupted. The worst affected were the fledgling bomber and night fighter pilots. In desperation at a still early stage of the war, Deichmann, Chief of Staff to the Chief of Training, suggested that the Ju.52/3ms be left to form specialised transport units, while the Junkers Ju.86s, unwanted by other elements in the *Luftwaffe,* be used to create a specialised training fleet. Parts existed for a thousand Ju.86s, and only wanted assembly, the substitution of a conventional aero-engine for their original diesels, additional tankage and dual controls to become an excellent instrument trainer, since the aircraft did handle well in the air, in spite of its other limitations. By contrast, the Ju.52/3m could seriously mislead advanced student pilots, having three engines rather than the two of German bombers and night fighters, and a steering wheel instead of a stick; and neither British nor American instructors would have been content to give advanced training on an aircraft with a fixed undercarriage. Göering, without even bothering to assess the problem, rejected the idea, and it found no support from Milch, a man who did at least know better, but who obviously needed to keep on the right side of his superiors; such are the dangers of life in a dictatorship!

Fuel shortages and the priority given to fighter and bomber production meant that the *Luftwaffe's* air transport capability declined from 1943 onwards. Even as defeat loomed, units were still committed to hopeless tasks, including a final airborne assault timed to coincide with the Ardennes offensive. As the Allies marched into Germany, the Ju.52/3m squadrons were supposed to re-supply beleaguered forces in spite of the near suicidal element of these missions, as at Bresnau in 1945. Other aircraft were used to ferry senior officers and officials around Germany as the surface transport system collapsed and pockets of resistance to the Allies became isolated, first by the flood of refugees and then by the spearheads of the Allied invasion.

After a late start, the Allies were in the process of showing the Germans how to make the best use of air transport and of airborne forces.

Chapter Three
The Allies Discover Airborne Assault

While the Allies had been burying their heads in the sand during the years before the outbreak of World War II in Europe, they could not be accused of delay once they had experienced the shock of the German advance into Scandinavia and through Europe to the Channel and North Sea coasts. Even before America entered World War II, American commanders and their political masters had come to appreciate the value of the parachute and of the glider. In the United Kingdom, the appreciation was just as keen, but the urgency of action was even greater. Even as France fell in June, 1940, the British Prime Minister, Sir Winston Churchill, stated that Britain "ought to have a corps of at least 5,000 parachute troops".

Action was swift, for as many commentators on airborne warfare have pointed out, the British had to acquire the knowledge and the skills which had been gained by the Germans over at least six years, some of it before the formation of the *Luftwaffe,* in as many months. Equipment had to be designed and tested, troops had to be selected and then trained, and so too had the aircrew for the inevitably specialised squadrons assigned to these duties. Rather than relying upon an imperfect knowledge of German practice, the British started afresh, and were ultimately to surpass the Germans in many of their developments.

Paratroops cannot drop in standard combat kit without some form of protection, partly to ensure warmth and dryness while dropping from an aircraft flying well in excess of 100 mph, but mainly to stop the standard combat kit from snagging the lines of the parachute. Standard German paratroop kit tended to be bulky, with a waterproof smock covering the battledress, plus padded knee and elbow sections and padded gauntlets, while the helmet was lighter in weight than the *Wehrmacht* standard, and offered minimal neck protection. Although the British kit appeared to be more complicated than that of the Germans, it was simple to wear and, even more important, easy to discard on landing, offering maximum warmth in the air and mobility on the ground, with a waterproof smock and jump jacket. An early difference from German practice was the tendency for the British to carry either a Thompson or Stirling sub-machine gun under the smock, so that British paratroops always landed armed, while the design of the parachute with its smoother opening characteristics enabled the British parachutist to jump with a 100 lbs kitbag dangling from his leg on a long line. The Americans used a combined combat and jump jacket, plus front-laced boots which became a distinctive feature of US paratroop dress.

Only the American paratroops made combat jumps with two parachutes, the reserve 'chute being carried on the chest, something which might not have been possible for the British when jumping through the floor of a bomber! The snag of having two parachutes was that jumps had to be made from a higher altitude if the reserve parachute was to be of any value, and so the faster and less exposed jump from around 400 feet favoured by the British and German parachutists could be unnerving for

While the Whitley was one of the early paratroop-dropping aircraft, the Albemarle was first choice as a glider tug for the British forces. Like the Whitley, it was an Armstrong-Whitworth product.

Paratroop training, for a jump through the floor of a bomber during the early days of World War II. There was a real risk of parachutists having their teeth knocked out when leaving an aircraft in this way.

Americans. Another drawback of a higher altitude jump was the greater dispersal of the troops on reaching the dropping zone, with even the standard British ten-man 'stick' from a Whitley bomber at 400 feet likely to scatter troops over as much as 600 yards! Officially, only one person died in British paratroop training during the war years as a result of an incorrectly packed parachute failing to open.

Parachute design was another problem. Initially, British paratroops trained on the standard RAF Irvin training parachute, but this proved unsatisfactory for automatic opening from a static line, an essential safety feature for low altitude drops. Raymond Quilter, of the Gregory-Quilter Parachute Company, produced a parachute which had rigging lines which withdrew from the parachutist's pack while the canopy remained folded inside, with the canopy pulling out as the limit of the static line was reached. The British development became known as the 'X' parachute, and is the basis of most modern paratroop parachutes. It was reliable, and allowed jumps from 400 feet so that the parachutists were exposed to enemy fire for just forty seconds; most of all, it opened smoothly, allowing the kitbag to be carried on an elasticated cord which unwound from the paratroopers' leg pockets, with a spring device which reduced the shock of the release. The German parachutes also used a static line which permitted a jump from 400 feet, but opened sharply with a violent jerk. The Americans used the T-5 and later the T-7, both of which were reliable, but slow, and this combined with the need to be able to use the

spare parachute meant that most American jumps were from 800 feet and higher, while the US 'chutes opened with a sharp jerk. The Russians, although not wearing reserve 'chutes on operational jumps, nevertheless did train with two parachutes, and so were taught to jump from 800 feet or more.

Standard practice on a British paratroop-carrying aircraft was for the aircraft to turn onto the approach, and reduced the speed to 100-120 mph. The paratroops would be ordered to "hook up", and would attach their static lines to the rail inside the aircraft. The command, "prepare for action", would come. On a red light being switched on, the order would be "action stations", with the first paratrooper standing, or sitting, in the exit, at attention. The next stage would be for a green light to come on, with the command "go", and the first man would jump. Even while jumping from the door of a transport aircraft, such as the Douglas C-47, British paratroops jumped feet first, while the Germans would dive out of the aircraft, head and shoulders first.

It was impossible for the British to create a dedicated fleet of transport aircraft during the early years of the war, and so the older and less effective bomber types were allocated both to parachute transport and glider-towing duties. The logic was understandable, given the technology of the day, transport aircraft could not make the contribution, day in and day out, which one would expect today, and given the relatively small number of jumps which each aircraft would operate on, it made sense to use bombers withdrawn for the occasion from their more usual duties. This meant that for the early years, most British paratroops had to jump through a hole in the floor of the bombers, with the door, if it existed, not being used; the Armstrong-Whitworth Whitley had a round hole, on which it was easy to have teeth knocked out on leaving the aircraft, the Armstrong-Whitworth Albemarle had a specially modified hole, which was, perhaps disconcertingly, coffin-shaped! Doors were used when the British eventually obtained C-47s of their own, or were flown in USAAF aircraft.

Some idea of the speed with which the British reacted can be gained from the fact that the first paratroop training establishment, the Central Landing School, opened on 21st June, the day before the formal surrender of France. A month later, the first jumps by No.2 Commando were made from converted Armstrong-Whitworth Whitley bombers. The Central Landing School became the Central Landing Establishment in August, 1940, before undergoing yet another name change to the Airborne Forces Establishment. Throughout this time it was based at Manchester's Ringway Airport. The organisation was part of the Royal Air Force, even though the troops themselves were part of the British Army, and for the first twenty years or so of the history of paratroops in the British Army, were men on secondment from other units. While this was happening, No.2 Commando also underwent several name changes, becoming No.11 Special Air Services Battalion before changing its name to the Parachute Battalion on 15th September, 1941, and later that year to the 1st Parachute Battalion, the last being necessary as, by the end of 1941, the British Army already had three parachute battalions.

Of all the British gliders, the General Aircraft Hotspur was the most attractive and the one which still bore some resemblance to the peacetime sporting gliders. These two belonged to No. 2 Glider Training School.

While pressing ahead with the training of an effective paratroop element in the British Army, the glider was not neglected, and examples were available from spring, 1941, for training. Initially, the RAF handled glider pilot training, but this arrangement was short-lived, with the British Army creating an Army Air Corps and, within it, the Glider Pilot Regiment, following which the Army handled its own glider pilot training. Contemporary critics described the RAF training of glider pilots as being "inefficient", but regardless of whether RAF- or Army-trained, glider pilots took almost three months to become fully trained, and received training on powered aircraft initially. Glider pilots were usually senior NCOs, sergeants or staff sergeants, and while initially the Regiment was operated with companies on Army lines, before D-Day it adopted the RAF and Royal Navy practice of being divided into two wings, each with nine squadrons which in turn had four officers and forty other ranks apiece.

In October, 1941, the return of the 31st Independent Brigade Group from India was marked by a change of name, to the 1st Air Landing Group. Although the paratroops were all volunteers, the glider-borne troops in the British Army were not, and often consisted of standard infantry battalions, sometimes with mountain training, and although it varied at times, at first there was little specialised training for the units allocated to this role. Both paratroops and air-landed troops were soon combined in one organisation, under the command of a former guards officer, Major-General, later Lieutenant-General, F.A.M. "Boy" Browning, as General Officer Commanding, Paratroops and Airborne Troops. His organisation reached divisional strength in August, 1942, with two parachute brigades and one air-landed brigade, each of three battalions.

The British, in spite of having to use bombers for all paratroop operations at first, and for most of them even

at the end of the war, did appreciate the need for specialised training, and in this, and in the allocation of specific units for paratroop and glider tug duties, were in many ways far more sensible than the Germans. The RAF assigned No.38 Wing to paratroop duties on 15th January, 1942, although the Wing was later expanded to become No. 38 Group. Initial equipment included the Whitley twin-engined medium-bombers, joined later by the Albemarle, again a twin-engined medium-bomber. The squadrons in the Wing became responsible to Army Co-operation Command, but were still expected to be available for bombing raids from time to time, and in between operations and training with paratroops, and dropping the odd bomb or two, also handled a

Most British glider operations included the Airspeed Horsa; this is a Horsa II being towed-off by an RAF Douglas C-47 Dakota, probably from No. 46 Group.

substantial volume of supply drops to resistance units in occupied Europe.

On 26th June, 1942, the Army and No.38 Wing, RAF, accomplished Britain's first drop of a complete parachute battalion in daylight, and the following day repeated the exercise but at night. On 22nd August, No.38 Wing

The most numerous transport aircraft of World War II was the Waco CG-4A, a glider known to the British as the 'Hadrian', with this one being towed by the second most numerous transport aircraft, the Douglas C-47 Dakota, possibly at the start of the Arnhem raid.

A Slingsby Hengist I Glider.

dropped a Polish parachute battalion. (The Poles were the only "free" forces from occupied Euope to be formed into a parachute unit of battalion strength, although former French paratroops were formed into units to serve with the Special Air Services Regiment in North Africa, mainly acting as ground troops and working with the Long-Range Desert Group).

Servicing of parachutes was also handled by the RAF, with these units serving as part of No.38 Group.

Similar developments were taking place in the United States, with the US War Department authorising the formation of the 501st Parachute Infantry Battalion on 16th September, 1940, followed by the formation of the 502nd in July, 1941, before the first unit was operational. Both units were later raised to regiment strength, the equivalent of a British brigade. During manoeuvres in September, 1941, the Americans successfully accomplished the dropping of a single parachute company of 200 men, repeating this performance in

The largest Allied glider was the General Aircraft Hamilcar, "the largest chunk of airplane", one US General had ever seen! Here the Hamilcar is discharging a Bren carrier, but it could also carry light tanks.

November for the benefit of the Press, when the exercise was a shambles, although a subsequent attempt worked well. By this time, air landing units had also been raised. By August, 1942, the Americans had two airborne divisions, each with two parachute regiments and one of air-landed troops, the 82nd 'All American' Airborne Division, and the 101st 'Screaming Eagles' Airborne Division.

As in Britain, the Americans ensured that developments in the Army were accompanied by similar developments in the Air Force, although the United States Army Air Force was still, nominally, a part of the United States Army. On 1st July, 1942, Air Transport Command was formed as part of the United States Army Air Force, although the United States Navy and Marine Corps both maintained their own independent transport units at this time. Air Transport Command was divided into two divisions, Ferry and Air Transportation formalising a command structure for the USAAF's existing transport squadrons, although so many additional squadrons were created that, by December 1942, the USAAF had the staggering total of 1,857 transport aircraft, more than the combined total of the

rest of the world's air forces at this time. In March, 1943, a new unit, Troop Carrier Command, came into existence, and by the end of World War II, this command alone was to account for thirty-two out of the 224 USAAF groups operating outside of the United States, providing specialised transport for paratroops, glider tugs and glider pilots, while also carrying troops on routine troop-carrying flights between battle zones and within the major theatres of war. Even before this, the USAAF's transport units had the advantage, compared to their RAF counterparts, of operating aircraft designed as transports, rather than bombers!

The first British, and indeed the first Allied glider of World War II, was the General Aircraft Hotspur, an elegant glider which gave the appearance of not having entirely forgotten its sailplane origins, and which was first flown on 5th November, 1940. The low and cramped fuselage provided accommodation for seven troops, sitting on a longitudinal bench on the starboard side, while the mid-wing configuration was unusual, and for a transport aircraft impractical. Almost a thousand Hotspurs were built, but the glider was devoted to training both pilots and glider-borne troops, and did not see operational service. A Twin Hotspur, two fuselages with a central spar, was built to increase the number of troops which could be carried, but this did not enter production.

Relatively few Slingsby Hengists were built, even though the manufacturer was a company with a strong peacetime connection with gliding. One of the more attractive gliders, out of the eighteen built, one was written off during the flight test programme.

Far more numerous, and far less attractive, was the Airspeed Horsa, of which 700 were built. As with the Hengist, the Horsa was all-wooden, but in some versions at least, this was taken to extremes, with even the controls fashioned from wood! A useful glider, the Horsa had room for up to twenty-eight troops, and some versions

Smaller gliders such as the CG-4A 'Hadrian' could be towed two at a time by a single aircraft, sometimes in tandem or sometimes side by side, as here, by a C-47.

Larger than the CG-4A was the 30-passenger Waco XCG-13, but this prototype was not followed by production aircraft in the same quantity as the smaller glider.

The Douglas C-47 also appeared with fixed undercarriage and faired-over engine nacelles as the CG-17 glider. Apart from having one of the largest carrying capacities of any American glider, the aircraft so built could later be upgraded to powered C-47s in the normal way.

could be used for dropping paratroops, but as with the Gotha Go.242, the glider was never used in this role. A howitzer, light truck and crew could be carried, while towing aircraft included such readily available types as the Albemarle or the C-47, with the Horsa substantially increasing the number of troops which could be deployed even by the exacting standards of the latter aircraft! In one of the more unusual but nevertheless successful, means of unloading bulky items of equipment or vehicles from an aircraft, many of the Horsas had cordite charges which enabled them to blow off their tailplanes, this was known as the 'surcingle', and it was most in use during the Normandy landings. Alternatively, other versions had tailplanes which could be shed using eight quick release nuts and wire cutters to cut the control wires. Yet another version had a hinged nose which swung open, but this did not gain the favour enjoyed by the tail-shedders because of the vulnerability of glider noses to damage on landing, either accidentally or because of anti-glider defences. An experimental powered version of the Horsa was built, and there were plans for larger versions of the glider, although none of these projects entered production. The Horsa served in all of the major theatres of World War II.

While the Russians and the Americans have the reputation for building large aircraft, the largest Allied glider of World War II was a British design, the General Aircraft Hamilcar. It was also, in view of the failings of the Ju.322, the largest production wooden aeroplane of the war. In the words of Colonel Frederick Dent, USAAF, in charge of the American glider procurement programme, it was "the largest hunk of airplane I have ever seen put together!"

Sensibly, the British believed that if airborne forces were to be deployed in strength, as opposed to small numbers on special missions, they would require a glider capable of air-landing tanks, larger guns and vehicles to enhance the effectiveness of the invading force. General Aircraft designed the Hamilcar, but it was produced in a railway workshop, after a half-scale flying model had been built and flown successfully early in 1941. The ability to carry up to sixty fully-equipped troops or an 18,000 lbs load, which could be two armoured cars or a light tank, was undoubtedly a useful asset. In spite of its bulk, the 150 mph towing speed was at least as good as that of any other glider, and although smaller than the Me.321, the Hamilcar could be handled by larger standard aircraft types, such as the Handley Page Halifax or Short Stirling heavy bombers, or when available, the Avro Lancaster. Clamshell doors in the nose made loading and unloading easy. The fuselage was built in two sections, and not assembled until shortly before it was needed. The undercarriage, as with many gliders, was jettisoned after take-off, with the glider landing on skids. The exhaust pipes of vehicles carried in the glider were linked to a pipe to the exterior, so that engines could be started before landing, reducing the time taken for the armoured cars, or whatever, to be operational, to just fifteen seconds after the glider came to a halt. Later versions retained the undercarriage to make ground handling after landing easier. Such a large glider needed two pilots. More than 400 were built, seeing action at Normandy and at Arnhem. A twin-engined powered version was also built, and known as the Hamilcar X. Vickers produced the lightweight Tetrach tank especially for deployment with glider operations.

The most significant American glider was the Waco CG-4A, known to the Royal Air Force and the other British Commonwealth air forces as the Hadrian. Out of 16,000 transport and training gliders built in the United States during World War II, almost 14,000 were CG-4As, more than the total for any other transport aircraft, before or since! More than 700 CG-4As were supplied to Britain, while the USAAF itself had almost 6,000 of these useful gliders available in the European theatre, with more than 2,000 in Burma and several hundred available for operations in the Pacific. The CG-4A was generally regarded as being easy to fly, taking thirteen fully-equipped troops in addition to one or two pilots. It could also carry jeeps, light trucks, anti-tank guns or a howitzer, which could be unloaded through the nose, which would lift complete with the cockpit, so that the vehicles or guns could be unloaded. Often wires were attached to the vehicles from the nose, so that the forward motion of the vehicles would automatically lift the nose, and in at least one accident, more of which in the next chapter, this feature saved the lives of the crew when the glider stopped, but its cargo didn't! While the early models could jettison wheels on take-off and used skids for landing, later versions retained the wheels for easier ground handling after landing, and it also enabled the glider to be "snatched" back, of which more later. Some CG-4As had a six-point combined towing hook and anti-crash barrier extending from the nose to protect the glider and its occupants on landing from obstacles, such as the anti-glider posts, known as 'Rommel's Asparagus' to Allied troops.

Amongst the other important American gliders was the CG-13A, also built by Waco and incorporating a lifting nose, although in this case the nose was raised by hydraulic rams, while up to forty troops could be carried. The XCG-17, and its production version, the CG-17, was a development of the C-47 transport, with a cheaper and lighter structure, but with a fixed undercarriage and the engine nacelles faired over so that engines could, if necessary, be retrofitted. The CG-17, built by Douglas, could still be towed by a C-47, while the smaller gliders, such as the CG-4A, could sometimes by towed two at a time, usually in tandem tow.

The British and the Americans were far more level-headed about gliders than the Russians and the Japanese, who also built gliders. Both of these countries even experimented with gliders which could aptly be described as 'winged tanks', but without success.

Not everyone regarded the advent of airborne forces, whether air-landed by glider or parachuted, as a boost to fighting capability. There was a tendency for many to regard such forces with caution, if not with outright suspicion or hostility. Many military commanders appreciated the training of paratroops and the fact that this made them an elite force. Especially in the Pacific, there was a tendency to simply regard such units as crack ground troops, which was also the fate of most *Luftwaffe* paratroops after Crete. Air Chief Marshal Sir Arthur 'Bomber' Harris, objected to such forces because he felt that weather and difficulties in landing, especially in Europe, made their operations costly and hazardous. General, later Field Marshal, Montgomery, regarded them as "waste of time", even though he was to push for paratroop assaults on occasion, because of the amount of time taken up by training and in preparation for operations, which meant, for instance, that many glider pilots made no more than two or three operational sorties. The general view, however, was that such forces had an important role to play, and that their effectiveness, especially in an invasion or if an advance had stalled, was out of all proportion to the numbers deployed. Nevertheless, much had to be done to improve the chances of success, since the difficulties were ignored at the peril of those involved.

Considerable attention was devoted to making drops more accurate. For this reason, Pathfinder units were specially trained, most notably by the British in their independent parachute companies, and these skilled teams would be dropped as close as possible to the glider landing zone or paratroop dropping zone by the best aircrew available. Later, the use of navigational and direction finding beacons, originally established to help guide bomber crews, made this part of the task more accurate and easier. The usual method of marking a dropping zone was for the troop carriers to fly in a line, although the Americans preferred 'V' formations, approaching two lights placed several hundred yards apart, and when these were at 90 degrees to port and to starboard, the green light was switched on and the troops jumped. Within a short time, radio beacons were also available, with the 'Eureka' ground beacon transmitting a signal to the 'Rebecca' receiver aboard the troop carrying aircraft, but this only gave a general direction, and the final decision on when to jump had to be visual. Glider landing zones were marked by a 'T' shaped flare path, with three lights 75 yards apart marking the head of the landing strip, which was itself marked by five lights, usually 50 yards apart. A flashing beacon, positioned 300 yards from the start of the landing strip, was usually taken as the release point. All of these arrangements had to be placed in position in as little time as possible, for it was not unknown for the activities of the Pathfinders to alert enemy forces. Whenever possible, lights were masked so that they could only be seen from the air. The Germans usually preferred to use Pathfinder aircraft, dropping two groups of incendiary bombs, to mark dropping zones, which was a quicker and simpler means of achieving the objective, but far less reliable than the methods preferred by the Allies.

Supplies also had to be flown in to airborne forces, and by 1944 the Royal Army Service Corps was using three different types of supply container for parachuting supplies to troops on the ground; these were a wicker pannier, a bombcell, and a pack. The pannier was ideal for loads of up to 500 lbs, and could be rolled out of aircraft fitted with a roller conveyor, making rapid drops relatively easy. The bombcell had two compartments, long enough to take rifles or machine guns, and could be carried in and dropped from a bomber or, occasionally, fighter bomber aircraft. The pack was limited to 200 lbs, could be manhandled to the door of an aircraft, and was most frequently used in the Burma campaign. Supplies could also be free dropped. Supplies were usually parachuted from 600 feet, sometimes less, while free drops could be as low as forty or fifty feet. The Germans used a form of bombcell.

Taking the war to the enemy

In developing the concept of airborne operations, the British in particular soon discovered that they had acquired another means of taking the war to the enemy, both by airlifting agents into and out of occupied territory and keeping resistance movements supplied from the air, and by mounting covert operations. During the early part of the war, when direct conflict between opposing armies was confined to North Africa, and the Royal Navy was on the defensive, fighting submarines and surface raiders, the use of airborne forces for covert operations was another way of undermining German morale and boosting that of those living under German occupation. Careful planning and training for each operation meant that the use of paratroops as airborne commando units was limited, but nevertheless this too did occur, and on one occasion at least it was spectacularly successful.

Agents were often dropped from transport, and even more frequently, bomber aircraft operating on behalf of the Special Operations Executive, but a more reliable means of achieving this was to use the versatile Westland Lysander army co-operation aircraft, the successor to the Westland Wapiti biplane, but these aircraft, and their operations, were under the control of Army Co-operation Command, and cannot really be regarded as air transport operations as such. Nevertheless, the task was also assigned to No.38 Group, RAF, which used bomber aircraft to drop supplies and agents.

Not every clandestine operation was successful, and even when success was achieved, it did not always provide the immediate support sought by the population of the area concerned, and could even work to their disadvantage.

The classic example of this occurred in 1942, when three Czech agents were dropped by the Royal Air Force for a successful assassination attempt on Obergruppenführer Reinhard Heydrich, the Reichs Protector of Bohemia and Moravia, as the Germans preferred to regard Czechoslovakia. A bomb was thrown into his car on 27th May, and Heydrich died a week later from his injuries. His assassins died after being cornered in a church with Czech resistance fighters, while the village of Lidice was razed to the ground and its population either killed or shipped to concentration camps.

Regular forces were often used on covert missions, and there was an element of seeking to use the forces raised, rather than see them wasted, but much was also learnt that was to be of value in more important and larger scale operations later.

A Hamilcar about to be towed off by a Handley Page Halifax bomber.

The fast development of the British Army's parachute units during 1940, eventually created a state of anti-climax, as highly trained and motivated volunteers, away from their own regiments, began to feel that they were without a role. Indeed, by early 1941, many of those involved appeared to want to return to their own units, with the chance of being posted to North Africa or Burma, rather than engaging in a succession of seemingly pointless exercises.

It was felt, at this particularly grey period of the war, that volunteers should be sought for a raid on enemy territory, and a force of thirty-eight officers and men was selected from the 500 men in the 1st Parachute Battalion. The objective of *Operation Colossus* was the destruction of the Tragino aqueduct in southern Italy; the aqueduct provided water for the major bases of Taranto, Brindisi and Bari in one of the driest parts of the country. Destruction of the aqueduct would seriously hinder operational efficiency and would affect the smooth running of the Italian Navy's main base at Taranto, while also making the movement of supplies from the area to North Africa that much more difficult.

The force was allocated eight Armstrong-Whitworth Whitley bombers, with two of these aircraft being assigned a diversionary bombing raid to provide cover for the activities of the paratroops, who were under the command of Major T.A.G. Pritchard, with Captain G. F. K. Daly in charge of the demolition party. The paratroops were carried in four of the aircraft, and two more were to carry the bulk of the explosives required for the operation. In preparation, the eight bombers and the paratroops were flown out to Malta, ready for the raid to start immediately after dusk on 10th February, 1941. The

aircraft took three hours to fly from Malta to the dropping zone, a distance of 400 miles, but technical problems prevented the two aircraft carrying the explosives from dropping these, while the aircraft carrying the demolition party dropped them in the wrong valley, two miles from the aqueduct and in difficult terrain. Another aircraft crashed. Even so, other members of the demolition party managed to use the few explosives dropped with the main party to damage one of the aqueduct's piers, and to destroy a bridge nearby, over the River Ginestra, so that there was a breach in the water supply to the southern ports by 03.00 on 11th February, 1941. Unfortunately, it was less extensive and more easily repaired than had been planned. After this first daring raid, all of the paratroops were captured and imprisoned, but they would not have been able to escape even if they had managed to evade capture, for the Admiralty, on learning that the mission's cover had been blown by the crash of one of the bombers, cancelled the submarine pick-up of the paratroops rather than risk the vessel and its crew close to an enemy coast. It is tempting to think that had the unit been landed by glider, with their explosives, they might have arrived together and the operation would have been more successful, but even gliders sometimes came down in the wrong place.

Complete success accompanied the next operation, even though this was far more complex, and more important too. Although the Germans had lagged behind Britain in the wartime development of radar, and their equipment was far less precise, they did possess a chain of radar stations which were proving troublesome enough for British bombers plodding across France on their way to bomb the industrial areas of the Ruhr and the Rhine. In January, 1942, Admiral Lord Louis Mountbatten,

then Chief of Combined Operations, suggested that a raid be mounted to capture an enemy radar so that more could be learnt about its operation. The station selected for a visit from the paratroops was that at Bruneval, and the operation was once again with the support of the Royal Air Force, with No.51 squadron flying-in the force in its Whitley bombers, while the Royal Navy was to use gunboats and landing craft to lift the force off the coast once the mission was completed.

The radar installation at Bruneval was located on the top of cliffs, with heavy coastal fortifications nearby and, in addition to the *Luftwaffe* technical staff, the site was defended by a hundred or so German troops. The unit assigned to *Operation Biting,* was C Company of the 2nd Parachute Battalion, and for the operation it was divided into three units, 'Rodney', 'Drake' and 'Nelson', each of about forty men. 'Drake' Group, with an RAF technician to assist them, was to dismantle and seize the vital components of the radar for subsequent examination in England; while 'Rodney' was to suppress the German troops who lived in a house called *La Presbytere*, and 'Nelson' group was to silence the shore defences and any German troops in a nearby village. The operation took place during the night of 27th February, in heavy snow, in spite of which the entire unit landed safely, although about half of 'Nelson' Group came down about two miles away from the dropping zone. The shore defences and the village were quickly taken, while the German troops defending the radar installation seemed to take some time to appreciate just what was happening — surprise was near complete. The force completed its task and was taken off the French coast by six landing craft and then transferred to the motor gunboats, in spite of the presence nearby of a German destroyer. Six men were left

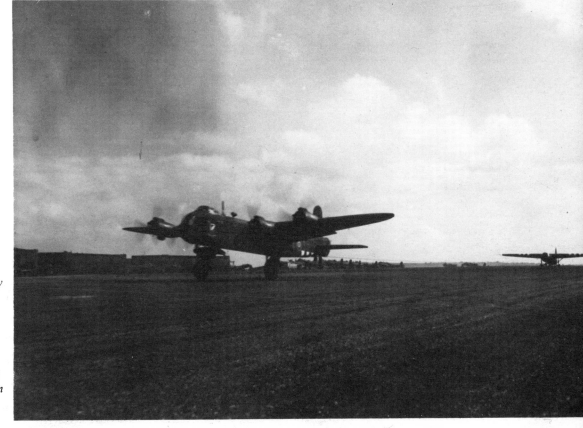

One of the first heavy bombers, the RAF's Short Stirlings were soon superseded by the more capable Lancasters and Halifaxes, but the aircraft made a good glider tug, and is seen here towing-off a Horsa glider.

behind after becoming isolated from the main force, while another three men had been killed, with seven wounded in action, but in addition to the radar components, the force took with them a captured German radar expert.

The success of the operation was impressive, and it could only have be accomplished by troops landing from the air, since forces landing from the sea would have had to fight their way past the extensive coastal defences.

Success often breeds success, but unfortunately this did not happen, with the next mission, *Operation Freshman,* which started on 19th November, 1942, and which was tasked with the sabotage of a German heavy water plant, some sixty miles west of Oslo, in Norway, to prevent the Germans from manufacturing an atomic bomb. The force of aircraft used was small, just two Handley Page Halifax four-engined heavy bombers towing two Airspeed Horsa gliders, and for the first time the force was to home-in on a 'Eureka' beacon. Unfortunately, the 'Rebecca' receiver in one of the aircraft failed, so after the 400 mile flight from Scotland, the first glider-tug combination missed the landing zone, with ice on the tow rope causing this to break so that the glider crashed amongst the mountains with the loss of eight out of the seventeen men aboard; the survivors from this accident were little better off, with the five who were uninjured being captured and executed, while their injured comrades were murdered in hospital by a Gestapo doctor. The second glider landed successfully, but all on board were killed in subsequent fighting, while the Halifax tug crashed into a mountain with the loss of all on board. The heavy water plant was subsequently destroyed by Norwegian saboteurs.

By air to battle

British and American paratroops were deployed in large numbers for the first time in *Operation Torch,* the Allied landings in North Africa during November, 1942, with the intention being that the troops were to undertake raids or be dropped in support of their own national units. Instead of using converted bombers, it was decided that USAAF Douglas C-47s transports would be used, and most, although by no means all, of the British troops, the 1st Parachute Brigade, were given a "crash" course in jumping from this aircraft, with which, of course, they were unfamiliar. The intention was for a combined seaborne and, if necessary, airborne assault to take Morocco, Algeria and Tunisia, so effectively squeezing Rommel's *Afrika Korps* between the combined British and American forces in the west, and the British 8th Army advancing across the Egyptian Western Desert in the east. The western part of North Africa was also strategically important since it held Vichy French forces whose allegiance was uncertain as the war developed, and who were in any case suspect due to the effects of political, and other, pressures on the population of Vichy France. The seaborne invasion consisted of three task forces under the overall command of the American General Dwight D. Eisenhower, with the eastern force, largely British, to seize Algiers; the central, American force, to take Oran, and a western force, again American, to land at Casablanca and occupy French Morocco.

On the night of the 7th and 8th of November, the US paratroops, of the 503rd Parachute Infantry Regiment, took off from England in thirty-nine C-47s for the flight of more than 1,000 miles to occupy the air bases at La Senia and Tafaraoni. The inexperience of all concerned was such that during the long night flight, the leading aircraft lost its way and had to land to seek directions from a French-speaking Arab! Running short of fuel, the force jumped at La Senia only to find that the base had already been taken by ground forces.

An advance party of the British 3rd Parachute Battalion flew into Maison Blanche airfield near Algiers, and were joined within a few days, by the rest of the battalion, who arrived on 13th November, the same day that the two companies of the advance party jumped on to Bone Airfield, strategically placed between Algiers and Tunis, and arrived just before a force of German paratroops in their Junkers Ju.52/3m transports; wisely,

An American CG-4A after a successful landing in Normandy on D-Day.

Last-minute decoration for a Horsa as British troops board.

rather than risk a battle at this point, the Germans decided to remain on board their aircraft and return to base. The British were unaware of the German presence, but it provided a good example of the way in which an airborne assault can quickly change the strategic picture — after all, what would have happened had the German *Fallschirmjäger* been in time to jump first? The following day the American paratroops jumped to seize and hold the airfields at Tebessa and Youks les Bains, but thick fog forced the British to postpone a jump onto the airfield near Beja, to secure the Souk el Arba Plain, until 15th November: Their sole opposition was the curiosity which their silk parachutes and weapons containers aroused amongst nomadic Arabs! Far less successful was the drop of the British 2nd Parachute Battalion to take the airfield at Oudna, near Depienne, there to await the arrival of the British 1st Army. Their USAAF C-47s, of which there were forty-four, dropped them twelve miles off the dropping zone, and after a forced night march to the airfield, they arrived to find that it had been abandoned. Worse, the British 1st Army had been stalled, leaving the paratroops fifty miles behind enemy lines. Faced with the choice of a fighting withdrawal to British lines or a surrender, the paratroops decided to fight, but only a quarter of the battalion eventually rejoined the British forces at Medjez.

The force of paratroops, not large by the standards of a major campaign, had made their mark. They then fought for the next few months as ground infantry. It was from their time in North Africa that the British 'Paras' received their nickname of the 'Red Devils', a reference to their berets, from their German opponents. In North Africa alone, they accounted for more than 5,000 German dead.

Allied victory in North Africa paved the way for an assault on southern Europe, and one which could only have been mounted after the conquest of North Africa and its base facilities. Malta was too close for the element of surprise, too vulnerable to aerial attack, and its

facilities too overcrowded for an invasion force. The RAF could base less than a third of the 120 plus squadrons of combat and other aircraft assigned to the invasion of Sicily at the island's airfields, Luqa and Hal Far. The invasion of Sicily was to require 140,000 troops, most of whom would arrive in the seaborne force of 3,000 ships of various sizes, although mostly fairly small. This force had to face the Italian 6th Army under General Guzzoni, which included 275,000 Italian and German troops, amongst them the *Luftwaffe*-manned Hermann Göering *Panzer* Division.

Preparations for such a major assault were, as one would expect, extensive. During May and June, 1943, No.38 Wing, RAF, was involved in *Operation Beggar,* ferrying thirty Horsa gliders to North Africa ready for the invasion. Over a period of six weeks, the Horsa gliders were towed by Handley Page Halifax bombers over the 1,400 mile route from England to North Africa, with most of the journey being over the sea. Nineteen of the gliders reached the base at Kairouan, near Sousse in Tunisia, while another four crash-landed in the sea after breaking their tows, another three crashed in the mountains along the coast of North Africa whilst flying in low cloud, and another four crash-landed at other points in North Africa, mainly in Morocco. For the glider pilots in particular, this must have been an epic flight, taking ten hours, vulnerable to air attack from the *Luftwaffe* over the Bay of Biscay and the Mediterranean, and in addition to the sheer duration of the flight and the strain of concentration, also enduring considerable cold and discomfort.

Fortunately, most of the the gliders required for the operation were shipped by sea and re-assembled in North Africa.

The one advantage which the Allies had for the invasion of Sicily, without which the operation would have been impossible, was a substantial measure of aerial supremacy for the first time in the war in Europe. The

British paratroops aboard a C-47 Dakota on their way to the ill-fated operation at Arnhem.

Allies could muster almost 4,000 aircraft of all types against the combined German and Italian forces in the area of 1,400 aircraft. Even so, the Axis forces could deploy a potentially troublesome quantity of aircraft, and the operation was preceded by major attacks on Axis airfields.

Ready for the invasion, code-named *Operation Husky,* the 1st Parachute Brigade was reinforced by the 2nd and 4th Parachute Brigades and the 1st Airlanding Brigade, which combined to form the British 1st Airborne Division. The Americans assembled the 82nd Airborne Division, comprising the 504th and 505th Parachute Infantry Regiments and the 325th Glider Infantry Regiment. The XII US Troop Carrier Command provided 331 C-47s, with 222 of these assigned to carry the US 82nd Division and the remaining 109 assigned to carry the British 1st Airborne Division, which also had No.38 Wing's aircraft, including twenty-eight Albemarles and seven Halifaxes, while there were also a total of 140 Waco CG-4A gliders, shipped from the United States, in addition to the nineteen surviving Horsa gliders. As in North Africa, the British and American paratroops were assigned objectives linked to the invasion plans of their own national forces. The initial airborne assaults to coincide with the amphibious landings on 10th July, 1943, were to be by the US 505th Parachute Infantry Regiment and by the British 1st Airlanding Brigade.

The 505th Parachute Infantry Regiment was to drop inland of the invasion beaches to support the US 1st Infantry Division by seizing the high ground, the Piano Lupo, in the Gela area, as well as undertaking a number of other specific tasks. They were to operate without Pathfinder units with the pilots identifying the dropping zones from aerial reconnaissance photographs, while their C-47s were to fly in 'V' formations of nine aircraft apiece, and rising to at least 600 feet for the final stage of the fly-in. In the darkness of the early hours of 10th July,

the aircraft lost formation and missed the few check points available to them so that they eventually approached Sicily from a number of directions, eventually dropping their troops up to sixty-five miles from the dropping zone, scattering them between Gela and Modica, with just 200 out of 3,400 men actually landing on the Piano Lupo.

The British 1st Airlanding Brigade was to capture the *Ponte Grande,* near to Syracuse, the bridge over the canal near Syracuse, and then the harbour itself. There were also a number of coastal batteries to silence. An advance party of two companies was to land in eight Horsa gliders close to the bridge and capture it, arriving at 23.15 on 9th July, while the remainder of the brigade were to follow at 01.15 on 10th July, in 136 Waco CG-4A gliders. Of the two battalions of the brigade involved at this stage, one, the South Staffordshire Regiment, was to hold the bridge, while the other, the Border Regiment, was to take the town of Syracuse. Seaborne forces were to come ashore and rendezvous with the airlanded units by 10.00

Taking-off from Tunisia during the evening, several gliders did not even reach the African coast and others were lost *en route,* while the plan for the gliders to be released from 2,000 feet, 3,000 yards off the coast of Sicily led to the inexperienced C-47 crews, who provided most of the tug aircraft, releasing 60 per cent of the gliders prematurely in a strong gale, with confusion further created by dust clouds off the coast of Sicily. Some seventy-five CG-4As and three Horsas landed in the sea, with the more fortunate occupants being rescued by the seaborne assault force, some swimming ashore, and 250 or so drowning. Just fifty-two gliders reached the coast, and of these, only twelve came down anywhere near the landing zone. Out of eight Horsas supposed to land near the bridge, just two did so, and of these, one hit the banks of the canal and set off the explosives aboard, killing all of its occupants. Luckily, the troops in the one glider which arrived close enough and intact seized the bridge, and

A Hamilcar after discharging its load at Arnhem.

men from three other gliders which came down a couple of miles away hastened to reinforce this small band. Although the demolition charges were removed from the bridge, it was overrun by an Italian counter-attack, and not retaken until the British invasion force arrived six hours late, at 16.15

The disaster of the first night was to be repeated on the second night. It was decided that the US 504th Parachute Infantry Regiment would fly-in on the night of 10-11th July to jump onto the US-held airfields at Gela and Farella, and to this effect, all anti-aircraft units ashore and afloat were advised of the plan and told to hold their fire. The first formations flew over a group of US warships without incident, but after a single gunner accidentally fired a few rounds, other gunners joined in, believing that an aerial attack was about to take place,

seriously damaging thirty-seven out of 144 C-47s, with eight of those so badly damaged that they had to return with their occupants still aboard, and out of 2,000 paratroops, there were 229 casualties during the fly-in. Matters then went from bad to worse, with many troops being attacked during the descent, so that by the time order had been restored, just over a quarter of the 504th's men were still able to fight. Many of their comrades had been dropped haphazardly, some of them too low.

The shambles of the British glider assault had led one paratroop officer to remark that he "thanked God" that he went "to battle by parachute and not by glider". The British paratroops were soon to have their chance.

The British 8th Army had the objective of pushing across Sicily to Catania. To ensure that reinforcements could not be hurried into the area by the Axis forces, and

Reinforcements at Arnhem; the Horsa gliders have blown-off their tailplanes for the speedy unloading of vehicles and heavy equipment.

An Arnhem supply drop.

that the key *Ponte di Primosole* was not blown in front of the advancing British, the British 1st Parachute Brigade was despatched in more than a hundred troop-carrying aircraft and sixteen gliders from North Africa on 13th July. Unknown to the paratroops, during the previous day, the German 1st Parachute Division had been dropped south of Catania to reinforce the defending forces, in a brilliant example of using paratroops to ensure rapid reinforcement for troops under pressure from an invader. The Germans also saw the *Ponti di Primosole* as a vital feature to be held.

The British force was to come down at four dropping zones and two landing zones, so that the bridge could be taken from both sides, while other units held the high ground around the bridge. In a vain attempt to avoid the problems of the previous nights, 1st Airborne Division's RAF adviser persuaded the American C-47 crews to abandon their 'V' formations and adopt the British technique of flying in line astern, not fully appreciating that their lack of experience forced them to follow their leader and that a long line of aircraft raised greater possibilities of their becoming lost. For the first time, Pathfinders were being used, from the 1st Independent Parachute Company.

Another near disaster followed. Confusion and dispersal led to the loss of two aircraft to Allied naval anti-aircraft fire, while another nine were damaged and returned to base, while Axis anti-aircraft fire shot down thirty-seven aircraft and damaged several more so seriously that they too had to return to base. Just thirty-nine aircraft dropped their paratroops within a half mile of the dropping zones, while another forty-eight dropped troops many miles off course. Only eight gliders landed intact, and another nine either crashed on landing or were lost over the sea. At dawn on 14th July, just 295 officers and men out of the 1,856 who had taken off from North Africa were close enough to the bridge to present an

effective fighting force. The force took the bridge, but was soon counter-attacked by the German airborne troops, who retook the bridge later that afternoon. British ground forces joined the battle on 15th July, but the bridge was not taken by the Allies until 16th July.

While the airborne units were not intended to take part in the Allied landings at Salerno in Italy, and indeed the British 1st Airborne Division was landed by sea at Taranto to seize the naval base there, a strong German counter-attack immediately after the Salerno landings on 12th September 1943 threatened to throw the Allies back onto the beaches. At just six hours' notice, the US 504th Parachute Infantry Regiment was dropped behind Allied lines as reinforcements, helping to turn the tide of battle. Rather less successful was the drop of units from the US 509th Parachute Infantry Regiment to block roads around the village of Avellino, twenty miles from the beachhead. There were no dropping zones as such and the surrounding hills meant that the necessary high altitude drop resulted in the paratroops being scattered over 100 square miles. It proved impossible to organise the force into an effective fighting unit, but by luck more than 500 out of the 640 men dropped eventually returned safely to the Allied lines.

The following June, in an attempt to accelerate the advance on Rome, sixty officers and men of the 1st British Independent Parachute Brigade were dropped from three USAAF C-47s, to act as saboteurs. The drop was accompanied by dummy paratroops in the hope of confusing the enemy still further. After a week of making raids behind enemy lines, causing some damage but doing little of substance to the outcome of the Italian campaign, this force withdrew to the Allied lines. Appropriately enough, the mission was termed *Operation Hasty*.

The next major event for both the paratroops and the air-landed troops was to be the main Allied invasion of

Europe, the Normandy landings on 'D' day, 6th June, 1944, *Operation Overlord*. The period immediately preceding the invasion was one of intense preparation, one which turned the whole of southern England into what was virtually one massive military base. For the Royal Air Force, this included the rapid expansion of No.38 Wing, which became No.38 Group on 11th October, 1943, with nine squadrons, four of which were equipped with Armstrong-Whitworth Albemarles, another four operated the large four-engined Short Stirling heavy bombers, and another had Handley Page Halifax heavy bombers. Each squadron was equipped with sixteen aircraft, and to maintain numbers as aircraft suffered heavy damage, there were another eight reserves in each squadron. The Albemarle squadrons were to tow Horsa gliders, while the Stirlings and Halifaxes would tow the larger and heavier Hamilcars. A second Royal Air Force Group, No.46, from the newly-formed Transport Command, was also assigned to glider towing and troop dropping duties with its C-47 Dakotas. Transport Command had been created in March, 1943, from the former Ferry Command, which had been engaged in transport and aircraft delivery operations from the first months of the war.

The airborne forces also underwent expansion in preparation for the forthcoming invasion, indeed the change to the RAF's units reflected the growth in the airborne corps and the greater demand for air transport support.

A second airborne division, designated the 6th Airborne Division in order to confuse the Germans, was formed on 18th May, 1943, incorporating elements of the 3rd Parachute Brigade, a Canadian parachute battalion and the newly-formed 5th Parachute Brigade and the 6th Airlanding Brigade. At this time, No.38 Group was still heavily committed to the war in the Mediterranean, and it was not until January, 1944, that both Nos.38 and 46 Groups were detailed to assist the new 6th Airborne Division in the crucial preparations for the invasion of Normandy.

Rubberised bags like this enabled the RAF to drop motor fuel to Italian Partisans. This one won't dare spill a drop!

Training and exercising reached a peak in March and April, 1944. On 24th April, the entire 6th Airborne Division underwent a full scale dress rehearsal for the invasion, followed on 1st May, by No.38 Group and the 6th Airborne Division conducting a major exercise culminating with more than seventy gliders descending onto a small landing zone at Netheravon. After this, training was scaled down, not only to allow the men to be refreshed for the invasion, but because of congestion in southern England. At the same time, during May, the aircraft of No.38 Group were heavily committed to making supply drops to resistance movements, mainly in

As the German position in northern Italy weakened, the Partisans and their RAF liaison aircraft aircrew became more relaxed – a friendly chat around an Army Co-operation Command Westland Lysander – something which would have been unimaginable during the fly-in of agents to occupied France!

As the German resistance collapsed, normal food distribution was also disrupted, and supplies were often seized by the retreating Germans. To stave off starvation in the occupied areas of the Netherlands, the RAF mounted 'Operation Manna', dropping supplies to civilians during April and May, 1945. The aircraft is one of the then new Avro Lincoln heavy bombers.

France, so that these could reach a peak of activity just before and immediately after the invasion. More than 200 sorties were mounted by aircraft from the Group for the dropping of agents and the supply of resistance groups.

In preparation for the invasion, the United States Army also moved its 101st Airborne Division to Britain, and the Free Polish units had by this time produced a Polish Parachute Brigade. The British 1st Airborne Division was also back in the United Kingdom by this time, but was to be held in reserve along with the Polish Parachute Brigade.

An airlift capability for two divisions was also being created. The IX US Troop Carrier Command had 1,166 Douglas C-47 transports, while the combined strength of Nos.38 and 46 Groups amounted to more than sixty each of Albemarles and Stirlings, and sixteen Halifaxes, plus reserves, while there were, for the first time in a major British airlift, 150 RAF C-47s, while the British and Americans could also muster a combined total of almost 2,600 gliders.

The role of the airborne forces during the invasion was to protect the flanks of the main seaborne assault by seizing strategic points of defence and communications, including major bridges, once again to hinder the arrival of enemy reinforcements and to prevent vital links from being destroyed as the enemy forces withdrew. It was realised that the first day or two would leave the amphibious forces dangerously exposed on a relatively narrow coastal strip. In making their landings, the airborne forces would be preceded by Pathfinder units, who would also help in clearing some of the anti-glider posts from the landing zones, in addition to their normal duties, for which they were to be accompanied by engineers. Because the Americans were planning to use both of their divisions to support their seaborne troops, it would not be possible for Nos. 38 and 46 Groups to move the entire 6th Airborne Division in one lift.

The invasion was arranged so that the British and Canadian troops of the British 2nd Army Group under General Dempsey would land at 'Gold', 'Juno' and

'Sword' beaches, lying between Arromanches and Ouistreham, while the American 1st Army under General Bradley landed at 'Omaha' beach, near Colleville, and 'Utah' beach, near La Madeleine. The British and American paratroops were once again assigned objectives within the invasion zones of their respective national forces.

The US 82nd and 101st Airborne Divisions were to land on the Cotentin Peninsula to prevent reinforcements arriving, with the 82nd south of Carentan, capturing the bridge over the Douvre River, while the 101st would be north of Carentan and inland from 'Utah' beach, securing both ends of the causeways leading inland from the invasion beaches, as well as taking several crossings over the Merderet River; finally both American divisions would link up and seal off the entire peninsula. These objectives were considered to be far more important than those of the British, so airlift capability was to be provided for each division to move three regiments and support units on the initial airlift.

The 6th Airborne Division would only be able to lift two out of its three brigades on the first airlift. The objectives were to capture the bridges over the Caen Canal and Orme River at Benouville and Ranville using paratroops from the 5th Brigade, while the 3rd Brigade, supplemented later by the 6th Airlanding Brigade, was to neutralise the coastal battery at Merville before the invasion fleet came within range of its guns, take the bridges over the River Dives at Varaville, Robehomme, Bures and Troarn, and to dominate the high ground between the Orme and the Dives, especially the ridge Le Plein-Le Mesnil-Troarn. Again, fears were expressed that this ambitious plan could lead to a futile slaughter, and certainly the experience in Sicily must have still been fresh in the minds of many.

While June had been chosen for the invasion, because this was the month most likely to produce the ideal weather conditions, the night of 5-6th June, 1944, was moonless and cloudy, with visibility of just three miles, while the windspeed, at twenty knots, was stronger than ideal for parachute landings. At 23.03, six Albemarles took off with sixty Pathfinders of the 22nd Independent Parachute Company, followed by six gliders carrying members of the Oxfordshire and Buckinghamshire Light Infantry and of the Royal Engineers, so that the dropping and landing zones could be marked with the 'Eureka' beacons and cleared of the *Rommelspargel* or 'Rommel's Asparagus'. American Pathfinders were also handling a similar role for the US 82nd and 101st Airborne Divisions. It was soon to become clear that the British Pathfinders had been dropped accurately and carried out their task successfully, while the American Pathfinders had been wide of the mark, frequently failing to mark the correct dropping zones. The men of the 82nd and 101st Airborne Divisions started to jump at 01.30 on 6th June, with their drops being widely dispersed and units having to fight a succession of isolated battles and failing to achieve their objectives until later: The 101st was scattered over an area some twenty miles wide, with 1,500 men either killed, wounded or captured. In spite of these difficulties, both divisions did what they could, and by dawn, running slightly behind schedule, they were on their way to achieving most of their objectives and in spite of a fierce battle developing west of the Merderet River

with German forces, had managed to join up by the following day. The American ability to overcome their initial setbacks was all the more noteworthy since more than half of their equipment was lost or damaged through being dropped into swamps and woods, while gliders bringing support units and heavy equipment also suffered, with a consequent loss of life and equipment.

The main problem for the British came with the force intended to neutralise the battery at Merville. The plan for this attack envisaged three gliders being used, with one landing on top of the battery itself, the glider-borne troops being reinforced by the 3rd Parachute Brigade. The paratroops were scattered on landing by the strong winds, and many were killed or wounded by a bombing raid intended to soften up the battery, while others were wounded by a stampede of cows, maddened by the bombing. The C-47 pilots of No.46 Group mistook the River Dives for the River Orme, contributing further to these problems, while a broken tow line meant that one glider came down to earth before crossing the English Channel; a second overshot the battery and crashed into woods, fortunately without any fatalities so that the occupants were free to take on a German patrol; and the third landed by mistake in a village more than half-a-mile away. Despite these problems, a force of 150 men from the 3rd Parachute Brigade's 9th Battalion succeeded in taking the battery.

This inauspicious start boded ill for the main part of the British operation, even though the 5th Brigade had been quick to seize the bridge over the Caen Canal and the town itself, but the 6th Airlanding Brigade came down in darkness and high winds within yards of their objectives. The main force landed so successfully that surprise was complete, some gliders coming so close to their bridges that they cut through the barbed wire surrounding the German defensive perimeters, so that the bridges over the River Orme and the River Dives were soon taken, in spite of the Germans flooding some of the meadows close to the bridges over the River Dives.

During the months following the Normandy invasion, more than sixteen parachute or glider operations were planned, and then cancelled, mainly because objectives were overrun before an airborne operation could be mounted, but on some occasions the reason for cancellation was different, and related more to doubts over the ability of ground forces to reinforce the paratroops before these would be overrun by a fierce German counter-attack.

A little more than two months was to pass before the Allies invaded the South of France in an assault timed to coincide with the break out from the Normandy beach-heads. The invasion, or *Operation Anvil*, started on 15th August, and was primarily an American operation, with the British 2nd Independent Parachute Brigade Group fighting alongside the American 1st Airborne Task Force, commanded by Major-General R. T. Frederick, which comprised five US parachute battalions and a glider-borne regiment, with 535 Douglas C-47s and 465 gliders of all types available to the force. The objective of the airborne troops was to cut off any German attempt to rush reinforcements to the invasion beaches. A successful drop by men of the 1st Independent Parachute Platoon at 03.30 to set up marker beacons was to little avail as thick fog and low cloud at dawn meant that the markers could not be seen from the air, while high ground meant that the gliders and paratroops had to be released from the relatively high altitude of 2,000 feet. In the event, only 60 per cent of the troop-carrying aircraft dropped their paratroops accurately, with men being scattered over twenty miles from the dropping zones in the region of Oraguigan and Le Muy. Some landed as far away as St. Tropez and Cannes. Fortunately, injuries were slight. The invasion was notable for the fact that twenty-nine planeloads of paratroops from the 509th US Parachute Infantry Regiment, dropped three miles outside of St. Tropez, captured the German anti-aircraft batteries and coastal artillery batteries defending the town, plus more than 200 infantrymen, before beating the seaborne invasion force into the town itself.

The lack of British participation in *Operation Anvil* was not simply as a consequence of the effort of *Operation Overlord,* but it was also because of the plan for another, in many ways more ambitious airborne assault in the Netherlands, *Operation Market Garden.*

In effect, *Operation Market Garden* was a combination of two operations which were closely related; *Operation Market,* the airborne assault to seize the bridges over the rivers Maas and Waal, and across the lower Rhine; and *Operation Garden,* the approach of XXX British Corps over the ground, with XII and XIII Corps on the flanks. It was felt that the outcome of the airborne assault would be to lay a carpet of paratroops through which the advancing ground troops could move quickly, leap-frogging German resistance in the Low Countries and possibly even bringing about the end of World War II before the end of 1944. The units allocated to this operation were the US 82nd and 101st Airborne Divisions and the British 1st Airborne Division, including the 1st Polish Independent Parachute Brigade Group. The aircraft would come from Nos.38 and 46 Groups RAF, as well as from the USAAF IX Troop Carrier Command. The 101st would drop north of Eindhoven to take the bridges at Eindhoven, over the Wilhelmina Canal at Zon, the Zuit Willensvaart Canal at Veghel, and over the River Aaj, while the 82nd would take the sole dominating land feature, the Groesbeek, as well as the bridges over the River Maas at Grave, over the Maas-Waal Canal just north of Nijmegen, and over the Waal; these objectives were regarded as being rather extensive for a single division, so the priority was given to the Waal bridge, with the remaining objectives to be taken by troops arriving on the second and third lifts. The British 1st Airborne Division was to drop and land six miles west of Arnhem, taking the bridge over the River Rhine. Alone of all the airborne forces, the British had their dropping and landing zones far enough away from their objective to lose the element of surprise, but this was done because of RAF objections to the heavy anti-aircraft defences in the immediate vicinity of the bridge. Worse still for the British, Dutch resistance reports of two German *Panzer* divisions refitting close by to Arnhem were discounted by the Allies.

The operation was one of the largest of World War II, with more than 2,000 gliders, tugs and troop-carrying aircraft involved. The aircraft were to take-off from seventeen airfields spread across southern and eastern England. The US 101st Division was carried in a first lift of almost 500 C-47s, plus seventy CG-4As, while the 82nd

used 625 C-47 troop carriers, while another fifty of these aircraft acted as glider tugs. No.38 Group RAF, now ten squadrons strong, six of them with Stirlings, two with Halifaxes and two with Albemarles, provided 205 out of the 353 glider and tug combinations required by the 1st Airborne, with the remainder being provided by No.46 Group. The fly-in was reasonably successful, although thirty-five C-47s and sixteen CG-4As carrying the two American divisions were shot down, there were no losses on the fly-in to Arnhem, where the Pathfinders of the 21st Independent Parachute Company had dropped from twelve Stirlings to capture a German platoon and mark out the dropping and landing zones.

The American divisions were able to take their objectives quickly, although one bridge was destroyed before it could be taken, after making a successful first air drop and landing on 17th September. The Americans had the advantage of having 75 per cent of their troops flown in on the first day of the operation, but even so, the German commander at Nijmegen, General Model, was quick to react, and in spite of the early American successes, they and XXX British Corps were stalled at Nijmegen by strong German counter-attacks. Unknown to the Allies, the Germans also had the advantage of finding a set of Allied plans on the body of a staff officer killed when his CG-4A glider crashed.

The British troops *en route* to Arnhem were far less fortunate. A little over an hour after the Pathfinders had dropped, at 13.15, the 1st Airborne's gliders homed in to the Pathfinders' beacons, smoke signals and orange and crimson markers. Two of the giant Hamilcar gliders nosed into soft soil and overturned, losing the British valuable anti-tank guns, while another thirty-five gliders failed to make the correct landing zones, including those carrying the armoured jeeps intended to take an advance party of paratroops to the bridge before surprise could be lost. The British paratroops had to march to Arnhem, but before they had covered more than a couple of miles, they became bogged down in a running battle with German troops. Unknown to them at this time, Germany's leading exponent of airborne assault, General Kurt Student, was also in the area, and there was none better equipped to deal with an airborne assault and to guess the likely intentions of the commander of an assault force. The vital element of surprise had been lost, and as British troops struggled to reach the bridge during the night, only a small force managed to assemble there, so rather than seizing the bridge, they became involved in a confrontation with German troops on the bridge itself.

A second lift of British troops was scheduled for 18th September, but this was delayed until 15.00 by dense fog in England and by low cloud around Arnhem, by which time the troops already landed were having considerable difficulty in keeping the dropping zones and landing zones open, and the troop-carrying aircraft encountered heavy anti-aircraft fire. A planned airlift of the 1st Polish Independent Parachute Brigade Group scheduled for 19th September had to be postponed to 20th September due to bad weather, and when they did arrive, the gliders carrying the Poles were attacked by Messerschmitt Bf.109 fighters.

Possibly the biggest disappointment of the operation was the failure of the air supply operation, due to heavy anti-aircraft fire, bad weather and the ever-tightening

German grip around the British force, which meant that only 7 per cent of the supplies dropped landed in British hands, as it became difficult to reset markers to show the areas still under British control. There was no lack of bravery amongst the aircrew of the supply aircraft, who had to fly a straight and level course along a pre-determined line through heavy anti-aircraft fire. On 19th September, the first day of the re-supply operation, with a hundred aircraft from No.38 Group and sixty-three from No.46 Group, thirteen aircraft were lost and ninety-seven seriously damaged. The same story was repeated during the two days which followed, with almost 200 casualties amongst the crews of No.38 Group alone. By 21st September, the operation was effectively ended, with the 1st Airborne Division having held the bridge for the planned three-and-a-half days, and during the night of 25-26th September, the surviving troops endeavoured to fight their way back to American lines; out of more than 10,000 British and Polish troops, just over 3,000 officers and men returned, the rest being killed or taken prisoner by the Germans. The operation had failed, due to the inability to lift enough men on the first airlift and get them close enough to the objective to maintain surprise, and the failure of the relieving force to reach the airborne forces quickly enough. The entire operation suffered from being over-ambitious.

The Germans were also to suffer from over-ambition in their offensive in the Ardennes region of Belgium in December, 1944, in which they hoped to throw back the American advance towards Germany. Just two paratroop battalion groups were available to the German commander, and only sixty-seven Ju.52/3m were ready for the operation, with little or no night navigation experience amongst the aircrew assigned to what was to be a night drop. One of the two battalion groups was dropped on Mont Rigiur at the Malmedy-Eupen-Verriers crossroads, to stop the movement of Allied reinforcements, but poor weather and the inexperience of the German pilots meant that less than a third of the force reached the correct dropping zone, and of those, many paratroops were injured in the 30 knot wind, dying of exposure or of their wounds, except for those fortunate enough to be taken prisoner by American troops. The operation was a complete failure, particularly as American forces reacted quickly to neutralise the paratroops, of whom just 200 were able to fight as a unit before their capture. The other parachute battalion had been held in reserve and was not deployed as the Ardennes offensive quickly ran out of steam.

An opportunity for the British and the Americans to put into practice all that they had learned about airborne warfare was to come with one final major operation, with the Allied crossing of the River Rhine in Germany during *Operation Varsity*, in March, 1945. The units involved in *Operation Varsity* were the British 6th Airborne Division and the US 17th Airborne Division, jointly forming the 17th Airborne Corps. The combined force was to be flown from England aboard aircraft of IX US Troop Carrier Command, with 1,696 transport aircraft towing 1,348 gliders, so that 21,680 troops could be flown-in in a single lift, escorted by more than 1,000 fighter aircraft and 2,000 aircraft to support the ground operations. Some 600 of the gliders were in double tow, and the massive formation of transport aircraft approached its objective, the dropping and landing zones, in broad daylight on 24th March, in three columns each nine aircraft across. The airborne troops were to seize the high ground between the Rivers Rhine and Issel, with the British 6th Airborne Division taking the village of Hamminkeln and the bridges over the River Issel, before linking up with the US 17th Airborne Division, which would have taken the bridges over the Issel canal and the town of Diersfordt. The British 3rd and 5th Parachute Brigades were to drop before the 6th Airlanding Brigade followed in their gliders, while the US 507th and 513th Parachute Infantry Regiments were to land in advance of the US 194th Glider Infantry Regiment. A forward observation unit was to accompany the paratroops to direct heavy artillery fire across the Rhine.

In contrast to many operations, *Operation Varsity* was scheduled to take place in daylight, and it can only be surprising that no German fighters appeared during the fly-in. However, more than 240 troop-carrying aircraft were shot down by heavy anti-aircraft fire, and 50 per cent of the surviving aircraft suffered damage from anti-aircraft fire. Yet, all but thirty-five gliders reached the landing zone, many more were destroyed on landing, and paratroops, British and American alike, descended through a hail of small arms fire. This was the first operation in Europe to see the new Curtiss C-46 Commando transports deployed in large numbers, with seventy-two of these aircraft included in IX Troop Carrier Command's fleet. The C-46 was a mixed blessing. It could carry thirty fully-equipped paratroops, more than the C-47, and they could leave by doors on either side of the aircraft, reducing the area over which they could be scattered, but no less than twenty-four of these aircraft were shot down in flames, although fortunately the paratroops got out of all but one. It soon appeared that the C-46 was a firetrap, fuel from ruptured tanks would run along the inside of the fuselage and the aircraft would explode into flames if hit by tracer.

In spite of the heavy defence put up by the Germans, the force flew in at 10.00 and by 15.00 had attained all of its objectives and linked up with ground forces. The US 513th Parachute Infantry Regiment was dropped by mistake over the dropping zones for the British troops, but joined them in their part of the operation. Yet, in spite of this apparent success, 25 per cent of the air-landed forces were killed or wounded. The aircraft of Nos 38 and 46 Groups, RAF, also on the mission, fared comparatively well, with just six shot down and forty damaged.

Mopping Up

As the war came slowly to an end, a number of isolated paratroop missions were necessary to retain control over territory being evacuated by the Germans. The reasons for these operations varied; there was the need to establish some framework of law and order in some cases, including stopping the local inhabitants from taking revenge on German prisoners, but in other cases there was also a need to forestall other forces, the Russians or at least Communist-backed revolutionaries in Greece, for example.

British and American paratroops were dropped over

Greece as the Germans evacuated that country in October, 1944, under growing Soviet pressure on the Balkans. The despatch of an Allied force to Greece was prompted by concern over Soviet intentions, and indeed, in spite of an unopposed arrival, before long British forces were to be engaged in fighting with Greek Communist forces. An advance force, a company from the 4th Battalion of the Parachute Regiment, dropped onto Megara Airfield, near Athens, on 12th October at 12.00, arriving in a gale, and, although unopposed, half of the company was injured on landing. Within two days, the remainder of the British group was flown in.

The last paratroop mission while hostilities persisted in Europe was the dropping of two Canadian parachute battalions in the northern part of the Netherlands in *Operation Amhurst* on the night of 7-8th April, 1945, using fifty of No.38 Group's Short Stirling heavy bombers. Jumping from 1,500 feet in low cloud, the operation was entirely successful.

World War II took rather longer to end in Europe than was necessary, as a fanatical German leadership refused to accept defeat, and German troops were reluctant to surrender because the Allied demand for unconditional surrender allocated the Soviet Union a substantial part of German territory. The desire of the Western Allies to reach Berlin before Soviet forces meant that pockets of German resistance were often by-passed, to be dealt with later, although *Operation Amhurst* was the one instance of paratoops being deployed on such a mission.

In an attempt to slow down the Allied advance, the German occupation forces in the Netherlands opened the sluices on the dykes, putting large areas of farmland lying below sea level under water. Following this, the Germans attempted to requisition all civilian food supplies for their troops, and in retaliation, and partly to prevent food supplies reaching the Germans, Dutch railwaymen struck. The result of this was that even after southern areas of the Netherlands had been liberated by the British and the Americans, the northern part of the country remained under occupation with millions starving. The situation became so desperate that, starting on 29th April, 1945, the Allied air forces mounted *Operation Manna* flying food to the Dutch. The operation lasted for ten days, until 8th May, by which time the RAF alone had assigned 145 de Havilland Mosquito light bombers, and 300 Avro Lancaster and Lincoln heavy bombers, to it, with a total of 3,156 flights dropping 6,685 tons of food.

As with the Berlin Airlift a few years later, several of the pilots dropped sweets to Dutch children, using handkerchiefs for parachutes. Most of the supplies were free-dropped, however.

On 'VE' day, 8th May, 1945, aircraft from No.38 Group, RAF, flew the 1st Parachute Brigade to Copenhagen on *Operation Schnapps* while the following day the remainder of the 1st Airborne Division was flown to Norway in the start of an airlift of 7,000 troops and 2,000 tons of military stores, with the object of accepting the surrender of and then controlling 350,000 German soldiers and airmen. The Norwegian operation was spread over several days, and after the advanced party arrived on the first day, bad weather delayed the fly-in of the main body of troops, although earlier plans to drop parachutists were not needed since the Norwegians had acted quickly to seize airfields so that the troops could be airlanded. The fly-in to Norway was not completed until 13th May, and bad weather, with difficult terrain, resulted in the loss of six airmen and thirty paratroops in accidents.

Throughout the final months of the war, the RAF had maintained supply drops to resistance movements, and after the Italian surrender, this had extended to supplying the Partisans in northern, German-occupied Italy. The collapse of the German defence meant that the Partisans increasingly managed to take whole areas under their control, patrolling these by horseback or, when Allied transport aircraft and bombers dropped fuel in rubber bags, motor vehicles. Supporting this effort were flights into and out of areas in which the Partisans were active by Westland Lysanders of Army Co-operation Command. The Italian Co-Belligerent Air Force was primarily engaged on transport and rescue duties with the Allies, and helped to maintain a supplies air bridge for troops in Greece, mounting more than 9,000 transport and supply missions in Italy and the Balkans on behalf of the Allies after the Italian surrender. A substantial element in the RAF's own air transport effort in the Mediterranean by this time was provided by Nos.28 and 44 Squadrons, South African Air Force, both of which were equipped with Douglas C-47 Dakotas.

As the war in Europe ended, plans were being made to move aircraft and men to reinforce the Allied operations in the Pacific and in India-Burma, although the situation was to change considerably before the planned invasion of Japan could be mounted.

Chapter Four
Transport and Assault in the East

The vast distances, much of them over water or inhospitable terrain, of the Pacific and the Far East would seem to have been made for the transport aeroplane. Yet, while there were major operations in the Far East, the Pacific and what is normally known as the India-Burma-China theatre, which were completely dependent upon the aeroplane for success, military air transport played a role in the region which was completely different from the way in which developments had taken place in Europe. One shouldn't be too surprised at this. There were still severe limitations on the technical performance of the aeroplane, while the Pacific islands seldom had airfields, with both Pan Am and Imperial Airways in pre-World War II days using flying-boats for their services in the area. Then too, the war with Japan had developed as a war between carrier fleets, with amphibious landings, and this type of warfare was so well suited to the conditions that even when paratroops and paramarines became available to military and naval commanders, they preferred to use these men as crack troops on amphibious assaults rather than using them from the air. Air transport did play a vital role in bringing urgently needed supplies and personnel to where they were needed, but with the exception of the air supply operation to China and the air re-supply of the Chindits in Burma, this role was seldom of strategic importance. Of course, given the massive air transport commitment in Europe, a similar role over the far greater distances in the East may well have been beyond the resources available, but there was another reason as well; the Japanese did not make as affective use of the submarine as had the Germans. Then too, it has to be accepted that fast-moving attack carriers and troop transports are more cost-effective than maintaining an airborne assault, and the force does at least arrive with full air cover and with heavy equipment ready for use.

This is not to suggest that the Japanese, who lost little time in casting themselves as the villains of the piece, had neglected air transport completely. At the outbreak of World War II in the Pacific, the Japanese Army Air Force was equipped with a variety of aircraft, both of Japanese design, such as the Mitsubishi Ki-57 Type 100, developed from the MC-100 civil airliner and known as 'Topsy' to the Allies, and the Tachikawa Ki-54C, known as 'Hickory' to the Allies, as well as of American design, including the Nakajima Ki-34 Type 97 transport, a development of the Douglas DC-2. Kawasaki also built Lockheed Super Electras under licence. Between the two wars, the Japanese armed forces had worked hard to obtain the best in design from the West, and had built many British and American aircraft under licence, and, as a former World War I ally of the United Kingdom and the United States, had benefited greatly from contact with officers from the armed services of these countries before Japanese moves in China sounded warning bells in the defence and foreign ministries of the West.

Primitive starting for a Japanese Army Air Force Tachikawa Ki-54 transport and communications aircraft, known as 'Hickory' to the Allies.

Dense jungle and paddy fields make poor landing zones for gliders, but the Japanese did build and develop a number of glider designs, with the Japanese Army Air Force and the Japanese Navy Air Force both developing their own designs in competition with each other. All Japanese gliders were designated 'Ku', from the verb *Kakku,* meaning "to glide", but only one design, the Ku-8, entered quantity production, with 700 being built; the Americans found many of these on Luzon after they retook the Philippines, suggesting that they were being prepared for a counter attack against Allied forces. The largest glider was the Ku-7, sometimes known as the 'Buzzard' or 'Flying Crane', which was similar in appearance to the Go.242 and could lift up to thirty-two fully-equipped troops, but most of those built, of which there were only about forty, were powered. Neither of these designs was available until mid-1944.

There was only one significant airborne assault during the Japanese push across the Pacific in the wake of their attack on the United States Pacific Fleet at Pearl Harbor, and that was at Palembang, the vital oilfield on Borneo which accounted for 55 per cent of all crude oil production from the Netherlands East Indies. On 14th February, 1942, more than 700 Japanese paratoops landed on three points around the oilfields, and were

While the Chindits were fighting behind enemy lines, American fighter squadrons in China were cut-off by the Japanese advance into Burma, and so were yet another call upon the USAAF's air transport resources. Here, a Curtiss C-46 Commando lands at a Chinese airfield.

soon engaged in fierce fighting with the Dutch East Indies Army, although the oilfields were taken by 16th February, after the defenders had destroyed most of the oil wells to stop these from falling into enemy hands.

The Japanese landing on the Dutch island of Timor on 19th February, 1942, was accompanied by the dropping of 630 paratroops, whose role was to act as snipers, hindering the Dutch and Australian troops defending the island, and during the four days before the island was surrendered, some 550 of the Japanese snipers were killed.

Over the "Hump"

In the Pacific, United States Army Air Force and United States Navy transport aircraft maintained a supply service to forward bases, supporting the seaborne effort. The relative absence of good airfields in many of the Pacific islands led to a role for transport flying-boats such as the Martin PB2M-1 Mars, which had originally been developed as a maritime-reconnaissance aircraft but which suffered from insufficient armour protection and a limited defensive armament, and was put to work as a transport instead, re-design being considerd unnecessary for its former role in view of the substantial number of Catalina and Mariner flying-boats available to the USN. The maximum speed of just 210 mph was good for a transport of the day, regardless of type, and the Mars was a significant design in other ways as well. Four 2,200 hp Wright Double Cyclone radial engines gave a range of up

Wingate's Chindits were completely dependant upon air supply to move food and ammunition into the theatre, although transport within the area was often by mule. Here, smoke flares from the Chindits guide a C-47 on its supply drop.

to 4,100 miles. Following a first flight in late 1941, the first transport version became operational in December, 1943, and one of these aircraft lifted a payload of 35,000 lbs over a distance of 1,200 miles before the end of the year. In January, 1944, another Mars carried 20,500 lbs from California to Hawaii!

Before this, an American Volunteer Group had arrived in China during September, 1941, and were at first officially part of the Chinese Nationalist forces under General Chiang Kai-Shek, fighting the Japanese invaders, although the members of the group, about a hundred or so pilots plus supporting personnel, were all former USN, USMC and USAAC pilots, flying Curtiss P-40 Warhawk fighters, supplied by the United States to China. The commanding officer, Captain Claire L. Chennault, was also a Colonel in the Chinese Air Force! The Japanese advance through South-East Asia in December, 1941, cut the group off from its supply lines, leaving its members with the alternatives of curtailing operations or being supplied by air. The one advantage available to Chennault was that the Americans were the only people with the resources available to make such an airlift a possibility at this stage of the war. The entry of Japan into the war had also brought the United States into the conflict, and the need for secrecy or disowning the volunteers' force was gone. The disadvantages were many, apart from the quantity of supplies needed, the transport aircraft would have to fly over a part of the Himalayas which rose to more than 16,000 feet, later known to the aircrew involved as the "hump", and sustain a regular and reliable operation in the face of difficult weather, indifferent base facilities, and the possibility of enemy air attack.

The airlift started, initially with Douglas C-47s flying over the "hump", and with each carrying about two-and-a-half tons of supplies, early in 1942. A network of bases had to be established in north-east India, with railways moving supplies forward to the bases from Calcutta. The operation would have been easier had the transport aircraft been able to take the most direct route to the American Volunteer Group base at Kunming, but the threat of attack from Japanese fighters based at

Myitkyina forced them to take a route across the Himalayas and south-east Tibet. The squadrons employed on the airlift were transferred to the new United States Air Force Air Transport Command in December, 1942, while Chennault's group became part of the United States China Task Force in July, 1942, with Chennault being promoted to the rank of Brigadier-General in the USAAF. The airlift monthly total rose from 2,800 tons during February, 1943, to 7,000 tons by December of that year, while it rose even further to 12,000 tons a month during early 1944. The increase in tonnage was helped by the substitution of Curtiss C-46 Commandos on the airlift, as well as a number of Douglas C-54 Skymaster four-engined transports and some Consolidated C-109s. There were the inevitable arguments between Chennault and the military commanders in the region, with the former wanting the bulk of the airlifted supplies to keep his force operational, while the then Commander-in-Chief of the India-Burma-China theatre, Lieutenant-General Stilwell, insisted on a 50:50 split of supplies between air and ground forces. There was opposition from the Japanese, but on one of the rare occasions when they decided to do something about it, as in March, 1944, when eighteen bombers and twenty fighters went to raid Chennault's base, the P-40s shot down all but one of the Japanese aircraft.

It was in the demands placed upon transport aircraft during the war years, flying over the Himalayas and across the North Atlantic, that the reliability and acceptability of transport for more arduous post-war operations was proved.

Behind Japanese lines

In spite of many difficulties in the Far East, the British Army was able to mount what may be regarded as the most impressive, and extensive, covert operation of any war, operating behind the Japanese lines in Burma. The operation was made possible by the availability of transport aircraft and gliders, and it was even more

Chindits aboard the rescue plane back to India.

The morning after! Gliders after accidents during night landings at 'Broadway', one of the Chindit landing fields, with US and British troops. The lift-up nose of the CG-4A can be clearly seen.

impressive in that it was conceived by a man who was not an airborne soldier, Colonel, later Major-General, Orde Wingate, described by the British commander in the India-Burma-China theatre at this time, General, later Field Marshal, Wavell, as a "genius for novel and unorthodox warfare". Wingate arrived in Burma during late 1942, after a successful campaign in Ethiopia, helping the Emperor, Haile Selassie, and his troops, in their fight against the Italians.

During 1943, Wingate mounted his first campaign against the Japanese, with the formation of a force known officially as the Long-Range Penetration Brigade, but more usually referred to as the *Chindits,* taking this name from the location of their operations on the east bank of the Chindwin River. In addition to the courage, planning and sheer nerve needed to mount such an operation and on such a scale, not the least of it was Wingate's ability to appreciate the effects on warfare of both radio communications and transport aircraft. This degree of open mindedness is all the more impressive if one bears in mind that most of the senior army officers of the day had been trained in an army centred around cavalry, infantry, artillery and horse-drawn transport. The background was not unique to the British Army, which could at least claim to have seriously attempted mechanisation during the late 1930s, having largely mechanised its artillery and transport, in contrast to the German Army of World War II, even if its tanks were slower and outgunned by the German *Panzers* at the beginning of the war.

Wingate's initial force comprised 3,000 men, divided into eight columns and each with a Royal Air Force liaison officer, which infiltrated their operational zone on foot in that first year behind enemy lines. Once in enemy-held territory, the force was kept supplied by Douglas C-47 Dakotas of No.31 Squadron, and by Lockheed Hudsons of No.194 Squadron, Royal Air Force.

The main effort by the Chindits came during 1944, when, in spite of other battles in the theatre, 2,000 additional Chindits were to infiltrate Japanese lines on foot, while 10,000 were flown in, either by glider or being dropped by parachute.

Wingate's objectives during 1944 were to capture and dominate the Indaw-Kaha area, close to the 24th parallel, and having secured this area, to hold it until eventually relieved by Stilwell's troops advancing over the ground.

Stubborn as a mule, especially one determined not to join a C-47 flight to follow the Chindit campaigns!

What comes down must go up again, if it is a CG-4A glider being pulled-off the landing strip at 'Broadway' by a C-47. This 'snatch' technique worked well and might have assured the glider a role in post-war transport fleets had it not been for the rapid development of the helicopter.

For this, Wingate's force was to include six Long-Range Penetration Brigades, each fully supported by auxiliary troops, and with a mixture of British, Indian and West African troops, including many Indians from the 3rd Indian Division. This time air support was to be on a relatively generous scale, supported by a USAAF air commando under the command of Lieutenant-Colonel Philip Cochrane. The then generous allocation of seven squadrons of C-47 Dakotas, as well as bombers and fighters and a small number of L-1 and L-5 liaison aircraft to airlift casualties out of jungle clearings, showed both the growing appreciation of air power in all of its forms and of transport in particular, but it also reflected the easier availability of aircraft to the Allies by this stage of the war.

The operations of 1944 were to be in three phases, with the first phase, the advance into the area of the 16th Infantry Brigade under Brigadier Ferguson, with 2,000 troops, to be over the ground, or at least through dense jungle, while being re-supplied from the air by C-47s of No. 231 squadron, USAAF. The Brigade left Hamtung on 5th February. The aircrew of No. 231 Squadron had had no previous experience of supply drops over difficult country, and yet had to drop their supplies into zones cut into the jungle; narrow and just sixty yards in length, with any supplies which missed the zone being lost in the dense tropical forest. The first drop was badly bungled, but the lessons were soon learnt, and by 29th February, the force had reached the banks of the Chindwin, where they were joined by Wingate, who landed on a sandbank aboard a UC-64 of the USAAF. Wingate's own arrival was followed shortly afterwards by four CG-4A gliders which brought bridging equipment, so that a bridge was erected across the Chindwin and ready for use by 5th March. This was also the date chosen for the start of the second phase, the fly-in of troops from the 77th and 111th Indian Infantry Brigades, from their despatch airfields at Lalaghat, Hailakandi and Sylhet in Assam, to the landing strips beyond the Chindwin, code-named 'Broadway', 'Piccadilly' and 'Chowringhee'; these were the strips for the initial airlift, and were soon joined by another airstrip, 'Aberdeen'.

The fly-in of the second phase was one of the more difficult operations of World War II, with twenty-six C-47s each towing two Waco CG-4A gliders on a flight path which provided a minimum approach altitude over mountains of 8,000 feet, while after releasing the gliders, the transports had to climb to 9,000 feet, again to clear the mountains surrounding the landing zones. The plan was that twenty-six gliders should be despatched to both of 'Broadway' and 'Piccadilly', and that these should be followed by a wave of fourteen gliders to each strip. At 16.30 on 5th March, just half an hour before the first gliders were to be towed off, an L-1 returned from a reconnaissance flight over the landing zone with photographs showing that the Japanese had blocked 'Piccadilly' by the simple expedient of felling trees across the strip. It was decided to reduce the glider force from eighty to sixty, and to divert all of these to 'Broadway', with the first eight gliders landing well ahead of the main force in case the Japanese had also discovered the second strip. The troops aboard the first wave of eight gliders, towed by four C-47s, were all engineers who could, if the strip had been damaged by the Japanese, clear it in time

Dropping supplies to the Chindits.

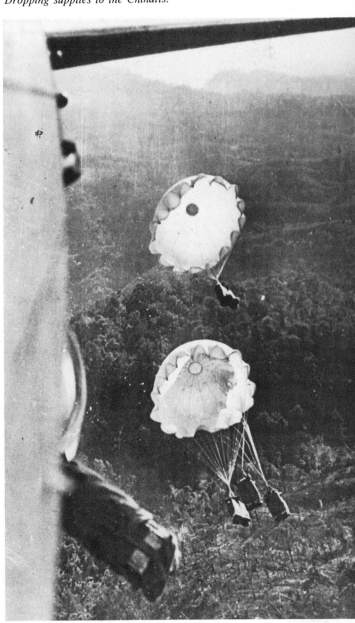

for the main wave. The first gliders left at 18.12, more than seventy minutes behind the original scheduled departure time.

A difficult and complex operation at any time, the fly-in was made more difficult by the fact that the gliders were having to land at night and the whole operation was taking place over extremely unwelcoming terrain. The technique called for the tug aircraft to fly as low as possible along a line of lights, oil-fired flares, with the glider pilots cutting their tow lines at a point half-a-mile short of the landing strip, which was marked by another flare. On landing, the gliders, which had retained their undercarriages, would roll clear of the landing strip. The eight gliders of the advance party landed successfully — the Japanese hadn't found the airstrip and the way seemed to be clear for an uneventful landing by the main body. The first two gliders of the next wave did land successfully, but the three pairs which followed all encountered a ditch on the landing strip, knocking their undercarriages off, spinning round, and blocking the landing strip. Before the flares could be realigned in an attempt to guide other gliders around the disabled aircraft, several more landed, crashed into the wreckage, and the lives of two men were lost and six injured. Two more gliders saw the accident in the poor light, and managed to glide over the wreckage before the lights were re-aligned for the rest of the gliders. A message sent to Lalaghat calling for the cancellation of a follow-up airlift was not received until almost 02.30 on 6th March, by which time nine gliders in single tow carrying heavy equipment had been despatched, and it proved possible to recall just eight of them. The sole remaining glider of

Wingate and an American liaison officer aboard a C-47 fitted out to carry mules.

this wave was released before it too could be recalled and landed too fast for the remaining unoccupied portion of the airstrip; it crashed into the jungle at the end of the strip, but its load, a bulldozer, continued to surge forward, although as it did so it raised the nose of the glider with the two pilots in it, so that miraculously they survived the incident while the bulldozer was wrecked in the jungle! After this night of chaos and wreckage, the strip was cleared again by dawn, with 400 troops in position to defend the airstrip, which had also been widened further so that the main force of troops could be flown in aboard C-47s from 20.00 that day.

One reason why 'Broadway' escaped Japanese attention lay in the fact that the only access to the strip was by air, with the nearest road many miles away in the jungle.

Although the first C-47 into 'Broadway' carried a reduced load of 4,500 lbs, this landing was so successful, in spite of being in the wrong direction, that subsequent flights carried a full load of 6,000 lbs. By 7th March, 'Chowringhee' was also ready for C-47s, although there was some confusion at the last moment as movements control doubted whether the strip really could be ready and recalled the first twenty aircraft; seven did not receive the message in time and landed, successfully! It was decided, however, that 'Chowringhee' was too close to the Japanese for safety, being just fifteen miles from a good road, so the decision was taken to evacuate the strip, with the last troops leaving on 10th March, just two hours before a raid by Japanese fighter-bombers; Japanese ground forces arrived the following day, to find the airfield deserted!

The fly-in of troops was completed by 11th March. It was decided that to accelerate the evacuation of wounded men, the L-1s and L-5s would be supplemented by gliders, with the CG-4As being snatched off the landing strips by the C-47s as they flew low over the gliders. In this technique, the glider's tow line was stretched between two lightweight poles, with the remainder of the line running through specially rigged loops, which provided some elasticity, to the glider. The glider was offset from the poles, which were in line with the approach of the tug aircraft, which had a hook mounted below the fuselage. As the tug engaged the tow line, the supporting poles collapsed, and as the tug revved up its engines to take the strain of the glider, the glider was snatched into the air. Developed in the United States, the operation was tricky and called for considerable skills on the part of the glider and the C-47 pilots, but it was successful on most occasions, and contrary to expectations, the general concensus of opinion amongst those involved was that less engine power was needed to snatch a glider off the ground than for a normal towed take-off from a runway. The technique was also useful for those instances when operations requirements were for heavier transport than could be provided by a light aircraft, yet could not find a suitable landing space for a transport aircraft. In late March, 1944, a patrol in the Kawlin-Wunthe area, aimed at disrupting Japanese supply lines, landed in five gliders, and after the completion of the operation, all five were successfully snatched back to base.

Wingate's forces were successful in tying down four Japanese divisions, a far larger force than that under his command and all of which were needed by Japanese

Briefing, with Wingate left and Lieutenant-Colonel Philip Cochrane, USAAF, right.

commanders on the front. The pressure on the Japanese intensified as the third phase of Wingate's campaign came into being, starting with the landing of United States Army engineers in six gliders to prepare an airstrip code-named 'Aberdeen', on which work began on the night of 22nd March. After two days of hard work, in humid tropical heat, the strip was ready to receive the first of the fleet of C-47s which were due to fly-in the 14th British Infantry Brigade and the 3rd West African Brigade to this strip in the Mega valley. It was originally intended to mount sixty C-47 sorties a night over six nights to airlift the two brigades, but the move coincided with a period of intense pressure on Troop Carrier Command as the 14th Army faced a major Japanese

counter-attack, and so only ten sorties a night could be flown, with the result that it took more than twenty nights from 23rd March to airlift the entire force into 'Aberdeen' The operation also suffered from disruption by bad weather. 'Aberdeen' was far from being an ideal base, it could only be approached from one end, and it was attacked by Japanese aircraft on several occasions, once just as a force of C-47s was approaching, although fortunately the Japanese aircraft and the transports did not actually meet in what would have been a hopelessly one-sided affair.

Even while 'Aberdeen' was being reinforced, the 77th Indian Division established a blockade across the main Japanese supply lines, calling this 'White City', and effectively cutting off the main Japanese forces. A landing strip was opened at 'White City', and in spite of becoming waterlogged by heavy rains on the first night, 5th April, twenty-six C-47s landed in darkness under the control of an Aldis lamp, with more than 250 men, four 25 pounder guns, six Bofors guns and a small number of anti-tank weapons.

After this major effort, other new bases were opened while some of the original bases were closed, so that the Chindits were effectively fighting a running battle with the Japanese forces struggling to pin them down. The 1st Air Commando was the mainstay of the supply line to the

The Chindit campaign showed many firsts, not the least of which was the use of one of the new Sikorsky R-4 helicopters for rescue duties; here is an R-4 in the air above one of the later R-5s.

Surrender! A Mitsubishi Ki-57, known as 'Topsy' to the Allies, brings Japanese Generals to surrender at Rangoon on 26 August, 1945.

Chindits throughout the rest of 1944 and into the first half of 1945, although by this time the strain was beginning to tell on the aircraft, and no doubt on the aircrew as well. One of the new bases was called 'Blackpool', and was located on the banks of Lake Indawguri, and this was supplied, and casualties evacuated, by two Royal Air Force Short Sunderland flying-boats on 25th May, 1945. At 'Aberdeen', in spite of its troubled existence, the base earned itself a place in aviation history as the location for the first wartime operational use of the helicopter, one of World War II's most successful and enduring inventions. Shortly after the base at 'Aberdeen' was established in March, 1944, Lieutenant Carter Harman, USAAF, flew one of the then new Sikorsky R-4 helicopters to 'Aberdeen' taking the frail machine over a 5,000 feet high mountain range, on a 130 mile flight from a forward air base. The positioning flight itself was only possible with the addition of extra fuel tanks, strapped to the machine above the head of the pilot. Whilst at 'Aberdeen', the tiny R-4 rescued three British soldiers and a downed fighter pilot, flying them out, one at a time, from a paddy field.

Meanwhile, tragedy had struck the Chindits with the death of Wingate on 24th March, when the North American B-25 Mitchell bomber in which he was flying crashed and exploded whilst attempting to land. Nevertheless, the force which he had built up had gained

a momentum of its own, and success was already assured.

There were other, perhaps more conventional, operations by airborne troops in the Pacific by this time. The first of these occurred in New Guinea during September, 1943, and was part of a joint American and Australian campaign to stop the advance by Japanese forces through New Guinea to a position which would enable them to threaten Australia itself. Difficult overland communications meant that the Japanese commander placed great value in holding the ports of Lae and Salamua on the Huon Gulf, at the eastern end of the island. Heavy fighting by Australian and American troops started in June, 1943, and led to an amphibious landing by the Australian 9th Division to the east of Lae on 5th September. Two days later, on 7th September, 2,000 paratroops from the US 503rd Parachute Infantry Regiment dropped from C-47 transports to cut the road into Lae through the Markham Valley, completing the encirclement by sea and by air of 20,000 Japanese troops. Although the paratroops had to fall back under a heavy Japanese attack, the overall Japanese position was such that Lae fell on 16th September with more than 10,000 Japanese casualties, including almost 3,000 killed.

American commanders placed considerable importance on the early liberation of the Philippines, but a far stronger than expected Japanese defence of Leyte delayed the retaking of the islands, with the entire operation taking almost a year from October, 1944, until the surrender of Japanese forces in September, 1945. When the US 11th Airborne Division arrived in Luzon on

Douglas C-47 Skytrain from the Jungle Skippers squadron of the 317th Troop Carrier Group drops a stick of paratroops onto the golf course at Corregidor on 16 February 1945. Many discarded parachute canopies from earlier drops litter the broken and cratered ground below.

31st January, 1945, they landed from the sea at Nasugbu Bay, some forty miles south of Manila. Determined not to suffer the major delays which were affecting operations on the nearby island of Leyte, the American drive through Corregidor on 16th February included a paratroop drop as well as an amphibious landing. The paratroops missed their dropping zone and suffered heavy casualties from a defending Japanese force of about 4,000 men. A further airborne operation occurred during this campaign, in late June, when the 11th Airborne Division was dropped onto positions around the northern end of the Cagayan Valley, an area of strong Japanese resistance, but these forces and three ground based divisions, were contained by the Japanese forces and made little further progress.

Japanese resistance knew few limitations. While the *Kamikaze* suicide attacks were the best example of this, the term is usually used to cover suicide attacks by manned aircraft. An unusual *Kamikaze* raid was mounted on Yontan Airfield at Okinawa in May, 1945, as

the Americans were securing their hold on the island. A small number of Mitsubishi Ki.21 Type 97 'Sally' bombers crash-landed to discharge Japanese troops who destroyed several fighters, bombers and transport aircraft before the USAAF guards at the base could stop them. The small Japanese force was soon eliminated.

Even as the tide turned against the Japanese, Allied forces often found themselves in difficulties, and on some occasions, transport aircraft resolved the situation. A good example occurred during early 1944, on the Arakan front, where the 7th Indian Division was surrounded by Japanese troops, but an airlift of supplies enabled the beleaguered force to fight off their Japanese attackers. Shortly after this success, the 4th British Corps, defending Kohima and Imphal, was surrounded, an air supply drop was maintained until this force could be relieved by troops advancing over the ground. As the Allied advance continued, in March, 1945, some 60,000 tons of supplies and 48,000 troops were flown into Burma, and 11,000 Allied casualties were flown out to India.

Unusual Allied operations included the landing of a troop of Royal Marines early in 1945 at Biluyen Island, with the troops being landed from a Catalina flying-boat to cause a diversion so that other forces could continue

Whilst flying 'The Hump' or supply dropping, the Skytrain and Dakota transports were always under threat from attack by Japanese fighters. This rare photograph shows Vickers 'K' machine guns manned by RAF Dakota crew members. The fuselage is littered with an assortment of vital supplies to be air dropped.

their advance, but the operation ran into difficulties as strong tides made the inflatable dinghies difficult to handle. In the event, the force withdrew with several casualties, and after the loss of its commander.

The one major airborne assault of the campaign in Burma arose from the need to seize the Japanese defences at Elephant Point, ready for an amphibious landing at Rangoon. The 50th Indian Parachute Brigade was not ready for a major operation at this time, with one of its battalions recently divided to provide the basis of two new battalions, while another had half of its troops on leave. In the event, an improvised battalion was created solely for the operation, drawing most of the paratroops from the 2nd and 3rd Gurkha Parachute battalions, while forty Douglas C-47 transports were obtained from the US 2nd Air Command, in spite of their crews never having handled paratroops! The American aircrew were

given some rather hasty training and their aircraft were as quickly modified with rails for parachute static lines. On 1st May, the Pathfinder force landed five miles to the west of Elephant Point, dropping from two aircraft, and were followed thirty minutes later by the main force dropping from two successive waves of C-47s, with a successful fly-in and jump into the dropping zone. The operation, so hastily assembled, soon gained an air of anti-climax, for as they advanced towards Elephant Point, they discovered that the Japanese battery crew had abandoned their position, which was taken without an encounter with enemy forces; one of the few instances of this happening during the war with the Japanese. Had the paratroops not been available, or if the Japanese had defeated them, it would have had serious repercussions on *Operation Dracula*, the taking of Rangoon.

Japanese surrender was more protracted than that of Germany with an acceptance of American surrender terms on 10th August, 1945, although the formal surrender did not occur until 2nd September. Meanwhile, American troops, drawn from the large force which had been poised to invade Japan, were prepared as an occupation force, which would later include troops from the other Allied Powers, notably Australia, although commitments elsewhere meant that a substantial British occupation force could not be provided. The original intention was for an advance party of American paratroops to jump onto Atsugi Airfield, some twenty miles to the south-west of Tokyo, on 26th August. However, when the first American troops did arrive at Atsugi that day, they were air-landed aboard a mixed fleet of ten Douglas C-54 Skymaster transports and Boeing B-17 Flying Fortress heavy bombers, and instead of paratroops, the 150 men were communications and technical specialists. Further communications specialists were flown in aboard a fleet of forty-eight C-54s which arrived the following day, although the first aircraft crashed with the loss of all nineteen personnel aboard — the death toll could have been higher but for the fact that most of the aircraft's load consisted of communications equipment. The first combat troops did not arrive until 29th August, when an advance party from the US 11th Airborne Division arrived, again at Atsugi, with the airlift of the main force starting at 06.00 on 30th August; and aircraft arrived at Atsugi at two minute intervals carrying the first of an occupation force of 150,000 men, all of whom were in the Japanese islands, arriving by air and by sea, by 21st September. Reports at the time made the point that Kadena Airfield on Okinawa had aircraft occupying two square miles of parking space! Had an assault been necessary, however, most of it would have come from the sea, for the United States and Royal Navies had planned a combined aircraft carrier force of 122 vessels, although two-thirds of these would have been small escort carriers or CVEs.

The Soviet Union had made little use of paratroops or of gliders during its advance through Europe and into Germany, except for the occupation of Rumanian Bessarabia. In the East, the Soviet Union did not formally declare war on Japan until 8th August, 1945, but gliders and paratroops were used for the Soviet advance into Japanese-held Manchuria, while the advancing ground forces also relied greatly on air transport, with huge distances of desert and grassland, few roads and railways, between the Soviet armies and their main base facilities.

Japanese forces were in retreat in Manchuria, with little opposition to Soviet troops from ground forces as the official date of surrender approached. During August, a combination of paratroops and air-landed troops using gliders, descended onto Chanchon, Harbin, Kirin, Mukden, and Tiensin, quickly taking a claimed 88,000 Japanese troops prisoner. Three days later, a similar operation resulted in the occupation of Dairen and Port Arthur, while 71,000 Japanese prisoners were claimed by Soviet forces.

After this, the first major peacetime operation for the Allied air forces was to be the repatriation of their own prisoners of war from the Far East, and elsewhere.

Chapter Five
Into a Cold War

The return of peace found the role of air transport aircraft more widely understood by the air forces and the armies of the world, with the aeroplane's potential for assault and supply from the air, and for other duties as well, such as movement and relief operations, now appreciated by many who would have ignored it only a few years earlier. There had been other changes as well, with the advent of the turbojet and the helicopter during the war years, while the gliders had pointed the way to a change in the shape of transport aircraft, especially for military transports, with the aircraft becoming rather more portly in appearance, and, over the ten or fifteen years which followed the end of the war, the need for rear-loading doors for easier supply drops or for loading and unloading vehicles, became a fundamental part of the specification for military transports. The situation was to evolve in which the military was no longer to be satisfied with converted bombers, nor even with military variants of commercial airliners, but was to require, and to obtain, transport types designed specifically for its own purposes, so successfully that some of these even found buyers amongst those airlines specialising in large items of air freight or operating away from the main airports.

Much of this was to come later, for at first many of the transport aircraft available during the surprisingly busy first few years of peace were to be converted bombers; the Lancastrian was an Avro Lancaster without bomb bay or guns, the Halton was a similar modification of the Halifax, while the Boeing B-17 Flying Fortresses and the Consolidated B-24 Liberators also underwent similar treatment. While the four-engined Douglas C-54, the military version of the DC-4 airliner, had entered USAAF service during the war, its four engines enabling it to lift three times the load of the C-47, and other similar developments were on their way elsewhere, these aircraft were not available in sufficient numbers. Retaining C-47s was only part of the answer, the aeroplane was still in demand, and commercial versions were still in production, for shorter routes and for smaller numbers of passengers or lower freight loads, but for longer distances, the speed and the range of other aircraft was needed, hence the appeal of the converted bombers. Cramped and uncomfortable they may have been, but even airlines, such as BOAC, had to inflict such aircraft on their passengers, operating them on the UK-Australia service, for example.

As in the early post-World War I period, part of the

As the war progressed, the RAF found itself operating a number of bomber types as transports, with gun turrets removed and faired over, and many of these remained in service during the early post-war years; this is a C-87, the transport conversion of the Liberator bomber.

Fairchild's C-82 marked a step forward in the air dropping of supplies, with a practical rear loading and unloading door, roller floor for the easy movement of cargo, which could either be free dropped or pulled from the aircraft by its parachute.

answer was to use bomber technology with a new fuselage more suited to air transport operations. Boeing used B-29 Superfortress technology to build the giant Stratocruiser airliner and C-97 transport, while Avro used the aerodynamic surfaces of the Lancaster on the York airliner and transport, and Vickers did the same, creating from the aerodynamic surfaces of the Wellington bomber the Viking airliner and its close relation, the Valetta military transport, with, later, a further development, the Varsity. The problem of retaining bombers in the transport role was not confined to Europe, the USN's R3Y transports were variants of the Privateer, the maritime-reconnaissance version of the Liberator.

Even the glider had a role to play in this. One late-war glider design under development by the American Chase concern led directly to the Fairchild C-123 Provider transport aircraft. The Bristol Freighter owed more to Bristol's experience with the pre-war Bombay than to any glider, but the Hamilcar glider almost seems to have inspired the layout of this aircraft, which was best known for its car-carrying and livestock transport operations, but which also served with many air forces, including those of Pakistan and New Zealand.

These aircraft were joined later by types with obvious

benefits for military air transport, notably the ability to carry bulky loads. By the end of the 1940s, the United States Air Force obtained the giant Douglas C-124 Globemaster, able to carry loads of up to twenty-five tons over long distances, while during the 1950s, the Royal Air Force received the Blackburn Beverley, with a twenty-two ton load and an impressive short field performance, which made up for its slow speed, a plodding 160 mph cruising! Smaller than either of these, but far more practical for the dropping of supplies, was the Fairchild C-119, known by the manufacturer as the Packet, but more affectionately and usually referred to as the 'Flying Boxcar', an aeroplane of twin-boom configuration able to lift more than five and a half tons. Other new arrivals were improvements of earlier tried and trusted designs, the Douglas C-118 Liftmaster was a pressurised development of the C-54, as well as the military version of the DC-6 airliner. Utility became the theme for military transport aircraft, and the French Nord Noratlas was a smaller aircraft of similar configuration to the C-119, with twin engines and twin boom fuselage, to be followed later by the British Armstrong-Whitworth Argosy, with four turboprops. The advent of the jet engine was to lead to faster transport in due course, but of more immediate benefit was the derivative of the turbojet, the turboprop, which was to be far more suitable and flexible for military transport applications. Even piston-engined aircraft benefited from the use of jet engines to boost their performance, removing some of the weight and other penalties experienced when operating from high airfields or in tropical heat. The C-119 frequently used this technique, with a single small jet engine mounted above the fuselage, and so too did the smaller Fairchild C-123 Provider, with two turbojets mounted under the wings.

The glider was the casualty in this, but the reasons were complex, going beyond the improved performance of transport aircraft, and their ability to use shorter and rougher landing strips, to the other major invention of the war years, the helicopter. As the helicopter emerged as an aircraft capable of lifting a reasonable load, experiments led to concepts such as 'vertical envelopment' to describe the rapid deployment of helicopter-borne forces to surround enemy positions, and 'vertical replenishment', for the re-supply of forces, and especially of warships, with many naval auxiliaries using helicopters to transfer stores rather than by using lines between the ships.

The airlift capability of the early helicopters, such as the Bell 47 and the Sikorsky S-51, was limited; in the transport role these machines were only suitable for communications or for CASEVAC duties, and both types proved their suitability for these operations, not least during the Korean War. Yet, as early as 1946, the twin-rotor Piasecki HRP-1 Rescuer was able to give some idea of what could be expected from the helicopter, able to lift up to one ton of cargo, which could be slung under the fuselage, or carry up to eight passengers. The Sikorsky rival to the Rescuer enjoyed far greater success, and it was also to outstrip the entire production of all earlier Sikorsky helicopters, this was the S-55, known as the H-19 by the USAF, and as the H-19 Chickasaw to the United States Army, and built under licence in the United Kingdom by Westland as the Whirlwind. The ten-passenger H-19, or S-55, used either 550hp Pratt & Whitney R-1340 or 700hp Wright R-1300 piston engines, and could carry up to ten fully-equipped troops at a cruising speed of 90 mph. That the helicopter was still limited was not beyond doubt, but nor was there any doubt about its potential, which was to be amply demonstrated on several occasions during the Korean War and during the emergency in Malaya. Large doors meant that troops could be unloaded quickly, while folding rotor blades helped in striking down into the hangar of an aircraft carrier, or in fitting the helicopter into a transport aircraft for long range deployment.

An early distinction of the S-55 was the first trans-Atlantic helicopter flight, with two H-19As of the Military Air Transport Service Air Rescue Wing positioning from East Hartford, Connecticut to the USAF base at Wiesbaden, West Germany. The fuel capacity of each aircraft was increased from the standard 180 gallons to 480 US gallons, and they left East Hartford on 14th July, 1952, flying via Greenland and Iceland to Prestwick in Scotland, arriving there sixteen days later, on 31st July, having spent forty-five hours, forty-five minutes in flying time crossing the Atlantic. The total journey time to West Germany was twenty days, with each H-19 spending fifty-two hours in the air.

This performance, and other performances during the

As the post-war demand for ever larger helicopters developed, the homeland of Igor Sikorsky was not to be left behind; this is the twin-rotor Yakovlev Yak-24 troop-carrying helicopter of the mid-1950s, known as 'Horse' to NATO. Russian utility extended to a tail ramp, for some reason a feature overlooked on Western designs of the period.

Successor to the C-82 was the more familiar C-119 Packet, or 'Flying Boxcar', an aircraft often used with turbojet engines to boost performance when taking-off from hot or high airfields.

Korean War, was impressive, but the trans-Atlantic flight was more of a novelty than a practical proposition. It could not have been used on the Bruneval raid, for example, although it could have been useful for the Normandy landings providing that the anti-aircraft fire had been adequately suppressed beforehand. The follow on from the S-55, the S-58, known to the United States Army as the H-34A Choctaw, offered a better performance and could carry up to sixteen troops, while many of those built outside of the United States, notably by Westland, as the Wessex, used turbine propulsion for extra performance.

In the Soviet Union, the twin-rotor Yakovlev Yak-24, code-named 'Horse' by NATO, entered service in 1954, and was able to take up to forty troops, although by 1960, this helicopter was being superseded by the Mil Mi-6, a helicopter able to carry up to sixty-five passengers.

Relief from the air

While these developments were exciting and were to enhance the air transport capability of the air force, it was very much a case of "jam tomorrow" for the units engaged on the early post-war operations.

As the war came to an end in Europe, the RAF and the USAAF helped to move displaced persons around the Continent, and after the disruption of communications and normal food distribution patterns in the aftermath of German defeat, these air forces also found themselves flying emergency food supplies at times. By August, 1945, transport had become one of the main tasks for the Royal Air Force, which was flying an average of 9,000 passengers between Europe and the Far East each month; the passengers were mainly returning former prisoners of war who had opted to return home by air, while there were also senior military personnel and diplomatic staff

for the re-opened overseas missions. Most troop deployments were still by troopship. As Japanese resistance collapsed, squadrons were diverted from bombing duties to reinforce the transport squadrons, with more than 400 Short Stirling and Consolidated Liberator bombers readied by the RAF to help fly released PoWs back to Europe; the London *Times* ran a headline on the release of the PoWs and their repatriation saying "Air Travel Preferred", almost seeming surprised that homeward-bound ex-prisoners would turn down the chance of spending several weeks in a slow troopship! The RAF conducted a similar operation in Europe, helped by the South African Air Force, which itself handled 100,000 former PoWs by the end of January, 1946.

There were other demands too, even as the strength of the RAF was being rundown to a peacetime level. The severe winter of 1946/47 in England meant that the aircraft of the much reduced No.38 Group, Royal Air Force, were heavily committed to flying both animal and human foodstuffs to villages isolated by heavy snowfalls. Such peacetime operations were not without risk, and a Handley Page Halifax bomber of No.47 Squadron crashed in Staffordshire killing all aboard, whilst flying in heavy snow.

Reductions in the size of the armed forces were inevitable, for after all, the wartime scale of manpower could not be sustained in peacetime. In the United States, there was re-organisation as well, with the United States Air Force finally being established as an autonomous air arm free of Army control in September, 1947, replacing the United States Army Air Force and having full equality with the United States Army and the United States Navy. This also left the United States Army free to develop its own organic air power, tailored to suit its own battlefield mobility needs, and inevitably this was to

73

mean the development of a large fleet — the Western world's largest — of helicopters of all kinds. Within the new USAF there were other changes, and on 1st June, 1948, the Air Transport Command was merged with the Naval Air Transport Service to establish the Military Air Transport Service, or MATS, as part of the USAF, which then assumed responsibility for all American strategic air power, although for a period there were a small number of transport aircraft still left in the USN and the USMC, just as one of the USAF's commands, Tactical Air Command, also maintained some theatre air transport capability of its own. Gradually most of these units were absorbed into MATS, with the exception of the USN's carrier onboard delivery transports, developed from anti-submarine and airborne early warning aircraft, to fly urgent supplies to carriers whilst underway at sea.

It was soon to be clear that peace was an illusion, and even the end of colonial responsibilities was to create problems in which military air transport aircraft would play a part.

The partition of India into India and Pakistan on Independence in 1947, created problems, with large numbers of Hindus resident in what was now Pakistan, and many Moslems in what was now an independent Hindu India. A large proportion of these were on good terms with their neighbours, but others were less fortunate. On independence, the Royal Indian Air Force had lost several of its squadrons to provide the basis of what was to be, for a period, the Royal Pakistani Air Force, leaving the post-independence RIAF with a total strength of just eight squadrons, seven of which were fighter units and one, happily as it turned out, a transport unit with Douglas C-47 Dakotas. The refugee problem, which resulted from inter-communal strife within India and Pakistan on independence, reached dimensions which have never been accurately totalled. Most walked to safety, many others risked rail travel, with the danger of ambush and murder in both cases, with pitched battles even taking place between columns of refugees moving in opposite directions. A fortunate few, in relation to the total number involved, were flown by the RIAF's transport squadron, No.12, which carried 30,000 refugees in almost a thousand flights from Pakistan to India.

The evacuation of refugees from Pakistan had hardly been completed with the RIAF having to airlift troops into Srinagar, after insurgents moving through Kashmir, a disputed state on the borders of India and Pakistan, had reached the outskirts of the city. The need to meet threats along India's borders from both Pakistan and China was to be a recurring theme of India's post-independence history, and one which ensured a high priority for transport units with the air force. Pakistan also had to accord air transport a high priority for as long as East Pakistan was a part of the country, using Bristol Freighters to fly the 1,000 mile long route over Indian territory to East Pakistan, before this 'province' seceded from Pakistan many years later.

World War II had itself hardly ended before a so-called 'Cold War' broke out between the former World War II Allies. The Soviet Union and, after a revolution, Communist China were on one side of an 'Iron Curtain', with the United States and the United Kingdom on the other. Soviet forces held those countries which they had "liberated" from the Germans as World War II had ended, while by contrast British and American forces had simply passed through on their way to occupy Germany.

The Avro York transport had an airliner fuselage, but owed much to the World War II Lancaster; this is an RAF example loading supplies for Berlin.

Berlin Airlift, and Avro Lancastrians, of Flight Refuelling, at the fuel discharge point at the Berlin end of the lift.

The Royal Air Force did not suffer quite as devastating a run-down in its strength as that which had followed the ending of World War I, and although overall armed forces could be cut, there could be no doubt about the strong defensive posture adopted. The most enduring of the alliances were the Warsaw Pact and the North Atlantic Treaty Organisation. The original members of the Warsaw Pact were the USSR, Bulgaria, Czechoslovakia, East Germany, Hungary, Rumania and Yugoslavia, with the last mentioned withdrawing early on, while Albania never joined, and Rumania managed to avoid having Soviet troops stationed in the country in later years. The North Atlantic Treaty Organisation, or NATO, included the United States and the United Kingdom, Belgium, Canada, Denmark, France, Greece, Italy, Luxembourg, Iceland, the Netherlands, Norway and Turkey, while West Germany joined during the mid-1950s, followed by Spain many years later, and France left the military command structure of NATO, while remaining a member of the organisation, during the late 1960s. Less successful defensive alliances promoted by the West were the Baghdad Pact, which was forced to change its name to the Central Treaty Organisation after a revolution in Iraq, and which gradually disintegrated under political pressures, and the South-East Asia Treaty Organisation, which fell apart as a result of British, Australian and New Zealand indifference, leaving the last two countries to seek a trilateral alliance with the United States. There were other agreements relating to defence with Malaysia and Singapore.

The growing tension between East and West was to result in a number of difficulties, the so-called 'Cold War Hot Spots', in the years which were to follow, with direct conflict between the major powers rare, except in Korea. For air transport, the most challenging of these problems was the greatest relief operation of all, the Berlin Airlift.

The partition of Germany which followed Allied victory in 1945 had given Britain, France, the United States and the Soviet Union responsiblity for pre-allocated areas of the country, while the former capital, Berlin, some distance into Soviet territory, was also administered jointly by the four Allied Powers. The Western zones of Germany were being welded into a new democratic state, with some of the impetus coming from the need to create a new and acceptable currency so that post-war reconstruction could progress. The Soviet Union had no intention of allowing democracy to flourish in its own part of Germany, but also made much of the fact that the British, French and American zones of Berlin were isolated from the rest of what is now the Federal German Republic, while the Russian zone of Berlin was the capital of the German Democratic Republic. This, and the need to reform the currency used in West Berlin, played a part in creating the international tension which led the Soviet Union to cut the railway link to Berlin on 1st April, 1948, for a period of a couple of days, while the road and rail links were cut on 11th June, again for two days, although on this occasion the excuse was given that the *autobahn* had to be close due to repairs on the Elbe Bridge, while rail traffic was reinstated after one day. Finally, on 24th June, all freight and passenger traffic to the city by road, rail and inland waterway was closed by the Soviet Union, followed the day after by a ban on food supplies to West Berlin from the farms of East Germany, leaving a city of 2.5 million inhabitants to starve and to freeze.

Appreciating the vulnerability of West Berlin to Soviet pressure, and anxious not to yield further territory and peoples to Soviet rule, on 1st April, the United States Air Force in Europe, USAFE, decided to operate thirty flights by C-47s of the 53rd Troop Carrier Squadron with military supplies for the US Army garrison in West Berlin. The aircraft flew from Rhein-Main, just outside Frankfurt, 275 miles from Berlin, along the southernmost air corridor to Berlin. The exercise was intended to demonstrate the intention of the Americans not to yield, but the Soviet Union also applied counter-pressure, with Yakovlev Yak-9 fighters harassing the aircraft during their flight. Less fortunate was a British European Airways Vickers Viking 1B airliner, flying to Berlin's British zone airport at Gatow along one of the approved air corridors on 5th April, 1948, with ten passengers aboard: A Yak-9 made a mock attack on the aircraft, narrowly missing the starboard wing, before making a climbing turn and, obviously intending to make another pass at the airliner, collided with it at 1,000 feet! There were no survivors.

On 26th June, 1948, West Berlin had supplies of grain and flour sufficient for seventeen days; cereal for thirty-two days; fats for forty-eight days; meat and fish for twenty-five days; potatoes for forty-two days; and skimmed and dried milk for twenty-six days. There were also cows grazing on farmland within the city limits, although not enough to provide for all of the city's fresh milk needs. To maintain these supplies, a daily food requirement existed of 13,500 tons, including 646 tons of wheat and flour, and three tons of yeast. An airlift remained the only option if the city was not to be abandoned, yet the United States Air Force in Europe estimated that its own daily airlift capability would be

just 700 tons, and that even with strict rationing, a basic sound diet would still require 5,000 tons of food daily. According to the same estimates, the use of other Allied aircraft and chartered commercial transports would lift the daily airlift total to 3,000 tons, although the difference between this and the required daily delivery could be closed by boning meat and dehydrating potatoes, reducing the weight of these essential items before transport by 25 per cent. By agreement with the Soviet Union, air access to the city was available through three air corridors, roughly linking West Berlin with south, central and northern Germany, but while each of these corridors was twenty miles wide, there was an altitude restriction of 10,000 feet, largely to prevent attempts at aerial reconnaissance and partly to avoid any severe restriction on Soviet military flights over the corridors.

The Royal Air Force was to call the airlift, *Operation Plainfare*, the United States Air Force was to call it *Operation Vittles*. This wasn't to be the only slight area of difference, the estimates by both air forces at the end of the operation were also to differ, with the USAFE calculating that the combined airlift had moved 2,323,067 tons of supplies, while the RAF, unusually for the normally conservative British, put the total as being slightly higher, at 2,325,809 tons. Only 30 per cent of the cargo flown into Berlin was food, some 60 per cent was accounted for by coal, and so that the economic life of the beleaguered city could struggle on, raw materials were also carried for Berlin manufacturers, and their products were ferried out to West Germany; one estimate considered that for every 260 tons of raw materials flown in, 100 tons of manufactured products were flown out again.

The airlift started just two days after the closure of the surface links, with Douglas C-47s of the 61st USAFE

The military transport element of the Berlin Airlift was augmented by chartered airliners, including this Avro York of Skyways and the Avro Tudor of British South American Airways behind the York.

Star of the Berlin Airlift, and, many years later, of operations to the former Belgian Congo, the Douglas C-124 Globemaster.

Transport Group flying just eighty tons of milk, flour and medical supplies into Tempelhof, the operation being limited by the three ton maximum load for these aircraft, which made thirty-two flights on that first day from the USAFE base at Wiesbaden. The Royal Air Force had despatched the first aircraft of its contribution, eight C-47 Dakotas, from Waterbeach, near Cambridge, the previous day. The outlook at this stage was bleak, with the USAFE having just 102 C-47s at its disposal and the RAF believing that it might be able to provide 150 aircraft, while the *Armée de l'Air* could only offer personnel, with all of its transport aircraft committed to the war in French Indo-China. By 29th June, the USAFE had Nos.60 and 61st Transport Groups flying 384 tons of supplies to the city, while the RAF had fully committed Nos.24 and 30 Squadrons, again with C-47s. The early performances were affected by chaos on the ground, and some unrealistic attitudes, for example, the air traffic control centre at Frankfurt insisting on a twenty-five minute separation between aircraft taking off for Berlin. Elsewhere, aircraft were parked nose to tail at Wiesbaden, and it could take up to thirty hours to make just two return trips to Berlin, with aircraft waiting an hour at Berlin's Tempelhof airport before unloading started.

Fortunately, both the British and the American governments were determined not to allow themselves to be defeated, and the necessary impetus for organisation and the provision of all of the resources required came from the President of the United States and the British

Prime Minister. The first of thirty-five additional Douglas C-54 Skymasters assigned initially to the Berlin Airlift from Alaska, Hawaii and the Caribbean arrived at Wiesbaden on 30th June, and were ready for operations a little more than ten hours after their arrival. Two squadrons of Short Sunderland flying-boats, ten aircraft in all, of Nos. 201 and 230 Squadrons, RAF, were moved from their base in Northern Ireland to Hamburg, arriving on 5th July. The Sunderlands were based at the old Blohm und Voss flying-boat factory, and operated to the Havel See at Berlin. By 20th July, the RAF had ten Sunderlands, forty Avro Yorks and fifty Dakotas on the airlift, while the USAFE had fifty-four C-54s and 105 C-47s, with the nine ton payloads and greater speed of the Yorks and C-54s providing a welcome boost to the daily delivery, which passed the 2,000 ton mark to 2,250 tons, two thirds of it in USAFE and one-third in RAF aircraft, that day.

The increasing tempo of the airlift was beginning to show up weaknesses. Construction of a new runway was started at Tempelhof on 12th July in anticipation of a long siege, while a new runway which had been under construction at RAF Gatow came into operation on 27th July, but even so the RAF had to move its C-47s from Wunsdorf to Fassburg in West Germany in an attempt to reduce congestion at the 'mainland' end of the airlift. Worst of all, the first of several accidents to airlift aircraft occurred at Wiesbaden on 9th July when a USAFE C-54 crashed, killing the crew of two USAFE pilots and one United States Army civilian employee. A further accident occurred on 25th July, when a C-47 struck a Berlin apartment block, killing the crew of two. Meanwhile, the C-54 force was raised to seventy-two aircraft, operating

Douglas C-54s of the USAF Military Air Transport Service on the Berlin Airlift.

in eight squadrons of nine aircraft each, while the overall command of the operation was vested in a USAFE officer, Major-General William H. Turner, the Deputy Commander of the new Military Air Transport Service, who took over control from the USAFE on 29th July.

Naturally, the Russians were determined not to cave in to this show of dedication by the Allies, with the Soviet Union threatening to fly military aircraft in the air corridors to West Berlin, the first of a number of actions designed to make the operation more difficult and dangerous, including the firing of anti-aircraft weapons close to the air corridors.

Air freight has always been at its best for transporting relatively low weight, high value goods, or perhaps items which are perishable, such as fresh fruit out of season or, perishable in their own way, newspapers. Bulk commodities have never been well-suited to air transport, and indeed such tend also to be low value in relation to their weight and even when moved by sea or by rail use the slowest means. Yet, the Berlin Airlift was forced to take the energy needs of the city into account, and with winter not too far away, this was in many ways as important as the airlift of food. Coal and oil both offered major problems, since neither the airports in West Germany nor those at West Berlin possessed the specialised handling equipment necessary for either commodity. In an attempt to solve the unloading problem for coal, a Boeing B-29 Superfortress made an experimental flight with coal in the bomb bay, opening the bomb doors to unload the coal in a free drop while flying low, but the coal was reduced to dust on impact. Coal had to be handled the hard way, and the first coal shipment was carried as early as 7th July in barrack bags aboard the C-54s, the bags helping to make loading and unloading easier. In spite of the start of the coal airlift, the following day 75 per cent power cuts were introduced, with the city's trams and electric underground trains not running at all after 18.00. Special aircraft and loading and unloading facilities had to be provided for oil, and a British company, Flight Refuelling, provided four Avro Lancastrian tanker aircraft, each aircraft capable of lifting 1,500 gallons, at a charter rate of £98 per hour. These were also the first commercial chartered aircraft to join the airlift, but they were soon to be followed by others, almost all of which were owned by British companies, offered £45 per flying hour for chartered DC-

3s or C-47s, which was £8 an hour above the prevailing rate on the charter market. The extra payments were made to allow for the risk element from Soviet intervention and higher insurance premiums, as well as the costs of maintaining aircraft away from their main base for an indefinite period. Apart from the Lancastrian tankers, converted from ex-World War II Lancaster bombers, the aircraft of what came to be known as the civil lift included a wide variety of types, including the extremely useful, and at the time new, Bristol 170 Freighters, able to handle bulky items.

Before long, the aircraft of the civil lift were to include Avro Yorks, Handley Page Haltons, converted from Halifax bombers, sleek Avro Tudor airliners, Short Hythe flying-boats, and the new Vickers Viking airliners, as well as the Freighters, Lancastrians and DC-3s already mentioned. In all, some twenty-five companies, many of them with just a single aircraft, joined the civil lift. They included Air Contractors, Air Flight, which had been founded by Air Vice-Marshal Donald Bennett, a retired RAF officer who had led the RAF's wartime Pathfinder Squadrons; Airwork; Air Transport (Channel Islands); Acquila Airways; British American Air Services; British Netherlands Air Services; British South American Airways; British Overseas Airways Corporation; Bond Air Services; Ciros Aviation; Eagle Aviation; Flight Refuelling; Hornton Airways; Kearsley Airways; Lancashire Aircraft Corporation; Scottish Airlines; Silver City Airways; Seivewright Airways; Skyflight; Skyways; Transworld Charter; Trent Valley Aviation; World Air Freight and Westminster Airways; while British European Airways, Air France and Pan American World Airways, maintained a regular passenger service between West Berlin and West Germany from the Berlin airports at Gatow, Tempelhof and Tegel. None of these British airlines remains today. British South American Airways was taken over by BOAC after the failure of its Avro Tudor airliners, but BSAA's managing director, Donald Bennett, used his severance pay to buy two Tudors for £4,500 and formed Air Flight as an expression of his confidence in the aircraft. BOAC and BEA were later merged to form today's British Airways, while Skyways was later absorbed by Dan Air, with Airwork and Silver City

*War in Korea brought the helicopter to the fore, with
spectacular achievements in helilift operations by Sikorsky
S-55s of the USMC and USN.*

becoming part of British United Airways before that
company merged with Caledonian Airways to form
British Caledonian Airways. Flight Refuelling was not an
airline at all, and continues to this day as a manufacturer.

Only British, American and French aircraft were
allowed to fly into West Berlin under the agreement with
the Soviet Union, but to ease the pressure on the crews of
the RAF's transport squadrons, aircrew were seconded
from the Royal Australian Air Force, Royal New
Zealand Air Force, and the South African Air Force, all
flying with the RAF's Dakota squadrons. The Australian
pilots flew a total of more than 7,000 tons of freight and
over 7,700 passengers during their spell on the airlift,
while the South Africans, on 1,240 flights, carried just
over 4,100 tons of supplies.

As the pressure of the airlift mounted, all three of West
Berlin's airports were pressed into use; Tempelhof in the
American zone, Gatow in the British and Tegel in the
French, the last being the least convenient of the three for
the city centre. Stacking over Berlin was avoided
whenever possible due to the limited airspace available
before aircraft found themselves straying over the
Eastern zone, and also because military aircrew and air
traffic controllers were unused to this procedure. In
desperation, the USAF recalled reservists to its air traffic
control units, and sent these men to West Germany and
to West Berlin, wisely judging that these men had the
required civil ATC experience to cope with the high
density of traffic. On 5th August, the first manufactured

goods were exported from the city, returning aboard
airlift aircraft, while two days later the combined airlift
delivered more than 4,000 tons of supplies to the city.
While the smaller aircraft of the day struggled to
maintain the airlift, an idea of what air transport was to
be able to achieve in later years came with a brief visit by a
solitary Douglas C-124 Globemaster of the USAF, which
first flew into West Berlin on 17th August with a load of
twenty tons, more than twice that of a C-54 or a York,
and almost seven times the maximum of a C-47! The C-
124 made twenty-four flights to Berlin between 17th
August and 24th September, carrying a total of 428 tons.
Before the C-124 departed, three Fairchild C-82s,
predecessors of the C-119 Packets, or 'Flying Boxcars',
arrived on the airlift on 13th September, able to carry up
to five and a half tons each; these aircraft were also useful
for bulky items and carried such things as steam rollers,
for runway extensions and repairs, and ambulances, to
West Berlin.

Additional airfields in West Germany were taken over
by the airlift aircraft, as congestion built up on RAF and
USAFE airfields, those of the *Armée de l'Air* were not
close enough to the border to be of great use. The RAF
transferred its C-47s to Lubeck at the beginning of
August, a few days before other British commercial
aircraft came to join those of Flight Refuelling, while
before the end of the month, the USAFE had to base
three of its C-54 squadrons at Fassburg in the British
zone to relieve congestion elsewhere, while later, British
commercial aircraft were transferred from Fassburg to
Lubeck. Major overhauls of aircraft could not be carried
out in Germany by this time due to the pressure on space,

and the diversion of the limited numbers of mechanics and fitters to routine servicing, so for heavy overhauls, Burtonwood in Lancashire, in the north-west of England, became the maintenance base for airlift aircraft, replacing Oberpfallenhofen in Germany.

By October, the demand for aircrew was so great that the USAF had set up a special pilot training camp at Great Falls in Montana to prepare aircrew for the airlift, and later that same month 10,000 reserve aircrew were recalled by the USAF to active duty. The end of the month saw President Truman directing the USAF to assign more than sixty additional C-54s to the airlift, while attempts were made to minimise the use of the USAF's C-47s in favour of the more productive C-54s, in the hope of reducing runway and airway congestion. USN R-5Ds, the Navy's designation for the C-54, arrived in early November, with a force of twenty-four aircraft built up before the end of the month, while at the same time the Royal Air Force started to introduce its new Handley Page Hastings four-engined transports to the airlift. Soviet pressure was maintained meanwhile, although it was not to be until the following April that the Russians actually "rustled" West Berlin's cows, creating an additional problem in supply of fresh milk for young

The other side of transport in wartime, evacuating casualties. The small Bell 47 Sioux was used on CASEVAC duties, and in this picture the perspex hood of the stretcher cover can be seen lying in front of the helicopters.

children. The citizens of West Berlin used whatever resources were available to them, and before the onset of winter had already started to fell trees in the woods around the city. Nevertheless, the airlift continued its relentless progress, with almost 7,000 tons carried by British and American aircraft on 18th September in a special effort designed to mark the celebration of Air Force Day by the yearling USAFE, which also invited 15,000 German guests to its main bases at Frankfurt, Rhein-Main, and Wiesbaden. This rise in the total moved daily continued until November fogs began to hinder, but never completely stopped, the airlift.

Winter brought many problems, and some West Berliners did die from cold, although for those who survived and lived in the right zones, there was the final confirmation of what the airlift really meant, with the division of Berlin formally into East and West on 1st December. By the middle of the month, ice on the sea and the lakes prevented continued operation of the RAF's Short Sunderlands and the Hythes of Acquila Airways; the latter well away from the warmer climes of their regular service to Lisbon and Funchal! In spite of the climate, and the occasional fog, by January, a weekly airlift total of 41,540 tons was reached, with a monthly total of 171,960 tons. Daily totals were often higher, and in spite of the pre-airlift estimate that the maximum daily total would only be 3,000 tons, by 11th April a record of 8,246 tons was airlifted, only to be broken a few days

Sikorsky S-51, or R-5, lands at a forward position in Korea.

later, with the so-called 'Easter Parade' special effort of 16th April, moving no less than 12,940 tons of supplies into the city. Larger aircraft also became available, with a Boeing C-97 Stratocruiser starting operations on 4th May, carrying ten-ton loads, before, on 12th May, the blockade ended almost as quickly as it had begun.

The end of the blockade did not mean the end of the airlift, for by this time West Berlin was subsisting on a hand-to-mouth basis, and to re-establish stockpiles, the airlift continued well into the summer of 1949. The end of the British civil airlift did not come until 16th August, 1949, while the RAF continued flying until 23rd September. The airlift had required the services of 75,000 people, including 45,000 German cargo handlers, who received additional rations for their vital work, 12,000 USAFE personnel and 2,000 from United States Army Airlift Support Command as well as 800 USN personnel, while the Royal Air Force and the three British Commonwealth air forces, had assigned 12,000 men to the operation. A constant reminder of what it really was all about came within the total numbers employed with the inclusion of 3,000 displaced persons from the Baltic States. The United States Air Force allocated a total of 441 aircraft to the airlift, of which no less than 309 were C-54s, in addition to the USN's twenty-four R-5Ds, while there were also 105 C-47s, five C-82 Packets, a single C-97 and the C-124 Globemaster. The RAF contributed a total of 147 aircraft, of which more than forty were C-47

Dakotas, as well as thirty-five Avro Yorks and twenty-six Handley Page Hastings, in addition to the ten Sunderlands. Civil airlift aircraft included a total of 104 aircraft, with forty-one still on contract by the end of the lift. The total number of flights amounted to 277,804, of which 189,963 were by USAFE aircraft, 65,857 by the RAF, including flights with British Commonwealth aircrew, and 21,984 were by chartered British commercial aircraft.

During the airlift, there were at least 700 cases of harassment by the Russians and East Germans, with a hundred or so of these being through the use of searchlights to dazzle pilots at night, and there were almost as many instances of close flying, as opposed to buzzing, of which there were almost eighty examples, with a similar number of instances of radio interference or jamming. Flares were fired at aircraft on more than fifty occasions, and balloons used to obstruct flights on eleven. Ground fire actually struck aircraft on fifty-five occasions. There were sixty-five serious accidents during the airlift, although it is not known whether any of these could be attributed to Russian intervention. Before the air traffic control systems were brought up to the required standard, two C-47s of the USAFE collided in mid-air near Ravolzhausen, whilst flying in thick fog. The first fatal accident to a British aircraft, an Avro York, was on 19th September, 1948 with the loss of all five crew members when the aircraft crashed on take-off at Wunsdorf. A British Lancastrian tanker crashed on take-off at Thruxton in England, while on an airlift

The core of the RAF's post-World War II strategic transport capability was built around the Handley Page Hastings, able to carry almost ten tons of cargo or troops, but the configuration of this aircraft made it far less practical than the C-119.

positioning flight, with the loss of all seven men aboard.

The proximity of all of the airfields in West Berlin to East Germany led to other difficulties. The worst instance came with the erection of a transmitter mast on the approach to the new airfield at Tegel in the French zone; but with free access by Allied troops to all parts of Berlin, something shared by the Russians too, the French disposed of the problems presented by the mast by simply blowing it up, to Russian consternation!

There was a lighter side to the airlift as well. On 20th December, 1948, the USAFE mounted *Operation Santa Claus* at Fassburg Air Force Base, carrying gifts for 10,000 Berlin children. As a result of an unofficial initiative by a USAFE pilot, Lieutenant Gail Halvorsen, who started by dropping handkerchief parachutes of candy through the ten inch flare tube of his C-54 to children watching the airlift, in an echo of *Operation Manna,* the USAFE mounted an exercise known as *Operation Little Vittles,* dropping sweets and chocolate to children. An attempt by some pilots to extend this largesse to the Soviet zone was strictly forbidden by the USAF after a few days.

This was not the sole instance of a relief operation being required due to tension between East and West. During May, 1950, the advancing Chinese Communists trapped a British frigate, HMS *Amethyst,* in the Yangtse River, demanding that the vessel be surrendered. Before the eventual break out of the ship, an RAF Short Sunderland twice landed on the river, at considerable risk of being destroyed by Chinese artillery fire, to take medical aid and supplies to the crew. It had originally been intended that the Sunderland should drop the supplies, but a landing proved to be necessary.

War in peace

Japanese surrender in 1945 provided the former colonial powers with the challenge of re-establishing administrations and re-asserting their authority in territories which frequently saw an opportunity for independence with the departure of the Japanese. British, French and Dutch territories had been over-run by the Japanese advance, and only the British were to enjoy any real success in reintroducing colonial administrations in a troubled post-war world.

The Dutch territories in the East Indies were too large and sprawling for the Dutch to have any real hope of a return to the pre-war situation. The Dutch economy had been weakened by the war, and perhaps, too, there was relatively little enthusiasm for a colonial war amongst those who had only just returned to their homeland, or who were enjoying the first breath of freedom after several years of German occupation. Indonesia attained independence after a brief struggle in the Netherlands East Indies, which ended in 1949, and which had, at the outset, involved Indonesian airmen flying abandoned Japanese aircraft. Air transport had only a small part to play, but the departing Royal Netherlands Air Force was able to bequeath a small number of Lockheed 12 transports to the new Indonesian Air Force, which initially used these elderly aircraft on internal communications duties and providing essential air services.

The French in Indo-China were even less lucky, since they found themselves facing an opponent, the Viet Minh, which enjoyed strong support from the Communists in China. A fierce war raged from 1946 until the eventual French surrender in 1954, as Ho Chi Minh and his military leader, General Giap, battled with French forces. This conflict was marked by a growing use of military air transport, and before it ended a small number of Sikorsky S-55 helicopters would also be deployed in support of the French Army and Foreign Legion.

Initially, the *Armée de l'Air* operated French-built

Republic (Egypt), Liberia, the Sudan and Mali, and amongst the non-African states deemed to be acceptable to African opinion, help was forthcoming from India, Pakistan, Indonesia, Ceylon, Ireland, Austria, Sweden, Denmark, Norway and Canada. Apart from India and Canada, none of these nations possessed air transport with sufficient range and payload to be effective in the emergency, and as a result, the UN force was to be largely dependant upon the United States Air Force and to a lesser extent the Royal Air Force, to help move troops and equipment to the Congo. There was also some Soviet involvement, but this tended to be more concerned with stirring up trouble than in helping the UN.

After the UN appeal for help, the first troops to arrive in the Congo, on 16th July, were fifty Ghanaian troops under the command of Major-General Alexander, a British officer on secondment to the Ghanaian Army, who arrived with their equipment aboard two Royal Air Force Handley Page Hastings transports which had been operating inside Ghana. Two days later, the first Tunisian troops followed, arriving at Leopoldville in USAF C-119s, while Ethiopian troops arrived in aircraft belonging to their national airline and Moroccan troops arrived in USAF aircraft. Within a few days, 3,500 UN troops were in the Congo, and by the end of July, this number had swollen to 9,000 with a total of 15,000 by mid-August and almost 20,000 by mid-September. Meanwhile, as the UN forces hastened to prevent a massacre of Belgian civilians on the one hand, or a Soviet take-over on the other, the Congolese Prime Minister was able to use a dozen Soviet Ilyushin Il-14 transports to move troops loyal to the Federal Government around the Congo. Eventually, the Soviet action provoked a strong American response, with the USSR backing down and removing its aircraft, and, without Soviet support, Lumumba was removed in a *coup d'etat* on 19th September. After this, the activities of the Soviet Air Force were confined to bringing reinforcements for the Ghanaian contingent.

Anxious to minimise the super power involvement inside the Congo, even though it recognised that international flights would have to be largely under the control of the USAF's Military Air Transport Service, the United Nations contrived to create its own air transport service inside the Congo, under the command of a Royal Canadian Air Force officer, Air Commodore Carpenter, using a seconded force of ten Fairchild C-119 Packet, or 'Flying Boxcar', transports, loaned and crewed by the RCAF and by the Italian Air Force. This force was supplemented by a similar number of commercial airliners, mainly DC-4s, on charter, while helicopters and light aircraft for liaison duties were provided by the USAF, but manned by volunteers from other nations. Even so, the USAF had to improvise an air traffic control system within the Congo, following the departure of civilian Belgian controllers on the outbreak of the civil war, and, with the dual aim of evacuating the 300 American civilians working in the Congo, many of them in Katanga, sent two Lockheed C-130 transports to Leopoldville, arriving there on 15th July with fifty men of a combat airlift support unit. This force eventually had to cope with the task of handling a large number of flights into and out of the Congo, as the initial airlift stretched into months, and the USAF also found itself faced with

the task of strengthening the air traffic control and movements control at other airfields, including Kano in Nigeria and Chateauroux, one of the main USAFE bases in France, as well as providing mobile units at Addis Ababa, Dakar and some other less important centres. Overall control of the operation came under the USAFE headquarters at Evreux, also in France at that time, which initially used three squadrons, each with sixteen C-130s for the airlift, leaving USAFE with just three squadrons of C-119s for its own operational requirements in Europe. At the peak of the airlift, five squadrons of MATS C-124 Globemasters were transferred from the United States, providing an extra sixty long-range heavy-lift transports. During the first three months, the USAF carried 20,000 troops into the Congo, evacuated 2,500 refugees and 1,800 Belgian troops, and carried 3,500 tons of cargo, divided almost equally betwen relief supplies and military equipment.

There were other problems in addition to those of air traffic control, and some of these only became apparent as the operation proceeded. The Globemasters, so useful, were limited by weak runways at many airfields inside the Congo, and in some of the African states which they visited when picking up troops for the UN force. There were also problems in finding aviation fuel of the right grades. The newer, turboprop Hercules seemed to be free of these problems, but the larger Globemaster and the smaller C-119s weren't. One of the focal points for the airlift, Kano in Northern Nigeria, normally handled 150 flights a week, but suddenly was faced with the prospect of handling more than 500 flights weekly. The supplies of fuel and spares at Kano, established under a bilateral UK-Nigeria defence agreement and considered adequate for three weeks sustained operations, were quickly exhausted. Globemasters often had to be routed through Accra or Dakar as a result. Some idea of the spread of the air transport operations may be gained from the fact, that by late September, thirty nations had military personnel in the Congo.

While the initial difficulties in the Congo had centred around the mutiny in the Army and the desire for cession from the Congo Republic of the Katanga leadership, the troubles in the Congo rumbled on for some years afterwards. A fresh source of opposition to the Leopoldville Federal Government appeared in Orientale Province and its capital, Stanleyville. Rebel forces took black and white hostages, and to free these, on 24th November, 1964, 600 Belgian paratroops dropped from C-119s onto Stanleyville in an attack co-ordinated with ground forces, rescuing 1,800 white hostages and 300 black hostages, although another twenty-nine hostages were murdered by the rebels before they fled. This was the last major airborne operation in the Congo, although the unrest continued even after this.

The French also had a difficult colonial situation before this in Algeria, where unrest during the late 1950s and early 1960s, followed civil war between French settlers, who saw Algeria as a part of metropolitan France, and nationalist rebels, and which at one stage put the French armed forces in the unenviable position of being caught fighting the two opposing factions. The war had far reaching consequences for the French domestic political situation, and for the French armed forces which suffered a mutiny at one point. Nord Noratlas and

Fairchild C-119 Packet transports of the *Armée de l'Air* maintained an air bridge of troops and supplies throughout this period of trial, while the *Armée de l'Air* and the *Aviation Legérè de l'Armée de Terre,* or French Army aviation, operated about one hundred helicopters, including nineteen Bell 47Gs, a similar number of Alouette IIs, fifteen Sikorsky S-55s and forty-four Sikorsky S-58s, out of a total aircraft strength in Algeria of more than 800.

Helicopters were also used by the British in Aden, centre of the South Arabian Federation, a confederation of small states under British protection opposed by the neighbouring Yemen Arab Republic. The Federal Army was supported by British Army and Royal Marine units in its fight against two terrorist organisations, the Egyptian-backed National Front for the Liberation of Occupied South Yemen, or NLF, and the Front for the Liberation of Occupied South Yemen, or FLOSY. The outbreak of hostilities followed a rebellion by tribesmen in the Radfan Mountains, north of Aden in 1964. Royal Navy Westland Wessex helicopters, a turbine-powered and licence-built derivative of the S-58, from the commando carrier HMS *Albion,* and Royal Air Force Wessex and twin-rotor Bristol Belvedere helicopters based on Khormaksar, operated in support of the ground forces, while reinforcements and rotation of troops was undertaken by Bristol Britannia four-engined turboprop airliners of RAF Transport Command. However, the

The RAF's first large helicopter was the Bristol Belvedere, which was an invaluable asset in both Malaya and Aden; one of the Belvederes is seen here in Malaya ready to lift part of a Westland Wessex fuselage.

situation remained difficult up to the granting of independence and Britain's withdrawal from the South Arabian Federation in November, 1967, after which a Marxist government swept to power.

A Legacy of Conflict

The ending of colonial rule certainly did not bring peace. In Vietnam, the overthrow of the pro-Western South was seen by the Communist North as part of the unfinished business of the Indo-China War. Rhodesia, now Zimbabwe, on the other hand, was never officially a British colony and had enjoyed self-government on internal matters, so that the civil war which resulted was as much between two opposing "liberation" movements as against the white settlers, whose position was complicated by a withdrawal of British support following a unilateral declaration of independence. The position in Nigeria, which also suffered a civil war, was simpler, and mainly tribal, although personal ambitions and some superpower involvement did little to help.

The Vietnam war was undoubtedly the most significant of these post-colonial conflicts, just as the war in French Indo-China had been the bloodiest and largest

The Lockheed C-130 Hercules has become the workhorse of the world's air forces, operating into and out of primitive strips, above, or carrying paratroops, below. Although designed as a military transport, a substantial number are also operated by freight airlines, especially those carrying bulky loads or operating in areas with basic airfields.

True strategic mobility requires the ability to airlift helicopters, for which the USAF used Douglas C-133 transports, seen here taking two Sikorsky HH-3s, one of the many variants of the S-61 family.

of the colonial wars. The war was not confined to Vietnam itself, and spread into neighbouring Laos and Cambodia, involving not only American and Vietnamese forces, but troops from South Korea, and Australian forces as well.

The peace won by the war in French Indo-China barely lasted ten years, by which time infiltration by guerilla forces from North Vietnam into the south, and into neutral Laos and Cambodia, was threatening the stability of the region. The United States provided military assistance and advisers, but within a few short years this had developed into a wholesale military and naval commitment. More than any other conflict, Vietnam was the helicopter war, reflected in the sorry statistic that, of 8,000 American aircraft lost in the war, no less than 4,600 were helicopters. In this war, the helicopter eliminated the need to deploy paratroops, with a wide variety of machines of all sizes moving troops far more quickly than the glider ever could, and yet still retaining the advantage of a glider-borne force in that the forces deployed as entire units ready to fight. On the other hand, the helicopter lacked the glider's great advantage, stealth. Large numbers of fixed wing aircraft were also employed, primarily Fairchild C-123 Providers

and Lockheed C-130 Hercules, while other aircraft of the Military Air Transport Service operated an airbridge from the United States, Hawaii, Japan and Hong Kong, a favourite rest and recreation centre for the US forces, and these aircraft included the McDonnell Douglas C-133B Cargomaster, which was superseded in due course by Lockheed C-141 Starlifter and C-5A Galaxy transports, and there were, sadly, also McDonnell Douglas C-9A Nightingale ambulance aircraft, a derivative of the DC-9 airliner. As helicopters became larger, and landing strips harder to defend against Communist Viet Cong forces, and in particular from heavy mortar attack, the helicopter assumed more and more of the duties which would previously have fallen to transport aircraft. Lockheed KC-130H Hercules tanker aircraft refuelled helicopters so that even longer missions became commonplace.

The war saw several major helicopter designs into service. The most significant of these was the Bell 204 and its development, the 205, known in United States service as the UH-1 after 1962, although its nickname was 'Huey', after the earlier designation from its first appearance in June, 1959, of HU-1. Outside of the United States, the helicopter was better known by the US Army's official designation of Iroquois. A succession of different versions of the UH-1 Iroquois entered service, with the 205 offering a longer fuselage and a cabin for up to twelve fully-equipped troops rather than the seven of the

original 204. Before long, the UH-1 series was carrying not only troops, but being armed with machine-guns, rocket pods and air-to-surface missiles, including anti-tank missiles, although such sophisticated weapons were seldom employed in the anti-guerilla role. The concept of the helicopter gunship emerged, while at the same time, C-47 transports had their side windows removed and machine gun positions installed as another measure designed to provide the maximum anti-personnel firepower, becoming AC-47s, while there were also AC-119 conversions of the Packet. In a reversal of the usual evolution of military transport aircraft design, the UH-1 series led to the development of attack helicopters, narrow fuselaged twin-seat helicopters based on the rotor blades of the UH-1, yet optimised for the attack role with stub winglets and pylons for a substantial warload.

While the small size of the UH-1 series and its high performance meant that this was the most common type deployed in Vietnam, and it was frequently used for the evacuation of troops, for assault duties and for CASEVAC, several other purely transport helicopters also endured a baptism of fire during the conflict. Sikorsky introduced their S-64, or CH-53, flying crane helicopter, a machine without a cabin fuselage, and the giant S-65, or CH-54 which could carry troops or move

Left: South Vietnamese airborne troops handling air-portable equipment during training with a Fairchild C-123 Packet, a theatre transport aircraft developed from a glider design. This picture was taken in October, 1962, at an early stage in the Vietnam War.

Right: Long range operations, including combat air rescue by HH-3 'Jolly Green Giant' helicopters of the USAF, meant that helicopters needed to refuel in mid-air, using Lockheed KC-130 Hercules tankers.

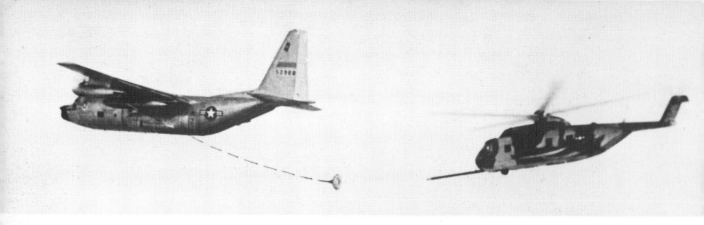

The sequence of an inflight refuelling session for a helicopter:
An HH-3 tops up from a KC-130.

Above: Difficult bush conditions prevent this Bell 205 Iroquois from landing during its errand of mercy in Vietnam – one of the troops on the ground steadies the helicopter.

Below: Panic, as a wounded Korean infantryman clings to one of the skids of an Iroquois helicopter as it takes off.

heavy underslung loads, while Boeing-Vertol introduced the large twin-rotor CH-46 Sea Knight for the United States Marine Corps, and the even larger CH-47 Chinook, able to lift up to sixty men, for the United States Army. These were all machines which could only be used in Vietnam in the transport role, although later developments of the S-65 were designed for the United States Navy for mine countermeasures operations.

It is difficult to isolate individual operations in Vietnam, since the availability of the helicopter and the flexibility which it bestowed upon ground commanders, able to react almost immediately to events, ensured that every day helicopters would be ferrying troops between battle positions as American and Vietnamese troops struggled to maintain contact with fast-moving guerilla units skilled in jungle warfare. The operations which at Suez and in Korea proved to be so noteworthy, became not just an every day event, but something which took place several times every day. There were a number of operations which can be identified as being more significant than most during the war, and perhaps at the same time, typical of many.

One such operation occurred during April, 1968, at a

Above: Even larger helicopters were pressed into service in Vietnam, including the Boeing-Vertol CH-47 series Chinook, one of which is shown here demonstrating its ability to lift fuel containers.

Below: Transport aircraft were modified to act as gun ships in Vietnam, including the AC-47 conversion of the C-47, and the AC-119 conversion of the C-119, shown here, which belongs to the 71st Special Operations Squadron.

Above: A practical feature of the CH-47 series is its rear-loading ramp; here American troops prepare to board a CH-47D.

Right: A USAF Sikorsky CH-3C brings some much-needed additional artillery to a Vietnam battlefield.

comparatively early stage of the war, with a combined assault by American and South Vietnamese units on the A Shua Valley, which had been firmly under Viet Cong control for some time. Code-named *Operation Delaware*, the usual term for this exercise was a "reconnaissance in force", and rather than holding the valley, as the French would have done, the objective was to displace the Viet Cong and prevent them from using the road through the Valley as a supply route. Commencing on 19th April, the United States Army used helicopters to fly in artillery to the hills overlooking the valley, with even fairly large artillery pieces presenting little difficulty for the Sikorsky CH-53 Tarhe flying crane or the CH-47 Chinook. On the first day, before the Viet Cong could react, little opposition was encountered but on the second day, twenty-seven American helicopters were lost in what was described as being a "disastrous start", with the highest daily figure for helicopter losses of the war at that time. Not all of the helicopters were lost to enemy fire; several were lost when they collided with other helicopters in the dust raised by their rotor blades. There were too few good landing sites, and many of these were rough jungle clearings which had been made by 'daisy cutter' 3,000 lbs bombs. Some CASEVAC helicopters had to hover above the jungle, winching the wounded to safety.

Amongst the aircraft lost to enemy fire was a Sikorsky CH-53 Tarhe flying crane, brought down from 6,000 feet, while a large Boeing-Vertol Chinook was shot down through the clouds. While some of the Viet Cong anti-aircraft gunners appeared to be using a simple form of radar, many Viet Cong simply lay in their shell or bomb craters, which acted as a sound reflector, and then fired upwards directly into the air as the sound of an approaching helicopter reached a peak.

The South Vietnamese forces also operated large numbers of helicopters, although there was a greater emphasis on light transport or utility and less on attack. Increasingly, as the war progressed and the Viet Cong mined rivers and roads or lay in ambush, the helicopter provided the safest means of reinforcing or resupplying besieged garrisons. New titles were coined for American and Vietnamese army units flying with the helicopters, with 'air cavalry' replacing the World War II paratroopers!

Although few in numbers, Royal Australian Air Force and Royal Australian Navy helicopter units were also sent to Vietnam, and the Australian contribution to the war, at odds with domestic political agitation in

A USMC Boeing-Vertol CH-46 Sea Knight at Nui Dang during the Vietnam War.

Australia, was rated highly. The Australians did, generally, enjoy greater success in the areas under their control than did the American or South Vietnamese forces, while commentators pointed out that the Australians did not blast or bulldoze their way through forests, but instead used the forests as the Viet Cong did, for shelter and cover, and unlike the Americans, the Australians did not wander around with transistor radios announcing their presence. More than any other army in Vietnam, the Australians worked on the basis of keeping the enemy on the move, wearing him down, rather than on a kill ratio. At the peak, 8,000 Australian troops, a fifth of the total Australian Army strength, served in Vietnam.

When the Australians first arrived in Vietnam, a Royal Australian Air Force Bell UH-1 Iroquois squadron was amongst the first units to be deployed, and later this was joined by a small number of Royal Australian Navy helicopters, sometimes operating from the light fleet carrier, HMAS *Melbourne,* while the elderly HMAS *Sydney* acted as a fast troop transport. As the Australian forces were withdrawn during 1970, the helicopter units were amongst the last to depart.

While South Korean units were also deployed in Vietnam, they did not bring any air power with them, and indeed depended on the USAF to fly their forces into Vietnam.

On the other side, few helicopters were used by North

Unhappy ending – a South Vietnamese Bell 204 Iroquois is flown into the sea after dropping its passengers onto an American warship during the evacuation from South Vietnam.

Vietnamese forces, although small numbers of Mil Mi-8 helicopters were available and occasionally spotted in action by American aircraft close to the border between the two warring parts of Vietnam.

While most American rescue units do not belong to the Military Air Transport Service, or Military Airlift Command as it later became, a number of rescue units are part of MAC. The reason for the arrangement stems largely from the limited need for the USAF to maintain substantial search and rescue helicopter units in the United States, where the United States Coastguard Service maintains a rescue service using Sikorsky S-62 helicopters and Lockheed Hercules transports optimised for the rescue role. Small utility helicopters are deployed as rescue machines at USAF bases, originally these were Kaman machines, but are now replaced by the ubiquitous Bell Iroquois. More significant than these in many ways are the larger helicopters used for combat air-rescue, with the Aerospace Rescue and Recovery Service using Sikorsky HH-3 helicopters, a variant of the S-61 family. In Vietnam, the HH-3 became known as the 'Jolly Green Giant', because of their green colour scheme and the prevalence of a certain brand of sweetcorn in the rations of the US forces. During the first five years of the war, more than a thousand aircrew were rescued by helicopter from behind enemy lines, sometimes flying to within forty miles of Hanoi. A larger, up-rated successor to the original 'Jolly Green Giant', has been the 'Super Jolly Green Giant', based on the S-65.

The helicopter also played a prominent part in the closing stages of the Vietnam War, a long-drawn-out process which saw defeat becoming inevitable as the political will of the South Vietnamese collapsed. While it had been agreed that neither side should receive arms to replace combat losses, only the United States obeyed this stricture, so that South Vietnam suffered while the North continued to draw upon the Soviet Union for supplies. On 20th April, 1975, nine aircraft carriers attached to the United States 7th Fleet converged on South Vietnam for the inevitable evacuation, and this force, equivalent to the then entire commissioned peacetime force of the United States Navy, was equipped solely with helicopters. On 22nd April, 7,000 United States Marines were landed, mainly by helicopter, to protect American nationals and also the 130,000 Vietnamese already cleared for immigration to the United States. The evacuation was still in full swing a week later, amidst an atmosphere of chaos and, occasionally, panic.

The better organised aspects of the evacuation saw a definite procedure established, with South Vietnamese

Above: The RAF used a force of ten Short Belfasts, originally designed to move ballistic missiles, they were an ideal transport for helicopters and other large items of equipment. In spite of the bulbous shape, the design of the aircraft owed much to the Bristol Britannia, most military versions of which were built by Shorts.

Below: The RAF's standard troop-carrying helicopter during the 1970s and 1980s has been the Westland-Aerospatiale Puma, three of which are flying in formation in this picture.

The withdrawal of the RAF's Short Belfast transports has left the RAF with a gap in its airlift capability, which is sometimes partially filled by chartering the aircraft back from their new owners, HeavyLift Cargo Airlines, which now operates several of these aircraft. Here a Westland Lynx helicopter is loaded, but on occasion the HeavyLift Belfasts have also carried RAF Chinook helicopters.

helicopters landing aboard the American warships, the passengers hastily unloaded, the doors ripped off so that the helicopter could sink quickly and the pilot escape easily before taking off and landing in the sea, after which the pilot would be picked up by waiting American helicopters. At the end of the operation, large numbers of South Vietnamese helicopters were also brought away aboard the American warships, but in spite of these having been American property as a result of being provided as military aid, the incoming North Vietnamese demanded their return, without success!

Not all of the evacuation was so carefully and coolly handled. On the morning of 29th April, South Vietnamese helicopters arrived before the warships were ready to receive them, and the USS *Blue Ridge,* a command ship, had to handle fourteen helicopters and their occupants during a period of ninety minutes on a landing pad able to take just one machine at a time. One helicopter landing on the *Blue Ridge* dropped on top of another helicopter taking off, sending whirling fragments of metal across the landing pad before the helicopter crashed onto the ship and the doors opened to discharge a crowd of frightened women and children. Another helicopter crashed onto the ship as the pilot jumped out before it landed!

Aircraft of the Military Air Transport Service were also involved in the evacuation, and with tragic consequences when a North Vietnamese surface-to-air missile shot down a C-5A Galaxy loaded with Vietnamese orphans. Almost all of those on the lower deck of this giant aircraft died, while most of those on the upper deck survived.

It would be easy to see the failure of American arms to stop the fall of South Vietnam as a defeat for the helicopter. In fact the real failings included the inability of the American forces to grasp the essentials of jungle warfare so well known to the British, the Australians and, elsewhere, the Portuguese. There was instead a policy of overkill, and insufficient attention was paid to gaining the support of the South Vietnamese. Ultimately, the Vietnamese suffered the consequences of American defeat, while their neighbours, especially those in Cambodia, fared even worse.

In another major counter-insurgency operation at this time, the government of the country concerned had to stand alone, albeit with some occasional, but very limited, assistance from South Africa. Following the Rhodesian unilateral declaration of independence, or UDI, on 11th November, 1965, there was little immediate internal opposition. Royal Air Force Gloster Javelin jet fighters were deployed to neighbouring Zambia at the request of that country's government; quite why this was done remains a mystery since there was never any declared or implied intention by Rhodesia to attack Zambia. Fuel for the Javelins was flown out to Zambia aboard Royal Air Force Bristol Britannia transports, one of which proved to be too heavy for the taxiways of the airport at Lusaka, but the deployment was of short

A Scorpion light tank is an easy load for a Belfast.

duration and the aircraft involved soon returned to the United Kingdom. The Royal Navy also maintained a blockade to prevent oil reaching Rhodesia, through the port of Beira, in Portuguese-administered Mozambique.

However, by the early 1970s, the situation inside Rhodesia had changed for the worse, with two terrorist groups fighting against the government, attacking white settlers and intimidating black villagers and workers in the towns. Against this was the small Rhodesian Air Force which, in addition to combat squadrons of Hawker Hunter jet fighters and English Electric Canberra jet bombers, with a mixed training and counter-insurgency squadron of piston-engined Percival Provosts, also maintained a squadron of Douglas C-47 Dakota transports and a small number of Aerospatiale Alouette II and III helicopters. The C-47s and the helicopters were engaged in operations primarily designed to react to terrorist activity by moving troops to the areas in which they were active in time for a "hot pursuit" operation to have some chance of success. It was yet another instance of the use of transport aircraft to enhance the efficiency of a relatively small security force faced with operations over a very wide area. Paratroops were deployed by the C-47s, usually dropping a stick of ten men, but sometimes taking a planeload for larger operations, but seldom with more than one aircraft deployed on one operation. The

aircraft would also, whenever necessary, conduct air re-supply operations for troops fighting in the bush. The helicopters themselves were usually the means of reaching the scene of a terrorist incident, and frequently went into action overloaded, with the Alouette IIIs being used with the dangerous practice of a running take-off, discarding the vertical take-off capability and attempting to use the helicopter as a short take-off aircraft, something for which it was never designed.

Once agreement had been reached on an acceptable political solution for the future of Rhodesia, British helicopters were shipped out to Rhodesia aboard USAF transports, mainly C-141 Starlifters so that these aircraft would be at the disposal of the British troops enforcing a ceasefire, assembling members of the guerilla groups in camps, and monitoring the conduct of elections. The need to use USAF aircraft to deploy the helicopters was a direct consequence of the British having sold the RAF's own heavy lift transport aircraft, ten Short Belfasts, whose size made them ideal for the transport of bulky items of equipment, including a Westland Sea King helicopter.

Even while the Rhodesian crisis rumbled on during the run-up to the elections of April, 1979, there had been another guerilla war which had overlapped with the conflict in Rhodesia, although coming to an end some years earlier, taking place in the former Portuguese colonies in Africa, of which two, Angola and

Mozambique, were near neighbours of Rhodesia. The Portuguese colonial wars had started some years earlier than the crisis in Rhodesia, and of the three Portuguese possessions involved in this conflict, which started during the 1960s and continued into the early 1970s, most of the fighting took place in Angola and Mozambique, with relatively little in the third colony, Portuguese Guinea. The deployment of large quantities of equipment was out of the question for the poorest country in Western Europe, and indeed the whole colonial involvement placed an enormous strain on the financial and manpower resources of a country with a population of little more than eight million. The Portuguese troops were, of course, supported by locally-raised units in all of these campaigns, which ran simultaneously. During these campaigns, Portugal must have enjoyed the distinction of being the last country to use cavalry in combat, because of the advantages enjoyed by mounted troops fighting in scrub land, offering a combination of speed and stealth. The Portuguese received little sympathy from the international community for these campaigns, and even less support, with the African commitments being used as an excuse to deny Portugal modern military equipment even to fulfil the country's NATO commitments. Harsher regimes have been treated better than that of Portugal during this period.

For all of the reasons outlined above, the Portuguese Air Force, the *Forca Aerea Portuguesa*, operated equipment which was primarily obsolescent, and even obsolete. The backbone of the air transport units was the veteran Douglas C-47 once again, with forty of these aircraft used for parachute drops and for air re-supply missions. Strategic air transport from Portugal to the colonies was handled by a handful of Douglas DC-6 transports, an order for Boeing 707 jet airliners raising an international outcry! There were also eighty or so Alouette III helicopters, with a few of the older and smaller Alouette IIs, with a few Sikorsky UH-19A Chickasaw helicopters. The only modern transport equipment was a squadron of twelve Aerospatiale SA-330 Puma helicopters. This said, the Portuguese armed forces enjoyed considerable success in what was a vast colonial commitment for a small country, and may even have succeeded had it not been for a combination of international pressure and revolution at home. Post independence, both Angola and Mozambique suffered continuing guerilla warfare, although that in Mozambique has been much reduced in recent years as a result of a withdrawal of South African support for the insurgents in 1984.

Military air transport played little or no part during the civil war in Nigeria which followed an attempt by the state of Biafra to secede from the Federation during the late 1960s, although a few chartered transport aircraft maintained an unofficial airlift of supplies from Europe to the rebels.

While the Rhodesian crisis rumbled on, and even after it had ended with the creation of the independent state of Zimbabwe, Britain had an internal security problem of her own in Northern Ireland, where the Irish Republican Army and the Irish National Liberation Army, were engaged in terrorist activities, supposedly in support of a united Ireland, but in reality also intended to overthrow the government of the Irish Republic. Both the British and the Irish security forces deployed helicopters for observation and communications duties, but the major instance of helicopters being used in the transport role came with the introduction of internment on 9th April, 1971. Troops and members of the Royal Ulster Constabulary were carried in Royal Air Force Westland Wessex helicopters on this occasion, arresting 300 wanted persons within a few hours. While small numbers of Westland Wessex helicopters were used, mainly of the Royal Air Force but also including some Royal Marine machines and many of these remain in use in Northern Ireland, in more recent years the province has seen the introduction of small numbers of Westland-Aerospatiale SA-330 Pumas. Much of the day-to-day work is handled by Westland Lynx and Scout helicopters of the British Army's Air Corps, carrying small numbers of troops or bomb disposal experts. The Irish Army Air Corps also uses Aerospatiale Alouette III helicopters to move the two bomb disposal squads based close to the border with Northern Ireland to incidents, and in one year, these and other Irish Army bomb disposal units answered some 600 incidents.

While the unrest in Ireland seems destined to rumble on indefinitely, problems emerge at regular intervals elsewhere. In emergencies, transport aircraft, including Lockheed C-130s of the South African Air Force, are used to move police and troops around South Africa, and these aircraft also help in air re-supply of forces deployed in Namibia, or South-West Africa, although most of these operations are handled by ground based troops. Helicopters are used to ferry troops around in Central America, the scene of many local wars in recent years, and most notably in Nicaragua and El Salvador, but it is too early to define any unusual or distinctive pattern of operations.

There have also been a number of small scale commitments by the French *Armée de l'Air* in Africa in recent years. Transall transport aircraft, sometimes known as the C-160, have operated in support of French forces deployed to help the armed forces of Morocco and of Chad to fight guerillas in those countries, but the operation in Chad was of very short duration during 1984. Neither operation bears any resemblance to those on a scale of Indo-China or Vietnam.

Given the balance of power between the alliances of East and West which have prevented global war over more than forty years, it seems likely that the tendency will be for wars to be fought by proxy, using terrorists. Already, counter-insurgency operations are the single largest commitment for transport aircraft for most of the time, and inevitably this means a continuing role for the helicopter in particular. While the helicopter does provide a faster reaction to events than any other form of aircraft, it does not permit an element of surprise because of the noise. It is also becoming increasingly vulnerable to portable anti-aircraft missiles, and the increasing availability of these will be a hazard to both fixed-wing aircraft and helicopters in the future, on counter-insurgency operations almost as much as in a major conflict.

Chapter Seven
Strategic Intervention

Sometimes regarded as a modern concept, and by "modern" one really means the post-World War II period, strategic intervention has been practised throughout the twentieth century and even during the nineteenth as well. The United States, that least colonial of all the great powers of the past two centuries, according to the Institute of Strategic Studies, sent troops into the small republics of central America on some thirty occasions between 1900 and 1934, after which the American stance became one of isolationism. For the major European powers, even when not directly concerned with colonial expansion, there was often a desire to intervene in the affairs of states bordering on those colonised or administered by themselves; sometimes there was the need to protect their nationals in the trading stations which had been created to supplement colonial acquisitions in those places, such as the mainland of China, where colonisation was likely to be more trouble than it was worth, an approach sometimes aptly described in the term "gunboat diplomacy". All of these matters were managed without the use of military transport aircraft until the British started to deploy troops by air in the Middle East and on the north-west frontier of India, in what is now in fact Pakistan, during the 1920s and 1930s; operations which may be regarded as having more to do with strategic intervention than counter-insurgency. For the British, the distinction between strategic intervention and counter insurgency is less clearly defined than for other states, simply because Britain's colonies were extensively supplemented by a network of protectorates and by treaties, some a direct result of the colonial era and willingly entered into for greater stability and trading advantage, while others, notably in Palestine, the result of a League of Nations mandate, and often these, which were thrust upon Britain, were the more difficult to deal with.

The ability of the transport aeroplane to become involved in this duty was a direct result not so much of changing political situations and of the broadening of the difficulties between East and West, but of the technological changes taking place as the aeroplane became larger, faster, and with a longer range. Governments no longer sent a gunboat, depending on the circumstances, it was a decision over whether or not to send a task force with aircraft carriers, or fly troops in; usually, the ideal solution required a combination of both, and certainly, effective air transport is not a substitute for the aircraft carrier and commando carrier any more than these are a substitute for air transport. Of the countries most likely to become involved in such operations, the United Kingdom, the United States and France all possess carriers and air transport, the Soviet Union is steadily developing a carrier force, just as it has massive air transport capability, but the effectiveness of either over a sustained operation at great distance from the USSR has still to be tested.

One element in the broadening of the role of air transport was the availability of in-flight refuelling, most often used by the British and the Americans to extend the range of their transport aircraft and for bombers and fighters as well; indeed, even when tanker aircraft were close developments of transport types, the in-flight refuelling units were often part of the bomber force, as with the USAF's Strategic Air Command. While the first major use of tanker aircraft by the Royal Air Force centred around converted bomber types, first the Vickers Valiant and then the Handley Page Victor, the Americans preferred transport aircraft, which were far more satisfactory and the only reason for the British use of ex-bombers was simply to avoid building new aircraft specifically for the tanker role. The first major tanker aircraft for the USAF was the Boeing KC-97, a military version of the Boeing Stratocruiser airliner, which was soon followed by the KC-135, from which the Boeing 720 and 707 jet airliners were developed during the later 1950s. The war in Vietnam saw the first major effort at in-flight refuelling for helicopters, and this required slower flying aircraft, able to perform satisfactorily at lower altitudes. The Lockheed Hercules proved to be ideal, with tanker versions designated as the KC-130, and in fact the popularity of the Hercules and the wide range of roles which this aircraft has come to perform means that often Hercules tankers are "topping up" Hercules transports! The RAF had to equip several of its Hercules as tankers for the air supply operation to the Falklands, while by this time the RAF had also received VC.10 tankers, its first converted airliner tanker, which was followed soon after by tanker Lockheed TriStars, both types being purchased secondhand from British Airways. The TriStar, and the similar McDonnell Douglas KC-10A Extender, developed from the DC-10 airliner, of the USAF, have dual roles, as long-range strategic transports and as tanker aircraft.

During the early 1950s, it appeared at first as if there was a gap emerging between the transport aircraft used by the military and those used by commercial airlines, with the latter seeming to have the faster and higher flying aircraft, especially with such types as the de Havilland Comet and the Bristol Britannia. The situation did not last for long, however, with both the Comet and the Britannia joining RAF Transport Command to provide a fast long-range transport element, while the USAF received its C-135s. Nevertheless, heavy transport aircraft were still slow and plodding, until the arrival of the Lockheed C-130 Hercules as the military transport

aircraft against which all other aircraft of the genre had to be judged. The large and capacious fuselage of the Hercules was adequate for many military vehicles and for artillery pieces, missile launchers and smaller helicopters, while the cruising speed in excess of 300 mph, considerable range and pressurisation, although not quite as good as that on airliners, was all complemented by a large rear-loading door and ramp, with roller floors so that supplies could be loaded and unloaded easily. The Hercules could carry between eighty and a hundred fully-equipped paratroops, or in the case of air-landed troops up to 120 could be carried; up to seventeen tons of cargo could be parachuted or free-dropped within minutes, usually on a single run over the dropping zone! Several versions of the aircraft were built following its introduction to USAF service in 1956 as the C-130B, including a solitary C-130C, which on one occasion managed to touch down on an aircraft carrier, and take-off again! The most popular version of this aircraft has been the C-130H.

That airliner derivatives have their role is also proven by the statistic that more than 700 C-135s and KC-135s have been built, with their original 13,750 lbs thrust Pratt & Whitney J57 turbojets having been replaced in recent years by CFM56 turbofans, reducing the noise level and fuel consumption, while also extending the life of these aircraft which, in common with many peacetime military transport aircraft, have relatively low annual utilisation rates. Several air forces operate Boeing 707s, although the *Armée de l'Air* has KC-135s. Some of the fast jet military transports are simply used as VIP aircraft for heads of state, but others do work as long-range transports for military personnel.

During the 1950s and 1960s, the RAF's long-range transport capability was boosted by a squadron of de Havilland Comet 2 jet airliners, which, in spite of the failure of the original Comet 1, proved to be a rugged and durable aircraft.

Larger aircraft with a high turn of speed have also been introduced by the military, including the Lockheed C-141 Starlifter, which first flew in 1963, and which can carry up to forty-two tons of freight or 130 fully-equipped troops, and the C-5 Galaxy, which first flew in its C-5A form but which went back into production for a second batch of C-5Bs during the mid-1980s. The C-5A first flew in 1970 and can lift up to 130 tons. Both of these turbofan aircraft have cruising speeds in excess of 500 mph, and ranges of around 6,000 miles. The Soviet Union has been developing a counterpart to the C-5, the Antonov An-124 *Ruslan*, which first appeared in the West at the 1985 Paris Air Show. Russia's earlier Antonov An-22, which enjoyed the distinction of being the world's largest aircraft before the C-5 appeared and took this title, lacked the speed of the American aircraft, and used turboprop engines; the Russians have had some difficulty in developing large turbofans. While these large aircraft were all designed with strategic intervention in mind, and the rapid reinforcement of American units in Europe, the aircraft which immediately preceded them, such as the Douglas C-133 and the Short Belfast, both turboprops, were originally designed for the movement of inter-continental ballistic missiles; in the case of the Belfast, the cancellation of the British Blue Streak missile led to the aircraft being completed as a strategic transport, and the original plan to have nose and tail doors for easy loading and unloading of missiles was reduced to tail-doors only.

One consequence of the steady upward rise in aircraft

A Short-built Bristol Britannia of RAF Transport Command, retracting its undercarriage after take-off.

size was the need to design specialised aircraft for theatre transport in the major air forces, and as low cost air transport types for the smaller air forces, although many of these have purchased the C-130 series in small numbers. The days when military air transport meant using a Ju.52/3m or a C-47 also meant that a single type would suffice, offering a certain flexibililty, but also limiting the potential of military air transport to the performance of these aircraft. Even if refuelling bases did exist for these smaller aircraft, the bases themselves were another burden to be defended in wartime, and as the Berlin Airlift showed, the use of many small aircraft could lead to congestion. By the late 1950s, military versions of the new small turboprop regional airliners were becoming available, notably with the Fokker F.27 Friendship, sometimes known as the Troopship in its military version, and the Avro, later Hawker Siddeley and then later British Aerospace, 748. In most cases, the military variant included a larger rear door for loading and unloading bulkier items, but only the 748 was developed to include a version with a tail ramp, known as the Andover; this aircraft also included a kneeling undercarriage for loading and unloading vehicles, and a stretched fuselage, but only the RAF bought this aircraft

new, with some of these sold later to the Royal New Zealand Air Force. There were relatively few specialised small military transports, partly because the larger size of the helicopter reduced the need for this type of aircraft in many air forces, while others found new or specialised aircraft too expensive, but notable amongst the specialised types have been the short take-off and landing -STOL- de Havilland Canada DHC-4 Caribou and its larger and more recent cousin, the DHC-5 Buffalo.

Gradually, a pattern has emerged. The major air forces of the superpowers possess large and fast transport aircraft able to deploy large numbers of men and bulky loads, including battle tanks and large helicopters as well as tactical ground-to-ground missiles, over very long distances. This means aircraft such as the C-141, C-5A/B and the projected McDonnell Douglas C-17, as well as the Russian An-124 rival to the C-5 series. Below this, most air forces of any size will have transports such as the Lockheed C-130 Hercules or the Franco-German C-160 Transall, capable of a limited strategic role and effectively, by the standards of today, serving as medium transports. The air forces of the major, but non-super, powers tend to complement their Hercules or Transalls, which are the paratroop aircraft as well, as the type for moving bulkier consignments, with fast jets such as the VC.10 or aircraft of the Boeing 707 and C-135 family.

Below these broad categories comes a third, the tactical

or theatre transport, often overlapping in performance with the larger helicopters, but at lower cost, especially at the bottom end where many smaller transports are of lower performance than even medium sized helicopters. As already mentioned, many of the aircraft in this third category are airliner derivatives, with the exception of the Caribou and Buffalo, and the airliner derivatives are cheaper, because of longer production runs, and also offer the smallest air forces the opportunity of having maintenance sub-contracted to airlines. The smallest of these types include the Short C-23A Sherpa, developed from the 330 and with a few changes, including a rear ramp; the Spanish CASA C-212, and somewhat smaller, the Short Skyvan and the Israeli Aircraft Industries IAI Arava. Even smaller still, and offering little scope for bulky items, are the Pilatus-Brittan-Norman Islander and Trislander, the Pilatus Turbo-Porter, de Havilland Canada Twin Otter, the Australian GAF Nomad, and the Dornier Do.228 and the earlier Do.28. A problem for any manufacturer seeking to enter this market is that while it is already overcrowded, there is a tendency for many developing aircraft industries to seek to start with projects aimed at this field.

The variety of helicopters on offer has been covered briefly in an earlier chapter. It is only sufficient to say that here too there is a growing range of aircraft available.

Since the early 1950s, the military air transport operations of the RAF and USAF have undergone certain major changes, partly reflecting the reduction in the overseas commitments of the RAF in particular, and partly because of the improved airlift capability of these armed forces and the aircraft which they employ. At first, an appreciation of the value of air transport led to the concept of trooping by air, usually contracting this work to charter airlines, but later, while still maintaining the concept of trooping by air, the air forces took over almost all of the work; partly because of the improvement in the performance of the aircraft available to them, and partly because of reduced overseas garrisons. Amongst the American airlines which handled this work can be included World Airways, Saturn Airways and Overseas National, operating within the United States, and from the United States to Japan and Europe. This work often accounted for as much as 60 per cent of the total business of these airlines, but the USAF wisely stipulated that the companies interested in military charter contracts should always have a minimum commercial charter workload of a third of their total business. British charter airlines flew military personnel and their families from the United Kingdom to Gibraltar, Malta, Cyprus, Singapore and Hong Kong, with the companies involved including several of the predecessors of today's British Caledonian Airways, such as Airwork, Hunting Clan, Transair and Caledonian Airways; as well as Dan Air, Eagle Aviation, Skyways and Scottish Airways. In one sense, the charter airlines provided an unofficial air transport reserve, but the USAF also included transport squadrons in its reserve units, the State Air National Guard squadrons.

Intervention by air

The first major airborne assault of the post-war period arose with the Anglo-French invasion of the Suez Canal Zone in Egypt in 1956.

The political and military background to the events at Suez in 1956 is complex, but in essence the operation became necessary after Egypt nationalised the Suez

A USMC CH-53 Super Sea Stallion disappears into a USAF C-5A Galaxy; a CH-46 Sea Knight is in the background, ready for shipment by air.

The substantial size and payload capability of the Lockheed C-5A/B Galaxy transport means that the rapid development of armoured units is a possibility, although generally armies still prefer to pre-position heavy equipment and fly-in reinforcing troops.

Until the arrival of the Antonov An-124 "Ruslan", the heaviest aircraft in the Soviet Union's transport force has been the Antonov An-22 'Cock'.

Canal, an international waterway, in July of that year, subsequently refusing to abide by the principle of free and uninterrupted passage of vessels through the Canal, regardless of nationality. Britain and France prepared to intervene, and at first international opinion was strongly in favour of their doing so. Unfortunately, the inability of these two nations to mount the campaign quickly led to this support waning, except from Israel, which continued to press for action as a result of Israeli vessels being barred from the Canal.

Continued friction between Israel and Egypt culminated in war breaking out between the two countries in October, 1956, as the British and French naval task forces were preparing to invade Egypt, and as air and land forces were assembled at the British bases in Cyprus. Israeli troops and aircraft repelled the Egyptian forces and Israeli paratroops were dropped from C-47s to cut off an Egyptian retreat across the Sinai Desert at the Mitla Pass. As the conflict began to threaten the security of the Suez Canal, Britain and France demanded that Egyptian and Israeli forces withdraw to lines ten miles on either side of the Canal Zone. As anticipated by Britain and France, Israel complied and Egypt refused, providing the two European nations with the opportunity to intervene.

The operation to take the Canal Zone was complicated by the still limited performance of all of the aircraft used, transport and combat types alike, which meant, for example, that British fighters could spend little time over the zone before having to return to their bases in Cyprus. On the brighter side, both the Royal Navy and the *Marine Nationale*, were able to deploy carrier-borne fighter, fighter-bomber and ground attack aircraft. The Royal Air Force was to operate Handley Page Hastings and Vickers Valetta transports, and the *Armée de l'Air* its C-119 Packets and Noratlases, but neither force could land a full airborne division because of the limited numbers of aircraft available for the operation. Both countries had other extensive worldwide commitments, and airfields in Cyprus, used by both countries for the operation, code-named *Musketeer* were also congested. Partly for these reasons, the paratroop assault was to be followed by a heli-borne assault using Westland S-55 Whirlwinds to carry Royal Marines from the light fleet carriers, HMS *Ocean* and *Theseus*.

RAF, Fleet Air Arm and *Aéronavale* aircraft attacked the Egyptian airfields in the Canal Zone on 1st November, and within forty-eight hours had achieved effective air supremacy. The invasion, planned for 6th November, was brought forward by twenty-four hours because of fears that a change in the weather could make a safe drop of paratroops onto Gamil Airfield at Port Said difficult, if not dangerous; the airfield had water on both sides, the Mediterranean on one side and a lake on the other!

The fly-in to the Canal Zone started before dawn on 5th November, with almost 700 men of the British 3rd Parachute Battalion, and a small quantity of light vehicles, artillery and anti-tank guns, taking off from Nicosia in Cyprus to arrive over the Canal Zone at 07.15, with the drop completed by 07.25. Coming under heavy fire on landing, the paratroops managed to secure the airfield by 08.00. Meanwhile, the two French battalions of paratroops and the 1st (Guards) Independent Parachute Company, were flown in and dropped to the south of Port Said itself and to the east of the Canal, seizing the bridges over it and holding these until joined by Royal Marine Commando units coming ashore in an amphibious landing. A second British airlift followed before noon, while the French dropped additional paratroops to take Fort Faud. The following morning, the original date for the invasion, 400 men of the Royal Marines were flown in by Westland S-55 Whirlwind, helicopters, seizing the pier and later reinforcing the paratroops at nearby Gamil Airfield, from where the Fleet Air Arm helicopters, of which there were twenty-two, started to fly-out casualties. The entire heli-lift took ninety minutes.

International pressure, including the withdrawal of American support for sterling and the French franc, brought a ceasefire later on 6th November, with the entire British and French forces withdrawing by sea on 13th November. There can be little doubt about the effectiveness of the military aspects of the operation, but real success was denied the British and the French by the delay in mounting the operation, which had involved the recall of reservists and demonstrated fatal weaknesses in the strategic mobility of the armed forces of both countries. The lessons were quickly learnt, however, and within a few years the Royal Navy had converted two of its aircraft carriers, HMS *Bulwark* and *Albion*, as commando carriers, while new transport aircraft entering service during the later 1950s and early 1960s saw an enhancement of the airlift capability of the Royal Air Force, including the provision of helicopter squadrons within RAF Transport Command. At the same time, the strength of British parachute forces was reduced from a division to a single brigade, with only two of the three battalions actually fully trained as parachutists. It could be argued, however, that the new, smaller, parachute element was more professional and better trained, with the Parachute Regiment no longer being dependant on officers and men seconded from other units, but recruiting direct, so establishing a greater *esprit de corps.*

British and American aims were not always so far apart, however, and within two years of the Suez crisis, the armed forces of both countries were once again acting in concert, and on this occasion the operations were an undoubted military and political success.

During the summer of 1958, civil war in the Lebanon threatened the stability of the Middle East and British troops were flown to Cyprus in Royal Air Force Hastings transports, ready to intervene if necessary. In the event, an even more dramatic crisis arose, with the bloody overthrow of the Hashemite monarchy in Iraq, involving the execution of King Feisal II and many other members of the Royal Family, in a left-wing coup which struck at the centre of the Baghdad Pact, the alliance set up by the United States and United Kingdom to help the states in the Middle East defend themselves against Communist attack. On 14th July, American marines were deployed in Lebanon to restore order at the request of President Chamoun, with most of the American force landing from the sea, but with reinforcements flown in aboard USMC Fairchild C-119 Packets staging through Port Lyautey in Morocco and Hal Far in Malta. A few days later, USAF MATS transports flew in 2,000 men of the US Army's 24th Airborne Brigade, mainly using C-124 Globemasters, while other troops from American units in West Germany were flown to Adana to act as a theatre reserve in the event of the situation escalating. At the same time, an advance party of the British 16th Independent Parachute Brigade was airlifted to Aman on 17th July and followed by the remainder of a force of 2,000 men, with their own artillery, with the entire force being assembled in Jordan by 20th July, ready to provide support for the Jordanian Government under King Hussein. This rapid intervention stabilised the situation,

and British and American troops started to withdraw in October. An idea of the build-up which took place during the early days of the operation can be assessed by the need to move American transport aircraft out of Adana on 17th July simply to ease congestion, as aircraft were parked nose to tail, and to allow B-66 Stratojet bombers to deploy to the airfield in case these were called upon by the commander of the American forces in the Lebanon.

In spite of this display of Western determination, the new regime in Iraq was soon to show that it intended to remain as an unsettling influence in the area, even though it was also to be largely unsuccessful in achieving its aims. On 25th June, 1961, the Iraqi dictator, General Kassem, claimed sovereignty over the neighbouring state of Kuwait, following up his claim with threats of punishment to Kuwait's ruler if his orders were not obeyed! Iraqi troops also advanced towards the border with Kuwait. The Emir of Kuwait appealed for British assistance on 30th June, by which time the commando carrier, HMS *Bulwark*, was already on passage from Karachi to the Gulf with 600 men of No.42 Royal Marine Commando aboard, and fifteen Westland Whirlwind troop-carrying helicopters. HMS *Bulwark* arrived off Kuwait on 1st July and her commandos were flown ashore, while tanks were also landed by two LCTs of the Amphibious Warfare Squadron. The following day, RAF Transport Command assigned seventy out of its total force of 200 aircraft to the support of the Army and RAF units based at Kuwait, which included Hunter jet fighters which had also been flown in. By this time Hastings and Beverley transports were already airlifting troops for Kuwait from Aden, Cyprus and Kenya, with most staging through Muharraq Airfield in Bahrain and the main RAF staging post for the Gulf at Khormakshar, before flying on to the still uncompleted airfield at Kuwait itself. The movement of troops was impressive; on 2nd July the airlift of two battalions of infantry from Kenya was started, with No.45 Royal Marine Commando being flown in from Aden, with a parachute battalion from Cyprus and an artillery battery from the UK being flown in through Turkey and Iran on 3rd July. Additional battalions and a field squadron of the Royal Engineers followed within a few days. This was only part of the picture, for as it happened, fresh troops were being flown in from the United Kingdom to Kenya, replacing units which had already left for Kuwait, where the new 9,000-foot-long runway was taking five transport aircraft an hour as well as providing an improvised forward base for the two squadrons of Hawker Hunter jet fighters; there were also additional combat aircraft aboard the two Royal Navy aircraft carriers, HMS *Victorious* and HMS *Centaur*. The intensive use of the airfield at Kuwait is the more impressive if one bears in mind that it had no ground control approach available for the aircraft, while additional problems were presented by frequent sandstorms. During the eight days from 2nd July to 10th July, Khormakshar and Muharraq handled 4,500 men and 900 tons of freight. Once again, a well co-ordinated rapid deployment of men and equipment defused the situation, and there was no conflict. The only casualty of the whole operation was one of the RAF's Blackburn Beverley heavy transports, which was destroyed on the ground at Muharraq in late October by a terrorist bomb.

The one weakness which manifested itself during this

deployment, was the lack of adequate numbers of helicopters to move British troops around what could well have become a theatre of war, and lorries had to be requisitioned locally to move men to the planned defensive line, at the Matla Ridge, some forty miles across the desert from the town of Kuwait. The problem has been a recurring theme for both the Royal Navy and the Royal Air Force, possibly being due in the main to the British Army not being allowed to operate helicopters large enough to provide a worthwhile transport effort. The one available commando carrier had just fifteen Whirlwinds operational, with five more as reserves, but the ten-man capacity of these machines meant that even a Royal Marine Commando required at least four lifts for a deployment ashore, or for battlefield mobility. The only squadrons in the RAF able to transport helicopters were the Beverley, with a total of just thirty-two aircraft between them, and these aircraft also had to transport heavy artillery and vehicles, while the Beverley's cruising speed of little more than 150 knots was of limited productivity, and the maximum load of twenty-two tons could only be lifted over a range of less than 500 miles. The Armstrong-Whitworth Argosy transports also entering service at this time were faster, but with a much lower carrying capacity and were too small for moving large helicopters. The Britannias and Comets were fast, but at their best as troop carriers, while only available in small numbers. Most of the troop carrying was still being handled by the elderly Hastings. There were only two helicopter squadrons with the heavy-lift Bristol Belvedere available worldwide to the RAF, and no aircraft capable of carrying them. Logistically, the entire force reflected an appalling lack of standardisation, too many types in too few numbers.

Further reinforcement of the Kuwait garrison took place in December, 1961, in response to the reinforcement by the Iraqis of their garrison at Basra; but this was a relatively small scale operation by the British forces.

Britain's success was undoubtedly made easier to achieve by the weakness of the Iraqi Air Force at this time, with its own troop-carrying potential severely limited to the capacity and speed of a small number of Mil Mi-4 helicopters, similar to the Whirlwind, and a few Antonov An-12 transports.

The operation also highlighted one of the major drawbacks of rapid deployment, that of acclimatisation of troops, and it was for this reason that most of the men deployed direct from the United Kingdom were sent to Kenya rather than to Kuwait. Even so, the troops arriving in Kuwait from Aden and Kenya, and the Royal Marines from HMS *Bulwark*, suffered in total several hundred cases of heat exhaustion of varying degrees of severity.

Trouble broke out in East Africa itself within a couple of years, early in 1964, with the armies of the newly independent African states of Kenya, Uganda and Tanganyika, now Tanzania, mutinying, while the Sultan of Zanzibar was overthrown in a *coup d'etat.* President Nyerere of Tanganyika appealed to Britain for help when units of his army mutinied, and No.45 Royal Marine Commando was embarked aboard the aircraft carrier, HMS *Centaur,* at Aden and despatched to East Africa. *Centaur's* marines were landed directly by helicopter from the carrier onto the barracks occupied by the rebel soldiers, and overcame the scant resistance offered with the loss of three Africans killed and nine wounded. RAF Bristol Britannias flew No.41 Commando direct from Britain to Nairobi, to quell the mutiny there, and later some of these men were flown from Nairobi to Lake Victoria in Uganda, to put down a mutiny by men of the Uganda Rifles, after which No.41 Commando was flown to Tanganyika to relieve the men of No.45 Royal Marine Commando.

The period before the formation of the Federation of Malaysia was also accompanied by disorder, largely instrumented by the Indonesian dictator, Soekarno, who not only opposed the new Federation, which at that time included Singapore as well as the Malaya states, but also entertained territorial ambitions in Borneo. On 8th December, 1962, a large scale revolt broke out in Brunei and in parts of neighbouring Sarawak and North Borneo, with the so-called North Brunei Liberation Army fighting the forces of the Malaysian Government and of the local rulers. The Sultan of Brunei, an independent state, appeal for British assistance, following which RAF aircraft flew No.42 Royal Marine Commando from Singapore to Brunei. Initially, the marines had to requisition lighters and small boats for transport, but they were soon joined by No.66 Squadron, Royal Air Force, with their Bristol Belvedere helicopters. The largest RAF helicopter at the time, the Belvederes of No.66 Squadron made one of the longest non-stop flights over water by a large formation of helicopters whilst being deployed to Brunei; flying 400 miles across the South China Sea from their main base at Singapore to Kuching, in Sarawak, where they refuelled for the 500 mile flight across dense forest and mangrove swamp to Labaun Island off the coast of North Borneo. Naturally, this was an empty positioning flight, and additional marines had meanwhile been moved to the area aboard the commando carrier, HMS *Albion*, being flown ashore by the carrier's squadron of Whirlwind helicopters, many of which remained ashore to support the marines. It took just one month to disperse the insurgents, proving once again the value of rapid intervention.

After the Federation of Malaysia became fully independent in September, 1963, Brunei was not included due to a dispute over the state's oil resources. The new Federation was faced with the increasingly violent opposition of President Soekarno and, by February, 1964, RAF and Royal Navy helicopters, including some of the then new Westland Wessex which were replacing the Whirlwinds, were operating from bases in Sarawak and Sabah to assist army and marine detachments in the jungles and swamps, fighting guerilla forces infiltrated by Indonesia across its 1,000-mile-long land frontier with Malaysia, while troops were rotated from the United Kingdom aboard RAF Britannias, and by chartered commercial airliners, including Britannias and DC-7s. The heavy freight movements were handled by Beverlies and Argosies, while theatre transport was handled by RAF Vickers Valettas and RNZAF Bristol Freighters, although by the time the confrontation with Indonesia ended, with the overthrow of Soekarno in mid-1966, Avro 749 Andovers, stretched versions of the civil 748 airliner, had started to replace the Valettas. After a successful campaign, with troops fighting in the jungle and supported by a "hearts and minds" campaign designed to gain the support of villagers, again using the CASEVAC capability of the helicopter to the full, British forces started to withdraw from Malaysia in September, 1966, the start of a gradual run-down of British forces in the area, which extended into the early 1970s.

Much of the ability to deploy forces rapidly in an emergency had come, as we have already seen, from the existence of garrisons and theatre transport aircraft outside of the United Kingdom. Faced with considerable local opposition to British withdrawal by the governments of Malaysia, Brunei and Singapore, a major exercise was conducted, perhaps one should say concocted, to demonstrate the ability of British forces to reinforce the region's own forces in an emergency. Named *Bersatu Padu*, the exercise included the airlift of RAF Westland Wessex helicopters of No.72 Squadron from RAF Odiham, in southern England, to Malaya, where they in turn transported troops of the 9th Royal Malay Regiment to an imaginary front line, spread across jungle-covered hills and low mountains. Once the Malayan troops were in position, the RAF helicopters commenced a major re-supply operation, providing this support for the Malay troops throughout June, 1970. The entire point of the operation was soon lost, however, for within a few years the RAF's force of ten Short Belfast heavy freighters was sold, leaving the RAF and the British armed forces as a whole, without the ability to transport helicopters other than small ones, using its own aircraft.

The Royal Air Force effectively reached a peak of capability in the transport sense during the late 1960s and early 1970s. Even during the early 1960s, the transport capability had been impressive, and effective as the events in the Middle East and East Africa have shown. The Soviet Union and the United States also both possessed massive airlift capability. The Soviet Union was able to airlift two divisions at once; while the term "division" varies in its numerical significance between armies, in the Soviet case it would amount to about 40,000 men in two divisions. The United States considered that it could airlift a single infantry division of about 20,000 men, including air portable tanks, or, alternatively it possessed an airlift capability of 21,000 tons. The MATS 1963 strength stood at more than 600 aircraft, with a number of additional transport units integrated with Tactical Command to provide support for strike and ground attack aircraft to provide for the rapid deployment of combat air power anywhere in the world. The RAF, still at that time with a separate Transport Command, had some 150 fixed-wing aircraft, including ten de Havilland Comet C-2s and twenty-two Bristol Britannias, as well as thirty-two Blackburn Beverlies for bulky items, and twin-engined Vickers Valettas for theatre transport; Transport Command, unlike MATS, also included transport helicopter units, mainly Wessex and Belvederes, giving a total of some 200 fixed and rotary wing aircraft. The French *Armée de l'Air* had some 200 Nord Noratlas transports, albeit with a short range compared to some of the British and American transports, with a maximum of 1,000 miles.

While the operations just mentioned had a colonial theme, there were other events also taking place in the world, which also portrayed a different type of strategic intervention, and one which was often more direct.

Trouble on the doorstep

Not all of the instances of strategic intervention were the preserve of the Western powers, and the Soviet Union was soon to show that it would not hesitate to intervene in its East European satellites. However, at first, the Soviet capability to extend its air power beyond Europe was limited. Much of the development both of the Soviet Union's military air transport capability and of its naval strength, dates from the failure of either to influence events during the Cuban missile crisis of October, 1962.

The Cuban missile crisis arose because of American opposition to the construction of guided missile silos in Cuba, threatening the southern United States, and also seriously affecting an American defensive posture based on the threat of Soviet attack over the North Pole or across the northern Pacific ocean. A blockade of Cuba by the United States Navy succeeded, in part because of the inability of the Soviet Navy to deploy an effective and balanced strength in the area at that time, and partly because of the inability of the Soviet Air Force to mount an airlift to by-pass the blockade. In contrast, starting on 19th October, MATS airlifted most of the 7,000 men and 3,000 tons of equipment that was moved to the southern United States to reinforce existing units in the area, and before the crisis ended, the 14,000 USAF reservists in the twenty-four transport reserve squadrons were activated, with 90 per cent of the men and 75 per cent of the aircraft fully operational by 28th October; these units were stood down in late November as the crisis receded. Although the Soviet Air Force's then force of Ilyushin Il-28 transports could not have flown direct to Cuba, the Tupolev Tu-114s could have done so, but without the ability to move the bulky items of equipment which an air supply operation would have demanded.

Soviet transport aircraft were to figure more prominently in Europe, however. Although there was little use of transport aircraft during the early 1950s when riots and demonstrations in both East Germany and Poland were ruthlessly suppressed, or in Hungary in 1956, when more than 75,000 Soviet, Rumanian and Czech troops crossed the borders in early November, ready for the ten day Battle of Budapest from 4th to 14th November, military transport aircraft did figure prominently in the Soviet invasion of Czechoslovakia during the summer of 1968.

The reforms of the so-called "Prague Spring" under Alexander Dubcek provoked a strong response from the Soviet Union, and once again Warsaw Pact tanks rolled across the frontier, as in Hungary twelve years earlier, to re-establish a less liberal and more enduring brand of Communism. During the night of the invasion, 21-22nd August, 1968, an entire Soviet airborne division was flown into Prague within the space of six hours, with 250 aircraft bringing 20,000 men and their equipment, taking the Czech capital by surprise, while another fifty aircraft landed during 22nd August, bringing additional Soviet and Polish troops. Aircraft employed on this operation included the new Antonov An-22 transport, known to NATO as the 'Cock', and at the time, the world's largest aircraft, capable of lifting a payload of up to eighty tons, while for the movement of personnel, there were large numbers of the Antonov An-12 and of Ilyushin and Tupolev transports.

It seems likely on this occasion, given the greater use of aircraft, that transport aircraft were also used to rotate Hungarian, Polish, Rumanian and Soviet troops used in Czechoslovakia, especially because the initial invasion force was soon withdrawn after morale was affected by the cool welcome extended to the Warsaw Pact forces by the Czechs; the surprise being the greater since the invaders had been expecting to be welcomed as liberators!

The West had come, by this time, to accept that the Soviet Union would intervene heavily in its East European satellites if it felt that Communist orthodoxy was threatened. Yugoslavia and Albania had escaped from the Soviet Bloc largely because they had a difficult terrain from which to mount an effective defence, and because they did so at a time when the Soviet military capability was insufficient for effective deployments over even medium distances. What did surprise the West was the Soviet intervention in Afghanistan, which, while it had moved towards a close relationship with the Soviet Bloc during the 1960s and 1970s, had still not been regarded as a part of the Bloc, and which did possess strong nationalistic elements amongst its population.

The Afghan monarchy had been overthrown in a *coup* during July, 1973, while a further *coup* in 1978 opened the way for Soviet "advisers" to take part in the running of the country. The conflict between Marxism and Islamic doctrines resulted in rebellion throughout most of the country during the following year, possibly inspired by the overthrow of the Shah of Iran by fundamental Islamic extremists at the beginning of that year. A new prime minister, Hafizullah Amin, was unsuccessful in curbing the rebellion, in spite of the army and the air force being supplied with modern Soviet equipment and large numbers of advisers, instructing the Afghan personnel in their use. The murder of the Afghan president in September, 1979, added to the growing tension in the country, and to Soviet fears of Islamic unrest spilling over into the Moslem areas of the Soviet Union. It may have been at this time that the Soviet Union decided to intervene, for certainly, given the massive size of the Soviet armed forces, the operation which followed at the end of the year was still too large and well organised to have been conceived and implemented on the spur of the moment. Unusually, it also appears that many of the original troops deployed may even have been reservists, with the exception of the crack airborne units, since it was decided to use units based close to the border with Afghanistan rather than reduce the forces available on the borders with China or in Eastern Europe. The forces in Soviet Turkestan and the Central Asian Military District were at a low state of readiness, and required mobilisation to bring these up to full combat strength, in marked contrast to the forces in Europe and the Far East.

Paratroops did not have to be dropped into Afghanistan, since the presence of upwards of 4,000 Soviet military advisers meant that an airborne assault was not neccessary, and that troops could be air-landed without difficulty. The invasion started slowly, with the arrival of an advance party from the 105th Guards Airborne Division who were flown into Bagram Airfield, a military base to the north of the Afghan capital, Kabul, on 24th December, securing this airfield as their main base for the airlift rather than the commercial airport at Kabul, which was open to foreigners. The next two days, 25th and 26th December, saw the main force of the Division arriving in Afghanistan, with upwards of 5,000 men, two regiments and their supporting troops, flown-in by almost 300 sorties of large Antonov An-22 transports, supported by the smaller Antonov An-12s and Ilyushin Il-76s, turning the airfield into a massive Soviet barracks and arsenal. Soviet paratroops drove into Kabul itself on 27th December, using BMD armoured personnel carriers and supported by ASU-85 airborne assault guns, and some fighting with troops loyal to the Amin government ensued, before Amin was killed and the Soviet Union's puppet, Babrak Kamal, took over. Meanwhile, other paratroops moved north to secure the strategically important Salang Tunnel for ground troops and armoured units to pass through on their way into Afghanistan. Within a few days, the Soviet Union had flown and transported by motor vehicle, some 80,000 troops into Afghanistan.

The distances involved and uncertainty over the security of convoys on the long supply routes, have meant that a substantial Soviet air transport operation is tied down in providing an air bridge into Afghanistan. The Soviet ground forces use helicopters, mainly Mil Mi-8s, for the transport of troops, and long chains of marker lights have been established to make it easier for helicopter pilots, with Mil Mi-8 transport helicopters and Mi-24 'Hind' attack helicopters to fly across the country. While the Mi-8 is vulnerable, the heavily armoured Mi-24s, which can carry troops in small numbers, have little to fear from poorly-armed rebel forces. While the Soviet intervention has raised the level of the rebellion amongst the naturally anarchistic Afghans, one of the main weaknesses of the rebel forces appears to be an absence of co-ordination, with jealous rivalries between tribal leaders or war lords.

Less direct involvement by Soviet forces outside of the recognised confines of the Soviet Bloc has also occurred in Africa, mainly in Angola and Ethiopia, with Soviet equipment and support being used to support Cuban troops propping up the Marxist regimes of these countries. A substantial part of the commitment comes from transport aircraft flying in men and supplies, although on the long flights from Cuba to Angola, civilian airliners, often Ilyushin Il-62s, are used to avoid any embarrassment which could occur if a military transport had to make a forced landing *en route*. Nevertheless, Ilyushin Il-14s of the Cuban Air Force have also been used, especially on flights to Angola, staging through Guinea. Theatre transport in the states receiving Cuban support, fighting the wars on behalf of the Soviet Union by proxy, include Antonov An-2 'Cub' and Mil Mi-8 helicopters, although in Ethiopia, the Soviet presence is the more obvious, with many of the transport aircraft and helicopters used within that country belonging to the Soviet Air Force.

Not all of the instances of strategic intervention have involved the major powers of East and West, or West, or the Soviet Union's puppets, such as Cuba. The intermittent wrangling between Israel and the Arab

Mainstay of the Soviet Bloc helicopter fleets is the Mil Mi-8 helicopter, known to NATO as the 'Hip'.

States, and between India and Pakistan, have also produced their share of excitement.

The wars between Israel and her Arab neighbours tended to amount to either guerilla campaigns, with sneak attacks by one side resulting in retaliation by the other, or to major conflicts in which fighter dog fights over the desert were matched by tank battles on the ground. Certainly, the terrain leant itself to tank warfare, because of the openness of much of the terrain, the stony nature of the Sinai desert, and the distances involved. Often, the conflict was between numbers, with Egypt and Syria possessing massive manpower, and technology, with Israel attempting to compensate for the small population by using their higher standard of technical education to use the latest American or French supplied equipment. To fight a war, Israel had to mobilise reserve forces, meaning that effectively the first few days of a war would always favour an attacker, before Israel could bring the maximum power to bear on her opponents. It was for this reason that Israel found the outcome of the June, 1967, war so satisfactory, for large areas of Arab territory fell into her hands, providing a problem in the greatly increased perimeter to be defended, but this was outweighed by the distance, the buffer zone, established between Israel and her neighbours. Neither Egypt nor Syria, the most militant of Israel's Arab neighbours,

accepted this. Egypt had lost most in territory, with Israel occupying the East Bank of the Suez Canal, but Syria had lost the Golan heights, making an attack on Israel difficult. An opportunity for the Arab nations to re-assert themselves came in 1973, with the decision to mount an attack on Israel at the time of the festival of Yom Kippur, when Israel's ability to respond would be at its lowest. The actual timing of the attack was a compromise; the Egyptians wanted a late afternoon attack with the sun behind them, the Syrians, attacking from almost the opposite direction, wanted an early morning attack, which would have given them the same advantage. In the end, they agreed to attack at 14.00, on 6th October.

The war took on a different flavour on this occasion as far as the Egyptians were concerned, mounting an amphibious assault across the Suez Canal. Of the many assaults across the Canal, the one which was most interesting was the use of the heli-borne assault in the north on the night of 6-7th October, with Mil Mi-8 helicopters carrying Egyptian troops to seize Baluza, and then withdraw again, for this position was to be beyond the furthermost limit of the Egyptian advance, which failed to cut off the few roads along which Israeli reinforcements would eventually come. The Israeli counter-attack ten days later was highly successful, but did not involve transport aircraft, with paratroops making an assault across the Great Bitter Lake using amphibious assault craft instead of transport aircraft to seize their objectives.

This reluctance to use air power was not shared in the conflicts between India and Pakistan which followed the independence of the two nations in 1947, and lasted until the defeat of Pakistani forces in East Pakistan, or Bangladesh as it was to become, in 1971. However, in spite of the Pakistan Air Force having developed the air transport capability to keep a direct route to East Pakistan following independence, this service was only operable with the goodwill of the Indians, and in time of conflict, East Pakistan could only be re-supplied by sea. Indeed, the effective use of air transport was an Indian prerogative.

The post-independence strength of the Indian Air Force, as it became after India became a republic, soon increased from one to three squadrons of Douglas C-47s, later augmented by two squadrons of Fairchild C-119 Packets and one of de Havilland Canada Otters for light transport. As India started to drift towards closer relations with the Soviet Union, a squadron of Antonov An-12s and then one of An-14s added further to the transport strength of the Indian Air Force, and even though a third C-119 squadron was raised later, Mil Mi-4 helicopters soon became the mainstay of the helicopter units rather than the Sikorsky and Bell helicopters introduced shortly after independence.

Not all of the Indian Air Force's operations were against Pakistan; China, on the north-east frontiers of India, was also a major cause of tension and of occasional border skirmishes, which erupted into outright warfare in October, 1962. While helicopters provided forward air mobility for Indian troops rushed to the scene, with re-supply and casualty evacuation operations high in the Himalayas, often under heavy fire from Chinese positions, there was also a major airlift operation by the fixed-wing transport squadrons. Fairchild C-119s operated into and out of airfields as high as 17,000 feet above sea level, often using jet booster engines to improve their performance, while the An-12s flew-in two troops of AMX-13 light tanks to Chushul airfield in Ladakh, 15,000 feet above sea level.

Pakistan had, of course, been divided into two parts on its creation as a result of independence, but, in addition to the problems of having a country divided in two and with another country in-between, the East Pakistanis felt that the nation's wealth was concentrated in the West, whose people had a virtual monopoly of the senior positions in the administration and the armed forces. It was often claimed that the East was treated as a colony by the West. Disorder broke out in the East after the Awami League obtained 298 out of 310 seats in the regional assembly, and also acquired a minority of seats in the national assembly as well, forcing the President to postpone the re-opening of Parliament. A year of violence led to refugees flooding into India, creating a succession of problems for the hard-pressed Indian authorities, with considerable economic, social and security problems of their own, especially with the history of conflict with both Pakistan and China, and with Chinese forces within easy striking distance of Assam, close to East Pakistan. India found itself being pushed towards intervention after the Awami League election victories of December, 1970, and planning commenced for war timed to coincide with the end of the 1971 monsoons in November, by which time it was thought that winter in the Himalayas would prevent

China taking advantage of the situation to invade India.

War broke out in the East and the West on 3rd December, 1971. Although far stronger than the Pakistan forces defending East Pakistan, the Indian Army soon found that the terrain favoured the defenders due to the large number of swamps and rivers in the area. At first, the Indians placed great store on their Soviet-built PT76 light amphibious tanks, until it was discovered that these were prone to overheating once submerged. It was soon clear that large numbers of Mil Mi-4 and Mi-8 helicopters would have to be used to provide both the means of making assaults on Pakistani-held positions and for providing air-bridges over enemy strongpoints and across the many rivers and swamps. The first major use of the helicopter in this war was to make an assault across the mile-wide Meghna River on 10th December, putting the IV Indian Corps, attacking from the east, within striking distance of Dacca, the capital of East Pakistan. Four days later, Pakistani forces were withdrawing from the northern areas of East Pakistan when a parachute battalion was dropped from a squadron of C-119s onto Taghail, after which reinforcements were airlifted in. On 16th December, Pakistani forces surrendered in the East, and the independent state of Bangladesh was declared.

Covert operations

Most attempts at intervention have taken place openly, or reasonably so, and in peacetime there have been fewer of the isolated raids which counted for so much during World War II, when these often presented an ideal way of engaging the enemy and attaining a limited, but important, objective. In peacetime, or what passes for it, some of the covert operations have in fact been supply missions, often using chartered commercial aircraft to fly in supplies, for example during the Nigerian civil war, the rebels in Biafra received much of their equipment in this way.

Then again, just as in war, so in peace, covert operations, even when planned and executed by supposedly highly trained personnel, have had mixed fortunes; possibly because these operations rely on small numbers of personnel and are conducted over long distances with little other support, and thus depend so much on a generous amount of good fortune.

One of the more ambitious operations of the post-war period was an attempt by the Israeli armed forces to free the hostages from a hijacked airliner.

On 27th June, 1976, an Air France *Airbus Industrie* A300B airbus was hijacked after taking off from Tel Aviv for a flight to Paris. The aircraft and the 247 passengers and twelve crew were forced by four hijackers to fly via Athens and Benghazi in Libya to Entebbe in Uganda, at that time under the rule of the dictator, Idi Amin. Three more men joined the hijackers when the aircraft landed at Entebbe, where the passengers and crew were taken off the A300B and held hostage in an old and disused terminal building at the airport, in return for the release of fifty-three Palestine terrorists in prison in Israel.

The Israeli response was to send three Lockheed C-130 Hercules transports with a force of commandos, estimated by some to be as many as 200 men, to Entebbe, landing at midnight after a 2,500 mile flight on the night

The most numerous military transport in the West today is the
Lockheed C-130 Hercules; this is a USAF example, above,
while below is a C-130K of the Royal Air Force, Europe's
largest operator of the Hercules.

Above: A Sikorsky CH-53 (or S-65) Super Sea Stallion of the USMC airlifts a self-propelled gun.

of 2-3rd July, 1976. As soon as the aircraft stopped, the rearloading ramps dropped and jeeps carrying heavily-armed men left the aircraft at high speed, overwhelming the guards detaining the hostages, killing twenty Ugandan soliders and all seven hijackers, as well as destroying at least six, and possibly ten, of the Ugandan Air Force's elderly Mikoyan MiG-15 jet fighters. The hostages were quickly removed and taken with the returning force to the waiting Hercules, before the entire force took off for Nairobi to refuel before continuing to Israel. This daring raid was not without its casualties, three hostages died, while another five were wounded, as were four Israeli commandos. The risk of injury and death to the hostages obviously had to be weighed against their possible murder if the Israeli Government had not bowed to the hijackers' demands, or, if they had agreed to the release of the terrorists, to the potential for further terrorist attack. At the same time, the raid could only have been conducted with the refuelling at Nairobi, and tension between Uganda and Kenya obviously helped the Israelis in mounting this successful operation.

A few years later, the opportunity for a similar raid arose after fifty-three American diplomats were held hostage at the United States embassy in Tehran by revolutionary "students", against whom the Iranian authorities refused to take any action. The Iranian Government seemed to be unmoved by diplomatic efforts to release the hostages, and an arms embargo appeared to have no success in changing Iranian attitudes.

Below: On their way to the Falklands, Royal Marine Commandos practising rapid roping drill from a Westland Sea King HC-4 onto the helicopter platform of the converted cruise ship, 'Canberra'.

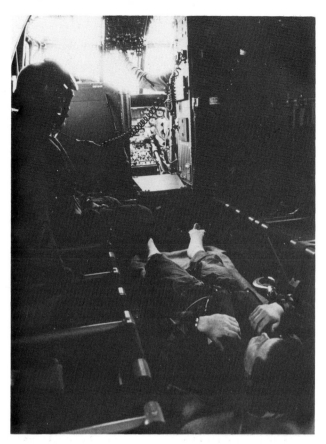

In a joint operation code-named *Operation Rice Bowl* between all four branches of the American armed forces, the nuclear-powered aircraft carrier, or CVN, USS *Nimitz*, arrived at the approaches to the Persian Gulf on 25th April, 1980. Included amongst her complement of some 6,000 men were ninety commandos drawn from the USAF, US Army, and the USN as well as the USMC, and eight large Sikorsky S-65 Sea Stallion helicopters. This force included men of the 'Delta Force', the US equivalent to the British Special Air Service, and was to be landed inside Iran in an attempt to rescue the hostages. Shortly after the start of the mission, one of the S-65s developed engine trouble and was forced to return to the carrier, while a second was also forced by technical problems to make a forced landing in the Iranian desert, with its crew and troops picked up by another helicopter. When the depleted force of six helicopters reached a desert rendezvous with six USAF Lockheed C-130 Hercules transports, from which the helicopters were to refuel, the assembled C-130s and S-65s were seen by the occupants of a bus, some fifty Iranian civilians, who had to be held in order that the secrecy of the mission would not be jeopardised. At this stage, yet another helicopter developed engine trouble, taking the helicopter force below the minimum of six machines considered essential to the mission's success, and forcing the commander of

Above: Falklands CASEVAC, an inside shot from the tail-end of a Sea King HC-4.

Below: One of the RAF's Falklands Chinooks survived the sinking of the 'Atlantic Conveyor'; it is seen here in flight over Goose Green.

the mission to abandon the rescue attempt. Unfortunately, confusion seems to have arisen after this, with a C-130 taking off, but in doing so it collided with a helicopter hidden by the dust raised by its rotor blades as it too prepared to take off, with this accident accounting for the deaths of eight American servicemen and the injury of four others. The five surviving helicopters were abandoned, with the force withdrawing in the five remaining C-130s.

As one would have expected, the failure of this mission precluded any further rescue attempts, with the hostages scattered to prevent rescue until they were released early the following year. The outcome was a propaganda triumph for the Iranians, and a humiliation for the Americans, with the burnt corpses of those killed in the accident paraded before the television cameras. Inevitably, an inquiry was held over the failure of the mission, accompanied by Press reports that there had been no special maintenance for the aircraft involved in the mission, and even one allegation that the helicopters had been accidentally drenched by fire hoses before the mission started. True or false, the drenching of the normally reliable S-65s could account for their failures during the mission, but then too, had the helicopters been refuelled in flight, the confusion which occurred on the ground would have been avoided, unless, of course, the ground rendezvous was required for another purpose, possibly to pick up Iranian agents, but if so, choosing a site within view of a road was hardly good planning. Most important of all, the mission was too complicated; all of the indications show that to succeed, an airborne mission needs to arrive as close as possible to its objective, and as quickly as possible; witness the Israeli rescue at Entebbe, which might have been impossible had the hostages been held away from the airport. Many have argued since that the rescue could still have proceeded, even with just five helicopters, which seems plausible given the large size of the S-65.

These are points which many critics have overlooked, but then they would, for the operation tempts comparisons with the slickness of that mounted by the Israelis.

Island Grabbing

While it seems unlikely that there will ever be another operation to compare with the German invasion of Crete, airborne forces have been involved in several smaller incidents during the 1970s and 1980s which have at least some relationship with the invasion of Crete; quite why this outbreak of "island grabbing" occurred is hard to explain, and indeed the factors surrounding the Turkish invasion of Cyprus, the Argentinian invasion of the Falklands Islands and their subsequent re-taking by the British, and the American invasion of Grenada, all differ. The objectives of those involved also varied considerably. With the exception of Grenada, all of the islands concerned were large, indeed, the Falklands comprises two large islands and many smaller ones, with a total land area of about that of Wales.

Although at first Cyprus resumed a peaceful existence following independence from the British, the calm did not last for long, and the tensions between the Greek and Turkish Cypriot communities on the island were too strong. The constitution bequeathed to the islanders by the British never really worked, and the death of the President, Archbishop Makarios and the resulting confusion as a new president was sworn in, and then almost as quickly replaced, amidst increasing violence between the two communities, finally led Turkey to invade the island on Saturday, 20th July, 1974. Turkish C-119 and C-130 transport aircraft dropped paratroops close to the Turkish enclave at Nicosia, the capital, and elsewhere on the island, although most of an estimated invasion force of 70,000 troops came ashore from landing craft and warships. The initial assault at 07.30 was followed by a re-supply operation later in the morning, while helicopters were used to move Turkish troops over the Kyrenia range of mountains, helping to provide a strong Turkish bridgehead behind this natural defensive position, after which the Turkish troops advanced to the Nicosia-Famagusta road, the so-called 'Attila Line', before a cease fire could be arranged.

There was little that the Greeks could do to stop this, Cyprus was close to the coast of Turkey, and the few Hellenic Air Force aircraft which flew to Cyprus ran the risk of attack off the coast of Turkey. In the confusion and panic which followed, one Greek C-119 making a supply run to Cyprus was shot down by its own side close to Nicosia. Confusion was understandable, both countries had been equipped with obsolescent aircraft by the United States, which tried to strike a balance between the NATO commitments of the two countries without providing either with the arsenals which would tempt them into outright warfare with each other. The fact that these were two of the three poorest countries in NATO also meant that aircraft procurement from other sources was out of the question.

The invasion provided a problem for the British, with a large number of servicemen and their dependants at the sovereign bases, with many Turkish-Cypriots caught in what became the Greek-Cypriot zone after the invasion. There were also British holiday-makers to be brought back to Britain. The British aircraft carrier, HMS *Hermes,* which had been converted from a light fleet carrier to a commando carrier before the invasion, was ordered to the area, evacuating British tourists and residents from Kyrenia, a largely Turkish-Cypriot town on the northern side of the island, by boat and by Westland Wessex commando-carrying helicopters, and then taking them to the RAF bases at the other side of the island. The British refugees were then flown back to the UK aboard Bristol Britannias while other RAF aircraft flew emergency supplies to Cyprus for the Turkish-Cypriots.

While the Cyprus problem centred around the continued demands for *Enosis,* Union with Greece, by the Greek-Cypriot community, a different set of circumstances prevailed some eight years later when Argentina invaded the Falkland Islands on Friday, 2nd April, 1982. There were no Argentinians living on the islands, despite Argentinian claims of sovereignty. The invasion of the Falklands was by an amphibious force of Argentine troops and marines, who encountered fierce, but ultimately hopeless resistance from a heavily outnumbered force of just seventy Royal Marines, the islands' garrison. After taking the capital, Port Stanley, the Argentinians used air force C-130 Hercules

Maintaining the air bridge to the Falklands, an RAF Hercules C-130K refuels over the South Atlantic.

transports and chartered civilian Fokker F.27 Friendship airliners to fly in reinforcements. The build-up of Argentinian forces on the islands included the deployment in the islands of light helicopters and utility aircraft for transport and liaison duties.

The following day, three Argentinian helicopters, an Aerospatiale SA.330 Puma and two Alouette IIIs, operating from the ice patrol vessel, *Bahia Paraiso,* landed an invasion force on the island of South Georgia, more than a thousand miles to the east and the south of the Falklands. Once again, the Argentinians encountered fierce resistance from the Royal Marines garrison, in this case a force of just twenty-two men, who missed shooting down the Puma with a 66-mm anti-tank gun by just inches. Not to be denied their prey, the defenders machine-gunned the Puma until it crash-landed after retreating across a bay. Within a few minutes, one of the Alouettes was also shot down.

An airborne assault by the British to retake the Falklands was clearly out of the question because of the distance from the nearest staging post, and the lack of aerial superiority over the Falklands. Reductions in the carrier strength of the Royal Navy, which twenty years earlier had included five aircraft carriers and two commando carriers, to just two ships, the relatively small, but new, HMS *Invincible,* and the larger, but older, HMS *Hermes,* also meant that a heli-borne assault from the sea was also out of the question, and the best that could be hoped for was an amphibious assault with helicopter support. Even this was more by luck than as the result of careful planning; HMS *Invincible* was under offer to the

Royal Australian Navy at the time, while the Royal Navy's two assault ships, HMS *Fearless* and *Intrepid,* were laid up awaiting disposal. On the other hand, the British task force despatched to retake the Falklands was assembled and sailed within 72 hours of the invasion. It was added to later with requisitioned merchant ships, including the liner *QEII,* the cruise ship *Canberra,* the *Norland,* a car ferry, and the container ship, *Atlantic Conveyor,* all of which were modified to a greater or lesser extent to accommodate the helicopter, which was to be an essential maid-of-all-work for the task force, in addition to the more glamorous role of anti-submarine protection for the fleet.

During the long voyage south, Royal Air Force Hercules transports dropped urgent supplies and mail to the task force, and additional equipment was flown to meet task force vessels *en route* to the Falklands at Ascension Island, where RAF helicopters acted as flying cranes, operating an onboard delivery service to the ships of the task force. A squadron of RAF Westland Wessex 5 helicopters and four of the RAF's newly delivered Boeing-Vertol CH-47 Chinook heavy lift helicopters were also sent to the Falklands, with some additional Harrier fighters, aboard the ACL container ship, *Atlantic Conveyor,* extensively converted to transport and operate these aircraft. Typical of the conversions to the merchant vessels was the installation of two helicopter landing platforms, fore and aft, on the cruise ship *Canberra.* As the task force voyaged to the Falklands, helicopters operated a steady stream of flights between the ships, moving supplies and personnel from one ship to another, although often bad weather severely curtailed flying. As conditions permitted, other helicopters worked enabling the troops and Royal Marines to continue training for the assault, with men practising rapid roping drills from helicopters hovering above the landing platforms and open decks of the troopships.

While a heli-borne assault was out of the question given the limited number of machines available, and the limited flight deck space available from the task force ships, which would have prevented a heli-lift of sufficient strength to overwhelm an entrenched opposition, the situation was made even worse by the loss of the *Atlantic Conveyor*. The ship was sunk on 25 May by an Exocet missile fired from an Argentinian aircraft, and with her went all but one of the Chinooks, and most of the rest of the RAF helicopter force assigned to the operation.

The invasion of the Falklands by British forces was conducted using landing craft, but during the final preparations for the invasion on 21st May at San Carlos, helicopters played an important part in moving men and supplies between ships, allowing the larger troopships to be kept clear of the immediate war zone. Eighteen members of the British Army's Special Air Services Regiment, the famous SAS, and two Royal Navy crewmen, were killed during the transfers when their Westland Sea King crashed on a flight from the *Canberra* to an assault ship.

Before retaking the Falklands, a small force of naval vessels was deployed from the task force to retake the

An RAF Hercules moves closer to the refuelling cone trailed from a converted Handley Page Victor bomber, whilst flying on the Falklands airbridge.

island of South Georgia. On 21st April, a small force of SAS men landed on South Georgia to reconnoitre Argentinian positions, but were forced to move due to appalling weather conditions, seeking transport by a Royal Navy Westland Wessex 5. The pilot of this machine flew on 22nd April through dangerous "white out" conditions to pick up the SAS team, but crashed after taking off from South Georgia, and another helicopter had to be sent to pick up the SAS men and the crew of the first helicopter, from which, fortunately, there were no serious casualties. The second helicopter took off successfully and returned the occupants of the first helicopter to the fleet off shore, flying with a massive overload of seventeen soldiers and airmen; for this, the pilot, Lieutenant-Commander Ian Stanley from the guided missile destroyer HMS *Antrim,* was awarded the Distinguished Service Order, DSO. The SAS men attempted a further landing on South Georgia that day, using five small Gemini inflatable craft; three of these reached the shore safely, one broke down and its crew were rescued by a naval helicopter, but the fifth, which also broke down, drifted away. The small craft remained missing for four days with its crew, before a helicopter homed onto a distress beacon, to find the crew on the southernmost tip of South Georgia, the last bit of land between the island and Antarctica!

Once the task force had placed the Army and Royal Marines units safely ashore, the wild and boggy Falklands terrain meant that helicopters had to handle most of the movement of supplies and munitions, with

Sea King HC-4 helicopters flying with artillery pieces slung under the helicopter, and ammunition in a net below that. As the British forces advanced, lack of helicopters and of fuel meant that most of the troops had to march, "yomping" or "tagging" across the desolate Falklands in cold and damp. Helicopters were used for the movement of Argentinian prisoners from forward positions, as and when space was available, and priority was always given for casualty evacuation. One operation at which the helicopters did play an important part in the speedy movement of troops was in the retaking of Bluff Cove and Fitzroy on the south coast of East Falkland. A telephone call by a British Army officer to a local resident ascertained that there were no Argentinian forces in the vicinity, before a flight of Army Air Corps helicopter gunships flew into the area, followed by a small number of troop-carrying helicopters, using a welcome thick mist for concealment. A few days later, when the main British force arrived at Bluff Cove, to unload men from the Welsh Guards, with supplies and heavy equipment, from the landing ships, RFA *Sir Tristam* and *Sir Galahad,* the Argentine Air Force mounted a heavy attack from McDonnell Douglas A-4 Skyhawk fighter-bombers, severely damaging *Sir Tristam* and crippling *Sir Galahad* when ammunition aboard the latter ship caught fire and blew up. More than fifty men from the Welsh Guards and the two ships' companies were killed, and more than seventy injured, many seriously. Amidst the heat, dense smoke and the dangers of exploding ammunition and Argentine air attack, Royal Navy Sea King anti-submarine helicopters flew close to the ships, often in zero visibility, to pull survivors out of the water, and then fly the injured to hospital, initially a field hospital and then on to the hospital ship, the converted educational cruise ship, *Uganda.* The anti-submarine Sea Kings had been helping with the movement of heavy equipment nearby at the time of the attack.

Argentinian prisoners taken at Goose Green, some 1,600 in all, were taken to San Carlos by helicopter, having a more comfortable ride than the paratroops who had had to march to their battle to take Goose Green.

Attacks by fast jet aircraft and ground fire presented a threat to helicopters of both sides. The Argentinians lost two Aerospatiale Pumas and a Bell UH-1 Iroquois to Royal Navy Sea Harrier fighters. During an attack, the best defence for the helicopters caught in the air was to hover close to the ground, allowing some freedom of movement rather than landing on often unsuitable and unlevelled peat bog, keeping well below the skyline, until the raid was over. Pilots of anti-submarine helicopters suddenly expected to perform battlefield movements tasks, for which they had had little training, coped well in spite of some difficulty in navigating overland; they also worried military commanders by parking their machines in neat, and highly vulnerable, lines as close as possible to headquarters, which was perfectly understandable in men used to parking on the limited space of a light fleet carrier flight deck!

As the Royal Navy attempted to enforce a blockade around the islands, the Argentine Air Force, the *Fuerza Aerea Argentina,* attempted to maintain a nightly supply operation using its small force of C-130 Hercules, although at least one of these aircraft was shot down. The Argentine Air Force appeared throughout the campaign

to be the sole repository of initiative and professionalism in that country's armed forces, and while most noted for their successful attacks with Skyhawk, Mirage and Super Etendard aircraft, the latter being operated by Navy pilots, the lack of adequate bomber aircraft led in one instance to the use of a C-130 Hercules as a bomber, with men throwing bombs out of the rear cargo doors in a fruitless attempt to hit the *Canberra*!

While most of the supplies and rotation of troops following the retaking of the islands had to be by sea, an airlift had to be established for personnel and urgent supplies, and this was hindered by the fact that the runway at Port Stanley could not take long-range jet transports. The airbridge to the Falklands was in two parts, until a new airport opened in 1985; before this, Royal Air Force British Aerospace VC.10s and Lockheed TriStars, ex-British Airways TriStar 500s, operated over the 8,000 miles from RAF Brize Norton to Ascension Island's Wideawake Airfield, sometimes direct but often staging through Dakar in Senegal, carrying passengers, many of whom would continue their journey south in the ex-educational cruise ship, *Uganda,* by this time a troopship until her withdrawal from the service in April, 1985. Passengers with priority continued to the Falklands in a Lockheed C-130K Hercules, with one, sometimes two, flights a day from Ascension Island over the 3,800 miles to RAF Stanley. While the range was within the unrefuelled capability of the Hercules, poor weather in the Falklands meant that as many as 50 per cent of flights had to abort their landing attempt and return either to Ascension Island or make for a diversionary airfield in Brazil. For this reason, the Hercules received fuel from a tanker aircraft at least once, and sometimes twice, on the outward trip, and many also received fuel on the northbound trip, especially if they were heavily loaded. The tanker aircraft, making a round trip far enough south to be genuinely useful, also had to receive fuel from another tanker, and it could in some instances, especially when Victor tankers were in use, take five tankers, both for refuelling each other and for refuelling the transport Hercules, to enable one aircraft to reach the Falklands. The minimum refuelling speed of the Victor was only slightly lower than the cruising speed of the Hercules, since these aircraft were originally converted as tankers for fighters and bombers, and below a certain speed, the refuelling hose drum unit would start to wind in. The normal practice was for the Hercules to refuel in a shallow dive, but this led to concern about the effects of fatigue on the fin of the Hercules as it was buffeted in the slipstream of the Victor. A 50 per cent reduction in fuel consumption occurred once several Hercules were converted to act as tankers. The flight time of almost thirteen hours in a noisy and cramped Hercules, and often cold as well, was something of an endurance test for all concerned, but it also had to be used by the Falkland Islanders, left without their regular Argentine Air Force-operated flights to Buenos Aires, and for those visiting Britain for major medical treatment. Would-be passengers were advised to take a hammock in which to sleep, while others found sitting on top of the cargo more comfortable than the canvas seats of the Hercules.

A major role did arise for transport aircraft of what had, by this time, become the USAF's Military Airlift Command, when the United States, along with forces from Jamaica, Barbados, St. Lucia, St. Vincents and Antigua, invaded the Caribbean island of Grenada, one of the Leeward Islands, on 24th October, 1983. The invasion had been prompted by suspicions that the island, which had had a history of political instability after a democratically-elected government was overthrown, was being used as a base by Cuba, for insurrection elsewhere in the Caribbean. Most of the assault was by amphibious forces of the United States Navy and Marine Corps, but reinforcements for the assault task force were flown out to Barbados. On the day of the invasion, USAF C-130s dropped a thousand paratroops at Pearls Airfield in the north of the island and a similar number jumped onto the new airport under construction in the south of the island at Point Salines. Transport aircraft also played a role in the re-supply of the American and Caribbean forces. Plans for a unit from the 'Delta Force' to land before the invasion had to be abandoned — the 'Delta Force' contingent was delayed!

The scale of these operations is not large, and indeed the troops from other Caribbean island states flown into Grenada provide some idea of the type of operation, with 120 Jamaicans, fifty Barbadians, and a total of 130 troops from Dominica, St. Lucia, St. Vincents and Antigua, while the USMC contribution probably only equalled that of the paratroops in numbers. This is a reflection of the type of warfare in which the major powers find themselves in an unsettled world. Yet, even while such operations are being mounted, there are others, sometimes routine, sometimes as a one-off emergency, for military air transport units.

Chapter Eight
Relief from the Air

The use of military transport aircraft on relief and for some rescue missions is taken for granted today. It was always right and inevitable that the aeroplane should come to play a major role in humanitarian work, and perhaps inevitable too that the military transport aeroplane should handle most of these missions, although the military have by no means an absolute monopoly of relief missions. By "relief" one is distinguishing between the re-supply missions mounted to assist beleaguered ground forces and those sorties which are intended to aid stricken civilian populations. There is another kind of relief to be borne in mind, the rescue operation, either using ambulance aircraft to return casualties to base and medical treatment, or picking up downed airmen or ship-wrecked sailors, professional and amateur, from the sea; this latter role is often handled by specialised search and rescue squadrons, which are more usually part of a maritime-reconnaissance organisation, or may even be primarily a rescue organisation, such as the United States Coast Guard service, but there are a number of instances in which this duty is performed by aircraft and aircrew belonging to a military air transport organisation, such as the United States Air Force's Military Airlift Command, as the former Military Air Transport Service has become in recent years.

The main reason for military involvement in relief operations is quite simple; the military effectively operate as a "fire brigade", waiting for something to happen, while commercial airline operators are usually heavily committed to regular services. Even those air charter companies specialising in air freight and willing to undertake *ad hoc* consignments have more or less steady markets which they dare not neglect for fear of losing to a competitor, which limits the numbers of commercial aircraft likely to be available, especially at short notice. Then again, the military is more likely to have the organisation to be able to move ground teams into improvised air bases at short notice, and to cope with operations over jungle, desert or swamp away from controlled air space. Indeed, such operations are not unwelcome, providing additional and sometimes realistic training opportunities with sustained operations away from the main bases. This is not to say that some operations are not mounted closer to home and the full back-up facilities, such as those winter relief flights required in the British Isles by the exceptionally severe winters of 1946/47 and 1962/63. It also makes sense to use military aircraft and personnel which are being paid for anyway rather than charter-in aircraft from commercial operators.

There is still more to it than this. As the military transport aeroplane has developed, in the way in which we saw in the previous chapter, it first moved away from its earlier close relationship with the bomber, and then the technical specification of the military transport and the commercial airliner diverged substantially as well. The military does have some aircraft which are close relations to those in airline service, the most obvious examples are the McDonnell Douglas C-9A Nightingale and KC-10A Extenders of the United States Air Force, military variants of the DC-9 and DC-10 respectively, and the Vickers VC.10 and Lockheed TriStar transports of the Royal Air Force, as well as the Boeing KC-135/707 variants in service with several air forces. Relatively few military types have made the reverse move into commercial service, although the most notable exception to this is the Lockheed C-130 Hercules, while the RAF's squadron of Belfast transports has disbanded, but several aircraft survive in service with a commercial operator, Heavylift Cargo Airlines. The reasons for the difference lies in the more varied requirements of the military. The need for high aircraft utilisation and the maximum payload means that even commercial transport aircraft operate between airports at which there are often extensive ground handling facilities, not to mention long paved runways, so that the aircraft can be turned round quickly and carry the maximum load. By contrast, military transports are designed to impose the minimum strain on ground facilities, with large rear loading doors and ramps, which would be so much unnecessary and unprofitable dead weight on a commercial aircraft, while many military transports, with such obvious exceptions as the C-5A/B, the new An-124 and An-22, are often smaller than the larger commercial transports, offering poorer economics but greater operational flexibility. The ability to be able to load and unload vehicles easily is important while the military techniques of dropping supplies with or without parachutes is useful on relief operations, but has no commercial equivalent! This is another instance of the way in which military operations are more directly suited to the problems and the conditions encountered on relief operations. Relief organisations do, sometimes, charter-in commercial aircraft, but often their role is more limited than that of those employed by the military due to their being less suitable. Airlines with aircraft such as the C-130 in their fleets, are often engaged in operations in the less well developed parts of the world, usually supporting mining or oil and natural gas drilling programmes in remote areas.

The helicopter does show a closer relationship between its commercial and military forms, and because of its vertical take-off ability, operations by commercial and military helicopter operators are more closely and obviously matched than has come to be the case with

fixed wing aircraft; commercial helicopters fly over difficult terrain or to offshore oil and gas rigs, or onto super tankers, sometimes acting as flying cranes with underslung loads. Nevertheless, the distances involved and the loads to be carried often preclude the helicopter from playing a major role in relief operations.

During the recent famine in Ethiopia, the bulk of the work was handled by military transport aircraft, with helicopters playing a supporting role, and commercial airlines limited to flying supplies into the country for distribution by the military.

Variety

The role of the military transport aircraft in relief and rescue operations is amongst the more varied, and nor are the numbers of aircraft deployed necessarily large. In 1955, for example, a single 1944 vintage Sikorsky R-5 helicopter of the USAF Military Air Transport Service's 4th Rescue Squadron, helped to quell an outbreak of yellow fever in Costa Rica, flying medical teams to inoculate a thousand people in the less accessible northern and central parts of the island.

Some parts of the world appear to require this type of support from the military more often than others. In 1960, a hurricane devastated the tiny Central American state of Belize, and RAF aircraft had to rush medical supplies to the territory. In that same year, RAF Avro Shackleton maritime-reconnaissance aircraft based on Gibraltar flew supplies to Agadir in Morocco after an earthquake, and Blackburn Beverley transports were used to help distribute food in northern Kenya and nearby Somalia after a drought had been followed by floods. Beverlies were again in action distributing supplies, assisted by Hastings, in May, 1962, after border raids by Laotian bandits disrupted the local food distribution systems in remote areas of Thailand, while

The biggest post-Berlin Airlift aid operation mounted by the Royal Air Force has been in Ethiopia, helping famine victims. Here, men of the Royal Corps of Transport prepare to free-drop supplies from an RAF C-130K Hercules.

later that same year, after heavy rains in Brunei had led to flooding, other Beverlies flew in aid, although local distribution was handled by small Scottish Aviation Pioneers. In 1963, supplies had to be flown into Sarawak, while elsewhere "east of Suez", in April, there was an air drop of diphtheria vaccine to Christmas Island in the Indian Ocean. These were a few amongst many relatively small scale relief operations which became almost a matter of routine, while the RAF seemed to be involved in more of these than any other air force.

One of the more significant operations came in Nepal, early in 1973, in an operation code-named *Khana Cascade*, which involved four RAF Lockheed C-130K Hercules transports and a single RAF Westland Wessex helicopter. The operation was a result of the failure of crops in the hill areas of Nepal leading to famine, and it was originally planned that the relief flights should be spread over two months. Operations started on 4th March, 1973, with three of the Hercules based on Bhairawa and the fourth aircraft at Biratnagur, with American-supplied grain and rice being dropped to villages around Rukum and Surkhet in West Nepal. The difficult terrain required the aircraft to fly low over razor sharp ridges and then drop to just 200 feet above the floors of the mountain valleys, often in uncertain weather, before discharging their invaluable cargo. In spite of the difficulties, the operation took just half the time originally scheduled for it, dropping 1,957 tons of supplies, against the planned 1,850 tons, between 4th and 30th March, in what an RAF spokesman at the time described as the RAF's biggest operation "since the Berlin airlift".

More than ten years later, a far grander operation, and one in which several air forces were employed, came in Ethiopia. After several years of drought, worsened by the effects of continuing civil war, the people of Ethiopia were struck by the effects of a particularly severe famine. The situation reached crisis levels during the summer of 1984, and under pressure from the relief organisations and public opinion, the Western nations were compelled to offer not only relief aid in the form of food and medical supplies, in addition to those distributed by charities, but the offer of transport aircraft as well. This was in spite of the fact that, at this time, Soviet support for the Ethiopian Government had resulted in substantial numbers of Russian transport aircraft being deployed to the country. A shortage of vehicles meant that, even as aid poured into Ethiopia's ports, distribution to the remote inland areas most severely affected by the famine was barely possible. Political problems also hampered relief operations, with initial political objections to the use of military transport aircraft being raised by the Ethiopians, who then sharply changed their attitude and demanded more aircraft than Britain could offer, with the offer of two aircraft on duty in Ethiopia for three months being rejected with a demand for a third aircraft! Once this was resolved, there were delays before the Ethiopians would allow the RAF space at Addis Ababa, followed by a particularly mean-minded insistence that the RAF would have to land to offload supplies rather than drop them: The need to land not only slowed up the pace of delivery, and made supplies to the worst affected areas impossible until this problem was overcome, but it also added to the extremely heavy wear and tear of operating out of unpaved landing strips, with tyres being

A despatcher's eye view of the supplies hitting the ground.

torn to shreds on sharp stones and rocks, and aircraft hulls suffering damage from stones thrown up during the landing and take-off runs, so that aircraft often had to have their fuselage bellies replated on return from a period in Ethiopia.

Eventually, what the RAF code-named *Operation Bushell* started on 1st November, with three RAF Hercules leaving Lyneham in Wiltshire and flying to Addis Ababa by way of the RAF base at Akrotiri in Cyprus, arriving at Addis Ababa at dawn on 3rd November. A total of seven aircraft were assigned to the airlift, with five acting as reliefs and maintaining an airbridge of spares from the UK, while two stayed in Ethiopia at any one time. After an initial three months, the operation was extended to late 1985 at a cost of £1 million per month. By this time, other air forces were also offering help, with the *Luftwaffe* basing C-160 Transalls at Addis, and the Soviet Union, amongst several Warsaw Pact states, finally pledging twelve Antonov An-12 transport aircraft and twenty-four Mil Mi-8 'Hip' helicopters. In addition, the International Red Cross started operations with a chartered commercial Hercules in September, 1985.

The civil war in Ethiopia also meant that the air forces involved could not station aircraft at the port of Assab, the entry point for most of the seaborne relief supplies, and instead had to fly a positioning flight from Addis Ababa each morning, carrying fuel and no cargo to Assab, before flying grain and other supplies, mainly to Makale, in north-east Ethiopia, and to Diredawa in the south-east. The aircraft made up to three flights daily with up to sixteen tons of supplies on each flight. In spite of the many difficulties, the two RAF aircraft allocated to the airlift managed to account for 30 per cent of all of the airborne relief supplies, air-landing 14.5 million pounds

An RAF Hercules drops supplies from forty feet.

of cargo during the first three months, after which one of the aircraft was allowed to air-drop supplies before the onset of the wet season, dropping supplies from 40 feet at altitudes of 9,000 feet above sea level in the mountainous and inaccessible areas of Ethiopia. Even the landing strips for air-landed supplies were often as high as 7,000 feet above sea level.

Amongst the cargo handled by the RAF were medical supplies, tents, blankets, motor vehicles and spare parts, as well as grain. Air drops of soft supplies such as flour, grain and sugar are well-suited to free drops without parachutes, being delivered safely and without loss if double-bagged. This also saved the cost of parachutes and presented less risk of supplies drifting off the dropping zone in strong winds. The RAF's involvement in Ethiopia ended in late 1985.

Not all military transport operations consist of dropping supplies to the hotter and drier parts of the world, with aircraft from No.40 Squadron, Royal New Zealand Air Force and from the United States Navy Squadron VXE-6, operating into and out of Antarctica. The RNZAF uses one of its five Lockheed C-130H Hercules to fly up to fourteen flights per year from Christchurch on the South Island of New Zealand, over the 2,000 mile journey from McMurdo Sound, carrying scientists for the Antarctic research station on the nine hour flight. Operating within Antarctica, VXE-6 flies six rocket-assisted and ski-equipped Hercules and six Bell UH-1N Iroquois helicopters on internal transport duties. The RNZAF Hercules does not have skis, and nor do the occasional USAF MAC Lockheed C-141 Starlifters

which are the largest aircraft to operate into and out of Antarctica. Rocket assistance is required for aircraft taking-off in the extreme cold and high altitudes of the Antarctic land mass, and if landing is not possible, the USAF and RNZAF aircraft make air drops of supplies, usually leaving this technique for supplying the smaller and less well-equipped bases. The UH-1Ns were used to recover wreckage, including the flight recorder, and the bodies of the passengers and crew of an Air New Zealand DC-10 which flew into Mount Erebus in 1979.

Sometimes too, military air transport operations take place in an atmosphere of high drama. One of the most notable came in May, 1972, when the British liner, *Queen Elizabeth II*, was on passage from New York to Southampton, when a ransom demand was made to the New York office of the owners under threat that six bombs onboard the ship would be detonated if the ransom of $350,000 (£134,500 at the then prevailing exchange rate) was not paid, At the time, the ship was 1,000 miles away from the British Isles, and had more than 1,400 passengers aboard.

The British response was to send a bomb disposal team, four men, two of whom were from the British Army's Special Air Services Regiment while the other two were from the Royal Marines, under the command of Captain R. H. Williams, to the area aboard a Lockheed C-130K Hercules of the RAF. The whole operation was mounted within hours of the bomb threat being received on 18th May, with Captain Williams having never made a

125

The USAF's Military Airlift Command operates McDonnell Douglas C-9A Nightingale ambulance aircraft, converted from the civilian DC-9 airliner.

jump from a military aircraft before, and having just thirty minutes' training before boarding his aircraft. An RAF British Aerospace Nimrod maritime reconnaissance aircraft flew low over the area before the jump, with the four man team jumping in sticks of two during two runs past the ship, jumping into fog and a ten foot swell, to land 200 yards off the ship, which picked them up in its boat. The special equipment needed by the team was also parachuted into the sea. The scare was a hoax, but the response was effective.

Of course, the need to provide effective support for the civilian population has resulted in air transport being the main function of many of the smaller air forces and air arms in the developing world. There are even air forces which can be fairly described as being nothing more than air transport organisations, including that of Nepal, for example.

Chapter Nine
On Duty Today

Even though the numbers may appear to be impressive on paper, in reality, no nation maintains armed forces of infinite strength; the truth is simply that the armed forces are massive swallowers of manpower. This fundamental truth is all the more relevant to the armed forces of the democracies, in which a balance has to be maintained between defence and other requirements, while for the smaller countries, the issue is not just one of a smaller population meaning smaller armed forces, but in addition the impact of devoting a substantial proportion of the nation's manpower to defence and its affect on industry and agriculture is increased disproportionately compared to the effect on countries with far larger populations. Again, the cost of maintaining large overseas garrisons which absorb vital foreign exchange is one which no nation cares to carry, and which only a few attempt to afford. The Soviet Union milks its European satellites, the United States and the United Kingdom do not do this, although in some instances contributions of one kind or another are made to help offset the cost of overseas garrisons. Yet, adequate defence cannot be maintained if forces fall below a certain level, and the larger countries have a commitment, often political and economic, but

one could argue, moral, as well, to come to the aid of those less able to defend themselves. In fact, no one country could resist a major assault by the Soviet Union by itself, hence the need to maintain collective defence. The penalty for not maintaining substantial overseas garrisons is a heavy investment in strategic mobility, in effect an up-dating and extension of the British tactics in the Middle East during the 1920s and 1930s, and the response is the same, a commitment to air transport by the military. This is not the complete picture, of course, Britain's early air transport units in the Middle East were complemented by a carrier force, and today amphibious warfare units and aircraft carriers also complement the combat air transport forces of the major powers, but it is the strength of military aviation and its transport squadrons which concerns us here.

No one can be sure just how or where a major East-West conflict would break out. One of the most widely accepted, but by no means the only, prospects is that of an advance by Warsaw Pact forces across the Inner German Border, which would almost immediately bring NATO and Warsaw Pact forces into heavy conflict on the Central Front. Other possibilities lie in an attack on NATO's flanks, either the northern flank, meaning Norway, or the southern, meaning Turkey and Greece; Britain and the Netherlands have the responsibility for reinforcing Norwegian forces, the United States provides the same assurance to Greece and Turkey. A Soviet push across the more remote parts of Anatolian Turkey to the

The new transport for the USAF's small transport fleet is the Short C-23A Sherpa, based on the Short 330 Commuterliner, which is present in many American airline fleets. The first Sherpa is seen here in flight over Northern Ireland.

Rapid exit for a tank from a C-130H Hercules of the USAF, the tank has been pulled from the aircraft by a parachute which also acts as a brake on its fall.

oilfields of the Middle East is another operation taken seriously by military planners. There could be any combination of these.

If such an eventuality should arise, or as soon as it appeared imminent, there would be a massive reinforcement by air and by sea of British and American forces in West Germany. As in the operations detailed in this book, the movement of heavy equipment would be mainly, although not entirely, by sea, with most of the manpower being moved by air. The problem of providing air-landed troops with adequate heavy equipment has been largely accounted for by positioning stocks of equipment and supplies in West Germany, a practice which enables substantial forces to be deployed in an emergency without incurring the difficulties of maintaining large overseas garrisons. In contrast with many earlier conflicts, the ability to lift substantial loads, including heavy artillery, tanks and missiles, is now a significant requirement for the United States Air Force. The ability to reinforce European forces in a crisis is an essential element in the policy of deterrence.

Even in an isolated conflict, calling upon the use of the

so-called US Rapid Deployment Force, consisting mainly of personnel from the United States Marine Corps, heavy equipment would be moved by sea from bases in the India Ocean, while the Marines would be flown in by the USAF. The extent to which the Rapid Deployment Force is viable depends on the location of any conflict, the planning pre-supposes that it must be in the Middle East, effectively marking the oilfields of the region as the most important priority for the Pentagon. The French also have plans for a similar, but smaller, force. The British maintain a Strategic Reserve, with a standby battalion ready to be deployed by air anywhere in the world at a few hours' notice.

These changes to Western strategy have only become possible as a result of an extensive use of air transport, with individual programmes for procurement of aircraft ranging as high as $35,000 million in one instance. There are weaknesses in the plans, not the least of which lies in the fact that such full scale mobilisations can seldom be properly conducted in peacetime, while after the onset of hostilities, transport aircraft would be at the mercy of attacking fighter aircraft, and over the long reaches of the North Atlantic, the opposing forces could include long-range Soviet 'Backfire' supersonic bombers armed with air-to-air missiles. For operations outside of Europe, notably on the Middle East, the problem of acclimatisation of troops would also be serious inhibition on efficiency and combat readiness: Artificial means of climatising troops have been used, but never for substantial numbers within a short period.

So, what are the relative air transport strengths of the world's air forces today, and their plans for the future?

NATO

Several members of NATO also have extensive additional responsibilities outside the NATO area, which only extends as far south of the Tropic of Cancer; these countries include both the United States and the United Kingdom, and France, although the latter is no longer a full participant in NATO's command structure.

The backbone of the West's airlift capability is that provided by the United States Air Force's Military Airlift Command, or MAC, the successor to the former Military Air Transport Service. In contrast to most Allied air forces, the United States Air Force has an extensive air reserve in the Air National Guard units, which are organised within each individual state, so that half of the MAC's total mobilised airlift capability comes from reserve units of which the Air National Guard units provide the core, but which also include the USAF's Air Force Reserve service and the airlines' Civil Reserve Air Fleet. MAC's standing airlift capability comes from its force of seventy Lockheed C-5A Galaxies, which are

being joined by fifty C-5Bs, and which are the only aircraft capable of moving outsized loads; these are supplemented by 234 Lockheed C-141B Starlifter transports and what will eventually be a force of sixty McDonnell Douglas KC-10A Extender tanker/transports. The payload of the massive Galaxy transports amounts to more than 120 tons per aircraft, enabling M-1 main battle tanks to be flown in if necessary, and the projected McDonnell Douglas C-17 transport will have a fuselage of the same dimensions as the C-5A/B so that this aircraft will also be able to move tanks, helicopters, artillery pieces and guided missiles, and play a part in increasing MAC's daily airlift capability from 32.4 million ton/miles per day to 66 million ton/miles per day. Airlift capability on this scale would have made light work of the Berlin Airlift. The C-5A/B and C-141B squadrons are organised into two Air Forces, the 21st and 22nd, but for inter-theatre tactical transport, the USAF also has more than 520 Lockheed C-130 Hercules transports of all types, planning to maintain many of the early models into the next century through reworking the airframes; 302 of the Hercules transports are assigned to Air National Guard units or to Air Force reserve units. At the opposite extreme to the giant C-5 and C-17 series transports are

The future of the Military Airlift Command will be centred around the McDonnell Douglas C-17A, of which this is an artist's impression.

the new Short C-23A Sherpa light transports, of which there may be more than sixty eventually, although the initial order is for eighteen of these aircraft, which are developed from the civil Short 330 commuter airliner: The role of the small transports, such as the C-23A, includes the movement of aircraft spares, such as engines, around USAFE (United States Air Force Europe) airfields. The importance of the Air National Guard Unit is such that in recent years the opportunity has been taken to buy secondhand commercial airliners, mainly Boeing 707-320s and 747s, taking advantage of depressed prices during the recession, to augment the strength of the ANG squadrons, and especially their strategic transport capability; the 707s are designated C-18As and the 747s C-19As, making use of ANG members who have civilian jobs with airlines, and also ensuring that the aircraft are not sold outside of the United States so that the USAF retains an adequate reserve airlift capability.

Other MAC responsibilities include the Aerospace Rescue and Recovery Service, the Air Weather Service and the Aeromedical Airlift Wing. The Aerospace Rescue and Recovery Service is currently replacing some of its HH-3Es and HH-53B/Cs with the first of sixty Sikorsky HH-60D having a lower mission capability than the 'D' version due to simplified, and cheaper, avionics. Smaller helicopters include Bell UH-1 and HH-1 Iroquois for base crash and rescue duties and for missile site support utility duties. The Aeromedical Airlift Wing operates C-9A Nightingale CASEVAC transports derived from the civil DC-9 airliner, while the Air

Based on the DC-10 airliner, the McDonnell Douglas KC-10A Extender is one of the new generation of tanker/transports. Receiving fuel is a USN Grumman F-14 Tomcat fighter.

Weather Service uses special versions of the C-130 Hercules. There are also many units operating executive aircraft as VIP transports.

Forty years after the formation of the Military Air Transport Service to replace the duplication of the independent air transport units of the American armed forces, it has not proved to be completely practical to leave the other armed forces without their own transport aircraft, and small numbers of aircraft up to C-130 size are maintained by the United States Navy and the United States Marine Corps, while the United States Army maintains its own massive heli-lift capability, the largest in the Western world. The logic for the USN maintaining transport squadrons of its own is certainly inescapable inasfar as the carrier onboard delivery, COD, units are concerned, using specialised transport aircraft to fly cargo, often urgently required spares, onto the decks of the USN's carrier force. The concept of carrier onboard delivery was developed during the 1950s with the building of a batch of Grumman C-1 Traders, developments of the Tracker anti-submarine and Tracer airborne early warning aircraft, and utilising the same skills in the aircrew selected. The Royal Navy at this time converted many of its Fairey Gannets, made redundant for anti-submarine duties by the introduction of ASW helicopters, to COD aircraft while new variants were built for AEW operations. The current USN COD transport is the C-2 Greyhound, a development of the Grumman Hawkeye airborne-early-warning aircraft, which is turboprop-powered. As the USN builds up to a 600-ship, fifteen carrier group, Navy, there will be a total of seventy C-2s, but meanwhile, with roughly half that number in service, several C-1s remain operational.

Seven C-130Fs are also used by the USN on transport duties, although many more aircraft of this type are employed on submarine communications and related duties with the USN, just as the USAF uses C-130s in the electronic warfare squadrons, where their tasks include confusing enemy command and control operations. The USMC uses three squadrons of KC-130s for transport and refuelling; these thirty-six aircraft mainly being available to provide inflight refuelling for Marine Corps helicopters, but can also provide theatre transport if necessary, a useful flexibility, although for the bulk of its airlift capability, the USMC now relies heavily on MAC. Both the USN and USMC have substantial numbers of helicopters in the support and transport roles, including

The US Army's battlefield utility helicopter is the Sikorsky UH-60 Black Hawk, seen here on exercises.

180 medium-lift Boeing CH-46E Sea Knight helicopters in thirteen USMC squadrons, and 144 Sikorsky CH-53A/D and E Sea Stallion helicopters in nine heavy-lift helicopter squadrons. As befits the West's largest helicopter operator, the United States Army includes a substantial heli-lift force amongst its total helicopter strength of some 8,300 machines. Medium-lift capability is provided by 436 Boeing CH-47A/B and C Chinooks,

Augmenting the heavylift C-5A Galaxy is the C-141 Starlifter, also a Lockheed product.

The USAF Military Air Transport Command has recently introduced a new colour scheme for its C-5 transports, first using this on the latest C-5B version, above, and replacing the original colour scheme on the C-5As, below, as these become due for repainting. In spite of its size, the C-5A/B can operate out of a wide variety of airfields, and can still taxi in heavy snow.

which are being up-graded to CH-47D standard, while there are also seventy-two Sikorsky CH-54A Tarhe Skycrane helicopters, but tactical transport is also often provided by smaller utility helicopters, including the Iroquois and the more recent Sikorsky UH-60 Black Hawk.

The large quantity of transport aircraft in the United States armed forces makes Canada's relatively small number of aircraft more marked, not least because the sparse population and the vast distances of Canada place an added burden upon the transport element of what is now the Canadian Armed Forces, or CAF, the unified defence force which replaced the individual Canadian forces. Canada spends just 2.1 per cent of its gross national product on defence, compared with 6.9 per cent for the United States and 5.3 per cent for the United Kingdom. Backbone of the CAF's Air Transport group are twenty-six Lockheed C-130E/H Hercules, known in Canadian service as CC-130s, augmented by five Boeing 707s, known as CC-137s, a small number of de Havilland Canada Dash 7 and Dash 8 short take-off transports; the Dash 7 is known as CC-132; eight Boeing CH-147 Chinook helicopters, and some elderly Convair CC-109 Cosmopolitans and even more elderly Douglas CC-129 Dakota transports. The Dash 7s are used to support the Canadian unit, 1st Canadian Air Group, in West Germany, and are likely to be replaced by some of the Dash 8s. De Havilland Canada CC-115 Buffalo short

Flying delivery van, a Grumman C-2 Greyhound carrier onboard delivery aircraft lands on USS "John F. Kennedy", a Kitty Hawk-class conventional aircraft carrier.

take-off transports are used on search and rescue duties, but these eleven aircraft could, of course, be used as transports in an emergency.

On the other side of the North Atlantic, the Royal Air Force no longer has a separate Transport Command. It currently operates four transport squadrons equipped with Lockheed C-130K Hercules transports, the C-130K being an Anglicised version of the C-130H, and thirty of the sixty-six RAF Hercules have been stretched to C-130-30 equivalent standard, the work being carried out by a British company, Marshall of Cambridge. Six aircraft have been converted to the tanker role for the Falklands airlift, and another sixteen, both stretched and unstretched, have refuelling probes to act as receivers for this operation. Thirteen Vickers VC.10 transports are operated in one squadron, but another nine ex-British Airways aircraft are operated as tanker/transports, and the RAF has also introduced nine TriStar 500s, six ex-British Airways and three ex-Pan Am, as tanker/transports, with some of the converted airliners being used to replace Handley Page Victor bombers converted to the inflight refuelling role some years previously. Light transport is handled by ten British Aerospace Andover transports, although for this role considerable emphasis is placed on thirty-eight Boeing Vertol CH-47D Chinook helicopters, which have as a major task the support of inaccessible forward bases for the Harrier vertical take-off attack aircraft in a war role, and for standard troop carrying and battlefield mobility, forty-one Westland-Aerospatiale SA-330 Pumas are operated. A replacement for the Pumas is under consideration. The Royal Navy operates twenty-four

A USN CH-46 Sea Knight makes a delivery aboard an American aircraft carrier.

Westland Sea King helicopters in the transport role, some of them with Royal Marine pilots, to provide support for Royal Marine commando units, while the British Army's Air Corps can use many of its 300 helicopters for utility and light transport duties, although anti-tank operations take prominence. Current plans for the Army Air Corps envisage a light transport or utility helicopter for the late 1980s, early 1990s, which could be the Westland WG.30 or the Westland-Agusta EH.101, or even, some Army officers suggest, the CH-47 Chinook. The opening of the new airport in the Falklands in May, 1985, although this did not become fully operational until several months later, has reduced much of the burden of air transport to the Falklands, although Hercules transports still handle much of the air freight traffic.

The strongest air forces on the mainland of Europe are those of the German Federal Republic and of France, and both maintain substantial heavy-lift capabilities within their armies, which do not suffer from the artificial ceiling on aircraft weights imposed on the British Army, although this may end. The *Luftwaffe* operates eighty-nine C-160 Transall tactical transport aircraft, which can lift up to seventeen tons of freight, the same as a Lockheed Hercules, but over a shorter range, about 1,000 miles. The German Army, or *Heeresflieger,* operates 107 Sikorsky CH-53G medium-lift transport helicopters, and

almost 200 of the smaller UH-1D Iroquois, which are in essence utility helicopters. Another Transall operator, the French *Armée de l'Air* has seventy-six of these aircraft, and fifty of the older and smaller Nord Noratlases, as well as eleven Boeing KC-135 tankers and a small number of Aerospatiale Caravelles as fast transports and VIP aircraft. Mainstay of the *Aviation Legérè de l'Armée de Terre,* or ALAT, is the SA.330 Puma, of which 130 operate as tactical transports, while another forty have a similar role with the *Armée de l'Air.* While France remains outside of NATO's command structure, it is clear that the country still regards itself as a part of the Atlantic alliance, and co-operation between NATO and French forces has become closer in recent years.

The *Aeronautica Militare Italiano* has a relatively small transport element, with just thirteen Lockheed C-130 Hercules and thirty of the small Fiat G.222 tactical transports, a twin-engined aircraft with a load capability of seven tons of freight or forty-four troops, less than half that of a Hercules. The Italian Army uses twenty-six Meridonali-built CH-47D Chinook helicopters, and many smaller Agusta-built Bell helicopters officially in

A 'flying-crane' helicopter, the Russian Mil Mi-10 "Harke".

the transport role, although such small machines are more usually regarded as utility types. Across the Mediterranean, NATO's newest member, Spain, has just seven C-130H Hercules transports and another four KC-130H tankers in the *Ejercito del Aire,* whose main transport element consists of thirty de Havilland Canada Caribou transports, which are to be replaced in the future. The Spanish Army has twelve Boeing-Vertol Chinooks, and a number of smaller helicopters, but in equipment terms lags some way behind those of other armies of comparable size. Next door, the *Forca Aerea Portuguesa* operates nine-C130H Hercules, of which four are the stretched C-130H-30 variety, and uses several of its fourteen CASA C-212 Aviocars on light transport duties; the Spanish, by contrast, confine this type to search and rescue, training and maritime patrol duties. Ten Aerospatiale SA.330 Pumas have to double up on transport and search and rescue duties. There are also plans to up-date the transport element of the FAP, but even while freed from the political constraints imposed during the period of colonial wars, economic difficulties are making this task slower than it might otherwise have been.

Concern over the relationship between Greece and Turkey has led to limitations on the equipment provided for both of these air forces in an area which is regarded as being one of the weakest in NATO's defences. The *Elliniki Aeroporia* has twelve Lockheed C-130H Hercules transports, but still operates fifteen Nord Noratlases and six Douglas C-47 transports, as well as six Japanese-built NAMC YS-11 light transports, although the Greek Army does have twelve Boeing-Vertol Chinook helicopters, built by Meridonali in Italy. The *Turk Hava Kuvvetleri* has just seven C-130E Hercules transports, but there are also twenty C-160 Transalls, and no less than forty C-47s and three C-54s. Both Greece and Turkey plan to modernise their air force transport elements, and for both there is a clear requirement for additional heavy-lift helicopter capability, with the Turks in particular being weak on this count, in spite of the importance of battlefield mobility for countries which border the Warsaw Pact states.

Belgium, a small country with a small population and close to NATO's Central Front, maintains a small but modern transport element in the *Force Aérienne Belge,* with twelve C-130H Hercules transports, two Boeing 727QC convertible passenger-freight aircraft and three British Aerospace 748s. The Dutch *Koninklijke Luchtmacht* has just twelve Fokker F.27 Troopship tactical transports. Further north, the small Royal Norwegian Air Force has six C-130H Hercules transports, plus a few light transports, including de Havilland Canada Twin Otters, and Denmark has just three C-130H Hercules in the *Kingelige Danske Flyvevaben.*

Several of the non-NATO countries in Western Europe also maintain small transport elements in their air forces, with the Swedish *Flygvapnet* operating eight C-130E/H Hercules, and the Finnish *Ilmaviomat* maintaining five Fokker F.27 Troopships alongside four C-47s! Austria, on the other hand, has just two very small Short Skyvans in the *Osterreichische Luftstreitkräfte* and Switzerland has no transport capability in its air force. Yugoslavia shows the country's history of flirtation with both East and West in its equipment, with the *Yugoslovensko Ratno Vazduhoplovstvo* having twelve Antonov An-12 'Cub' and ten each of Antonov An-26 'Curls' and Ilyushin Il-14 'Crates' in its transport element, operating alongside two Douglas DC-6Bs and a single Boeing 727-200. The helicopter force includes eighteen Mil Mi-4 'Hound' and twelve Mi-8 'Hip' helicopters with two Westland Whirlwind 2s; newer equipment consists mainly of Pilatus Turbo-Porter liaison and communications aircraft.

The Warsaw Pact

The largest armed forces within the Soviet Bloc are, of course, those of the Soviet Union, and this is reflected in a substantial air transport element which can be accounted for partly by the size of the country which has for long made it ideal for air transport, and partly due to the ambitious and expansionist attitude of the Soviet Government. Of course, the USSR also plays much the same role as the USA with regard to providing air transport support to its Allies, over and above what the country may itself need. The size of Soviet forces is such that while other countries may allocate different commands to individual aspects of military aviation, the Soviet Union maintains what almost amounts to different air forces, with the VTA or Military Transport Aviation backed up by a national airline, *Aeroflot*, which is run more on military than commercial lines. The Soviet Union's helicopter force is deployed as a part of Soviet Frontal Aviation.

Currently, the VTA is receiving the first of the new Antonov An-124 'Ruslan', an aircraft similar in appearance to the Lockheed Galaxy and with a similar performance, although slightly larger, enabling the USSR once again to lay claim to the distinction of building and operating the world's largest aircraft. Meanwhile, the long-range heavy-lift element is sustained by fifty or so of the large four-turboprop powered Antonov An-22 'Cocks', which are the largest aircraft in Soviet service until the An-124 becomes fully operational during the late 1980s. This is not to suggest that modernisation has not already taken place, for the medium-range, medium-lift fleet is currently being updated by the introduction of the four-turbofan Ilyushin Il-76 'Candid,' which is being introduced at the rate of thirty or so aircraft a year, with well over 200 delivered so far, and which is replacing the Antonov An-12 'Cub' fleet of some 450 aircraft. Smaller, the Antonov An-72 'Coaler' is also being produced and appears to have supplemented rather than replaced the relatively small force of fifty Antonov An-24 'Coke' and An-26 'Curl' tactical transports; 'Coaler' is powered by two turbofans while the 'Coke' and 'Curl' have twin turboprops, and while 'Curl' remains in production, it has since been joined by a development, the An-32 'Cline', modified for operation from hot and high airfields. Another numerous type in Soviet service is the small Antonov An-2 'Colt', a single-engined fourteen-seat biplane, used for utility operations and light transport duties, and of which more than 400 still remain in service. A number of other types make up a total of some 1,200 transport aircraft, including Antonov An-14 'Clods', Ilyushin Il-14 'Crates' and Il-18 'Coots', along with the VIP fleet of Ilyushin Il-62 'Classics', Tupolev Tu-134 'Crusty' and Tu-154 'Careless' jets. Soviet Naval Aviation also maintains its

Mil Mi-6 'Hook' helicopter takes-off. While in the background are several Soviet Lisunov Li-2s (licence-built C-47s).

own transport element, including Ilyushin Il-14, Il-18 and Il-76 aircraft, and Antonov An-12, An-24 and An-26 transports.

Just as the Soviet Union has a reputation for size in its fixed wing transport elements, it has also maintained a similar reputation with the helicopter, with the newest arrival, the twin-rotor Mil Mi-26 'Halo', capable of lifting a twenty ton payload, including armoured vehicles, through twin rear clamshell doors, and with a fuselage of similar dimensions to that of the Lockheed C-130 Hercules. The eventual total of Mi-26s in Soviet service can only be guessed at, but it may be relevant that a previous giant helicopter, the Mi-6 'Hook', is still in service in quantity, with almost 400 available to ground commanders. The most numerous Soviet helicopter type remains the Mil Mi-8 'Hip', of which almost 2,000 are in service as transports and gunships. The Mil Mi-8 'Hip' also remains the main helicopter in most of the Warsaw Pact countries, with thirty in the Polish Air Force, or *Polskie Wojska Lotnicze,* PWL, and a similar number in service with the East German *Luftstreitkräfte und Luftverteidigung,* LSK. The PWL also operates a number of fixed-wing transports, with some twenty Antonov An-12 'Cubs' and a dozen each of the Antonov An-26 'Curl' and Ilyushin Il-14 'Crate', with a number of smaller aircraft, including An-2 'Colts'. The Il-14 'Crate' also figures in the LSK, which has twenty of this type, as well as thirty An-2s. The *Ceskoslovonske Letectvo* has a similar mix of aircraft, with thirty Mi-8 'Hips' operating alongside sixty of the older and smaller Mi-4 'Hound' helicopters, and about twenty An-24/An-26 transports as well as forty Il-14s. The Bulgarian Air Force has some forty transports, again with An-24s, An-26s and Il-14s predominating, and about the same number of Mi-4s and Mi-8s in the helicopter force. Smaller still is the Hungarian Air Force, which is amongst the smallest in the Warsaw Pact, with about thirty transports and the same number of helicopters, again with the mix already found in those countries just mentioned.

Outside of the mainstream Warsaw Pact countries, and the only one not to permit Soviet forces on her soil, in spite of remaining a member of the Pact, Rumania also has about thirty Mi-4 and Mi-8 helicopters, and about the same number of An-24, An-26, Il-14 and Il-18 transports in the *Fortele Aerienne ale Republicii Socialiste Romania.*

The isolated Communist Albania operates its air force as part of the Army, and with scant contact and no alliances with the other European Communist countries, and having since abandoned its earlier links with Communist China, is forced to remain dependent on elderly equipment. A small number of Lisunov Li-2s, Soviet-built DC-3s, remain in service with some slightly more modern An-2s and a few Il-14s, while the helicopter force has nothing more modern than the Mi-4.

Although not part of the Warsaw Pact, the Mongolian Air Force is under Soviet control and operates what almost amounts to the standard package of thirty or so Mi-4s and Mi-8s, and a similar number of An-24s and Il-14s, with a number of An-2s.

The Far East and the Pacific

The largest armed forces in the Far East are, as one would expect, those of Communist China, the Air Force of the People's Liberation Army is the world's third largest air arm, but it is also one with little modern equipment as a result of the rift between the Chinese leadership and their Russian counterparts during the late 1960s, which effectively froze Chinese aeronautical development into licence production of the then contemporary Russian designs. A closer rapport with the West in recent years has done little for the Chinese military inasmuch as a shortage of hard currency has prevented the purchase of Western military technology. The force of some 500 transport aircraft is a mixture of elderly Russian and even more elderly Western types, including a hundred or so Lisunov Li-2s and twenty Curtiss C-46 Commando transports, a few Douglas DC-6s and eighteen ex-Civil Aviation Administration of China Hawker Siddeley Trident airliners. There are twenty Antonov An-24s, a similar number of An-26s and ten Ilyushin Il-18s, with forty or so Il-14s. The single most numerous type is the Antonov An-2 'Colt', built in China and designated locally as the Harbin Y-5, while a small number of Antonov An-12s were built as Harbin Y-8s. The 250 or so Y-5s provide half of the transport force, and are being slowly replaced by the Chinese-designed Harbin Y-11, a twin piston-engined utility aircraft which is itself rendered almost obsolescent by its turboprop derivative, the Y-12 Turbo-Panda. The transport helicopter force consists mainly of more than 500 Harbin H-5, licence-built obsolete Mil Mi-4s, although thirty Mil Mi-8s are also in service. The An-24 is now being built as the Y-7. Suitable Western designs may be selected for licence-production in the future.

By contrast with China's foreign exchange shortage and large armed forces, Japan post-war has been prosperous but has kept defence spending down to around 1 per cent of GNP for political reasons, although the United States is now urging Japan to play an active role in the defence of the West. A small transport element in the Japanese Air Self-Defense Force operates thirty of the new Mitsubishi C-1A tactical transports with four turbofans, while there are eleven of the long-discontinued NAMC YS-11 twin turboprop transports and just six C-130H Hercules. The Japanese Ground Self-Defence Force operates a handful of Boeing-Vertol CH-47D Chinooks and sixty of the older Vertol KV-107s, built in Japan. There is relatively little modern equipment in the Japanese armed forces, and a tendency to rework and modernise older aircraft rather than build newer and more up-to-date types; this even extends to combat units modernising F-4 Phantoms and maritime-reconnaissance units doing the same with Neptunes.

There are relatively few military aircraft of any kind in the former French colonies in South-East Asia, although a small number of An-2s and An-24s, with ten Mil Mi-8s operate in Laos alongside some old C-47s, and a similar selection, although in larger numbers, operates in Vietnam. The old Cambodian Air Force, in what is now Kampuchea, no longer exists. Douglas C-47s are still operated by the Royal Thai Air Force, which has twenty, along with forty Fairchild C-123 Providers and three C-130H Hercules and two C-130H-30 Hercules. However, the air force is only one of four legs for the Thai armed forces, and the Royal Thai Army operates Short 330 transports and some Boeing-Vertol CH-47D Chinook helicopters, while the Royal Thai Border Police also has a Shorts 330 and three de Havilland Canada DHC-4 Caribou transports, as well as a substantial number of utility aircraft and helicopters. It would seem possible that either additional Short 330s or Sherpas might be obtained to replace the C-47s of the Royal Thai Air Force. Of the other pro-Western nations in the area, the Royal Malaysian Air Force operates a transport element of six C-130H Hercules and sixteen DHC-4 Caribou, as well as forty Sikorsky S-61 transport helicopters, while the adjoining island state of Singapore operates eight C-130B/H Hercules and six Skyvans, augmented by utility helicopters while the larger Super Puma helicopters are confined to search and rescue and anti-submarine warfare.

Non-aligned Burma has a serious counter-insurgency problem, yet low defence budgets and economic problems have combined to produce a small air force with little modern equipment, with a transport element consisting of four Fairchild FH.227 turboprop transports — essentially American-built Fokker F.27s — and two de Havilland Canada DHC-5 Buffalo tactical transports, as well as a number of Pilatus utility machines. China and the Soviet Union have competed to provide equipment for the small Air Wing of the Bangladesh Defence Force, although the transport element is entirely Soviet, with four An-24/26s, some An-12s and six Mil Mi-8 helicopters, while utility helicopters include a number of Bell machines supplied by the United States.

The Indian Air Force continues to maintain one of the

Above: A Meridonali-built CH-47 Chinook shows its 'flying crane' potential.

Below: A recent arrival in the transport fleets of the Soviet Union and of some of its client states, notably India, is the Ilyushin Il-76 'Candid' transport.

A bleak backdrop for a Short Skyvan of the Sultan of Oman's Air Force. These rugged utility transports are used on internal security operations.

world's largest air transport fleets, and certainly the largest of any non-aligned nation, but in recent years the force has come perilously close to disappearing, with fatigue problems with the thirty-eight Fairchild C-119 Packets and other problems in keeping the twenty-five C-47s fully operational, while Antonov An-12 'Cubs' also lacked the performance required. The thirty An-12 'Cubs' have been replaced by a fleet of twenty-five Ilyushin Il-76 'Candid' transports, while ninety-six Antonov An-32s, 'Cline' to NATO but known in India as the *Sutlej,* after a major river, are being introduced to replace the C-119s, C-47s and, eventually, twenty DHC-4 Caribou transports. Other Indian Air Force transport aircraft include forty Hindustan-built Hawker Siddeley HS 748 twin turboprop transports, while there is the possibility of an order for up to forty Lockheed C-130 Hercules. The helicopter element includes forty-five elderly Mil Mi-4s and fifty Mi-8s. Utility aircraft, Dornier Do.228s, are being built in India to satisfy the large Indian commercial and military market.

By contrast, freed of the need to maintain an air bridge to East Pakistan, the Pakistan Air Force operates a small, but reasonably modern, air transport force, with twelve Lockheed C-130B/E Hercules transports plus a commercial version L-100-20 Hercules, and two Fokker F.27-200 Friendships, while a helicopter transport force in the Army consists of ten Mil Mi-8 and thirty-five Aerospatiale SA.330 Pumas. The traditional hostility with India persists, but meanwhile Pakistan has gained a fresh source of tension following the Soviet invasion of Afghanistan, and claims by the Soviet Union that Afghan resistance to the occupying forces has been sheltered by Pakistan. Most of the operational aircraft in Afghanistan are operated by Soviet units, but, with the addition of a large number of Soviet advisers to the Afghan Republic Air Force, this air arm operates a number of ground attack and transport units, with the latter operating a squadron each, about ten or twelve aircraft, of Antonov An-2s, An-12s and Ilyushin Il-14s, as well as Mil Mi-4s.

Given the vast spread of the Indonesian archipelago, it is perhaps not surprising that a substantial proportion of the aircraft operated by the *Tentara Nasional Indonesia-Angkatan Udara* are transports, although this force has been boosted to its present strength in comparatively recent times; partly because of the Government's policy to relocate the population from over-crowded areas of the main islands to new townships on outlying islands, and partly because of the emergence of an indigenous aircraft industry to reduce the foreign exchange costs of aircraft procurement. Currently, the TNI-AU operates twenty-four Hercules of different versions, including three L-100-30 stretched civil versions, as well as six C-160 Transalls, an unusual combination, eight Fokker F.27 Friendships and nine C-47s, to which have been added eighteen locally-built CASA C-212 Aviocar light transports and deliveries of fifty CASA-Nurtanio CN.235 transports are also under way; these may replace the C-47s. The small helicopter element includes thirteen Pumas and Super Pumas as well as four Sikorsky S-58s, which are being re-engined, and a single S-61, as well as many utility types. By contrast, the Philippine Air Force, which receives aid from the United States, has a much smaller transport element, with seven Hercules of different versions, including several commercial types, and nine F.27s, while the only large helicopters are two Sikorsky S-70 Black Hawks. Indonesia's neighbours, Papua New Guinea and Brunei, have small transport elements, with the former including six ex-RAAF C-47s and the latter a squadron of eleven Bell 212s.

As one would expect from a large country with a sparsely populated interior, the Royal Australian Air Force devotes a substantial proportion of its strength to transport, with twenty-four Lockheed C-130E/H Hercules, twenty-two de Havilland Canada DHC-4 Caribou transports and twelve Boeing-Vertol CH-47C Chinook helicopters, as well as a number of communications, VIP and utility types, with the Australian Army Aviation operating small GAF Mission Masters, military versions of the Nomad commuterliner, of which thirteen are in service.

New Zealand's relatively small size, at least by Pacific standards and even smaller population, means that the Royal New Zealand Air Force has a transport element of just five C-130H Hercules and six ex-RAF Andover tactical transports, augmented by two Boeing 727-100s and a number of utility aircraft. The Hercules and the Andovers augment the five aircraft of the single maritime reconnaissance Orion squadron as necessary, especially for search and rescue duties.

The Middle East

The Middle East has been a constant source of political and military difficulty throughout much of the present century, with the sensitivity of the region increasing since the end of World War II and the growth in importance of the area's oil. The other major element in this instability has been the withdrawal of colonial influence by the British and the French, and the inability of any American substitute to compensate for this; few of the nations in the region were formally colonised, but many were protectorates of one kind or another and clearly closely linked to the European powers.

Amongst the many conflicts which have swept across the Middle East in recent years, the one which combines intensity and longevity is that between Iraq and Iran. Since the revolution in Iran, and more especially since the seizure of the US embassy staff as hostages, a lack of spares from the United States has meant that much of the Islamic Republic of Iran Air Force's equipment is no longer fully operational, and in addition to this there must be the inevitable losses of a sustained and bloody war. Under the Shah, no expense was spared to create a highly effective Imperial Iranian Air Force, and this extended to the provision of eleven Boeing 747 transports and fourteen Boeing 707 tanker/transports, as well as fifty Lockheed C-130E/H Hercules, of which as few as fifteen may still be operational, while there were also eighteen Fokker F.27 Friendships, with additional aircraft of this type with the Iranian Navy. It is believed that the Iranian Army may have only forty of its original ninety-six Boeing-Vertol CH-47C Chinook helicopters still operational. In addition to the trade embargo and war losses, operational efficiency may also have been seriously affected by purges of the armed forces, especially of the officer corps. By contrast, the *Al Quwwat Aljawwiya Aliraquiya,* or Iraqi Air Force, has been in receipt of supplies from the Soviet Union, and operates ten Antonov An-2 'Colts', six An-12 'Cubs', twelve An-24/26 'Cokes' and 'Curls', thirteen Ilyushin Il-14 'Crates' and seven Il-76 'Candid' transports, as well as thirty-five Mil Mi-4 'Hound', fifty Mi-8 'Hip' and fifteen Mi-6 'Hook' helicopters. The other major Soviet client state in the Middle East, Syria, has in the Syrian Arab Air Force a transport element with a wide variety of Soviet-built aircraft, with three or four examples each of the An-12, An-24, An-26, Il-14, Il-18 and Il-76, as well as more than fifty Mi-8 and ten Mi-6 helicopters. A small number of C-47s also remain operational.

Compared to the very large numbers of combat aircraft in service with the Israeli Defence Force/Air Force, transport aircraft are present in very small numbers indeed, largely reflecting the small area of Israeli territory, and perhaps the vulnerability of a substantial transport element in a country in which there can be little advance warning of air raids. A force of twenty-four Lockheed C-130E/H Hercules and two KC-130Hs, eight Boeing 707s and eighteen C-47s is accompanied by eight Aerospatiale Super Frelon medium-lift helicopters and thirty Sikorsky S-65/CH-53D helicopters, as well as liaison and utility aircraft and helicopters in small numbers. Egypt, a former enemy, and now the nearest thing to an ally in the Middle East that Israel has got, has a mixture of aircraft in the Arab Republic of Egypt Air Force, demonstrating that country's change of allegiance from the Soviet Union to the West. As far as the transport element is concerned, this includes twenty-one Lockheed C-130H Hercules, ten de Havilland Canada DHC-5 Buffalo and four Antonov An-12 'Cub' transports, as well as fifteen Boeing-Vertol CH-47C Chinook helicopters, and more than sixty Mil Mi-4 and Mi-8 helicopters. Recent arrivals have included twenty-one Westland Commando helicopters.

A long time ally of the West, Saudi Arabia has developed a strong air force with the latest American equipment. The need to maintain interceptors and airborne early-warning E-3A Sentry aircraft on station for long periods has led to the recent introduction of KE-3A tankers, of which there are ten, based on the E-3A or Boeing 720 airframe and modern CFM56 turbofans, augmenting eight KC-135 tankers already in service, thirty-six C-130E/H Hercules and nine KC-130H Hercules, as well as two VC-130H Hercules hospital aircraft. A small transport force includes forty CASA C.212 Aviocars, while there are a number of utility helicopters. Other states in the region also maintain a transport element in their armed forces, including the

Kuwait Air Force, with four L-300-30 Hercules and two DC-9-30s; the Sultan of Oman's Air Force, with three Hercules and fifteen Short Skyvans, and the Qatar Emiri Air Force, with ten Westland Commando helicopters and six Pumas, as well as two Boeing 707s and a number of liaison and communications types. Bahrain operates mainly communications aircraft in a dual air force and police role, but the United Arab Emirates Air Force, with aircraft from Abu Dhabi and Dubai, has five each of various versions of the Lockheed Hercules and DHC-5 Buffalo, as well as eight Puma helicopters and many more aircraft and helicopters in the VIP transport and communications roles. The Royal Jordanian Air Force has six C-130B/H Hercules, three C.212 Aviocars, and a number of small helicopters in the communications and liaison role.

Two of the smaller Soviet-backed nations, North Yemen and South Yemen, the former Aden protectorate, also possess a selection of Russian transport types in their air forces, while there have been discussions over a merger of the two nations. Both the Yemen Arab Air Force and the Air Force of the South Yemen People's Republic, operate a small number of non-Russian aircraft, with two Lockheed C-130H Hercules and three C-47s in the former plus four C-47s in the latter. However, most of the aircraft are of Soviet origin, and include six Antonov An-24/26 and four Il-14 transports in the Yemen Arab Air Force, while the Air Force of the South Yemen People's Republic has four Il-14s and three An-24s. North Yemen has twelve, and South Yemen eight, Mil Mi-8 helicopters.

Africa

The post-colonial era has seen the creation of a large number of independent African states, most of whom maintain at least a small air arm charged with communications duties, while for others, counter insurgency is an important and unending task, with others still concerned with promoting insurgency on a neighbour's territory, an activity which is not confined to those countries bordering South Africa. The contrast between the air forces of the largest and smallest of the African states is considerable, but a substantial number rely heavily on Soviet supplied equipment, while armaments generally appear to have a high priority on African shopping lists, certainly ranking far higher than the relief of famine amongst their own people!

To the north, amongst those countries bordering the Mediterranean and the Red Sea, including land-locked Sudan, countries can be divided superficially into those allied with Libya and those opposed to that country. One of Libya's allies is Ethiopia, and with Libya and North Yemen on the opposite shores of the Red Sea, Ethiopia is a party to a Tripartite treaty intended to overthrow the existing governments of the Sudan, Djibouti and Somalia. Large numbers of Soviet aircraft are operating inside Ethiopia helping the Government in a war against separatist Eritrean forces, but the Ethiopian Air Force also has a small number of transport aircraft of its own, including twelve Fairchild C-119 Packets and a similar number of C-47s, as well as a couple of C-54s and two DHC-5D Buffalo short take-off transports. Libya itself,

in the *Al Quwwat Aljawwiya Al Libiyya*, maintains a substantial transport element, doubtless to keep abreast with the colonial ambitions of the country's ruler. Seven Lockheed C-130H Hercules have been joined by six Ilyushin Il-76 'Candids', largely because of American resistance to supplying military equipment to Libya, while for tactical transport there are twenty-two Fiat G.222s and forty CH-47C Chinooks, most of which have been built in Italy, as well as twelve Mil Mi-8 helicopters.

On the receiving end of Libyan intentions are a number of states, including those already mentioned. Of these, the *Force Aérienne de Djibouti* is an exclusively transport force, but apart from a handful of communications aircraft and helicopters, the only transport aircraft worthy of note are two ex-French Noratlases, fortunately, the strategic value of the country to the west is such that a substantial and well-equipped French presence is maintained. Somalia, on the other hand, is largely on its own and its air force, the Somalian Aeronautical Corps, has suffered from a switch from using Soviet equipment, most of which is grounded for lack of spares, to Western equipment, which is available in limited quantities. The backbone of the operational transport force consists of six CASA C.212 Aviocars and four Fiat G.222s, as well as three C-47s, while there are also some An-24s and An-26s, and some Mil Mi-4 and Mi-8 helicopters, supported by a variety of light aircraft and helicopters. The Sudanese *Silakh Al Jawwiya As Sudaniya* operates six C-130H Hercules, seven DHC-5 Buffaloes and six CASA C.212s, although some of these will be used on maritime-reconnaissance, as well as ten Mil Mi-8 helicopters; a number of Pumas may be ordered from France. Another country which has suffered from Libya's unwanted interest is Chad, and again this is an instance of French intervention to curb Libyan territorial ambitions in a former colony; apart from the French forces, the *Escadrille Tchadienne*, operates two C-130H Hercules, three DC-4s and nine C-47s, two Noratlases and four SA-330 Pumas, as well as a number of smaller types in what is a purely transport force. Apart from a number of small aircraft, including light helicopters, the Tunisian Republic Air Force's transport element consists of just two C-130H Hercules and a Puma helicopter, the former being supplied under American military aid to help Tunisia resist Libyan intervention.

It would be an over-simplification to suggest that Libya is the sole cause of conflict and unrest in North Africa, since in another post-colonial confrontation, Algeria is providing support for the Polisario Front guerillas in the Spanish Sahara against Moroccan forces. In spite of this campaign against an ally of the West, Algeria received fourteen C-130Hs from the United States for its part as a successful mediator in the release of the American embassy hostages from Iran, and these aircraft provide the backbone of what was previously a small air transport element operating a variety of elderly Soviet types with a sprinkling of more modern European aircraft. The rest of the *Al Quwwat Aljawwiya Aljza'eriiya's* transport force includes eight Antonov An-12 'Cubs' and four Ilyushin Il-14 'Crates', as well as a VIP Il-18, while there are also eight Fokker F.27s with a helicopter force which consists mainly of forty Mil Mi-4s, twelve Mi-8s and four Mi-6s, as well as five SA.330 Pumas. On the other side, the *Force Armées Royales*

Marocaine operates nineteen C-130H Hercules and three KC-130Hs, as well as a Boeing 707 tanker/transport, while there are thirty-two SA.330 Puma helicopters with twelve Boeing-Vertol CH-47C Chinooks: The Hercules also maintain border patrols around the Spanish Sahara in addition to their transport duties, keeping an eye on the combined trench and embankments built along the borders of the Spanish Sahara by the Moroccans in an attempt to keep the Polisario out of this disputed territory. Moroccan units also receive support from French air and ground forces.

The other main area of conflict in Africa comes at the other end of the continent, around South Africa. The South Africa Air Force itself operates a strong, but mostly ageing, transport force, which includes more than forty C-47s and seven C-54s, as well as seven early version C-130B Hercules and nine more recent C-160 Transalls; the latter type being possible due to French disregard for embargoes on South Africa in recent years, while the other partner in the Transall programme is West Germany, not a member of the United Nations. A modern helicopter force has also been possible due to French co-operation, with more than sixty Aerospatiale SA.330 Pumas and fourteen of the much larger Super Frelon medium-lift helicopters. Neighbouring Zimbabwe is still largely dependant upon former Rhodesian Air Force aircraft, including thirteen C-47s, and has still to acquire up-to-date troop-carrying helicopters. Zambia has received some half-hearted aid from various Warsaw Pact countries, but these would appear to have lost interest since the creation of neighbouring Zimbabwe, so that the air transport

element consists of six C-47s, and five each of DHC-4 Caribou and DHC-5 Buffalo, as well as a number of smaller aircraft, while there are eleven Mil Mi-8s heading a mixture of small helicopters. Not all of the Zambian Air Force's equipment can be regarded as fully operational at any one time. The former Portuguese territory of Mozambique has a small air force, the *Forca Aerea de Mocambique*, which is now heavily dependant upon the USSR for support, including the provision of a number of transports of An-24 or An-26 standard which are flown by Aeroflot crews, but the air arm has eight Mi-8 helicopters of its own, as well as a Tu-134A and an Il-62 for VIP duties, which would appear to be impressive equipment for a small and impoverished African state! On the Atlantic side of the continent, the other major Portuguese colony is Angola, which operates a variety of Eastern and Western types in the *Forca Aerea Angolana*, including two commercial-variety L-300-30 Hercules, five An-26s, three C-47s, a Noratlas, a Fokker F.27 and a Tu-134A 'Crusty' VIP transport, as well as seven Mi-8s, and many smaller aircraft and helicopters, including thirteen Rumanian-built Islanders. Another southern African state, Malawi, the former British colony of Nyasaland, has a small Air Wing, with transport aircraft including four C-47s and six Pumas, as well as liaison and VIP aircraft.

For many other African states, the concept of an air force is virtually unknown, with small communications, transport and VIP Air Wings being more usual, with the last-mentioned role often assuming the greatest

The South African Air Force operates a small number of C-130s.

Many air forces and army or navy air arms find small utility aircraft useful, including the de Havilland Canada Twin Otter; this one belongs to the Argentinian Air Force.

importance. Over the last fifteen or twenty years, there has, nevertheless, been an upsurge in interest in military aviation amongst African states, and instead of the typical former French colony, for example, being content to operate a couple of Alouette II helicopters and a Broussard liaison aircraft, with perhaps a C-47 or something similar as the summit of its ambitions, larger aircraft are now becoming commonplace, with such purchases sometimes being through necessity or sometimes as a result of left-wing governments coming under Soviet influence. Of the former French colonies, one of the most substantial air transport elements is now that of the *Armée de L'Air du Cameroun,* with three C-130Hs, including a stretched -30H version, and four C-47s, four DHC-5 Buffalo, a single DHC-4 Caribou and two HS 748s, while the *Force Aérienne Gabonaises* is another Hercules operator, with three C-130Hs and a single L-100-30T, as well as a DC-6B, three C-47s, three Nord 262 tactical transports and six Puma helicopters. The *Force Aérienne du Niger* is another Hercules operator, with two C-130Hs as well as three C-47s, although the *Force Aérienne de Guinea* has demonstrated its closer relationship with the Soviet Union by operating four Il-14s, two Il-18s and four An-14s. While the *Force*

Aérienne de Cote d'Ivoire operates five F.27s and two F.28s in its transport element, as well as a number of VIP aircraft, the *Force Aérienne Centrafricaine* has four elderly C-47s and one slightly newer C-54, as well as seven Puma helicopters. In the former French Congo, the *L'Armée de l'Air du Congo,* has three C-47s and a single Puma. The *Armée de l'Air du Madagascar* has in recent years added to its original five C-47s with four Antonov An-26s and two Mi-8s.

The former Belgian colonies of Rwanda and Zaire (the old Belgian Congo) provide a contrast, with the Rwandan Air Force operating only two C-47s for air transport work, although there is a VIP Caravelle III jet airliner, while the *Force Aérienne Zairoise* has five C-130H Hercules and two DHC-5D Buffalo as well as four C-54s and twelve C-47s, and the helicopter element consists of eleven SA.330 Pumas and a VIP Super Frelon. Liberia, founded by former negro slaves, does not have an air force, but operates aircraft within the Liberian Army, just two C-47s.

Army control of the air force has been introduced in the former British colony of Kenya, following an unsuccessful coup attempt staged by air force officers in 1982, with the new Army-controlled unit known as the Kenya '82 Air Force. A small but fairly modern air force, the transport units include eight DHC-5D Buffalo and six DHC-4 Caribou transports as well as six Puma helicopters. The Senegambia Air Force, created on the

Some idea of the huge size of the Lockheed C-5A Galaxy can be gained from this photograph. The size and speed of the Galaxy enables heavy items of equipment or heavy weapons to be deployed easily, including, for example, cruise missile launch vehicles, moved from the USA to the Western Europe aboard C-5A transports.

formation of the combined state of the Gambia and Senegal, now as six F.27s and five C-47s, as well as three Pumas in its transport force. Also in West Africa, the Federal Nigerian Air Force is one of the largest and best-equipped, even though the country is no longer being borne along on rising oil revenues; the transport element includes six C-130H and three C-130H-30 Hercules, five Fiat G.222s and two F.27s, five Boeing-Vertol CH-47C Chinook, fifteen Puma and three Whirlwind helicopters, as well as large numbers of utility aircraft, including twenty Dornier Do.28 Skyservants. Ghana, which has also suffered instability in recent years, has in the Ghana Air Force five F.27s and six Short Skyvans operating on transport duties.

The demands of African operating conditions would favour practical tactical transports such as the C-23A Sherpa, but the lack of foreign exchange and the extent of Soviet influence may prevent this, even though the aircraft would not only be the ideal C-47 replacement, but also offer a worthwhile improvement in overall capability at a reasonable cost.

Latin America and the Caribbean

Although long under American influence, Latin America has continued to live up to its reputation for instability in recent years, and indeed if anything the situation has become worse. At the same time, the former British colonies in the Caribbean have proved to be more stable, although low populations and economic difficulties have prevented the creation of substantial armed forces. In spite of sometimes considerable natural resources, countries such as Mexico and Brazil have vied for the distinction of being the world's greatest debtor nations, and Argentina has also run into the economic difficulties which were exacerbated by the abortive attempt to seize the Falklands from Britain. As in Africa, many countries operate air arms or air wings which are primarily transport and communications units or extensions of the police rather than of the armed forces, with typical examples including Costa Rica, Guyana and Jamaica. The difficult terrain of many countries in Latin America and the Caribbean provides a constant challenge which requires the effective deployment of military transport aircraft to maintain communications and counter insurgency elements.

In no small part due to the country's intervention on behalf of the Soviet Union in many African states, Cuba has within the *Fuerza Aerea Revolucionaria* the largest air transport fleet of any air force in the Americas outside of the United States. Mainstay of this force consists of twenty Ilyushin Il-14 'Crate' and twenty An-24/An-26 transports, while there are a number of Antonov An-12 'Cubs' and twenty of the small LET L-410M Turbojets, with a helicopter force based on sixty Mi-4s and thirty Mi-8s. Commercial airliners from the national airline provide most of the airlift capability to overseas war zones. The only other islands in the Caribbean with an air transport element worthy of the description are the Dominican Republic and Haiti; the former operates five C-47s, five C-46s and two Sikorsky S.55s in the *Fuerza Aerea Dominicana,* an air force with a marked World War II air about it, while the latter has three DC-3s and two Sikorsky S-58s.

On the mainland of Central America, the *Fuerza Aerea Guatemalteca* faces a small RAF presence in Belize, over which territory Guatemala has territorial ambitions, with a few combat aircraft and an air transport fleet which consists mainly of five C-47s and a C-54, as well as a small number of IAI Arava light transports, three Sikorsky H-19s (S-55s) and some smaller Bell helicopters for utility duties. The slightly larger and more up-to-date *Fuerza Aerea Hondurena* also includes a number of transport aircraft, of which the most recent arrivals have been two C-130 Hercules which joined two Lockheed Electra airliners and fourteen C-47s, as well as a number of utility aircraft and helicopters. In Nicaragua, where the *Fuerza Aerea Sandinista* is fighting against American-supported and supplied rebels, the few remaining aircraft of those supplied to earlier regimes by the United States includes a solitary C-47, while the Soviet Bloc have provided a number of the inevitable Mi-8 helicopters. Fighting on the other side of the political divide, the *Fuerza Aerea Salvadorena* is opposing attempts by Communist terrorists to seize control of the country, with two DC-6s, twelve C-47s and three ex-Air National Guard (USAF reserves) Fairchild C-123 Providers as well as a large number of utility helicopters, mainly Bell UH-1H Iroquois, of which as many as 100 may have been supplied by the United States. Panama, on the other hand, has only in recent years introduced its first combat aircraft for light attack duties, and has been mainly a transport and coastal surveillance force with the *Fuerza Aerea Panamena* operating a Lockheed Electra airliner, three C-47s, and some Twin Otters and Skyvans as well as Aviocars, utility aircraft and helicopters.

Although the largest state in central America, Mexico, maintains the *Fuerza Aerea Mexicana* primarily as a transport force, with two transport squadrons flying two C-118s, a Douglas DC-7 and five C-54s, twenty C-47s, and three DHC-5D Buffalo, as well as ten Aravas and twelve Islanders. A utility helicopter force is spearheaded by five Puma transport helicopters. The Presidential Squadron operates five Boeing 727-100s/200s, including some in the QC convertible cargo-passenger role, and two Boeing 737s, as well as a One-Eleven, an Electra, and a number of executive jets. The Mexican Navy, or *Armada* has its own transport element, with five C-47s and two Buffalo.

The four major air forces in South America, and indeed in Latin America generally, are those of Brazil, Argentina, Peru and Ecuador, with the first two having the added advantage of home-based aircraft industries, reducing the foreign exchange burden of aircraft procurement and making larger, modern forces more sustainable. The *Fuerza Aerea Argentina* has eleven Hercules of different types, including some commercial versions and two KC-130H tankers, as well as four

Boeing 707s, seven Fokker F.28 Fellowships, of which two are used on VIP duties, and eleven Fokker F.27 Friendships, some of which were used to operate a regular air service to the Falklands before the Argentinian invasion in 1982. The FAA also has a number of helicopters, including three Boeing CH-47C Chinooks. Transport aircraft are also operated by the Navy, with three Skyvans and a number of Lockheed L-188 Electras, while the Army has three Fiat G.222s and thirty-three SA.330 Pumas. Brazil has ten Lockheed C-130E/H Hercules and two KC-130Hs in the *Forca Aerea Brasileira,* with twelve Hawker Siddeley (British Aerospace) 748s and twenty-one de Havilland Canada DHC-5 Buffalo tactical transports, and for light transport duties and utility operations there are more than a hundred of the Brazilian-designed and built Embraer EMB-110 Bandeirante twin-engined turboprops. There are no medium or heavy transport helicopters in service, although there are rescue machines and many utility types. By contrast, Ecuador has a relatively small air transport element in spite of maintaining substantial numbers of combat aircraft and having the operation of an airline, TANE, *Transportes Aereo Nacionales Ecuatorianos,* under the control of the *Fuerza Aerea Ecuatoriana.* The one consistent theme for combat and transport types alike is that the air force has small numbers of a large variety of aircraft types; transport aircraft include a single C-130H Hercules, four DC-6Bs and six C-47s, four Boeing 707s, three 720s, and one each of 727s and 737s, four HS.748s, two DHC-5D Buffalo, four Electras and two Pumas. The Army has five Buffalo of its own, as well as a Puma and some Arava light transports. Neighbouring Peru has a larger air force, and unusually for South American countries operates a mix of Western and Soviet types, which, in the *Fuerza Aerea del Peru* includes seven commercial Lockheed L-100-20s, sixteen Antonov An-26 'Curls' and a similiar number of Buffalo, as well as small numbers of C-54s, C-47s, and other miscellaneous types, while the helicopter units are equipped with Mil Mi-6s and Mi-8s, with six of each of these types, although the Army has another forty-two Mi-8s.

A mixture of transport types is also maintained in the *Fuerza Aerea Venezolanas,* with five C-130H Hercules, four Fiat G.222s and a single HS.748 being accompanied by fifteen C-47s and twelve Fairchild C-123 Providers, while a number of G.222s are also operated by the Army. There are few large helicopters in the FAV. Colombia is another country with an air force-operated airline, SATENA, which has five HS.748s, and eight DC-3s with an equal number of DC-4s, while the *Fuerza Aerea Colombiana* has in its military role, another sixteen C-47s, eight C-54s, four C-130B/H Hercules, and a number of other types including a Boeing 707 and two Aravas, as well as some commercially-configured DC-6s and DC-7s. Economic problems have prevented Chile from creating a substantial and modern air force, although there are many elderly aircraft on the strength, with two C-130H Hercules being accompanied by five C-54s and five C-47s, and a solitary Buffalo, while the helicopter element includes a small number of Pumas and six Westland Whirlwinds. Another elderly collection is operated by the *Fuerza Aerea Boliviana,* with a single Lockheed 100-30 Hercules and an Electra, as well as six Fokker F.27s, operating alongside twelve C-47s, seven Convair Metropolitans, usually 440s, although some have been up-dated to 580 standard, and four C-54s and DC-6s. The *Fuerza Aerea del Paraguay* has more than twenty C-47s, a handful of C-54s and DC-6s, and a few other elderly types as well as some utility aircraft, while the C-47 also figures prominently on the strength of the *Fuerza Aerea Uruguaya*, which has twelve, plus a small number of Fokker F.27s and Fairchild-Hiller FH.227s and CASA C.212s.

That so many air forces struggle to maintain an air transport element in spite of obvious economic difficulties, and operational problems as well with such elderly aircraft surviving in so many of the smaller air forces, shows that over the past fifty years, air force and army commanders have come to be convinced of the contribution which transport aircraft make to military success. The real question mark which does arise is just whether many of these aircraft could be deployed effectively in strength on a major operation, but fortunately, this is something which few of the operating countries are likely to require!

Chapter Ten
Tomorrow's Transports

Looking ahead is always difficult and uncertain, and in few areas of activity is prophecy so uncertain as in aviation. There are two reasons why this should be so, one is the degree of technological change which can occur over a relatively short period, while the other, almost contradicting the first, is the long production and service life of much equipment. This means that any look forward must be for a substantial period, and not just for the ten years or so which would be regarded as extreme in most other types of activity. Examples are easy to come by. Who, during the mid-1930s, would have foreseen not just the immense military success of the DC-3 in its C-47 guise, but the fact that fifty years later there would still be several hundred of these aircraft in air force service? Did anyone really expect the Lockheed C-130 Hercules to be in service and production thirty years after its first flight? During the late 1960s and early 1970s, before oil prices began to rise rapidly, vertical take-off transports were seen as providing enhanced flexibility for military aviation, overcoming the performance limitations of the helicopter; in the event, V/STOL has enjoyed limited success in combat aircraft, in spite of its advantages for air forces and navies, and as a transport option it is now largely forgotten.

There are political and geographical constraints as well, and economic problems which are especially difficult in terms of defence equipment procurement because of the tendency for military equipment to outpace the rate of inflation because of growing sophistication. The policy in many countries to order equipment in small batches over a period of years is not the way to obtain the lowest possible price, nor are larger orders when spread over an unrealistically long delivery period.

The way in which the political map has changed over the last forty years also has a bearing on the importance of military aircraft and their performance, Since the end of World War II, almost all of the colonies built up during the eighteenth and nineteenth centuries by the major European powers have gained independence, and their use as bases cannot be taken for granted. Over the same period, all of Eastern Europe and a substantial part of South-East Asia has come under Communist control. It may be argued that there is no foreseeable need for overseas bases, but it is the unforeseen which causes the major political and military difficulties. Had the Falklands been given an airport of international standard when the original airport at Port Stanley was built, economic links with Argentina may have been less and seizure would have been less tempting, not least because of the ability to fly in reinforcements at the first sign of tension. On a wider strategic point, no one starts a war or military adventure without the firm conviction of success, and deterrence, be it conventional or nuclear, depends for its credibility on convincing possible opponents that such a success will be denied them.

Of course, the role which military air transport can play depends on the resources available, and there has been some wishful thinking by politicians over the ability to fly troops to different crisis points around the world. In Britain, a Labour Government said that it would not deploy forces unless bases were available, excusing a planned rundown of the Royal Navy's carrier force. One has to accept that many operations are best performed by carriers and amphibious forces if bases ashore have become untenable, or the terrain makes an airlift impractical. In others, carrier-borne aircraft can secure local aerial superiority for long enough for airborne forces and shore-based combat aircraft to be deployed. Air transport is a component of strategic mobility, but it is not the entire answer. Of course, bases can be secured overseas, but one advantage of strategic mobility is the ability to dispense with fixed bases or forces *in situ* because of the costs, and the risk of having troops in the wrong place when a crisis does arise. Fixed bases also offer a target for a pre-emptive strike; the first USAF aircraft destroyed in the Korean War was a MATS C-54 caught on the ground.

Geography might appear to be rigid in the strictest sense, even if politically we know that this is not so, but technological change does redraw the map effectively. Allowing West Berlin to survive at all was a gamble by the Allies at the end of World War II. The Berlin Airlift seemed to be asking the impossible, but today such an operation would be far easier. The NATO countries can have at least some faith in the idea of a trans-Atlantic airbridge in a crisis, so long as the political will is there.

Defence is a balancing act between the likely threat and the resources available, and between manpower and equipment. There is another balance to be achieved, however, and this is the one most frequently overlooked, that of using whatever opportunities present themselves to create a genuine advance in capability. The United States Air Force has been reasonably successful in ensuring that Military Airlift Command has benefited from this type of development, helped by a more sympathetic administration than in earlier years. In the United Kingdom, this has not happened. When the RAF replaced its Hastings transports with the Hercules, this was done against an overall reduction in aircraft numbers, with the total transport aircraft strength of the RAF being more than halved between the early 1960s and late 1980s. Admittedly, the higher speed, increased payload and higher utilisation of the turboprop Hercules compared to the Hastings meant that the aircraft became

more productive, and that it could also replace the Argosies and Beverlies because of its greater fuselage girth, but the scope for rationalisation, fine for logistics reasons, was also taken to include reductions in the numbers of aircraft available rather than strengthening British airlift capability. There should have been room for a compromise.

There will continue to be a need for air transport units for as long as the Western democracies are prepared to resist Soviet expansion, and for as long as these countries are willing to provide assistance in the event of man-made or natural disasters. That is one side of the picture. There will also be a need for military transport units in the East for as long as the Soviet Union remains set on carving out a worldwide empire for itself. It can also be argued that many countries would still require air transport even if there was a less serious external threat, simply because of distance.

So the need is there, what of the aircraft?

There can be little doubt that many of the aircraft now in service will still be operating into the next century. Even early versions, such as the C-130B, of the Hercules are being reworked so that these will last well into the 1990s, longer in many cases, especially for those aircraft brought up to full C-130H standard. Aircraft of more recent build certainly have at least twenty years' life left,

Change will come slowly, but not for the want of trying, since designers have been working to close the gap between the conventional aeroplane and the helicopter; this is Bell's answer, the XH-95A.

and possibly as much as twice that. No doubt the same will be true of the Transall. The greater durability of modern aircraft with failsafe structures, and the lower utilisation in peacetime of transport aircraft in military service, combine to ensure long service life, especially if aircraft are sold in late life to smaller air forces in the less affluent nations. While there have been proposals for a "Herc replacement" turbofan in the past, most operators would accept that the best replacement would be a newer, and possibly stretched, Hercules. Given the developments in turboprop technology, the Hercules successor appears likely to be equipped with new technology turboprops, perhaps six or eight-bladed propellers, and with more extensive use of modern materials in the airframe with development and construction shared with European manufacturers. The problem of devising an improved Hercules is one which is already occupying designers in Europe and North America. During 1985, four companies, Lockheed in the United States; British Aerospace; Aerospatiale of France; and Messerschmitt-Bölkow-Blohm of West

Another Bell solution, the XV-15 goes through its paces.

Germany, joined forces under the designation of FIMA, the Future International Military/Civil Airlifter, to study designs suitable as Hercules and Transall replacements. As one might expect, the most widely publicised configuration for a FIMA project is that of an up-dated Hercules. A planned twin-engined small Hercules, but with the same fuselage dimensions as the original aircraft and many common parts, did not attract sufficient interest to enter production when mooted a few years ago. There may be a need for a smaller aircraft for cargo which cannot be satisfactorily handled by the current generation of lightweight or tactical military transports, or by medium and even heavy-lift helicopters, but this market may be too small for a specialised type, as indicated by the lack of interest so far in military transport derivatives of the British Aerospace 146 airliner, which with exceptionally short take-off and landing characteristics would appear to be the ideal aircraft for this slot. Perhaps too, Hercules range/payload performance is sufficiently flexible for operators to consider the occasional cost of operating below the optimum payload as being cheaper than introducing another aircraft into the inventory.

Certainly, standardisation, an economic advantage for civil operators, is at least as pressing for air forces, especially because of the logistics problems which could occur in a crisis when aircraft were being operated at full

stretch and supply lines stretched, if too many types were being operated. Air forces with too many different types, such as some of those in Latin America, suffer fundamental weaknesses which inhibit full operational efficiency. The new McDonnell Douglas C-17A transport for MAC will offer considerable flexibility for the USAF, replacing the C-141s in regular squadrons, possibly reducing the frontline Hercules force, and already this aircraft has enabled a ceiling to be placed on the numbers of C-5B Galaxies being built. Had the aircraft been available much earlier, and the programme not delayed by funding, one might speculate that the KC-10A Extender programme might not have been initiated, and that additional C-17As might have been ordered instead. Yet, against this, even the elderly KC-135 force has been re-engined and its life extended almost indefinitely.

Economics have a major role to play. The high cost of new aircraft has prevented many of the poorer countries from equipping their air forces with modern types. The simple balance of payments problems which confront nations such as New Zealand are made even worse for those countries which have a *per capita* income a tenth or worse than that of the industrialised nations, whose labour costs effectively set the pricing structure for new aircraft. This is why there are still so many C-47s in service, and it also means that the possibilities for C-47 replacements, such as the Sherpa, which is simple, of similar size, and has the advantage of a rear loading ramp, are reduced. The building of transport aircraft in Indonesia and Brazil will help to reduce the cost of new equipment for these countries, and also limit European and American manufacturers to what may be described as the "top end" of the market. The simple solution many might say would be for many of the poorer countries to do away with military aircraft altogether, even transport aircraft which can have a humanitarian application. Instead, what does happen is that these countries are sold Soviet aircraft, cheaper than their Western counterparts, but still more than they can afford, and often purchase technology which is far in excess of their needs for the sake of prestige.

For the future, it is clear that the market will continue to be served by aircraft of C-17A type for the USAF and possibly a few aircraft of this type might be purchased for the RAF, if funds permit, to reinstate a genuine strategic mobility. Below this, there will be up-dated developments of the Hercules, although serious competition may emerge from Europe at some stage. Suggestions of a military version of the A.320 and A.310 Airbuses are possibly unrealistic, however, since neither aircraft has the ideal configuration for military use, which really requires the lower floor which is permitted by a high wing, while high winged aircraft also tend to keep their engines further off the ground and so less likely to suffer fan damage from ingested particles from unpaved runways. At the lower end of the market, there will continue to be a large number of utility aircraft, many of which are derivatives, and some close derivatives, of current civil types, including the British Aerospace ATP and the Fokker F.50, the HS.748 and F.27 successors respectively. Possibly the BAe.146 will get into this market, especially if it could be built under licence in China, Brazil or Indonesia, all of which have substantial requirements for aircraft of this size, and distances, as well as economies, which would not lend themselves to heavier helicopters.

The extent to which the helicopter can be developed will dictate the future planning of many air forces and armies. Boeing-Vertol is working on a larger development of the Chinook, while several other manufacturers are looking at tilt-rotor, X-wing and advancing rotor projects as means of accelerating the helicopter first, and providing the basis for larger machines as well. It would seem that helicopters will become larger, but as they do, the market for each successive size increment is lower than that for the size beneath it, as fewer countries require the biggest machines, while others find greater flexibility in larger numbers of smaller helicopters, and the unit costs of the largest machines being spread over fewer aircraft, tend to be too high for many to justify. Detachable fuselages on the largest machines will enable these to operate in a dual role as more productive flying cranes, enhancing their heli-lift capability for vertical envelopment, but on

Rising fuel costs have condemned designs such as the Dornier Do.31E.

Above: The US Army plans to resurrect the XCH-62 heavy lift helicopter, a Boeing design.

Below: One possible successor for both the Hercules and the Transall military transports is FIMA, or Future International Military/Civil Airlifter. The design is being developed by Lockheed, British Aerospace, Aerospatiale and Messerschmitt-Bölkow-Blohm.

current production and aircraft life so far, it would seem that there will be many Sikorsky CH-53s and Boeing-Vertol CH-47 Chinooks in service at the turn of the century.

It now appears unlikely that the gap between helicopters and conventional transports will be bridged by the building of vertical take-off transports. Had the Fairey Rotodyne, the closest any country or manufacturer ever came to providing a practical VTOL transport, been put into production, such machines may have been a matter of course today. The demise of another possible development, the V/STOL Hawker Siddeley HS 681, during the late 1960s, although a short take-off aircraft with the prospect of occasional conversion to vertical take-off capability, followed by the fuel crisis of just a few years later, has meant that such machines are seldom seriously considered today. Even if these were built, the market might be far smaller than many might expect, largely because of the extra cost of such aircraft, and this remains an inhibiting factor in approaching the problem from the other end, by making helicopters ever larger, faster and more capable. There are even those who object to purchases of the existing generation of heavy-lift helicopters, of the size of the Sikorsky CH-53 and the Boeing Vertol CH-47, on the basis that medium or smaller helicopters offer greater flexibility, and less chance of losing a significant element of an airborne infantry force to anti-aircraft fire or fighter attack.

At the other extreme, the use of supersonic transports, including the concept of HOTOL, horizontal take-off and landing space shuttle-type vehicles for global travel can be ruled out for military use because of the relatively small number of occupants these would carry; which makes them even less likely to be used in military service than the Concorde supersonic airliner, no longer in production. If nothing else, the military appreciates practicality in its aircraft!

Since the many applications for military transport aircraft and helicopters includes that of assault, even though in terms of the proportion of flying hours consumed, this role may appear to be minor, any review of the future must include surface effect ships. In effect, these offer a compromise between airborne and amphibious assault. Variations on this theme, notably the hovercraft, were used in South Vietnam for patrolling rivers, showing a welcome ability to pass over minefields without detonation. The limited carrying capacity of such craft meant that their role was that of patrol rather than assault or battlefield movement, and their high noise

levels and relatively limited speed also removed the element of surprise! The Saudi Arabian Coast Guard has also found the more modern and capable British Hovercraft Corporation BH-7 hovercraft ideal for coastal patrol duties, especially in areas where extensive shallows and sandbanks hinder conventional marine craft.

Most of the military hovercraft used so far have been of the truly amphibious variety, using flexible skirts rather than sidewalls, and so have been able to operate equally well over land or sea. Ideas for developing the hovercraft for assault and patrol duties, including helicopter-carrying frigates such as the USN's now abandoned SES 2000 hovercraft frigate, have centred around the sidewall hovercraft, which can beach itself, but which cannot operate over land, although it can operate without difficulty in very shallow water or swampland. Doubts remain about the capability of such craft, and other high speed marine transports such as hydrofoils and jetfoils, to cope with bad weather in the open sea. Costs tend to be high, especially in terms of fuel and maintenance, in which such vessels are, if anything, more expensive than large aircraft, yet lack the poor weather capability and the flexibility of the aircraft. True, hovercraft in particular can loiter, or at least ride at anchor, something denied the transport aeroplane when away from base, and the hovercraft is relatively immune from minefields and torpedo attack, although the sidewall variety with water rather than air propellers, is less immune than the skirted variety. Perhaps the hovercraft is reduced to being a highly specialised and marginal contender most of all by the fact that it is only useful for assault rather than transport and relief, and in its chosen role, it is still slower than helicopters or transport aircraft, and lacks their ability to land attacking troops on the other side of coastal defences. This has not stopped the Soviet Union from working on large assault hovercraft, but the Soviet system means that the planners have to be less accountable for the cost-effectiveness of military equipment than their counterparts in the democracies of the West!

Indeed, to look ahead realistically, one has to accept that tomorrow's military transport aeroplanes are likely to be those of today, with a few new arrivals and developments of existing types. The more ambitious projects, including the American C-17A and the Soviet An-124, will be confined to a few operators, and may not even be seen in air forces other than those of the United States and the Soviet Union.

Index

DUBLIN BAY

from Killiney to Howth

SPONSORED BY

DUBLIN PORT

DUBLIN BAY

from Killiney to Howth

BRIAN LALOR

THE O'BRIEN PRESS
DUBLIN

DISTRIBUTOR
OUR EDITIONS
STER SPRINGS,
A 19425-0449
15) 458-5005

First published 1989 by The O'Brien Press Ltd, 20 Victoria Road, Dublin 6, Ireland.

British Library Cataloguing in Publication Data
Lalor, Brian
Dublin Bay.
1. Dublin. (County) Dublin bay. Natural History, History
I. Title
508.418'3
ISBN 0-86278-203-1

Drawings and maps: Brian Lalor
Editing: Íde ní Laoghaire
Book design: Michael O'Brien
Jacket design: The Graphiconies, Dublin
Jacket separations: The City Office, Dublin
Jacket illustration: Brian Lalor
Typesetting and computing: Ivan O'Brien at The O'Brien Press
Main type set in 11½/13½ Times Roman with headings and prelims
set in Palatino
Printing and binding: The Camelot Press
10 9 8 7 6 5 4 3 2 1

Contents

for

Ayelet, Allegra, Caoimhe, Eve

Introduction

Hamlet. Do you see yonder cloud that's almost in shape of a camel?

Polonius. By th'mass, and 'tis like a camel indeed.

Hamlet. Methinks it is like a weasel.

Polonius. It is back'd like a weasel.

Hamlet. Or like a whale?

Polonius. Very like a whale.

OBJECTS OF THE LANDSCAPE tend to exist only in a very marginal manner in the human consciousness until they have been perceived in some particular way which invests them with meaning. The eighteenth century discovered ruins as fascinating voices from the past rather than convenient heaps of stones to be cannibalised for the construction of milord's manor house. So enthusiastic did they become for broken-down walls, that no gentleman's park was considered complete without a fake priory or a rustic hermit's cell. Ruins could be said to have 'arrived' in the sense of being socially acceptable - a very important point in the eighteenth century. For the nineteenth century, mountains were the discovery, and while one could not for obvious practical reasons construct a range of peaks to enclose the vista of one's land, mountains might

The bay from the Hill of Howth with the Dublin Mountains and Wicklow Hills fading into the distance on the far side.

be collected and savoured at second hand. They could be drawn, painted and climbed, and from Wicklow to the Himalayas artists were dispatched to draw, paint and engrave anything which rose above a few thousand feet. Things do depend on how you see them or fail to do so.

Dublin Bay tends towards a chameleon-like existence in people's minds, visible to some, merging totally with its background for others. It tends to be perceived as the sum of its parts rather than a more definite whole. To the fisherman and the sailing enthusiast it is a clear concept, focused on the home port. To the land-bound it is more likely to be seen as a few areas centred on one's base.

The concern of this book is the totality of the bay rather than its well-known constituent parts. The sheet of water enclosed between Howth and Killiney encompasses so much of architectural, environmental, recreational, natural and historic interest that its waters lap on the shores of a truly vast subject and a uniquely beautiful location for an ever-growing city.

Geography plays a part in people's approach to the bay, and the division of the land into northern and southern shores by the river Liffey has had a decisive effect on the development of separate communities on opposite sides of the bay. This may have been less definite prior to the mid-nineteenth century when travel by boat was achieved with considerably more ease than travel around the bay on dangerous and inadequate roads. The scant existence of bridges by which to cross the river greatly restricted movement and the necessity of having to travel far into the city from one side in order to reach the other restricted movement. Access would have been more practical across the bay, weather permitting. The result of such long separation has led people to conceive of the bay as those parts which might be reached without having to cross the river. Bull Island and Dollymount Strand are emphatically northside, as much as Sandymount and Seapoint are southside. Tidal and navigational considerations also contribute to the separation of the shores of the bay, and unlike the landlocked lakes of Northern Italy and Switzerland, where ferries constantly cross and skirt the shoreline uniting the surrounding suburbs, the bay totally lacks any cross traffic. The fact that the bay is open to the Irish Sea and susceptible to constantly changing depths of water and to violent weather conditions unfortunately precludes the possibility of such a service ever being a success other than on a seasonal and sporadic basis.

Further complications are introduced by the fact that at an administrative level the bay is divided into a number of independent fiefdoms, the rationale for which is totally archaic. A colour-coded administrative map of the bay would resemble the hide of a piebald pony, with little relationship between the spots. City Corporation and borough council, government ministries and departments, planning boards and shipping authorities all have control of sections of the waters and shoreline. Much of this subdivision is appropriate, being based on the specialised needs of lighthouses, shipping, planning and the environment. The situation may be preferable to the existence of some organisation with overall power, as the further bureaucratising of the administration of the bay is not a recipe for clarity of thought.

Two schemes, an oil refinery and an underground gas cavern, were promoted by private industry in the past. While these schemes were defeated one does not know what future antisocial proposals may be lying around.

The public has become more vigilant and knowledgeable about the threat that industry can present to the amenity aspect of the bay.

Fortunately, the only industry of substance to be found in the bay is Dublin Port, something which is integral to it and absolutely appropriate.

Dublin Bay emerges from the obscurity of the past in the beginning of the eighteenth century

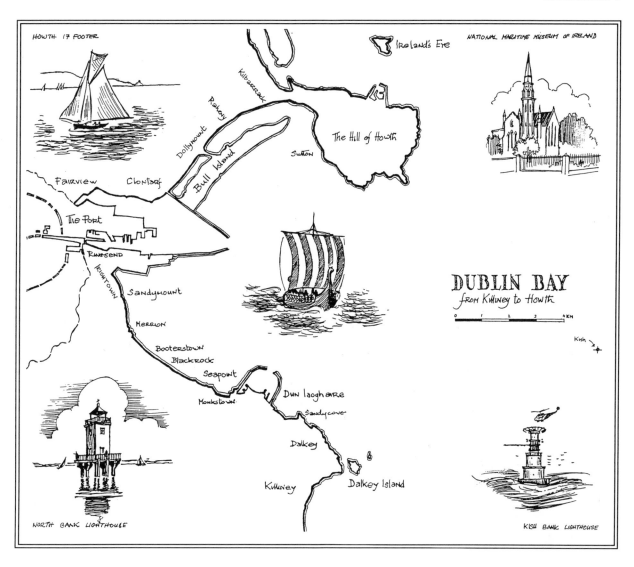

HOWTH 17 FOOTER

Kilbarrack

Raheny

Dollymount

Bull Island

Sutton

The Hill of Howth

Ireland's Eye

NATIONAL MARITIME MUSEUM OF IRELAND

Fairview   Clontarf

The Port

Ringsend

Irishtown

Sandymount

Merrion

Booterstown

Blackrock

Seapoint

Monkstown

Dun Laoghaire

Sandycove

Dalkey

Dalkey Island

Killiney

DUBLIN BAY
from Killiney to Howth

0   1   2   3   4 KM

Kish

NORTH BANK LIGHTHOUSE

KISH BANK LIGHTHOUSE

with a positive welter of representations of itself in maps, drawings and paintings. The impression is that of a stretch of water, tranquil or turbulent, with a forest of masts belonging to shipping of all sizes from full rigged sailing ships to barges, lighters, tiny sail boats and rafts. On the land stretching behind the seascape and enclosing it, are to be seen green fields fading into the distance, with a sparse scattering of buildings among them, and the occasional fishing village on the shore, composed of a few houses and a diminutive harbour. The human activity is all on the bay, with the bustle and energy generated by the trade and life of a thriving Georgian city framed by an idyllic pastoral landscape.

Today the order of things has been reversed, with a seething mass of occupation on the land stretching around the bay. Hardly a hill is unencumbered by densely packed housing and the fields have been totally submerged under the complex of roads and buildings now surrounding the waters. The pastoral scene has vanished under an intensity of urban expansion. But the waters of the bay have become much less densely occupied, and in a very different way from the past. With the development of container shipping a vast bulk of goods can be freighted on a single vessel which even twenty years ago would have required quite a number of smaller cargo boats. Although probably more yachts are owned around the shores of Dublin Bay than in any other part of the country, their activity is mainly confined to weekends and the summer months.

Scale is a major change since the eighteenth century. In the paintings of the period there is harmony between the marine landscape and the architectural one. The proportions are consciously human and both ships and buildings designed around the possibilities of human activity. Whether it is the Custom House or a timber raft conveying goods from a ship to the quayside, there is a like relationship to the surrounding world. Today extraordinary behemoths float on the surface of the bay like great water-borne catafalques containing department-store quantities of merchandise in their tightly packed containers. The ferries too have adopted this gargantuan scale, conveying townloads of passengers and their inseparable automobiles to and from the city.

Public perception of shipping has also altered. Nowadays it is identified with ferries and freight. Oil tankers, container ships, Guinness boats - bulk shipping of various kinds - are what pass through the bay. From the city's genesis up to the development of flight, freight was merely one aspect of what shipping represented, and the public interest in sea passage was on a level with contemporary involvement with air travel. This leads to a current estrangement of interest on the part of those who live around the bay.

Shipping on the bay was once seen as a lifeline of movement, travel, business and goods. When a Georgian or Victorian citizen of Dublin looked at those paintings of the bay crowded with shipping they saw something which we cannot experience, a symbol of not being cut off from the rest of the world.

> In Dublin they'd be glad to see
> A packet, though it bring in me.

Jonathan Swift's lines, written in irritation at being held up because of insufficient passengers for the packet boat at Holyhead in 1726, refers to the avidity with which the boat was greeted as a source of news from beyond the Irish Sea, a much more confining body of water then than it is now. This sense of anticipation related to the arrival of word from outside has no contemporary parallel.

Dublin Bay represents the city's very reason for being and has undoubtedly contributed to the generation and growth of its life through its history, bringing invaders and saviours, tyrants and revolutionaries, as well as being the medium for the arrival of the new in style, ideas, fads and follies and above all providing the means of trading successfully into and out of the country.

Dublin, like many another city, has attracted to itself a share of epithets, scabrous and dignified, relating to aspects of its past. Architectural grandeur of the eighteenth century or wattle huts in the eleventh have equally spawned an epithet, as have the literary revival of the late Victorian period, and the slums of that period and later. Dear and dirty, Augustan and arrogant, jewel and strumpet, a fair cross-section of the accumulated layers of personality and as different as the cultures and conditions they imply. All are true of course or at least sufficiently apposite to define some aspect of the city's inherited and corporate self. Yet the conditions described are exclusively urban in concept and no hint is given of a wider concern. No 'Bride of the Adriatic' here or even 'City of the Bay'. Dublin lived on and from the bay, yet appears not to have been associated with it. The treacherous nature of its waters may be a partial explanation.

The city's superb natural setting was greatly praised by Mr and Mrs S.C. Hall in their 1841 *Ireland, Its Scenery and Character* where they enthuse to a point of hyperbole about the surroundings of Dublin. Allowing for the fact that at that time the population was under a quarter of a million, the resources of the bay must have presented a less fraught aspect than they do today.

Killiney Hill and Sorrento Point from Killiney Beach.

There are few cities in the World, and perhaps none in Great Britain, so auspiciously situated as the city of Dublin. The ocean rolls its waves within ten miles of the quays, the Bay is at once safe, commodious and magnificent, within a variety of coast from the soft beach of sand to the rough sea promontory, from the undulating slope to the terrific rock, and there are several lighthouses to guide vessels into the harbour.

This was written when all the advantages of the bay had been harnessed in a manner which previous generations had aspired to but never succeeded in achieving. The silting problems of the Liffey had, after the best part of a thousand years, been solved. A harbour, enormous by contemporary standards, had been provided for ships in peril - this was completed a year after the Halls' visit. The railway to Kingstown was in place and the economic slump which followed the Act of Union had been overcome. Surprisingly, a century and a half later, despite the enormous growth in the population of the city, the enthusiasm which its relationship with the bay evoked in 1841 can still be experienced, and while the natural environment of open fields and uncluttered shoreline is gone forever, the strength of the landscape and its relationship to the bay continues to hold its own and to dominate the spread of the city.

From the Poolbeg Lighthouse, equidistant from either shore of the bay, one can see a number of areas of the surrounding contour which constitute separate and individual landscapes. Moving from the rugged cliff face of Howth to the gentle flow of the dunes on Bull Island, the eye travels round the rim of the land, passing over the angularity of the city with its high rise and dockland cranes to the extended sandy shore of Sandymount, out over the citadel of Dun Laoghaire and up to the tree-filled and manicured heights of Killiney Hill. Each area is an environment in itself and they grow naturally out of each other. At high tide the expanse of Bull Island contracts upon itself, becoming a knoll rather than a plain, and on the southern shores the sandy flats vanish altogether, the myriad of tiny figures who walk on the sands disappearing also.

The need to be alone in the out-of-doors cannot be answered by the public parks of the city, crowded as they are with people, children, dogs and noise. Remarkably for a city of a million inhabitants, one can walk with freedom and alone over many portions of the shoreline and find solitude, whether on man-made causeway or on the remaining fragments of natural landscape.

The graving dock, Dublin Port.

The replica Viking longship, Dyflin, *built in 1988.*

The language by which the physical form of the bay has been altered is one which uses stones and mortar, cast iron and concrete, wood and stucco, to provide all manner of structures which now surround it. The ways in which these elements of the architectural language have been used to express the imperial, the totalitarian, the frivolous and the functional, and respect as well as contempt for the inhabitants of the bay area, show themselves quite clearly in the expression of the many changes of style from the Georgian period down to the present.

Architecture - and by that I mean engineering, design and the planning of the environment - is a language of communication, and the manipulators of these associated disciplines have at their disposal the ability to communicate much which is conscious as well as concerns which exist on a more subliminal level in the way the requirements of any building problem are answered. A contrast of the late twentieth century with the late nineteenth shows clearly the existence of totally different styles of expression. The Victorians, despite the confusing variety of styles at their disposal, ranging between Romanesque, Gothic and Greek Revival - all to be found in the environs of the bay - were able to produce a more humanist environment in most of their civic concerns than is being achieved today.

The environs of the bay are a rich hunting ground for topographical names which evoke the whole of past preoccupations as well as occupations both political and sedentary. The nomenclature of the bay separates the Vikings from the Celts and Normans. A European consciousness, developed from the Grand Tour, brought about the renaming of considerable portions of the coastline of the bay, both north and south, as souvenirs of a wider term of reference than those which had been previously available. Howth, from the Scandinavian 'Hovat' (a headland) contrasts nicely across the bay and also across the span of eight centuries with Sorrento Point, from some presumed resemblance with that part of the Italian coastline. Nice that the Vikings went in for topographical descriptions as did the Celts, rather than naming parts of the Dublin coastline in so far as they resembled parts of Denmark. It is confusing enough to have Marino and Sorrento, without having remembrances of Scandinavia as well.

The Hottentot fig, the bar-tailed godwit, Bindon Blood Stoney - all these are or were inhabitants of Dublin and its bay. They sound like *dramatis personae* in a Restoration comedy, but other than the resonance of their names they have nothing in common beyond being plant, bird and man. The plant, a tropical one, is found on Howth, the bird on Bull Island, and the man was one of the more significant holders of the post of chief engineer to the Port and Docks Board.

Two people can be associated with Dublin Bay whose relationship is firmly located on opposing shores, Lord Charlemont on the north and James Joyce on the south. Both appropriately have their memorials, which are similar in that they embody the cultural core of their respective ages: the Casino at Marino, commissioned by Charlemont and on which he lavished his wealth and taste in order to create a model villa of the Age of Enlightenment; and Joyce's Martello tower at Sandycove, which in the refining processes of his reflections in Zurich and Paris he transformed into the stage setting for his novel *Ulysses*, which like the Casino was to be a model of the world as Joyce wished to consider it. The Casino and Martello are both similar and totally unrelated. The similarity lies in their standing now as monuments to the strength of character and achievements of two generative individuals, one a patrician patron of the arts, the other an impecunious creator who unlike Charlemont had to leave Dublin in order to recreate it. Their monuments differ in the way the Casino remains today, although uninhabited and unfurnished, substantially as it was in Charlemont's time, still reflecting its position as a symbol of an age and cultural concept. The Martello tower exists as a museum bearing no relationship to the purpose for which the building was built - as a battery - but representing Joyce's ideas in the personal and the whimsical. Joyce called the tower the Omphalos, from a curious carved stone at Delphi, somewhat resembling the form of the tower and regarded by the Greeks as representing the navel of the world. To Lord Charlemont the same idea may be inferred, in creating a stylistic and intellectual Omphalos at Marino.

Substantial studies have been made of the area of Dublin Bay from an environmental point of view, concentrating on the issues of pollution, water purity, recreation and amenity. These studies correspond with an era of unparalleled growth and the consequent accentuation of all the pressures which a large body of water adjacent to a developing urban area may experience. The purpose of such studies was never visual, so this aspect of the totality of the bay has remained unrecorded. My concern is with a visual record of Dublin Bay as it now is, representing both much which remains unaltered from the last two centuries as well as all that has happened since. This is not the bay in a state of suspended animation, and it does not require a great exercise of the imagination to predict developments likely to take place in the future, based on even a conservative estimate of trends over the past twenty years. The combination of man-made and natural topography within the confines of the bay gives the city a unique, invaluable and delightful location which can only develop and change beneficially if seen as an entity instead of as a meeting place for unrelated suburbs and conflicting interests. The pressures of population, pollution, recreation and trade are at this point too intense to be accommodated without the emergence of an intelligent consensus directed towards the pursuit of excellence rather than compromise.

This collection of drawings developed, not from an impulse to provide Dublin Bay with an image of itself, but as a result of a more casual series of reactions. I was engaged in drawing the area of the shoreline between Vico Beach and Scotsman's Bay, and having begun this sequence became aware that the topographical richness of the area was continued without interruption right around the shoreline of the bay in a diverse and complex manner, full of interest. Carried along by the attraction of the subject, I had in fact begun this collection of drawings before I was aware that I was doing so. From the Poolbeg Lighthouse as far out into Dublin Bay as one can go while remaining so to speak on *terra firma*, one has the sense of being a pivot around which the horizon of the bay circles, and it was from this point that I really began the task of presenting the bay.

My preoccupation in this sequence of drawings is with Dublin Bay as it is at present, but it is impossible to be involved in the subject in any way without being aware of its past history and the various plans which exist concerning its future. The act of looking purposefully at the whole area from primarily a visual point of view gives one a somewhat different perspective on the matter from the many which have already been expressed regarding the particular needs of individual areas. It is a remarkable fact and certainly relevant that although books exist on the subject of the bay as an environment, nothing has been published on the subject considering it as a place with an overall visual identity. This is extraordinary, considering the number of books on

Eighteenth-century houses on Church Street in the old village of Howth.

the city itself, and relates to the conceptual divorce which seems to exist between the city and its marine environment. I have covered an abundance of well loved places between Killiney and Howth and attempted to give coherence to the individual and distinctive sections of landscape which hug the bay. These areas have a variety as distinct geologically as socially and contain a range of changes of tempo and texture remarkable in so small an area of the earth's surface. From Victorian imperial marine architecture to gorse-covered scarps and sand dunes,the journey passes by way of Italianate landscaping, *bijou* residences and megalithic monuments to rocky cliff faces and those who go down to the sea in ships, in this bay of abundance.

For me the experience of doing these drawings was simultaneously an exercise in artistic interpretation and also an exploration. No matter how well one knows a place, the fact of having to look afresh at every aspect of the bay, its landscape and activity, has been a source of continual satisfaction and stimulation.

My journey around the shore of the bay which begins on Killiney Beach, follows the coastline fairly rigorously, with the occasional permissible digression where circumstances seem to demand it. The river Liffey itself is within and yet outside the bay, but it has to be included within the context of the bay. Also those landlocked areas once on the shoreline and now left behind by the receding waters cannot be ignored. This demands the exercise of some restraint, for depending on how far one wishes to go back in time, these lost shorelines could bring one to Merrion Square or even to the medieval city. Another major digression, or rather excursion outside the limits of the bay, is the inclusion of the northern shore of the Howth peninsula. To have ignored this would have meant that an important fragment in the history of Dublin Bay and an area of immense historic interest would have to be omitted.

The need exists to assess the present by more

exacting standards than those applied by the practitioners of environmental design today, and I intend to evaluate the state of the built and natural environment in the light of developments of a more leisured age, not purely because it appeals to me, but because I feel that the nineteenth century managed to strike the correct balance between the needs of the various pressures under which urban and suburban development takes place. One can reasonably assume that had the expansion of residential Dublin not taken place in the last century but that the growth had in fact occurred in the middle years of this one, the results would have been imaginatively vapid, and in most respects dismal, excepting the quality of the public drains. There would have been no elegance, form, focus or centre to anything, and these are the qualities which make the built environment of the bay so distinguished today. The great attraction of the bay comes from the successful combination of the natural environment with the man-made, and in both to experience levels of excellence and beauty. For the future the dilemma is how these qualities can be preserved and enhanced.

Looking towards the industrial skyline of the port with the dominating feature of the Poolbeg stacks. In the foreground, Bull Island Bridge, customs cottages and the Dollymount shore.

Killiney

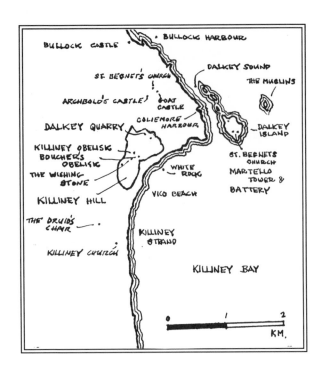

Killiney is a landscape of contrasting forms and textures associated more with the hill country of Tuscany than with the Irish landscape. This is surprising when old views of the area are examined, for the landscape which these show was almost entirely barren of trees prior to its development first as a number of estates and then as a residential quarter. The habit of the Grand Tour, and the naming of so many Irish demesnes from some memory of Italy, characterises the aristocratic properties which were developed all around Dublin Bay in the eighteenth and nineteenth centuries, and provides it with a liberal sprinkling of Italian placenames - Sorrento, Frescati, Maratimo, Casa Bella, Marino, Mount Olive, Bellmount, Montpellier, Tritonville and many more.

Of course, the fanciful naming of a few Irish fields with an Italian address does not create Italian topography, and these small manor houses surrounded by parkland were indistinguishable from the body of similar estates in other parts of the country. In Killiney, however, the combination of a steep and rugged landscape with the aspiration to create a semblance of the Mediterranean coastline found greater success, and without wishing to suggest that there is any resemblance between Killiney Bay and the Gulf of Sorrento (an often mentioned comparison), the topography of the hill did lend itself admirably to the desire for Italian allusions and also, perhaps, illusions.

The natural contours of the land provided a basis for an inspiring arrangement of varied planting, transforming the previously bare slopes into a stunningly successful example of man-made landscape gardening on the grand scale. The English eighteenth-century tradition of enhancing the natural topography to provide a foil to the architecture is here utilised to the full, even though there was no overall plan to coordinate and oversee the development. What exists today on Killiney Hill is the remnant of a great estate,

Page 17: Killiney Hill with its crowning obelisk seen from Uplands Road. The hill has been called various names over the past two centuries, Victoria Park, Mount Mapas and Scalp William amongst them.

Left: The entrance to Ayesha Castle, one of the principal houses of Victorian Killiney. The public road now passes under the arch.

Top: The White Rock, Vico Beach.

Above: Bathing ziggurat at Vico Beach, one of the many bathing shelters built around the bay in the 1930s.

with the addition of many villas to produce a splendid blending of rocks, trees, shrubs and houses, which together make a rough hilly terrain into a most habitable place.

The obelisk on the summit is the pivot around which the whole composition circulates. From all locations it identifies this particular hill as clearly from Clontarf and Howth as from the sands below the Vico Road. Although the obelisk at close quarters is rather ugly in detail and proportions - and far inferior to its counterpart in Obelisk Park, Blackrock - from a distance its relationship to the hill looks well balanced, and its steps and pinnacle conclude the landscaping of the hill to perfection. A saddle of parkland joins Killiney Hill to Telegraph Hill. Here is situated the quarry from which came the stone for Kingstown Harbour.

Below the summit the broad sweep of Killiney Bay curves westward to meet the coastline of Dublin Bay at Sorrento Point. The point forms a watershed in the demarcation of the shoreline, with the sandy beaches which run along below Killiney Hill stopping abruptly before the point and giving way to the deep waters of Dalkey Sound. Difficult access has prevented these beaches from becoming as popular and populous as Dollymount, and in fact one could pass above on the Vico Road without being aware that there was a fine stretch of beach directly below the precipitous cliffs, which can only be approached by walkways both above and below the railway embankment.

Of all the journeys which can be made around the bay, the rail journey along this section, poised above the water on the edge of the cliffs, is certainly the most exhilarating. Elsewhere the coast is seen in glimpses, but here, as between Dun Laoghaire and Merrion Gates, one shares the sensation of those early rail travellers of seeming to skim the bay. The element of height above Vico Beach gives this section an added feeling of the limitless expanses of the bay as one levitates along, before a tunnel suddenly cuts off the view.

If one were to single out a particular Victorian housing development anywhere in the area of Dublin Bay to illustrate the nineteenth-century developers' ability to conceive of dramatic location and luxurious living, then Sorrento Terrace must be the most remarkable. This terrace of four-storey houses faces out to sea across Killiney Bay, with the whole eastern coastline fading into the distance. Like the slope of Killiney Hill, this was a barren landscape of rock before it was built on, and it required a great leap of the imagination to consider a speculative development of a residential nature on a windswept cliff as exposed as the Baily Lighthouse on the northern shore. Yet the result was a stunning success and remains one of the most interesting elements of the Victorian development of the bay and a very characteristic fragment of the coast when seen from the sea.

It is part of the character of Killiney that it abounds in houses whose siting is singularly beautiful, and from any point on the beaches below the hill as one looks towards the obelisk, the houses blend into the planting, protruding and receding with angles of roofs, gazebos and garden temples all competing for attention from the viewer in a splendid mixing of the built and the sown.

One of the best-known mid-nineteenth-century views of Dublin Bay is the W. Bartlett steel engraving used to illustrate one of Mr and Mrs S. C. Hall's Irish travel books, and captioned 'from Kingstown Quarries'. This view is taken from an elevated point overlooking the bay, with the characteristic features of the harbour piers dominating the southern coastline. Howth looms darkly on the far side and a distant glimpse of Portmarnock can be seen over the isthmus of Sutton. In the immediate foreground of Bartlett's view is an array of pinnacles of rock, rising in Gothic splendour over the quarry and forming a screen through which the harbour can be seen. These pinnacles and precipices are deeply redolent of the early Victorians' love of the profound in nature and often represent a heightened vision of what the artist has actually observed. The authority of the Romantic poets of the period, too, could be invoked to indulge the passion for chasms, crags, torrents and ruined towers, anything which expressed the brute majesty of nature.

Between the shoreline, defined by housing and ruins (what else?), and the quarry, Bartlett shows a virtual *Arabia deserta*. In this empty landscape of rolling downs, the only feature is a single rugged tower with a row of cabins to the right and another row of larger gabled buildings to the left. This of course is Dalkey village, displaying clearly the essentially linear form of most rural settlements, laid out along a road, and, typically for the period, composed mostly of single-storey thatched cabins. The 1843 Ordnance map of the area, which is roughly contemporary, corroborates the general accuracy of Bartlett's view, but indicates a greater density of housing in the built-up area of the coast and around Dalkey village.

A century and a half later I thought it would be interesting to see what can be observed from the same point as that chosen by Bartlett. Although I had on many occasions drawn the bay from Dalkey Hill and was quite familiar with that view, the idea of working from the exact spot chosen by another artist, and one working in a time influenced by very different sensibilities, struck me as at least holding out the prospect of forming an interesting comparison. In Bartlett's engraving, the points which might be taken as constants, given the Victorian propensity to 'improve' the landscape, are the built rather than the natural features, for the reason that while their proportions may differ from reality their relative positions and relationships are easy to ascertain. Taking the Poolbeg Lighthouse and lining it up with the inside of the elbow on Dun Laoghaire's east pier, as in Bartlett's print, should, I felt, give

Above: The view from Killiney Obelisk, showing Sorrento Point, Dalkey Island (with St Begnet's Church and Martello tower, and the Muglins behind), the Wishing Stone, the tip of Boucher's Obelisk, and in the distance, Bray Head on the right.

Below: Looking north from Killiney Obelisk towards Telegraph Hill with Howth Head on the horizon and the Poolbeg Lighthouse on the extreme left.

*Bullock Harbour at low tide. The rounded stonework of the harbour mouth is
particularly notable. Beyond, to the left, is the east pier of Dun Laoghaire Harbour,
berth for the Sealink Ferry and for the largest fleet of yachts in the country.*

me the position from which to compare the landscape as it exists now with the mid-nineteenth century version.

This simple principle proved to be less easy to execute than I had anticipated. I quickly established my north-south axis for the drawing, but finding the correct altitude was a more difficult matter. The cliff of the quarry is quite vertical on its north-facing side and I found myself clambering over the cliff face below the tower on Telegraph Hill, seeking my observation point. Armed with drawing equipment, binoculars and a volume containing Bartlett's print, I descended from above, ascended from below, edged along ledges, hung from branches of saplings with a precarious foothold in the vertical cliff, squatted on slippery slopes - and all to no avail. Yes, Poolbeg Lighthouse and the east pier aligned themselves perfectly, and the gabled houses of Dalkey related correctly to the mass of Bullock Castle on the coast. Sandycove and Dalkey Martello towers also maintained their correct positions as in Bartlett's view. But after that, artistic licence took over. Proportion and position in Bartlett's view appear to have been seriously affected by the virus of grandiosity.

The problem is that his view is a synthetic one, based on the requirement of producing an accurate drawing of a particular landscape which must not only correspond to what exists but also fit into a set format - the plate size of the book it was intended to illustrate. Howth, in fact, lay outside the confines of the picture, so this had to be moved into a more favourable position and much enlarged in height to make it look more convincing. The fantastic frieze of pinnacles in the foreground of the print appear to be largely imaginary, a very splendid rendering of the rather more prosaic forms of this particular cliff face. Bartlett's view is an improvement on the reality, a fitting synthesis of the parts into a more romantic version of itself.

My view, done from a position half way up the cliff, represents the same material as Bartlett's without the 'improvements'. The greatest currently visible difference is the infilling with housing of the entire plain and foothills up to the very mouth of the quarry. Also, the maturing of much of the planting of the last century has filled in the view with a great deal of vegetation. The bay appears to have got smaller - as of course it has - because of a massive enlargement in the size of Bull Island since 1840, quadrupling its length, as well as the growth of the port continually eastwards, and the infilling of the shoreline of Clontarf, Ringsend and Sandymount.

The only fragment of open landscape visible in Bartlett's view and still to be seen is a small scrap of open space at the base of The Metals - the paved route for the transport of the quarried stone down to the site of the harbour. The quarry has thus far resisted any manicuring hand, and seems an anomaly among the trimmed lawns and fragrant shrubberies formed out of what was rock and agricultural land in the not too distant past. As late as the 1950s, this same view showed much open land preserved by the existence of big houses. Now, development has absorbed all this land and in some cases - as in the housing scheme above Bullock - seems to be aspiring to a Hong Kong-like density of occupation. Probably this is preferable to the alternative of the city spreading ever outward until it reaches Clonmacnoise and ceases to have any meaningful form.

Two of the group of castles which were a notable feature of Dalkey in the medieval period have survived, one, Archbold's Castle, as an antiquity and the other, Goat Castle, as the Town Hall. In the nineteenth century their precise age was a source of remarkably wild and wide-ranging speculation. In J. J. Gaskin's *Varieties of Irish History*, published in 1869, a poem is included in which the poet speculates on the probable age of the historic ruins. The decrepit figures of Time, Fame and Oblivion are encountered, apparently in the Main Street, and questioned concerning the

The panoramic view from Killiney Beach, stretching from the obelisk on the top of Killiney Hill to Dalkey Island. The variegated nature of the landscape of this area makes it particularly attractive, with its exciting combination of woodland, formal planting, architecture and wilderness.

origin of these ruins. They are less than communicative and the author comes to the conclusion that the towers may antedate the Danes, a margin of error of at least five hundred years. The description of Oblivion is so striking that I was constantly on the look out for him in Dalkey.

I saw OBLIVION step from stone to stone.
His ancient vest the twisting ivy bound,
His oblong chin the wild-moss crept around.
Jealous and sour his looks, I could descry
Disdain and anger flash from either eye.

Unlike any other part of the bay, the area between Dalkey and Dun Laoghaire enjoys a mythology which writers have woven around it. From the strange twilight world of Flann O'Brien to the more tangible creations of James Joyce and L.A.G. Strong, there is a world other than that seen by the casual passer-by. No other part of the bay has been so lovingly worked over and recreated. The innocent lump of stone which lies on the Vico Beach, the White Rock, and the Sandycove Martello on the shoreline of Scotsman's Bay have been invested with a significance quite apart from their ordinary existence. Both Strong and Joyce describe early twentieth-century Kingstown in careful and minute detail, writing about approximately the same places and period. Like the different sides of a contemporary stereoscopic photograph of the same object, the two views between them present a durable and tangible picture of life in pre-First World War Kingstown. It is surprising in how many ways things have not altered a great deal, and how traditions and habits prevail.

Coliemore Harbour lies tucked into the base of the hill of Killiney, separated from the bay by the rugged outline of Dalkey Island and protected by it from high winds and storms. Between the mainland and the island runs the deep channel of St Begnet's or Dalkey Sound. The deep water of the sound once provided harbour facilities for ships unable to negotiate their way into the Liffey. In the nineteenth century, proposals were made to enclose this area as a deepwater harbour, an alternative to constructing a harbour at Dun Laoghaire. Although not now used by ocean-going shipping, the passage of Dalkey Sound once provided a short-cut to the open sea and was used even by the B&I mailboat as its approach to Kingstown. L.A.G. Strong in his novel *The Garden* describes the image of the B&I ship making its way through the narrow declivity of the sound, in the early years of this century.

A faint cheer of welcome came from the houses above the shore, handkerchiefs and white napkins began to be waved from the windows, as the boat, looking huge and noble in the narrow channel, came past the point and breasted her way down the sound. The cheering grew, the waving doubled, then as she came fairly under the houses, a faint plume leaped from beside her funnel, and there rang out the stately, musical note known to all along the coast, her answer to the welcome. Three times it sounded, three long, full blasts, filling the space between shore and shore, leaping from hill to hill, peopling the lazy afternoon with echoes.

Nothing so dramatic passes through Dalkey Sound today. It is a region of small boats, fishing craft and pleasure craft. The diminutive harbour, and its neighbour Bullock, are idyllic sanctuaries of the personal and the accessible. There is a sense of quiet and tranquility in the small span of water enclosed by the gently curving walls of both these harbours, and they are protected by their smallness from the avaricious scrutiny of development proposals. The brash and flamboyant, so much in evidence in Dun Laoghaire, are out of keeping here where the activities and traditions of the local fishermen still prevail in the midst of conspicuous wealth and a burgeoning

*Sorrento Terrace and Sorrento Point
from the heights above, with the battery on
Dalkey Island between the Martello tower and the sea.*

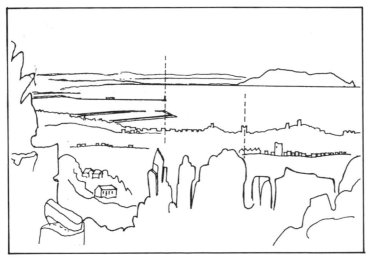

Above: 'Dublin Bay from Kingstown Quarry', a redrawing of Bartlett's mid-nineteenth-century view showing the changes which have taken place since then.

Left: Diagram based on Bartlett's steel engraving.

Above: Busy traffic in Dalkey Sound on a Sunday afternoon, with the launch Ingot *bringing sightseers from Dun Laoghaire.*

Below: November day at Sorrento Point with a lone yacht passing the Muglins.

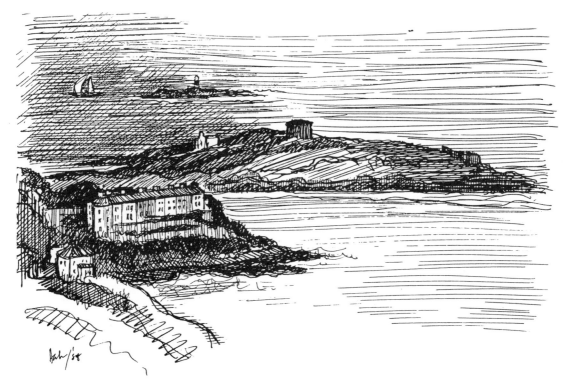

population.

Killiney and Dalkey are characterised by a lushness, the product of generations of planting and only barely controlled wilderness. Behind high walls are grouped some of the most interesting nineteenth-century houses on the bay, lavishly sited and overlooking the sweep of Killiney Bay, a location as magnificent as many in the Mediterranean. A landscape such as this can only be produced by time and the conscious fostering of varied planting. From the top of the hill both towards Bray and inland, the changes which have been wrought almost overnight are dramatic - not because so much has been built so quickly to provide much sought-after housing, but because of the impossibility of estates, laid out like the grid of a roll of chicken wire, ever being able to develop and mature to provide a visually rich and interesting environment. Much of the landscape around Sorrento Point has the merit of being a product of chance and inspiration. These are the criteria which await most opportunities for development in the environment of the bay. On the flat plains of Ballybrack the chance element has far less potential than on the hills of Howth and Killiney, yet the same bland approach is to be found in both places, as though they shared the same physical conditions.

Killiney and Dalkey Hills which formed the demesne of Killiney Castle, are now the only areas of open land, other than cabbage-patch parks along the coast, on the southern shore of the bay. This mixture of woods, open parkland, sheer rock face and gorse-covered slopes is in total contrast to the upland heaths of Howth Head. The sense of the demesne lingers even after a century of being a public park, so strong is the concept of nature simultaneously organised and let go wild. This is the ideal park, the product of at least two hundred and fifty years of human effort. In today's immediate terms its history covers the emergence of the entire modern world from before the Industrial Revolution to the present, a

Top: Rock climbers training in Dalkey quarry, which provides sheer cliffs within easy access of the city.

Above: Evening at Bullock Harbour, with boats returning from a day's sea fishing. Above the harbour looms the shape of Bullock Castle, built by the Cistercian monks in the twelfth century to protect the harbour.

Right: Coliemore Harbour in Dalkey Sound, a haven for small boats, and the point from which trips may be made to Dalkey Island.

rather daunting span of time. This is the timescale necessary to produce an area as rich in variety and plant life as Killiney Hill. For the bay to be a fruitful place in which people may pleasurably live generations hence, a look into the long-term future is a prerequisite for making the Killineys of the future some adequate mirror of the Killiney of today.

Dun Laoghaire

Left: Between the lighthouses at the mouth of the harbour, and seen through a screen of yacht masts, is the Sealink ferry, St Columba, *and in the distance, the Hill of Howth.*

Above: Across the span of Scotsman's Bay a cannon points at the Martello and is the sort of armament, usually a 24-pounder, which would have been positioned there.

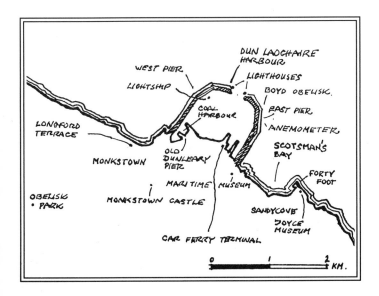

LIKE A CHARACTER in a nineteenth-century Russian play, Dun Laoghaire's existence and history are complicated by a succession of patronymics, separated by time yet overlapping geographically and chronologically. From a submerged beginning as a unnamed part of the parish of Monkstown, the place emerges as Dunlary, graduating to Dunleary, a village of a few houses and a small fishing harbour, before achieving apotheosis as Kingstown. This pose was held for a century before it metamorphosed into a variant of its former self, purged of imperial allusion yet royalist still, the new allegiance being to the memory of an earlier monarch. The final designation as Dun Laoghaire, fort of the High King Laoghaire (Leary), seems to be the lasting one.

While the geographic location on the south shore of Dublin Bay which was the eighteenth-century fishing village merely elided from one naming to another without ceasing to be the place it had been on the previous day, the change of naming had a profound influence on perceptions of the place. Over the course of some two hundred years the whole coalesced into a complex and interlocking series of interrelationships, broadly enclosed in the latest name in the sequence. For all this change, some of the original personality is still to be found.

The essence of Dun Laoghaire is its harbour, the visual, geographic and organisational core of the borough. Within the majestic granite embrace of the harbour is a sheet of water larger than the medieval city of Dublin, but, unlike that settlement which was hemmed in by slob land, the Liffey and the Poddle, Dun Laoghaire's harbour has been from its beginnings unaffected by constricting surroundings. It is at the point where the west pier touches the land that the original village was located, and a fragment of the pier of this settlement was included within the waters of the new harbour. What remains of the original village today is a single row of two-storey houses back-

ing on to the bay and wedged between the mass of later periods - high Victorian Longford Terrace on the west side and low twentieth-century on the east, the banalities of a filling station. This row of buildings might well be a section of the main street of any rural Irish country town. The façades are simple, a rhythmical arrangement of doors and windows, with arches leading to stores at the rear. Above plain plastered walls, the roofs run in a straight line, regularly marked by chimneys. It is not difficult to complete the picture with a corresponding other side to the street and an offshoot leading down to the harbour. There are myriads of similar places all over the country where time has stood still and the initial development has proved to be the ultimate one.

Not so for Dunleary, for time was developing a momentum at the end of the Georgian era which would sweep this area, and the fishing village with it, into the position of the fastest-growing town in Ireland, and one of the most important. The author of the *Post Chaise Companion*, a mile-by-mile guide to the Irish countryside, writing in 1813, takes his readers along the coast from Dublin towards Bray, pausing at everything he considers worthy of interest. Monkstown and Dalkey are mentioned and described, but Dunleary is not - a measure of the great change which was to take place by the middle of the century. This was written of course before the new harbour was begun, although there had been a stone pier and cove at the village since 1767. Evidently this did not impress the compilers of the directory sufficiently to warrant mention.

With the creation of this maritime city-state on the outskirts of Dublin, the old hegemony of the Viking establishment was for the first time broken, and the bones of Greater Dublin, as it now exists, began to be laid out. There had been a gradual tendency since the beginning of the city's existence to expand both northwards, on the far bank of the river Liffey, and more significantly, eastwards, in the direction of the bay and the sea

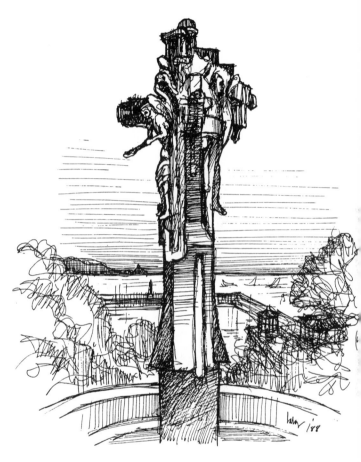

Left: The National Maritime Museum of Ireland. Amongst the major exhibits are the longboat from the frigate Résolue, *part of the French expedition which sailed into Bantry Bay in 1796. Wolfe Tone was on board the* Indomitable, *another ship of the fleet. Also on prominent display is the optic or reflecting light from the Baily Lighthouse, which was installed there in 1902 and worked for seventy years. It has a candle power of 2,000,000.*

Above: The extraordinary bronze sculpture of Christ The King by Andrew O'Connor which overlooks the harbour.

coast. With the establishment of an important residential and transport centre at a remove from the city towards the south-east, the balance was changed, and the gradual development of the areas in between was merely a matter of time. Kingstown became the first significant link with elements of the modern world, where the concepts of speed, convenience, transport and fresh air supplanted the concerns of the old city, centered on Castle, Parliament and trade.

The combination of optimum timing, advanced technology, economic growth and an appropriate architectural idiom coincided to produce the marvel of Victorian Ireland.

The nineteenth century begins with the two major problems which had beset Dublin for centuries still unresolved, although they were to be so within a generation. These problems were the silting tendency of the port, making it inaccessible to ships of any depth of draught, and secondly the absence of a safe and deep harbour for the mailboat and for shipping caught in stormy weather. The first of these problems was solved with the completion of the Bull walls which enclosed the channel and caused it to deepen itself by the process of self scouring. The second was resolved in favour of building a packet harbour at Howth and a post road from there to Dublin. The road was a success but the harbour proved to be a disaster, silting up before its construction was even complete. Howth's disadvantage was Dunleary's opportunity, and those propagandists who claimed that the Howth project would fail were shown to have been correct. Howth Harbour was begun in 1807 and completed in 1818. A mere sixteen years later, in 1834, the packet service was transferred to Dunleary.

A further problem, and one which concerned the ordinary citizen quite as much as the traders of the city, was the horrifying loss of life and property occurring in and around the bay from the wrecking of ships unable to sail into the Liffey,

and at risk because of the dangerous nature of the coast and the presence of sandbanks. The list of ships wrecked within or near the bay during the nineteenth century makes an impressive toll of disasters, and the accounts of survivors as well as eye witnesses from the shore make harrowing

Left: The beautiful neo-Egyptian mausoleum which houses the Anemometer, a device to check the wind speeds in the bay. Built in 1855, it is one of the most perfect of Dun Laoghaire's many architectural gems.

Left below: Isis on the east pier! More strange Egyptianesque structures on the shores of Scotsman's Bay, built as bathing shelters in the 1930s but looking more like the necropolis on the Nile.

Below: Sandycove in January. The bleak and empty sea becomes thronged with sails during the summer season. The James Joyce Museum in the Martello tower is the dominant feature of the headland.

reading. Something had to be done, and given the sense of public spirit in the period and the availability of limitless Government funds, what was done was done splendidly.

Between 1817 and the middle of the century when the enormous undertaking of the harbour was completed, an army of men and wagons was used to move the stone for the construction of the piers of Dun Laoghaire Harbour. From above Dun Laoghaire the slope of the hill runs down from Killiney Obelisk towards the sea, with the gentle curve of the rock suddenly interrupted by a great rectangular bite out of the surface, scarring the smooth fall of the landscape. Here the granite for the harbour was quarried, then cut, transported and chiselled to produce some of the finest stonework to be seen around the bay - indeed, this

work became the major architectural feature of the bay. Though a great feat of engineering, it is as architecture that such phenomena as Kingstown Harbour have to be regarded. It demands to be taken seriously on an aesthetic level, and not seen as merely functional. We do not speak of the Pont du Garde or the Colosseum as Roman engineering despite the very evident non-residential and functional nature of these structures.

Kingstown Harbour is an architectural monument no less impressive than anything the eighteenth century has to offer. It is not just the strength and size of the harbour which impresses, but also the quality of the masonry and the manner in which the details of the finishing have a thought-out appearance, the work of stonemasons and designers well versed in the capacity and unique possibilities of stone.

From the beginning, the new Kingstown Harbour was a success, and when the railway, Ireland's first, joined it to the city in 1834, the social potential of the area took a path of development which is still continuing - the colonising of the piers of the harbour as places of recreation, although they were constructed for more practical concerns. Indeed, it can be said that all the great recreational features of Dublin Bay are those designed by engineers for functional needs, or are the few surviving fragments of natural topography.

By the late nineteenth century the harbour was firmly established in the social calendar and in 1894 in *The Real Charlotte*, Somerville and Ross wrote

> The Kingstown people walk there because there is nothing else to be done at Kingstown, and the Dublin people come down to snatch what they can of the sea air before the short afternoons darken and the hour arrives when they look out for members of the St. George's Yacht Club to take them in to tea.

Top: The delicate form of the bandstand on the east pier, forever a reminder of the colourful life of regimental bands and naval activity in the harbour.

Above: The bandstand has a corresponding shelter for the listeners, poised like a pagoda on the edge of the pier.

Above: This lightship is now used as a base for the Sea Scouts in Dun Laoghaire. The Commissioners of Irish Lights, who maintain all the lighthouses around the coast, have two other similar lightships in service off the coasts of Co. Down and Co. Wexford.

At all hours of the day, and late into the evening, strollers promenade on the east pier of Dun Laoghaire, as they have done for a century and a half, with crowds on Sunday afternoons and solitary walkers communing with the moonlight after dark. The east pier attracts on a number of levels - physical, social, aesthetic, and perhaps more subliminally, spiritual. For the majority of those strolling on the granite sweeps of the harbour, the experience is a renewing one, an antidote to the pressures and inhumanities of daily life. Such facilities allow the people of a congested urban area to breathe and not just in the physical sense.

Although less frequented than the east pier, the western arm of the harbour provides the counterpoint to the more vigorous voice of the former. This is the resort of anglers, whose characteristic silhouettes can be observed daily, poised along the top of the breakwater at the end of the pier, patiently waiting for a catch. They are so still and regularly placed that one might mistake this line of figures for sculpted replicas of human anglers, the only difference between one day's sighting and another being that the number does change.

Dun Laoghaire is a place of *things*, and nowhere around Dublin Bay can there be such a remarkable variety of objects to look at where the craftsmanship and level of interest is so high. The piers of the harbour are themselves punctuated by a rich sprinkling of these phenomena, memorials to the heroism, follies and foibles of past generations. Each is an essay in an appropriate architectural language. Between them the Boyd obelisk and the Anemometer represent the nineteenth-century's striving to create its own mythology and finding an apt image for the need. The bandstand and its attendant shelter represent the faded glory of the days when regimental bands entertained the citizens of Ireland's premier township on Sunday afternoons, when the sun had not yet set on the Imperial consciousness of

Blustery weather over Scotsman's Bay. The spires of Dun Laoghaire's churches form a satisfying relief to the low-lying landscape and small-scale architecture of Victorian Kingstown.

the day. The two lighthouses, at the bottom of each pier, are themselves splendid examples of the superb stonework which characterised the period of their construction. The lighthouse proper is on the east pier, surrounded by the protective wall of the harbour battery; that on the west is the answering light, but its detailing is a joyous example of stonework, splendid for its own sake. Placed like a chessman on the end of the pier, you have to get fairly close to it in order to observe how the smaller of the two lights has been compensated for its more diminutive size. The slender pillar of granite masonry which supports the lantern stands on three concentric steps which gradually widen the circle, until at its base it suddenly fans out over almost the entire area of the end of the pier into the most splendid radiating circles of granite paving. On the seaward side the paving meets the wall, which also follows the line of the lighthouse, and appropriately this wall curves round towards the town, ending in a smooth round surface. Unfortunately, in the electrification of the lighthouse two crude channels have been cut through the fan pavement, at variance with the radii of the circle.

The piers look at each other across a short strip of sea. In James Joyce's *Ulysses*, the facetious Stephen Daedalus is teaching a class at a private school in Dalkey. He asks the children a riddle to pass the time, baffling their disinterested minds.

Tell me now, Stephen said, poking the boy's shoulder with the book, what is a pier.

He answers it himself.

Kingstown pier, Stephen said. Yes, a disappointed bridge.

Amongst the many interesting *things* in Dun Laoghaire are some which are more than they seem. The Martello tower at Sandycove and the Mariners' Church on Haig Terrace provide star-

tling contrasts of current usage and original intent. The dining tables of comfortable middle class citizens of the nineteenth century were laden with silverware, and had the necessary and appropriate container for everything. The squat

Below: The spiral staircase which connects the interior rooms of the tower.

Right below: 'In the gloomy domed livingroom of the tower Buck Mulligan's gowned form moved briskly about the hearth to and fro, hiding and revealing its yellow glow.' The room where Joyce, Gogarty and Trench slept and in which claustrophobia must have been endemic. It now houses the Joyce family photographs, with the museum proper housed in the rooms below.

round condiment sets of the period graced every table in the land - and what does one do when a dragon appears at the end of the garden? Grab the salt cellar of course! The threat of a Napoleonic invasion galvanised the War Office in London into dealing with the threatened dragon, and what did they decide to do? Place stone salt and pepper sets all along the threatened coasts of England and Ireland to ward off the invader, and the Martello tower at Sandycove came into being as part of these dragonian measures.

The invasion never occurred and the towers which appear periodically around Dublin Bay were not called upon to use their guns. They have stood abandoned and deteriorating for so long that despite their strong construction it is remarkable that so many have survived. Some, in an ecstasy of despair, just slid into the sea, others were removed to clear a path for the railway or for some improvement such as the People's Park, and a few just languished. The Sandycove tower became a museum and archive of the memorabilia of James Joyce in 1962 and is an object lesson in the admirable re-use of an impor-

'*Solemnly he came forward and mounted the round gunrest. He faced about and blessed gravely thrice the tower, the surrounding country and the awakening mountains.*' This platform is the stage set for the opening of Ulysses, and visiting it one can appreciate how precise are Joyce's descriptions. The central platform had a pivot, and supported between this and the iron rail which runs around the wall was a tressel upon which the cannon was able to traverse 360 degrees, during the period between 1804 and 1900 when the tower was a battery.

tant yet redundant piece of architecture.

This museum forms the hub of a different level of consciousness from the prevailing marine associations of Dun Laoghaire, and is the only physical proof of the continued literary associations which the area has had in abundance from the beginning of the literary revival in the late Victorian era to the present. The Joyce Museum shows what might be done elsewhere.

Remarkably, Dun Laoghaire has another museum also re-using a redundant building in a perfectly appropriate way. Tucked away in a quiet street above the harbour is the National Maritime Museum, filling a Gothic Revival church with relics of the country's often heroic struggle with the sea. If the Joyce museum is devoted to *objects d'art*, the Maritime Museum's concern is with *objects trouvés* - sea wrack and relics of ships lost, of lives gone down in the deep and the bravery and ingenuity of the captains and crews of everything from the Great Eastern to lifeboats and currachs.

Within the museum the basic structure of the nineteenth-century church has been overlaid with models, pictures, remains and information of most of the principal trends in the maritime history of the previous two centuries. The atmosphere is that of a temple to some vanished race. Under the chancel arch of the church with the tall lancet windows shedding sunlight on the display, rotates the optic of the Baily Lighthouse. The slow and rhythmic turning of this maze of prisms flashes beams of reflected light across the space and transforms what might be merely a reliquary of vanquished seamen into a magical interior of glazed containers, each of which reveals some stage in the long history of ships and of the sea.

Passing from the enclave of museums at the eastern side of Dun Laoghaire, the promenade runs behind and above the water thronged with yachts and the three most handsome of the bay's yacht clubs distributed along the shoreline of the harbour. These three buildings, representing dif-

Top: Longford Terrace, Monkstown, with the spires of St Patrick's and the Moorish Gothic turret of St Mary's beneath the mountains.

Above: The west pier lighthouse, another lovely piece of Victorian marine architecture, rarely without the company of some anglers.

ferent facets of classical inspiration, established a trend which lamentably died with them, to be resurrected a century later by the sole example of Howth Yacht Club. In Dun Laoghaire the most recent addition to the existing trinity of clubs, the Motor Yacht Club, shows no recognition of the fine tradition which exists, architecturally, in the harbour. The much smaller lookout station of the RNLI, in contrast, has been designed with great care, as though it were not concerned purely with saving life at sea.

The richness of Dun Laoghaire's architectural past needs enhancing, not the opposite, but frequently it is the latter which occurs. When the harbours of Howth and Dunleary were being considered in the early years of the nineteenth-century, the quality of the harbour facilities was what people were concerned with. It could be taken for granted that the works would be constructed of stone and to workmanship of a high standard, although occasions arose to query these

aspects when the work was in progress. Today one can have no such assurance that new structures will be built to such high standards, and there is much cause for trepidation when some new scheme is announced. When the public is alarmed and the officials complacent, the signs are that all is not well.

Plans have been discussed for some years for the development of a yachting marina within the piers of Dun Laoghaire harbour, and a number of schemes have been made public, to be greeted with dismay by those who use the harbour as a place to walk and experience the sea air. Despite universal car ownership, the advent of universal boat ownership can be seen to be a very unlikely event. The marina is therefore a boating and mooring facility for only a minority of the many thousands who walk on the piers every day of the year. With the first marina will come the second and the third until the entire area of the harbour has become a series of pontoons with the mass of

Above: The outer coal harbour, with a small fleet of trawlers berthed at Traders' Wharf.

Below: The harbour of Dun Laoghaire encloses 100 hectares of water, and is protected by two piers, the east 1070 metres long, and the west 1500 metres. Begun in 1817, it was finished in 1842, and was one of the largest man-made harbours in the world. Killiney Hill with its obelisk, the Sugarloaf and the Dublin Mountains form the backdrop to the harbour.

yachts which a large marina will inevitably attract. At that point, the aesthetic destruction of the harbour interior will be complete, the greatest harbour of the Victorian age will have been relegated to the status of parking facility of the yacht clubs, and public access will be greatly diminished.

There is a challenge to be seen here and it has been at least partially answered by one of the proposals for development, that which places the marina to the west of the west pier, outside the old harbour. The challenge is in the designing of a new marina which would take the existing standard of excellence in the original Kingstown Harbour as its point of departure. Anything new in the area of the Dun Laoghaire Harbour which does not accept the existence of an admirable beginning threatens to cannibalise and destroy the chief glory of Dublin Bay.

Civic pride oozes through the joints in the masonry of Dun Laoghaire Town Hall, as it does from most of the public buildings of the Victorian period. The predominant style of architecture of the southern shore of Dublin Bay eloquently expresses the Victorian concern with the improvement of their area in the terraces which run along the shore from Dun Laoghaire to Blackrock and

Dun Laoghaire Harbour under a heavy fog, with a single intrepid boat preparing to sail. The spires of the churches, characteristic from any angle, become accentuated in the miasma of the fog.

in the residential squares and terraces which mount the hill behind the township. Houses arranged in rows are the *modus operandi* of nineteenth-century Kingstown, and their stucco façades form pleasing links between the various schemes which were developed from the mid-century for the gentry and traders migrating from the congestion and filth of the city.

The house form of the eighteenth century, the four-storey brick terrace, became the basis for all the domestic developments in Kingstown, with a gloss of South-of-England watering places in the introduction of Regency stucco. This form of terrace and plastered façade is still the unifying feature of much of the southern coast of the bay and gives it an overall cohesion without diminishing its individuality. Monkstown and Blackrock developed in the same manner, the nucleus of a village street becoming surrounded by the squares of the more affluent residents. This line of Victorian expansion has left the area devoid of open spaces, with the exception of bits of coastline, small squares and the harbour piers, all the more precious for the absence of open land. Public parks are few and on the pocket-handkerchief scale, demonstrating the importance of not letting the same thing occur on the far side of the bay on the Hill of Howth.

But for Dun Laoghaire there is always the sea and the life it contains. The power of the bay is more evident here than almost anywhere else, and as an immense marine park it rivals the human occupation of the shore for diversity and continual movement. The many species of birds attracted by the ideal overwintering sites and feeding areas on the shore populate the entire circumference of the bay with teeming activity, and the waters, despite shipping and pollution, have not ceased to be a thriving habitat for fish and shellfish. The seats along the outer side of the breakwater on the east pier provide a opportunity to sit quietly and contemplate the sea and the gulls that wheel over Scotsman's Bay. The sighting of seals is not unusual. They loll in the water, scrutinising the watchers on the shore and staring with apparent intent as though they recognised a face among the crowd or perhaps attracted by a child's wave. As he leaves the Martello tower at Sandycove for the last time, Stephen Daedalus is attracted by a sound from the shore.

A voice, sweettoned and sustained, called to him from the sea. Turning the curve he waved his hand. It called again. A sleek brown head, a seal's, far out on the water, round.

Longford Terrace, old Dunleary.

Seapoint to Sandymount

In Carrickbrennan Graveyard, Monkstown, there is a small monument on the right of the entrance, commemorating the heroism of the captain and five crewmen of HMS *Ajax*, which went to the rescue of the brig *Neptune* off the east pier of Kingstown Harbour in 1861. This monument is decorated on the top by an immensely evocative broken mast with a rope coiled around its base, and below this is a *bas-relief* of three seamen in sailor suits, hauling on a rope played out to a tiny barque floundering in the waves. From behind, another man with a coiled rope comes to join them, and the location is identified by the presence in the background of the east pier lighthouse.

Two of the worst shipping disasters to occur in Dublin Bay took place around Seapoint in the winter of 1807 when the packet *Prince of Wales* and the transport ship *Rochdale* were driven on to the coast between Seapoint and Blackrock and totally wrecked with the loss of hundreds of lives. These disasters hastened the decision to build the asylum harbour at Kingstown and the provision of a refuge for shipping caught by difficult conditions in the bay. The tranquil shoreline of Seapoint nowadays appears to be far removed from this kind of shipping tragedy.

The Martello of Seapoint acts as a nucleus for an area of bathing and water sports and whatever the weather it has, like the Fortyfoot at Sandycove, its group of intrepid bathers braving the icy waters. On a scorching summer's afternoon the narrow space around the tower swarms with life, the cacophony of radios, children and dogs all blending into the nimbus of sound which surrounds the tower. Offshore, the graceful and often apparently pilotless sailboards angle their way across the water, bright colours rising and dipping, travelling effortlessly on the surface of the sea. Farther out the speedboats and water skiers add to the activity and the noise, making this tiny fragment of shoreline one of the most intensely packed when the weather beckons.

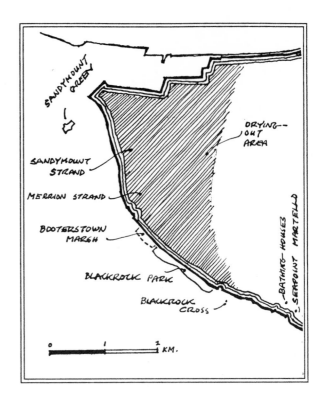

Page 51: The Martello tower at Seapoint and the bathing place, sympathetically connected by curving ramps and walls. Seen on a February day, the area is never without a few intrepid swimmers or sailboarders. In the background is the Poolbeg electricity station and a section of the Great South Wall, ending with the Poolbeg Lighthouse.

Right: Booterstown Marsh from behind the DART Station, with the embankment of the railway separating it from the waters of the bay. A good place for spotting birdwatchers and also to see mallard, moorhen, snipe and many waders and seabirds who either feed, roost or breed in the marsh.

Above Seapoint the façades of stucco march past with regimental precision - a product of the age of maritime victories commemorated in their name, Trafalgar Terrace. Another and earlier memory is marked by the name Monkstown, which covers the whole area from Dun Laoghaire to Blackrock. The Cistercian monks who came here in the wake of the Norman conquest established a castle, remnants of which still stand at Castle Park on Carricbrennan Road. There never was a monastery in Monkstown, but the castle served as a grange or out-farm of the immensely rich and important St Mary's Abbey on the north bank of the Liffey within the city of Dublin. At Monkstown Castle, the monks farmed extensively - commemorated in the area now called Monkstown Farm - and ran a fishery at Bullock Harbour. The produce of the farm was used both in the abbey and for trade. The Cistercians held their lands in Monkstown for nearly four hundred years until the dissolution of the monasteries under Henry VIII. Subsequently, the land passed

Below: A modern steel-sheet sculpture reflects the forms of sails on the bay and behind it the west pier of Dun Laoghaire Harbour. The three 'spires' are, from the left, the Customs Building in the coal harbour, the Town Hall and the mid-Victorian St Michael's Church.

Right: Seapoint in August. One of the worst of many shipwrecks in the bay occurred here in November 1807, when the Rochdale *was driven on the rocks with the loss of 265 lives – the entire crew and passengers of the ship.*

into secular private ownership, and remained an estate until the nineteenth century.

The Early Christian cross which stands on the main street of Blackrock may indicate the existence of an ecclesiastical settlement in that area also. If this is the case, no records or remains exist to substantiate the possibility other then a holy well on the east of the town which is not in itself either dateable or necessarily of any great antiquity. By the beginning of the eighteenth century the area had become established as a popular bathing place, and substantial houses were built along the coast. These have given their names to parts of Blackrock - those of the Duchess of Leinster at Frescati and Lord Cloncurry at Maretimo being among the more notable. A beautiful late nineteenth-century pastoral painting by William Ashford, entitled 'A Carriage passing Frescati', gives a glimpse of Blackrock in its heyday, as a quarter for the country houses of noblemen. In this picture a coach-and-four, painted a bright yellow, dash down a country road, with the entrances to villas on one side. Great trees overshadow the scene, with cattle and

drovers in the roadway. Some of the substantial houses are still to be found in Blackrock, others have vanished to be replaced by modern housing or supermarkets, so intense is the pressure for land in the area. Yet there is still a village atmosphere about its streets once the main highway has been left behind.

An interesting proposal, which predates the development of the railways, was the idea of constructing a navigational canal along the coastline from the old harbour at Dunleary to the recently completed Grand Canal Docks in the city. Seapoint, Blackrock and Booterstown would all have been affected by this plan and seaside villas would hardly have been built had the scheme been carried out. The railway, built for trade, quickly transformed itself into a public transport system. The canal scheme would have lacked this adaptability, and as there were not sufficient backers for the scheme it was quickly abandoned.

The railway track runs straight towards the city, cutting off the foreshore of Blackrock and Booterstown and leaving loops in the coast which

Sandymount Strand from the Martello to the edge of Irishtown. The Three Rock Mountain with its TV beacons looms behind and the tower of St Vincent's Hospital rises on Merrion Road. The Dublin Mountains appear to emerge from directly behind the houses, although a considerable spread of suburbs lies between them.

were still tidal pools after the building of the embankment to carry the track. One of these pools has become Blackrock Park, the other Booterstown Marsh.

Originally called Butters Town, this small portion of marshland, now hemmed in on all sides, is a fairly sad spectacle. On the north and south it has the Rock Road and the DART track as its boundaries, and east and west a tarmac car park and office buildings. Yet in the midst of all this is an important bird sanctuary, under the control of An Taisce. Booterstown can hardly compare with the much larger and better protected North Bull Island reserve directly opposite, but it is important as the only surviving fragment of the salt marshes which were common along the southern coast of the bay, a habitat for snipe, moorhen, mallard and other birds, as well as a variety of sedges and grasses. At present the whole area is under threat from a planning scheme to build a road overpass above and through the marsh, a scheme which could disturb the wildlife sufficiently to destroy the marsh as a breeding ground, without actually relieving the traffic congestion, but rather exacerbating it. The birds of Dublin Bay are not so hard-pressed for a breeding area that they will choose to nest under a flyover.

From Seapoint, when the tide is out, it is possible to walk to Irishtown or across to the Poolbeg side of the shore. This is a rich hunting ground for bait diggers, and their stooped forms are to be seen dotted out over the sands, excavating for worms. This inner area, or rather what remains of it, has been for centuries the closest place for sea bathing to the city, and still remains a popular resort for those who live nearby, but now more for walking, horse riding, jogging and cycling than for taking to the waters, particularly the closer the sands are to the city. Of those traditional pastimes which have over many generations been an attractive source of sustenance and relaxation in the bay, the one which has totally disappeared is the gathering of 'cockles and

Below: Sailboarding off the west pier at Dun Laoghaire. Sailboarding and water skiing are very popular in this shallow corner of the Bay.

Right: Sandymount Green on a hot July afternoon. The bust of W.B.Yeats is by the railings under the trees.

Right below: Villa by James Gandon. This little house, sited on Strand Road at an angle to the shore line, has a stupendous prospect of the entire bay looking directly towards the horizon. It was built by Gandon for the artist William Ashford, an important landscape painter. The house is now part of the headquarters of the Rehabilitation Centre (Rehab).

mussels, alive alive oh', much associated with Dublin. These shellfish are still to be found there, but nobody eats them now, and probably there is no better gauge of water purity in the bay than when it again becomes possible to eat shellfish taken from its waters. The cockle and oyster beds indicated on the eighteenth-century maps have disappeared, but it should be possible to restock them if the water conditions were adequate.

Strand Road suggests by its name something recreational, with seaside villas lining a promenade. To some degree this is the case and certainly was so in the past, the road forming the perimeter of Sandymount and concealing the existence of a village with its green surrounded by houses, an enclave of Victorian calm. However, since the construction of the toll bridge across the Liffey at nearby Alexandra Road, the traffic to the port coming from the south takes this route, along with all the commuter traffic which flows across the bridge - convenient for the commuters, yet destructive for those residents of the houses on the front. The dilemma of what to do with all the cars in a city not built to accommodate the traffic requirements of today besets this area as it does many other parts of the city. The choice appears to be between the expensive solution of building an underground rail system, thus relieving the traffic congestion, as has been done in other cities with evident success, and a cheaper, more piecemeal answer of wider and wider roads, destroying more and more urban and residential areas. Dublin, unfortunately, has opted for the above-ground solution, allowing the fabric of the city to be decimated without any prospect of ultimately solving the traffic chaos.

Across from Strand Road the reclaimed land has a perimeter of dumped boulders, looking, as Joyce said of those which in his day lined the South Wall, like 'piled stone mammoth skulls'. From this viewpoint the handsome Regency and Victorian house fronts on Strand Road look much as they did a century ago. Beneath them the

Left: Poolbeg Electricity Station from Sandymount Strand. On a rare windless day the plumes of smoke from the stacks rise straight up in the air, but more normally they are blown by the prevailing wind. The hillocky land between the stacks and the strand is recently reclaimed.

Above: Laying the Marine Drain at Sandymount Strand with the hills of Killiney in the background.

Below: Sandymount Strand at low tide. Small rivulets remain on the sands when the tide is receding. Behind is the Hill of Howth and the Baily Lighthouse.

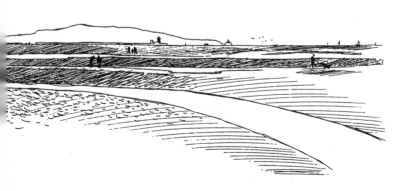

expanse of Sandymount Strand opens out towards the horizon and the sea. At high tide the strand is entirely covered by water and its presence unmarked by any piers or objects which might suggest the existence of low water other than the hulk of Sandymount Baths. When the waters begin to recede, the beach suddenly becomes populated with people, as though they had been under the water, submerged in the sands like the lugworm.

The old Sandymount Baths, which now stand marooned on the strand, are a remnant of a substantial bathing establishment of a type which preceded the pools of today. What can now be seen is just the pool structure. This is merely the base of an elaborate sea-bathing facility for gentlemen which was connected to the shore by a cast-iron causeway. This enabled swimmers to safely take advantage of fresh sea-water bathing at a constant depth and a considerable distance from the shore. The bathing establishments along the shores of the bay were promoted by the railway companies. Tickets to particular railway stations included admission to the baths, and the popularity of sea-bathing meant extra revenue to the companies.

Across this last open space of shoreline, motivated by the worthy desire of improving the traffic flow from the suburbs to the city, the planners have suggested putting a road, lower than the present one. The cost in the destruction of amenities which would be wrought by such a scheme is the final severing of the link between the city and the bay on the southern shore, with the annihilation of a vital piece of uncluttered beach.

I was sitting on the steps which connect the promenade of Strand Road with the beach, doing a sketch of the view from that point. The tide was out at its furthest limits and it looked as if one could walk right across the bay to Howth, a possible premonition of things to come. The South Wall and its bright red lighthouse hardly intruded to break up the vast expanse of sea, sand and sky. Children with dogs, women and men with dogs, packs of dogs on their own, lost by their attendant humans, careered past me, and interweaving with them were cyclists, horse riders, and conventionally walking couples. Out further on the horizon a sulky with horse and rider appeared, suspended between sea and sky like a mirage, the haze of the distance softening the definition of elements. For all this myriad of people, the bay seemed empty and the immense space absorbed people and animals. It was a typical Sunday morning on Sandymount Strand. In the immediate foreground stood a tall structure of steel posts displaying a sign which warned the public against the danger of being cut off by the incoming tide.

Vaguely aware of the Sunday walkers, the joggers and the dogs, I continued to draw until I noticed a figure creeping down the steps beside me, bent double with age. She asked would I mind her shoes while she walked on the sands. Feeble and tottering, she set off boldly across the sands looking as though she might collapse into a puddle at any moment. I anxiously followed her progress into the distance until she merged with other people on the beach, evidently spurred on by determination and courage. When she returned, the purpose of my drawing seemed trivial, and I, metaphorically speaking, tottered off, seeking another subject. The thought of the projected four-lane highway traversing the sands where I had been drawing seemed the ultimate affront to the idea of a city for people to live in, whether the people move at the speed of a sulky or with the slow motion of the old and the disabled.

Unlike the small public parks which are scattered around the bay and the linear promenades on both northern and southern shores, Sandymount Green has retained the form and atmosphere of a real village green. It is a delightful place to sit on a warm summer's afternoon under the mature trees. The area was developed from a brickfield in the eighteenth century to become the core of a prosperous suburb by the nineteenth. It stood in sharp contrast to its less salubrious neighbours, Ringsend and Irishtown. The Pembroke Estate, owners of the land, promoted the growth of a high-quality residential area, and this character is maintained today. Although the green is only a few minutes' walk from the heavy traffic of Strand Road, it has a sense of secluded peace.

The houses which surround it are a mixed collection of buildings, beginning in the early nineteenth century on the eastern side. These houses form a curious centrepiece of two-storey castellated villas, more like the gate lodges of some vanished country estate than the substantial suburban houses they are. Tucked into a corner of the green is one of the most gorgeous curved Victorian shopfronts to be seen anywhere in the Dublin area. This graceful series of arched windows, with a baroque pediment over the entrance, surrounded by decorative ironwork, has a fairy-tale grandeur, not easy to associate with contemporary business but which the Victorians obviously saw as in no way incongruous.

In Sandymount Green the bronze bust of W. B. Yeats represents an anomaly in Dublin's suburbs in being a substantial memorial to a literary figure erected where that person lived or, as in Yeats's case, was born. Strange remembrances exist in parts of Dublin, such as an enclave of literary street names in Bayside, Kilbarrack. I am not suggesting that Oscar Wilde Court and James Joyce Court would be better called something else, but that such namings acquire more meaning by having some historic origin in the events of the lives commemorated. There is a potential bonanza in such memorials for Sandymount, with the possibility of commemorating not just the famous poet but also his father and brother - the artists John B. and Jack B. Yeats, perhaps less influential than W. B., yet residents of whom any community might justifiably be proud.

Ringsend

John Dunton, the London bookseller, writing to friends in England in 1698 about his impressions of Dublin, is less than enthusiastic about Ringsend. His description, however, has a topographical quality to it which is interesting in the light of the changes which were to take place in the area over the next hundred years.

> We saw Ring's End which is compared to a neck of mutton in breadth, because it lies in the sea environed by its waters. ... When the tide is in, 'tis a peninsula having but one avenue to it by land from the south, 'tis a small village with three or four tolerable brick houses covered with tile or slates, besides several other less ones; it has no shelter, nor gardens and consequently a very bleak place, exposed to all winds and weather; upon the highest part of this neck of land is a gibbet lately set up...

He goes on to say that the gibbet was decorated with the corpse of a German doctor hanged for dismembering a Dutch skipper whom he had lured to his lodgings, apparently for the seaman's silver waistcoat buttons. Events hardly remarkable in any seaport, given the bloodthirsty manners of the period.

The physical amalgamation which has occurred to the previously separate areas of Irishtown, Ringsend and the Great South Wall enables them to be treated under one heading, although the consciousness of their being distinctive communities still exists. Eighteenth-century pictures show two clusters of houses perched on the 'neck of mutton', clearly separate yet also remarkably close together. Today no such physical separation is visible, and, as for being 'environed by its waters', the landfill and reclamation work of more recent years has pushed the shoreline of the bay so far away that only the end of Irishtown Park at high tide has any credible claim to being even near the bay.

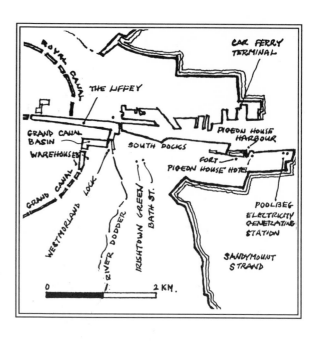

Page 63: Beach Street runs as a narrow old-fashioned street between the open spaces of Sandymount and Ringsend and is full of the life of a long established community.

Right: Westmoreland Lock of the Grand Canal, finished in 1796. The long passage from the Shannon across the midlands of Ireland ends here, where the canal enters the Liffey. The name and date of the lock are carved in a monumental inscription on the inner sides of the walls. The canal basin is now hardly used but would form a splendid centre for boating on the river if it were developed.

The Pigeon House Hotel, an important and neglected Georgian building which stands on the edge of the Pigeon House Harbour. Built as a hotel for passengers on the packet ships it is the only major eighteenth-century building in the city which has retained a semblance of its relationship to the landscape of the day, in this case, the Liffey in front and the Sugarloaf Mountain in the distance. At the base of the hotel is a section of the wall of the Pigeon House Fort.

The Grand Canal Basin, surrounded by tall brick-built warehouses and Boland's Flour Mills, from the window of Brian Lalor's studio in the nineteenth-century Sugar Mill, now developed by the IDA as an enterprise centre.

Between the small triangle of grubby land which is Irishtown Green and the 'Celtic interlace' of roads at the junction before Strand Road, runs the narrow declivity of Bath Street, confined between two areas of feverish traffic activity. Half-way down its length, and wistfully facing the river, is the Beach Tavern, now like the Ark on the summit of Mount Ararat, left behind by the receding tides. Once within a stone's throw of the sea, it now languishes almost a kilometre from the bay, surrounded by shabby houses and an air of seediness. Its façade, so at variance with its surroundings, attracted me even before I noticed the legend high up on the front of the building. This proudly proclaims its vocation as

hostelry to the watering place, now long gone and very hard to visualise in the narrow confines of Bath Street. In style, this building would be perfectly at home on the esplanade at Bray, with stucco ornamentation and extravagant gables. No better example could be required of the gradual changes which have occurred in the contours of the river mouth, caused by two centuries of reclamation.

On the city side of Bath Street, Irishtown and Ringsend occupy a wedge of land between the Dodder and the Liffey. Here the Dodder enters the Liffey, having joined forces with the Grand Canal.

Around the Grand Canal Basin lie the eastern-

Strollers in the distance on the Great South Wall on a winter's day.

most reaches of the Georgian city. The Grand and Royal canals were the culmination of one of the most ambitious plans of the businessmen and engineers of the Georgian period to unite the Shannon Estuary with the Liffey and make cross-country passage of freight possible without having to rely on the still unsurfaced roads. The canals were never a great success, coming at the end of the eighteenth century and soon to be superseded by the railways. However, we must respect the initiative and energy of their promoters, and also cherish the fact that inadvertently, as in the case of the Bull Wall and the harbours of the bay, facilities which were designed for functional reasons of trade and safety of sea passage have become some of the principal recreational areas of the city and bay. The waters of the Grand Canal Basin are now redundant, the place for the mooring of an occasional barge, and much of the property which surrounds them is derelict. This could all become an area of new life in a part of the city which has had little care or improvement in all its history, other than in its Georgian heyday. It ought to be adopted as a precept that no open waters which exist in our time should be filled in or used in a way which would diminish their character.

The development of Dublin in the Georgian period did not really extend beyond the limits of the canals, and this made areas on the periphery very suitable for the establishment of industries. Boat building and glass manufacture were prominent among the industries of Ringsend into the nineteenth century, and the latter is still a significant source of employment in the area. With the glass houses, salt and lime works, rope manufacturing, distilling, chemical works and electricity generation, there is an intense industrial tradition, which entirely dominated Ringsend throughout the nineteenth century. Most of the buildings devoted to these industrial concerns have vanished, although one, the sugar mill on Grand Canal Basin, has been handsomely refurbished by the Industrial Development Authority (IDA), while others await re-discovery.

The eighteenth-century sense of order is apparent everywhere on the Liffey and particularly here where the Grand Canal docks open on to it, with the corresponding entrance of the Royal Canal on the other side. It was of course easier then than it is now, without the countryside being built up, to engineer such schemes, and for the city to grow around them. All the developments which took place on the eastern side of the city used open farmland or reclaimed land. This shows in its rectangular planning, unencumbered by the old and crooked street patterns of the past.

Directly across the Liffey from the Canal Docks is the Point Depot, built as a railway goods terminus a century after the opening of the canals. This is, after the Custom House, one of the two most handsome façades between the bay and O'Connell Bridge. Built in a beautifully balanced combination of brick and limestone, there is a grandeur about the way the simple elements of the building are organised.

The other building of note in the river estuary is the forgotten wraith of the Pigeon House Hotel, an eighteenth-century hostelry doomed to a fate much worse than that of the Beach Tavern. When the South Wall was constructed it effectively cut off Ringsend from the channel of the river, passing by the point where the gibbet had once stood. The intervening stretches of land were gradually filled in, and what had been a peninsula became an indistinguishable part of the mainland. Halfway out the South Wall a harbour was built to accommodate the packet boats. On the reclaimed land which surrounded this, the Pigeon House Hotel was built, the only structure other than the Poolbeg Lighthouse out in the midst of the bay. This dignified building gets no mention in the many books which deal with Georgian Dublin, despite the fact that it is the only eighteenth-century hotel to survive and remains an important building of the period.

There is something inspirational about the siting of the Pigeon House Hotel, but in order to appreciate this, one's senses of sight and smell must be curbed. The harbour on which the hotel stands was constructed at a setback in the causeway of the Great South Wall. The harbour acted as the station for the packet boat before it became redundant, like Bullock and Ringsend before it, and was transformend into the city sewage works. The harbour, hotel and Pigeon House Fort were all purchased by the Corporation and now the smells from the sewage waft around the hotel. If the nose is assaulted, then so are the eyes. On the seaward side of the hotel the Corporation built the original of a series of electricity power stations, now long superseded and crumbling at the water's edge. Between the defunct power station and the odiferous pit, this fine building remains remarkably intact and worthy of the fitting rebirth it is now experiencing as the centre of the Bolton Trust. This trust was set up by lecturers from Dublin's institutes of technology in 1986, and is involved in promoting a working environment for small companies in the area of information technology and allied spheres. It would be good to see the sewage treated in some less archaic manner than that still practised here, and the air restored to a more palatable state. Below the hotel a fragment of the Pigeon House Harbour remains, and around the road sections of the fort wall have survived also, yet all are dwarfed by the latest development of electricity generation, the Poolbeg station.

From any point in Dublin Bay, on its shoreline, and also for many kilometres both out to sea and inland, the dominating feature of the landscape are the sixty-metre high pair of chimneys which rise out of the latest of the three electricity generating stations on the South Wall at Poolbeg. In practically any weather, whether the bay is shrouded in mist, or the city clotted with a pea-soup fog, the tips of the two chimneys will be seen rising above the haze, with an elegant curlicue of

Above: Following the construction of the Martello towers earlier in the century, the Pigeon House Fort was built in 1813 as part of the Harbour defences, but none of these forts ever saw any action. Fragments of the perimeter wall of the Pigeon House Fort and one side of the entrance way remain on either side of the road to Poolbeg on the edge of the harbour.

Right: At the corner of Pigeon House Road can be seen elements of four of the important stages in the development of this area. In the left foreground, the wall of the 1813 fort and behind it the original electricity station run by the Corporation with its decapitated brick stack. Inside the gates the fine cut stonework of the Georgian hotel building and dominating the whole group of buildings are the tall stacks of the modern Poolbeg Power Station.

smoke trailing like a pennant from one or occasionally both of them. Depending on the time of day or night and the light conditions, the chimneys can assume a variety of aspects, advancing or receding from the viewer as the atmospheric conditions change. If they were minarets or the campanili of a cathedral, they would be considered beautiful, but as factory chimneys their appeal is less immediate. The industrial landscape has been effectively interpreted by artists of the impressionist and later schools, and presented with compelling beauty. The reality frequently falls short of the artistic vision, less poetic somehow. In landscape terms the Poolbeg chimneys do have a virtue in the way they contrast and act as a foil to the predominant horizontality of the environs of Dublin. On a larger scale and in the idiom of our own time (that is, devoid of anything which might be considered decorative), they correspond to the eighteenth-century love of obelisks, and function as a defining presence.

In the brief period since their construction the Poolbeg chimneys have become ubiquitous with any view of the bay, and clearly mark the position of the river channel. The Victorians would have cloaked such chimneys with some decorative effect in order to give them some grace, and I think that they had the right approach, or at least a better one than the twentieth-century's infatuation with 'honesty of form'. This spurious notion that if something honestly expresses its function then it will be good architecture has been seen to be lamentably false. Perhaps in the hands of a master architect a factory chimney may be metamorphosed into a work of beauty, but such genii, if not an extinct species, are certainly an endangered one.

Driving round the perimeter of Sandymount Strand on the Poolbeg side one day, I was impelled to pull in to the side of the road so abruptly that a driver behind me quite justifiably blared on his horn with annoyance. The cause of my sudden

The entire width of Dublin Bay, from Killiney to Howth, can be seen from the beaches near Poolbeg. Here in the blustery weather of October the bay is almost bare of yachts, and the sea birds and migrants are beginning to gather on the shores.

swerving off the road was a new sight upon the horizon, a mirage of extraordinary 'Heath Robinson' form. It was high tide, and out on the surface of the water was perched an incredible and ridiculous sight. A machine or engine of strange appearance and unknown purpose was decorating the marine landscape where I had expected, at the most exciting, a few lugworm diggers. On closer inspection there were two of these contraptions, different in detail but otherwise similar, with tall smokestacks and a multitude of bits and pieces sticking out in every direction. What were these things - the product of a fevered mind, a hovercraft from the age of steam? All was made clear by a sign thoughtfully provided by Dun Laoghaire Corporation. The 'Heath Robinson hovercraft' were in fact engaged in the important but rather prosaic task of laying the marine drain from Blackrock to Ringsend across the drying-out section of the inner bay. For this task it seems that the technology of the space age is inadequate.

The road which joins Ringsend with the Poolbeg area now runs in a stuttering manner around the power station, much of the South Wall having been absorbed into the various industrial and shipping concerns along its length. Between the wall and Strand Road in Sandymount there are several small sandy coves along the new shoreline of the reclaimed land. From here the wide span of the bay stretches across the horizon, guarded on either side by the projecting outlines of the Hill of Howth on the north and Dalkey Head on the south. Between the strand and Howth, the Great South Wall runs like a dark line on the surface of the waves, the brilliant colouring of the Poolbeg Lighthouse a statement of human affirmation in the midst of the elements. Behind the wall, and marked by the Green Lighthouse of the North Bull, emerges the channel of the Liffey,

looking from here so narrow that the viewer expects the busy river traffic to end in imminent collision. The balance of the man-made and the natural, always a precarious one, is particularly evident from here. With the mass of Poolbeg station behind one, things look busy but unbrutalised. A slight rotation of the head brings the power station into view and with it the discordant development of everything which has been done on the southern face of the wall since 1900. It might have been worse. A plan for the development of the city published in that vintage revolutionary year, 1916, would have placed a 'power citadel' roughly where the tall stacks stand today, and infilled the entire shore of the drying-out area with housing, with a similar treatment of the northern shore, 'organising' Bull Island and filling in the Clontarf shore - development quite as revolutionary as anything which did actually happen in a different sphere.

The most positive thing to be seen in the Ringsend area is the new Corporation housing, built on reclaimed land. Unlike attempts at major housing schemes from the past, and what might have been expected had the 1916 plan been implemented, this development has the look of having grown in the way cities do, by degrees, with a varying skyline and different orientations. What is evident in the 1916 plan and absent from the new Ringsend housing is an obsessional regard for geometric forms which will organise, order and subjugate human aberrations, or any expression of the individual. Current planning philosophy has not moved very far from the 1916 mode of thinking in that all the streets must become wide boulevards for cars and the houses must be regimented like the tesserae of a vast and featureless mosaic. Now if Heath Robinson had submitted a city plan, *that* would have been interesting.

Dublin Port

The National Library of Ireland possesses a manuscript of Gerald of Wales's 'History and Topography of Ireland' illustrated with a map of Europe as it was thought to be in the early thirteenth century. The shape of the European landmass in the map resembles a table drawn by a small child in which two legs support a generally rectangular top. Transylvania is represented by the left leg and Spain by the right, and between these projections a number of sausage-like balloon shapes float in the empty space and are indicated as representing England, Ireland and Iceland. Such maps are nothing if not concise. The Irish 'sausage' shows four rivers, the Shannon which flows in at Galway Bay and out again at Kinsale, and the three others all located on the east coast - the Slaney, the Suir and the Liffey. This latter is marked as Auenliffus. Cartography at the time depended on the information of word-of-mouth rather than any precise observations, and although the manuscript is contemporary with its author's lifetime, the map represents Ireland in a most schematic manner. Nonetheless, it does contain much of interest in the quite sparse choice of information. There are three port cities represented equally on the east coast - Dublin, Waterford and Wexford - and each is designated by a little chessman-like castle to indicate a city or fort.

A thousand years before this map was drawn from contemporary information, the Greek geographer Ptolemy included Ireland in his Geography, indicating only the Liffey and the Boyne as rivers of the east coast, with the loughs of Belfast and Carlingford. Here the Liffey appears as Oboka, sounding like a place in West Africa, but Dublin is not mentioned at all. At least by the thirteenth century the city had arrived, in the cartographical sense of being worth mentioning. Gerald of Wales, who accepted rather credulously much nonsense fed to him by the mischievous subjects of his history, believed that the tide flowed out of Dublin port and into Milford

Haven, and then back again the other way, leaving either side high and dry in turn, as though the same waves crossed the channel between Ireland and Britain and then returned homeward. Once I was detained in Fishguard due to the ferry finding itself without enough water to sail, and I assume that Gerald had the same experience and accepted the explanation that the water was all on the other side!

In Dublin's rise from being one of a number of ports on the east coast of Ireland to occupying the position of pre-eminent port of the Republic lies a very chequered history. Repeated and vain attempts to find a satisfactory point from which passengers and goods might be conveyed across the Irish Sea occupied the citizens of Dublin from its inception as a city until the solution of the problem was reached a good eight hundred years later. Like a game of aquatic rounders, the search for a safe and secure harbour did a circle of the entire bay. At one time or another the port of Dublin was effectively operating from Dalkey, Dunleary, Ringsend, the Pigeon House, Poolbeg and Clontarf. From everywhere, in fact, but the river Liffey, up which the traders and citizens wished the ships to be able to navigate, but which was often inaccessible due to the sand bar in the bay being un-navigable and to the shallowness of the channel.

The solution to this apparently inextricable problem, continually exacerbated by the increasing dimensions and deeper draught of the sailing ships calling to the port, was brought about by a clever harnessing of the forces of nature combined with marine engineering. The prospect of dredging a navigable channel from outside the bar and up the river was only a temporary solution, and even today dredging is still occasionally necessary to shift the sand accumulating on the bed of the bay. Between the great mud flats of the North and South Bull Walls a channel existed for the river which provided limited access at high tide to the city quays. This was first separated

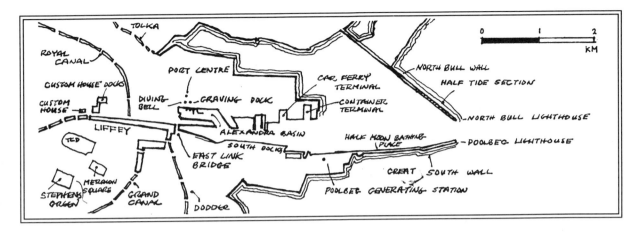

Page 75: The No. 1 graving dock with the lightship, the Kittiwake *being repainted. The graving dock is similar to others of the mid-nineteenth century, but it is the only structure of its kind in Dublin. These lightships have no form of propulsion and have to be towed to and from their station, either at* South Rock off Co. Down or Coningbeg off Co. Wexford. The lightships are automatic and can be monitored from the land, doing a two-year tour of duty before being returned for servicing.

The Academic Boris Konstantinov *moored at the end of Ocean Pier in the Liffey with, in the background, one of the great transporter cranes which load and unload the container ships.*

from the surrounding drying-out area during the eighteenth century by rows of timber piles driven into the South Bull in order to prevent further sands being swept by the tide into the navigable channel. The piled area was subsequently replaced by a wide stone-built causeway towards the end of the century, and twenty years later a similar wall was constructed on the corresponding Northern Bull. Between these walls the outgoing tide flowed at greater force than would occur without these constraints and thereby carried with it matter which might otherwise be deposited on the river bed. This flushing system maintained an accessible channel to the city, but the problem of ships of increasing size continued to pose a dilemma as it still does today.

As you pass over the East Link Bridge, the road to the north runs along below a high stone wall which marks the western boundary of the Dublin Port estate. Directly inside this wall, at the western end of Alexandra Basin, are the old and now mostly disused graving slips where ships were built throughout the nineteenth century. This is now an area of small boats and has the look of a forgotten boatyard, a backwater. The slip nearest to the road slopes down into the water, its concrete incline displaying a rich growth of seaweed as well as much detritus washed in by the tide. On the far end of the slip stands what looks like the amputated funnel of a steamship, half-submerged in the water, its surface pitted and corroded with rust. Seagulls perch on its top and the waves from a passing pilot boat lap on the metallic surface of the base. A small motorboat nearby is bright green in the sunlight, covered with a smooth fur of weed from ages spent under the water - forgotten places, forgotten things, as the port moves resolutely towards the sea. This heap of rusting iron is one of Dublin's few important Industrial Revolution survivals and deserves a more appropriate and important place in the modern port. It is in fact destined for preservation. This is the great diving bell designed by Bindon

Top: The Dyflin *under sail in Dublin Bay. This replica of a Viking longship was built to celebrate a thousand years of the city's history, which was marked by the Dublin millennium. The boat was the inspiration of the East Wall Watersports Group and its construction was sponsored by Dublin Port, the harbour authority. Under sail the* Dyflin *can reach a speed of twelve knots and can reach up to six knots under oars.*

Above: 'The Mariner' by John Behan, Maritime House, North Wall Quay, 1973. (Bronze.) Of the twenty sculptures grouped around the bay, this is the only one which deals with the theme of shipping, and its vigorous presence makes an heroic statement of the courage and commitment of the seamen who for centuries have formed the only link between this island and the outside world.

Blood Stoney, chief engineer of the Port and Docks Board, and used in the 1860s for the construction of the North Wall extension. The bell was lowered to the bottom of the harbour from a specially designed barge, and a team of men inside it were able to prepare a level surface for the base of the wall. The experience of working within this diving bell must have been horrendous and not for the faint of heart or those prone to claustrophobia. In the Engineering Museum at Trinity College there is a model on display of the barge and bell, showing how they were built, and these render the frightening cage of the bell less formidable than must have been the case to those confined inside it excavating the bottom of the harbour. There is a grandeur in this mass of iron which in its design is not without finesse, and while it could not be considered beautiful in the way much of the stone-built docks and piers are, the immediate impression is that here is some kinship with the Great Eastern and other pioneering creations of the Age of Steam.

Some few hundred yards further along the road the skyline of Victorian port facilities is broken by the clear voice of the late twentieth century declaring itself. This is the new glass-sheeted nerve centre of the modern port, Port Centre, to which the administration of the old Port and Docks Board moved from the Ballast Office in 1976. In a building which identifies more with the contemporary aspirations of a modern port than with the traditions which stretch back over a thousand years, the development of passenger and freight facilities is coordinated. From the upper floors of Port Centre the whole of the dockland area is visible. Looking back towards the Custom House, the former hub of port activity, and around a full sweep of the bay, everything which now concerns shipping from Dublin is visible from here and the coming and going of the massive container and bulk carriers take place virtually beneath the office windows of the Port Authority.

It was from the roof of Port Centre that I spotted the diving bell as I was engaged in drawing a panoramic view of the port, and puzzled over it for a few days before I realised what it must be. The form was familiar, but where had I seen it before? It was a bit like encountering the skeleton of the great Irish elk for the first time in the Natural History Museum, having previously known it only from pictures.

Two graving docks lie inside the perimeter wall which cuts off Alexandra Basin from the city, and to the east of Port Centre. These are not to be confused with the graving slips mentioned earlier. The graving slips were used for building ships, the graving docks for the repainting and repairing of ships too large to be brought up on a slipway. The No. 1 graving dock is the more interesting, No. 2 of the same species being a modern version of the earlier - deeper, wider, longer, but devoid of detail and less stimulating visually.

The earlier graving dock is a dry dock, giving the general appearance of a Roman stadium, with rather steeper sides. A more apt comparison would be with the Ziggurat of Ur, turned inside out and inverted. The manner in which the function of the dock has been organised is positively sculptural and there can be few structures of stone built in Dublin in its time where such complexity of detail is so successfully co-ordinated into a form which is at once instantly comprehensible yet also far from simple. The basic shape is that of a long pit with a flat end opening by lock gates to the basin and the other end rounded, reflecting the prow of the ships which it was built to contain. Within the simple shape of an oblong with one curved end, all manner of subtleties are engaged in, with the basic element of the stepped sides merging and separating into a complex geometry of walls, steps and ramps, fascinatingly controlled.

Apart from the sheer beauty of the stonework, which one comes to expect in all those constructions produced to answer the maritime requirements of the city, the marvel here is in the way no pains have been spared to delight the eye, while providing all manner of access for men and materials to the ships being worked upon. The modern graving dock by comparison is a mere opening in the ground with vastly less adequate means of access. Various unfortunate changes have been perpetrated upon the older graving dock, such as the blocking with concrete of some of the access ramps, but for something which has been in continual use for over a century it has in fact survived in a way which is a pleasurable surprise.

The factor which preserves this graving dock is that it still has a function which it can fulfil. Should it become redundant, what then would be its fate? The likely answer is that it would be filled with rubble and then promptly disappear under some more necessary structure such as warehousing. The fact that this is possible with an architectural masterpiece, not visible to the public, not fitting into any acceptable category of preservable buildings, in the midst of a functioning commercial area where every square metre of space is valuable, is a serious and constantly threatening consideration. The Pigeon House Harbour, with the exception of a token corner still open to the river, is now filled with sewage tanks, and the Great South Wall has disappeared under the accretions of later industrial needs. Georgian Dublin does not stop at Merrion Square, nor does the city's rich architectural heritage end with the Act of Union. This heritage is a far wider and more varied body of buildings than those for which Dublin is generally known. The No. 1 graving dock of Dublin Port deserves a place in the pantheon of important architecture from the previous centuries, all the more so as it must be one if the few to maintain the function for which it was conceived.

While I was working on the drawing of the graving dock and the South Rock lightship, the

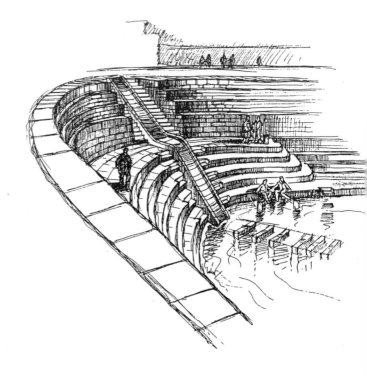

Kittiwake, which it contained at the time, the days were rainy and I frequently had to abandon the drawing until yet another shower had passed. These interludes provided me with the opportunity to wander around the surrounding berths and get a better idea of the activities of this section of the port. The graving dock opens into Alexandra Basin, although it in fact predates the basin considerably. Although ships are no longer built here, repair and refitting still form important activities in what now is the oldest part of the area controlled by the Port Authority. Other sections of the old port, such as the Custom House Docks, are no longer within the port estate and are being developed for commercial purposes.

Out in the waters of the basin project a number of piers and jetties, including one free-standing concrete mooring platform reached by a narrow wooden gangway. I walked out to inspect them and to get a better view of the landscape of cranes and ships which surround the basin. As I approached the platform, which was apparently only occasionally used, a flurry of seabirds rose into the air and flew around in a circular motion above the concrete slab. Not taking too much notice of this, I walked to the edge of the platform, to find the birds swooping and scolding vociferously. They must be nesting somewhere nearby, I thought, and looked around for a likely spot. As the platform was totally surrounded by water, I could see nothing which I could imagine as a potential nesting place. By this time the birds

Left: Diving bells were used since the eighteenth century for salvage from wrecked vessels but had not been utilised for construction until much later. This diving bell, dating from the mid-nineteenth century was used to clear the seabed for the base of the North Wall extension.

Left bottom: The 'prow' of the graving dock.

Below: Dublin Port at twilight from the Half Moon Bathing Club. The South Wall stretches back towards the city and the skyscape across the river is of the modern docks. Away in the distance on the left can be seen the spires of the medieval city of Dublin, now a long way from the port.

The southern face of the Great South Wall which protects the river channel from encroachment by sand carried by currents in the bay. All the stones for the wall were transported by barges across the water from the quarries on the southern shore.

- common terns - were in paroxisms of distress, screeching shrilly and liberally shooting their droppings on me. My eyes had to adjust to the camouflage before I was able to see their eggs at my feet on the cold concrete without a wisp of straw or a feather to soften the spot. In little groups of threes they were dotted around the platform, almost indistinguishable from the spotted dull colouring of the ground, and from a distance quite invisible, yet looking dreadfully vulnerable when observed. Hastily I withdrew and within a few minutes the birds had settled again on their 'nests'. Looking back from the main quayside, the birds had merged with their surroundings, visible only when in flight.

The entire *terra firma* of the port is reclaimed land as is most of the area between Amiens Street on the north and Merrion Square on the south and the present western shoreline of the bay. Exceptions to this are the lands around Ringsend which projected into the bay on a narrow spit of raised ground before reclamation absorbed them as an indistinguishable part of the shoreline. By the process of redefining the shoreline, Dublin Port has much increased its area in the past twenty years and is still engaged in a process of land reclamation if the necessary Government authorisation is granted for further infill. These intentions have proved very controversial for the residents of the Clontarf and Sandymount areas who see their sections of the bay diminishing before their eyes and industry moving gradually closer to their homes.

The spokesmen for Dublin Port advance the most cogent arguments for further expansion of the port into the bay, based on the vital need for

Through a screen of wild plants colonising the reclaimed land near the B&I terminal on the northern side of the Liffey, the transporter cranes of the South Bank Container Terminal can be seen. In the distance are the spires of the city churches and the Ringsend gasometer with, in the foreground, the Dublin Port Radio Centre and, beside it, the black-painted Eastern Breakwater Lighthouse. The Poolbeg Lighthouse was also painted black before being changed to its present bright red.

land. In order that the facilities will exist for Dublin Port to provide services comparable with those which exist in other modern and competitive ports, room for expansion is a prerequisite. The continual growth in the size of ships and the needs of containerised shipping demand deep-sea moorings and an uncluttered storage area totally unlike the warehousing of earlier centuries. It is a fact also that there has been a gradual seaward movement of the port since medieval times. However, there is another side to the question, which is the fact that the context has also changed. The reality is that the city, that is the residential part of it, has also moved resolutely towards the bay and now totally surrounds it, and it is into this residential context that the port wishes to expand. Obviously if the port were to expand as it has done in the past and wishes to do

still, pursuing the same valid arguments, then the whole drying shore is under threat as a potential area of reclamation.

A striking difference between current port development and that of the past is in the abandonment of the former clearly defined perimeters of stone-built quays in favour of imprecise and ragged outlines. This difference comes from the different methods of construction, the earlier being the building of strong retaining walls of stone or concrete which were subsequently infilled. The contemporary method is to work from the existing land area, dumping rubble until the desired level has been achieved, giving a totally different profile, that of a ragged boulder-strewn line of a very indifferent aspect, turning the Liffey into a sheet of water which resembles more a filled-in quarry than a river.

Sitting amongst the weeds and wild growth along the verge of one of the later bodies of infill which surround the B&I Terminal, I was engaged in drawing the view looking back towards the city in which the characteristic spires of the cathedrals are only dimly visible in the background between a screen of transporter cranes. Directly on the south bank of the Liffey opposite me was the Ringsend Coal Depot, an unattractive Industrial Revolution throwback in the midst of twentieth-century shipping technology. As I drew I became aware of an irritating amount of wind-blown grit descending on my clean white sheet of paper. This situation rapidly grew worse and every movement of my hand caused the grit, which was of course wind-blown coal dust carried over from the enormous heaps on the other bank, to smudge my paper. After an hour I had accumulated enough coal dust to form the basis of a statistical study of visible air pollution in the port, somewhere beneath which swam the now distinctly 'Pointillist' drawing of the river.

Concepts of the port of Dublin must include what these words currently imply along with those areas which both recently and in the more distant past were thought of as being the port. The excavations carried out at the Viking site of Wood Quay showed the existence and development of quay walls in successive stages. This process has been continued for the following millennium all along the banks of the river, between the original site of the city and the most recent new berths, projecting closer into the channel than anything which would have been feasible earlier. The eighteenth century was the beginning of the port as we know it today, with the organising of the system of quay walls and the harbour breakwaters to direct the flow of the river out into the bay. The building of the new Custom House during that period on reclaimed land brought the axis of the city eastwards and allowed the city to expand unencumbered by the constrictions of the medieval plan. Between the new Custom House

and the bay three extensive basins were constructed and surrounded by bonded warehouses under the control of the customs authorities. This area, recently cut adrift from the contemporary Dublin port, is in the throes of commercial development as a centre for international financial services, again beginning the process of moving the axis of the city further to the east.

The Custom House Dock site is emerging from the ravages of reconstruction and I found it difficult to decide on some satisfactory features which might be drawn amongst the ruins of what had been and the skeletons of what was to be. I concentrated on recording some aspect of the former use of the extensive site when it was the bonded warehouse section of Dublin port. Around the two basins (the third was filled in years ago for the ubiquitous road-widening), connected by a narrow canal, are the remaining nineteenth-century warehouses, long spacious structures of stone walls and cast-iron pillars.

Beneath two of the surviving buildings are vaults which support the superstructure and are of interestingly different forms of vaulting. Under stack A, there is a continuous series of barrel vaults with cross walls subdividing the space and without access of natural lighting. These vaults appear to extend away into infinity and sepulchral darkness. The other building, stack C, has an uncluttered understructure with groined vaults supported on columns and what appeared to be a system of borrowed natural lighting through shafts from above, although these had at some stage been blocked up. I proposed to draw both of these spaces, although they were dark as tombs and equally silent.

The B&I Bison *heads down the fairway from the port and closer up the* Kittiwake *lightship is being towed by the tug* Ben Eadar *to a mooring in Dun Laoghaire Harbour. The crane platform is on its way to the marine drain construction project at Sandymount. The channel of the port is busy all day with ships, from the largest containers to pilot boats, plying its waters. From the balcony of the Poolbeg Lighthouse the Great South Wall divides the channel from the shallows on the left hand side.*

I started with stack C, and despite being only barely able to see the white paper on which I was drawing, managed to capture some semblance of the space. The eventual plans for this area are as some kind of shopping precinct. To me they had all the damp attractions of a sea cave, moist underfoot, with water dripping somewhere in the distance.

Beneath stack A it was a totally different matter. The vaults here are dry and lofty. They lie beneath the building which was used to house a banquet for the Irish regiments which had returned in 1856 from the Crimean War. This event is well known from contemporary wood engravings, showing the wide parallel rows of columns decked with flags and garlands, the entire space packed with the dining veterans, seated on tiers, rising virtually to the roof of the building. Access to the vaults below is by a narrow flight of stairs which descend into a passageway running around the outside of the building, lit by occasional openings to the ground above. From this passage the vaults extend inwards under the warehouse, and I waited for my eyes to get accus-

tomed to the darkness before I began to draw. At some stage in the use of the building, a shaft for hoisting had been penetrated through the roof vault to communicate with the space above, and I edged slowly towards this, looking for an appropriate angle from which to commence drawing. I began, as in the other stack, to draw, literally in the dark. These vaults have a pleasing effect of receding into the distance, their arched openings illumined as a pale line of disembodied light in the distance. Somewhere from the building site outside a rather eerie laugh echoed down through the dark passages to discomfort me, but I could not even judge from what direction it had come.

For an hour I drew, cut off from the world, and now able to see with some degree of accuracy the details of the rooms and passageways, stopping occasionally to venture into an adjoining vault, then returning to my drawing. At this point the gloomy atmosphere began to impinge upon my senses and I started to imagine things - movements behind me, breathing in the distance, a single word uttered indistinctly and very far away. I began to feel decidedly uneasy in the near darkness and submarine isolation of the place. At the end of the series of receding arches which separated the vaults, a spot of light illumined a small area of the floor and noiselessly into this slab of brightness a feline form glided, black and full of menace. Hastily I slid back along the passageway and out into the brightness of the day, followed by a friendly-looking tabby cat, silently

Left: The Holyhead and Chester Railway warehouse, Wapping Street, North Wall. The name of this company expresses the close links which existed between British and Irish ports, and the company was largely engaged in the transport of itinerant harvesters from the West of Ireland to England - the lower end of the passenger trade.

Below: Between the two lighthouses of the port, the B&I car ferry M.V. Leinster *makes its way out towards the sea. The half-tide section of the North Wall are visible here at low tide. In the distance right across the bay, Killiney Obelisk can still be seen.*

padding along behind me.

Much of what has remained of the Classical world in terms of their built structures survives by virtue of being built of or supported by some variation of the arch, an immensely strong and stable constructional system. Domes, vaults and arches are all variations upon a single theme, discovered in the Eastern Mediterranean and used by the precursors of the Romans but only brought to fruition as an idea in the period of the empire, the first few centuries of the Christian era. In the Custom House Dock warehouses is to be found the latter end of this venerable tradition stretching back over a period of two thousand years. Not only is the system essentially a Roman one, the atmosphere also reminds the viewer instantly of baths, tombs and aquaducts of the Roman world.

From the arch to the circle is a small construc-

From the roof of Port Centre the bay, the river and the port are laid out with an industrial intensity unparalleled elsewhere in the city. In the botton left the lightship can be seen in the graving dock and, stretching right across the foreground, the ship loading jetty with lead and zinc conveyor overhead. Behind this are the waters of Alexandra Basin opening into the Liffey, and beyond the South Bank docks and the Poolbeg station. With ships coming and going and cranes constantly moving, this is the busiest section of the port.

Above: Stack A glimpsed through a winching shaft from the vaults below. The large space above was used in 1856 to hold a banquet to welcome home the Irish Regiments who fought in the Crimean War.

Above right: Looking towards the centre of the vaults under stack A.

Right: The vaults beneath stack C, which was used as a bonded warehouse by the Customs. On the ground at the right are the rails on which the barrels were stored.

Far right top: North Bull Lighthouse, which is now controlled from Poolbeg, is seen here through a magnifying window from the Poolbeg Lighthouse.

Far right bottom: The walls at the base of the Poolbeg Lighthouse are three metres thick and access to the lantern is made by a flight of eighty steps.

tional step; and buildings which are circular in plan partake of the same principle of strength in repose as do arched and vaulted structures standing up. Poolbeg Lighthouse, constructed in order to identify the entrance to the channel, had to be able to withstand the fury of storms in the bay. It is one of the most distinctive features of the bay and because of its pillar-box red colouring, visible in virtually all conditions of weather. The lighthouse occupies the position which was earlier held by a moored lightship, a method of identifying the position of the river channel which was unreliable. Situated in a position which is almost the centre of Dublin Bay, the Poolbeg Lighthouse is the culmination of the splendid harbour works which throughout the eighteenth century were a constant source of concern and public expenditure. While the completion of the South Wall did not finally solve the silting propensity of the Liffey - that had to await the completion of the corresponding Bull Wall which enclosed the channel from the northern side - the south wall and lighthouse itself between them made it possible to conceive of controlling the river in a manner which previously was unimaginable. The bright red exterior of the Poolbeg Lighthouse conceals walls of granite, three metres thick at the base which rise to the viewing platform and lantern in a very gradual inward sloping curve. The original eighteenth-century Poolbeg Lighthouse, of which this is an adaptation, was not as tall and had a distinctive balcony half way up on the outside of the building. The previous form of the lighthouse became a popular symbol of the port and it appears on maps and in many prints throughout the nineteenth century. At one stage the current lighthouse was painted black, which can hardly have increased its visibility.

From the balcony of the lighthouse, looking back to the city, the scale of the task of building the lighthouse itself and the Great South Wall is more easily appreciated. The broad stone ribbon

has a meandering course following the line of the
sand bars, as it runs back from the lighthouse for
about three kilometres before the Pigeon House
Harbour is reached and a further kilometre and a
half to the Grand Canal Docks. The Custom
House on the northern bank of the Liffey, begun
twenty years after Poolbeg, is seven kilometres
away. Perhaps these do not seem considerable
distances today when mechanical equipment has
much increased the speed of construction, but in
the eighteenth century, when every stone of this
vast undertaking was cut, transported across the
bay from the southern shore, and laid by hand, it
was with some justification that they called the
wall 'Great'.

In the comparatively narrow channel of the
port where it meets the bay between the containing walls, pilot boats dart back and forth like a
fleet of water taxis, or perhaps more aptly an
exclusive team of major-domos. From their berth
in the port, the pilots attend all those ships passing
over the bar who are not regular users of the

*Up to the early 1980s there was a jetty below the lighthouse
where this old crane still stands.*

channel. Dwarfed beside a gargantuan car transporter or container ship, the tiny and swift pilot boats accompany their charges before releasing them to the safe waters of the Liffey.

Eighteenth-century innovative skills and commitment to improving the port of Dublin meet the world of contemporary international shipping on the fairway of the Liffey, the latter benefiting from two hundred years of effort to make the city accessible to the sea. The painstaking labour with which the Great South Wall was constructed may appear primitive when compared with the sophisticated technology of the passing ships, but they are both part of the same tradition which received an apt reminder of how far back it goes with the launching of a replica Viking longboat during the Dublin millennium. When this boat, the *Dyflin*, sails sedately down the river and into the bay, it forms a further link in the historical progression uniting a thousand years of involvement between Dublin and its bay.

Above: A container ship passes Poolbeg heading up the river with a pilot behind it and another going towards the bay.

Below: Dublin's low-lying position is seen from the bay with only the tall stacks of Poolbeg breaking the skyline. A pilot boat heads out into the bay.

The Poolbeg Lighthouse at the end of the Great South Wall, a favourite place for anglers, and equidistant between the north and south shores. This is a splendid point from which to view the bay.

Bull Island

mongst the austere, venerable and dignified areas which surround Dublin Bay, Bull Island is an interloper. It is an anomaly, and having come about by happy accident has survived in its present form also by chance. It is now unlikely that the future of Bull Island will be one of 'development' since current taste tends towards the protecting of areas of wilderness, so few being now available for preservation. Plans do exist from the twenties to turn the island into a park in the manner of St Stephen's Green, complete with radiating walkways and excesses of Parks Department order. This chance to ruin an area of natural coastal environment was fortunately passed over and now the bay can boast of possessing an important nature reserve and an immense recreational strand within easy access of a large portion of the population.

The way to approach Bull Island is not from the broad modern road which enters opposite St Anne's Park, but over the old timber bridge from the Clontarf Road. Like the island itself, the bridge has many times been under threat of 'improvement' and even now there are periodic rumblings in Corporation offices. As the only other bridge that can join the Ha'penny Bridge in being the subject of popular esteem, it is to be hoped that it will survive long enough until an era emerges when the merits of such structures do not have to be championed by the public before the authorities become aware of them. Under the bridge flow the waters of the now truncated lagoon, and, in contrast to the roadway approach, the moment you step onto the bridge you know that this is another world. The causeway which projects directly beyond the bridge continues out into the bay, the later and smaller counterpart of the Great South Wall on the other side of the river mouth. Once past this point change is obvious all around you.

There is about the whole of the island, once you have left behind the area from which the oil

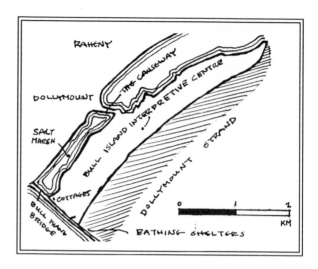

Page 95: The lagoon in winter is thronged with many species of migratory birds who feed on the mud flats during low tide and roost on the salt marsh to the left of the water. It is possible to see up to forty thousand birds feeding here at one time during the winter and one can birdwatch from the top of a passing double decker bus.

Below: Establishing the presence of the Port and Docks Board is the kiosk of the Harbour Police on Bull Island Bridge.

Right: The channel which divides Bull Island from the mainland has been successively called Raheny Lake and Crab Lake Water and is now known as the Lagoon. Here at low tide bait-diggers search for ragworm in the mud flats. In the foreground is the headquarters of the 5th Port of Dublin Sea Scouts, known as the Crows' Nest.

section of the docks is visible, a feeling of being cut off, adrift from the city and of being projected out into the bay. The ships which ply the fairway of the waters are at your feet, great container ships gliding up towards the port and the small pilot boats as well as yachts, tugs, trawlers, passenger boats, all bustling past out of the narrow confines of the channel. While you sit on the dunes or on the Bull Wall, there is a continual passing show of fascinating marine entertainment for your diversion. From the lowlying sands the city is barely visible and Howth lacks the bleak aspect which it maintains when seen from the southern shore. The mountains of Wicklow and Dublin dominate the scene on that shore, creating a landscape in which the urban element has been altogether diminished. The forms of Dalkey, Killiney, Dun Laoghaire and the inhabited coastline run like a dark band along the foothills of the mountains and do not intrude on the dominance

of the hills. The mass of Howth, a rolling contour of grey and brown, with bright speckles of housing scattered on the lower slopes of the hill, looks like it might be a more distant extension of Bull Island itself, rising as it does abruptly from the dunes.

Looking back towards Dollymount from Bull Island, across the tidal mud flats at low tide, with a few small sailing boats lying on the slob, there is an air of some remote nineteenth-century fishing village about the scene. The sounds of the ever-present traffic have been muted by the distance and the crying of gulls becomes the dominant noise. An occasional fisherman digging for bait at the water's edge emphasises the feeling of some little coastal port from a sepia photograph at the turn of the century. The bridge also has an other-worldly presence when viewed from the slob. A thin band of timber surmounted by a frail wooden rail and supported on spindly pillars, it spans the waterway in silhouette against the setting sun, an ethereal construction of spindles and spokes. A small kiosk on the bridge has a crudely lettered sign reading Harbour Police. The size of this establishment fortunately does not suggest a burgeoning crime rate on the island and it represents the only institution of the state or its agencies to be found anywhere on Bull Island other than the Interpretive Centre whose role in the future of the nature reserve is an entirely generative rather than repressive one.

From the waving motions of the dune grasses at the centre of the island, a pyramidal roof peeks up unexpectedly, revealing a two-storey building whose yellow dashed walls are a mass of projections and recessions, like some old coastguard outpost, yet here merging effectively into its background. The Interpretive Centre is not a museum filled with stuffed and dried representatives of the local flora and fauna as might have been expected in the past, but a study and information centre, devoted to the conservation

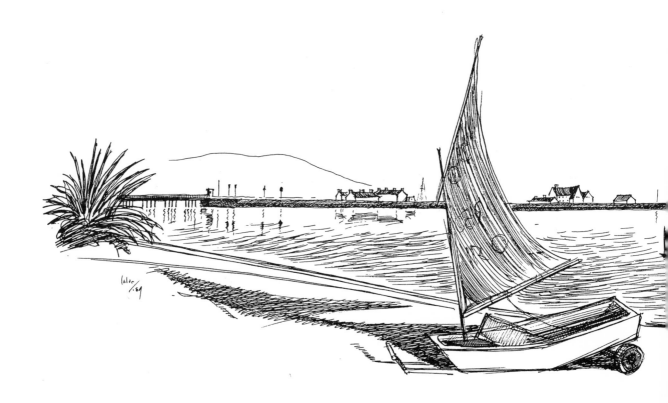

Above: The Coastguard cottages on Bull Island. Although the island belongs to Dublin Corporation the narrow strip of land along the Bull Wall is controlled by the Port and Docks Board.

Below: The full length of the North Bull Wall from the bridge at Dollymount to the tripod which marks the beginning of the half-tide section, seen from Clontarf Marina at the slipway of the Clontarf Yacht Club.

of the island's natural resources and the use of the place as an educational facility. Half a century after the island became a nature reserve in the 1930s, the building of the Interpretive Centre is the culmination of the official upgrading of the site from the product of tidal eccentricity to the major over-wintering place for migratory birds in this country. In 1981 UNESCO declared Bull Island a biosphere reserve, indicating the status it holds internationally as a natural habitat and study resource. For such a reserve its position is unique in being so close to a city and also for its minute size when compared with other national parks which have the same status in scientific research, parks such as the Camargue National Reserve in France.

Architecturally, the Interpretive Centre is the most distinguished of the small number of buildings on the island. The club buildings of the Royal Dublin Golf Club look more like a substantial villa, borrowed from the Clontarf shore, with

prominent gables visible from a considerable distance. And on quite a diminutive level, the bathing shelters which regularly punctuate the horizontal thrust of the Bull Wall are of interest as rare examples of the idiom of the thirties, as evocative of that era as the Victorian bandstands on the mainland are of the late nineteenth century. If one compares these little structures to the Casino at Marino, they appear tawdry and poorly finished, yet they have about them a distinct character. Together with those on the Clontarf promenade, this is an interesting group of little sculptural essays in mass concrete, indicating that someone was quite conversant with the current movement in design being experimented with in Europe, while the majority of the population was looking inwards. The bathing shelters are still eminently functional and distinguished enough to be worthy of conserving. Their frivolous and holiday personality contribute to the away-from-it-allness of the Bull Wall as much as the Victorian bandstands do to the parks and promenades around the bay.

The appearance and growth of Bull Island, having occurred within the last century and a half, has been well charted from its beginnings and makes an interesting subject for study, showing the manner in which it and similar areas, like the Sutton isthmus, have developed naturally. When the North Bull Wall was completed in 1825 and the river channel became self-dredging, the tidal flow outside it changed and sedimentation began to occur, with the clockwise motion of the tides in the bay depositing sand on the mud flats which previously had been submerged at high tide. The accumulating sand is constantly blown inland and builds up into sand dunes. These are stabilised by the growth of marram grass and later colonised by other plants which can thrive in such dry conditions. The highest of the dunes, those on the eastward tip of the island, have reached about nine metres above sea level and, although the island shows no tendency to grow closer towards

Left top: With the chimneys of Poolbeg in the background a constant stream of people passes along the causeway of the Bull Wall.

Left: Yachts from Dun Laoghaire race in Dublin Bay with the North Bull Lighthouse in the foreground.

Above: Bathing shelter on the North Bull Wall.

Left: Surrounded by the dunes, the Bull Island Interpretive Centre is devoted to the conservational and educational aspects of life on the island, an important national and international nature reserve.

Above: Between the dunes and the sea runs the 4.5 kilometre-long Dollymount Strand which can accommodate most of the ten thousand people who visit the island on a summer weekend.

*From Bull Island Causeway the receding tide brings the feed-
ing birds to the shoreline. Clontarf promenade
forms the background.*

The bathing shelters of the Bull Wall, as in other parts of Dublin Bay, are an interesting relic of the modern architecture of the early twentieth century.

Howth, the width is constantly expanding, leading to the enormous stretch of beach which now runs the full length of the seaward side of Bull Island.

Between the island and the Dollymount-Raheny shore, the situation is also one of increase. Since the building of the roadway which cuts the channel, the precious balance of nature has been altered. This lagoon, at an earlier stage called Crab Lake Water, is open to the tides at both ends and bordered by a salt marsh on the inland side of Bull Island. The mud flats have been invaded since the late fifties by spartina grass, which destroys the feeding area of the migratory birds who throng this lagoon in the early months of the year. Attempts are being made by the Corporation to restrict this growth and preserve the open channel from such encroachment.

The numbers of birds which overwinter here make an impressive show, with up to forty thousand of different species feeding at any one time. This is a familiar winter sight along the road from Raheny to the Bull Island Bridge, with the birds constantly flying and landing and feeding on the exposed mudflats of the channel. The Brent geese who have come from the Arctic regions of Canada are the most well known of the fauna of the island and also the most prominent numerically. Less obvious, because either nocturnal, shy of people or solitary, are the fox, rabbit and hare who also inhabit it, but are hardly likely to put in an appearance when there are ten thousand people on the beach of Dollymount Strand on a summer Sunday afternoon. The capacity of the wildlife of the island to satisfactorily co-exist with such massive influxes of people and cars is precarious, yet that it is possible at all is a remarkable testament to the growing realisation on the part of the public that this survival depends on their awareness. Since the new approach road was constructed in 1964 there has been an increase in the numbers visiting the island and a consequent deterioration in the dune cover, so important to the maintaining of the island and its wildlife. Obviously with even more holidaymakers coming to Dollymount Strand, the pressure will be greater and consequently the need more vital for public awareness of the fragile nature of this environment.

Although Bull Island is a nature reserve protected by the Game Preservation Act of 1930 and various other subsequent Acts, its position is a curious one, lacking the protection of permanent reserve status. Both the Special Amenity Order of the Corporation relating to the island and also the Ministerial Order relating to the sanctuary require periodic renewing, leaving a loophole for some tidy-minded administrator of the future to see Bull Island's openness as the answer to a now unforeseen pressure of housing or other civic concern. Such ideas have been voiced in the past and without the protection of permanent reserve status might be considered again.

Both the north and south Bull walls end in their respective lighthouses, but the half-tide section of the North Bull Wall is visible only at low tide. This section of the wall is constructed of boulders piled on the mud flats which surround the river channel and are now completely covered with a dense growth of seaweed, with some very drunken telephone poles swaying between the lighthouse and the end of the paved section of the road. Here in the river at low tide people swim, with the heavy shipping passing behind them and the wash from the traffic in the channel furrowing the waters. Despite the existence of frequent signs on both shores stating that the water does not come up to EC standards, there is no shortage of bathers, and swimming must be amongst the most popular forms of recreation around Dublin Bay. Many people to whom I talked at the various centres of sea bathing - excepting those in the Blackrock area who were very unhappy with the local water quality - assured me that the water, being constantly renewed by the sea, was perfectly safe and clean. There were many of those 'I have swum here, man and boy' responses, which had also an air of defiance about them, implying the determination to continue swimming, whatever the EC might think. A bather at the Half Moon Bathing Club on the South Wall expressed what many others had said, but with a succinct afterthought, 'The waters of the bay are perfectly clean and free from pollution, at least any that you can *see*.' What could not be seen they were prepared to overlook.

Another commentator on the question of pollution called out to me as I stood on the North Bull Wall watching the swimmers battling in the heavy swell. Assuming that I was contemplating the advisibility of entering the waves, he said, 'Tap water - I wouldn't touch the stuff', and plunged joyously into the sea and swam off.

Fairview to Sutton

On the northern shore of Dublin Bay the road runs parallel to the water's edge in a long gentle crescent, mostly bordered by a linear park of grass and shrubs in which the exhausting passions of the joggers are constantly displayed. Fairview Park ends at the railway embankment of the Skew Bridge and beyond this there is an unadorned stretch of grassland opening directly onto the waterfront at Clontarf. From here the waters are not left until one reaches the foothills of Howth peninsula. But the openness of the Clontarf foreshore gives way to a tidal channel at Bull Island, and although one knows that the bay is merely beyond the sand dunes, the character of the area changes into one more tranquil until the island has been passed and Sutton Creek appears below the dark uplands of the Ben of Howth. However, this takes into account only the seaward aspect of the road; something altogether different can be observed when one looks inland.

The eleven kilometres of road which stretch between Fairview Park on the borders of Clontarf and end on the isthmus at the approach to the village of Sutton contain an interesting sequence of examples of Irish domestic architectural styles, arranged as in an exhibition, running from the late eighteenth century to the immediate present.

Every facet of public taste is here displayed, not as they are usually found, arranged in streets and squares and as the constituent parts of towns and villages and suburbs, but in the curiously expanded form of a seaside promenade, a street with only one side to it. In fact, if one were to extend this linear display to include some outsiders such as the adjacent Casino at Marino and Clontarf Castle, a short walk from the front, two examples of the more influential upper echelons of taste can be added. But the arrangement of this 'exhibition' is certainly rather haphazard and must be judged on its cumulative effect rather than for any consistency of tone.

Although the road changes its name four times between Fairview and Sutton Cross, being successively Fairview, Clontarf Road, James Larkin Road and Dublin Road, it can be taken as a single entity, and the variety of its buildings seen as a concertinaed presentation of all the fads and fashions of the last two hundred years. In particularly marked contrast to the southern shore and specifically to the developments on the city side of Dun Laoghaire, where a single style and horizontal skyline provide unity, here the piecemeal development of two centuries is united only by a like scale and seaward orientation. Buildings come more in sets than as individuals

Left: Marino Crescent, 1792, a fine late eighteenth-century terrace of houses which originally looked directly on to the bay. Their presence indicates the beginning of the spread of residential areas outside the city in the form of suburbs instead of individual manor houses or villas surrounded by parkland.

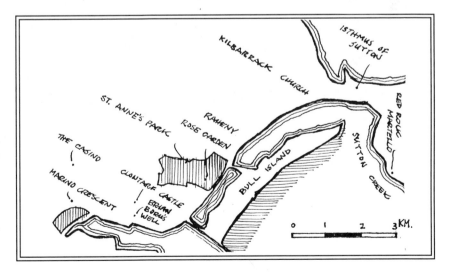

Above: From the roof terrace of the Casino a magnificent view of the bay and the Dublin and Wicklow mountains could be seen before the city developed around it, blocking the view. The beautifully carved urn on the parapet is both a decoration and the chimney pot of the flues concealed in the walls. The external Doric columns contain the drainpipes.

Left: The Casino at Marino, entrance hall. Designed by Sir William Chambers in 1758, it was built between 1762 and 1773 at the then extraordinary cost of £60,000. Commissioned by James Caulfield, later Earl of Charlemont, who spent eight years on the Grand Tour in Europe and the Aegean furthering his antiquarian and cultural interests.

on the seafront and the same themes of bay windows and gables are repeated with many variations for the full distance of the promenade. Amongst all these seaside villas are some which are notable, as much for the sense of the style of their times as the determination with which they ignore their neighbours. Late Georgian and Victorian villa make up much of this seafront, as do stuccoed cubes of whiteness from the thirties and post-war pebble-dashed bungalows. Recent years have seen the addition of sculpturally decorative flourishes to some of the houses along the front, and their choice makes for some curious juxtapositions.

Concealed behind a dense growth of trees which form its park, and directly opposite the more orderly lawns of Fairview, is Marino Crescent, the finest crescent-shaped housing development to survive from the eighteenth century in the Dublin area. Originally this grand curve of houses faced directly onto the bay, separated from the water only by the public roadway. Now the sea has departed and the fairview with it, and parkland, a railway embankment and the industry of the port and Ringsend have come between the houses and their spectacular view of the Dublin and Wicklow mountains on the far side of the bay. Change in the contours of the shoreline is not the only trouble afflicting Marino Crescent. Like all the residential areas of the city which were built before the modern era of universal car ownership, no provisions were made for the accommodation of parking spaces, and the residents of the crescent have taken what measures they think necessary to solve the problem. This usually requires either totally or partially removing the railings which surround the houses in such a decorative and previously practical manner, and turning the garden into a carpark. In a single-occupancy house this may be done without the total destruction of the ironwork, so much an integral part of the design of all eighteenth- and nineteenth-century buildings. In houses of multiple occupation, as are many of those in the crescent, the garden becomes the site of a sheet of tarmac and the wonderful cast-iron railings and gateways end up in the rubbish skip. When this happens on a large scale to an important group of houses, it becomes obvious that there is little point in preserving the buildings when they have been denuded of all the decorative touches which lent finesse to the design and are an integral part of the original conception.

As a 'spite fence', Marino Crescent makes a substantial statement of intent. Built, according to legend, by a developer who wished to annoy Lord Charlemont whose Marino demesne lay directly behind where the crescent now stands, the crescent effectively blocked the view of the bay from Marino House and the Casino. Now the crescent is being dismembered, with its eastern end already replaced by a block of modern flats. Marino House, the Charlemont residence, is totally gone, its presence echoed by fragments of the demesne wall. Only the Casino, Lord Charlemont's principal artistic achievement, has

Top: Fairview Park occupies a section of the bay cut off when the railway embankment of the Belfast line crossed the foreshore from Amien Street Station.

Above: The railway track crosses the road diagonally at Fairview by a double-arched bridge, known as the Skew Bridge. The internal ribs of the arches are laid at an angle to the ground, and the construction was much admired when it was buit in 1843.

Two shelters on the Clontarf promenade.

survived, intact and generously refurbished. It looks as though it had landed from another planet, and in a sense it has, surrounded as it is by the pretty brick council houses of contemporary Marino. It is a relic of an Augustan age, quite as distant as that of the Pharaoh's Egypt from the preoccupations of those who now live on the Charlemont estate.

Charlemont's contribution to eighteenth-century Dublin, conceived at the meridian of its splendour, presents a sophistication and sensibility beyond anything else achieved in the city in the Georgian idiom, and it represents not just the vanished glory but one of the actual glories of Dublin Bay in terms of man's treatment of building and landscape as an exercise in creation. This is all very difficult to appreciate now with the Casino torn from its natural habitat, or rather vice-versa, yet the restoration does capture some of the magic of this intellectual concept made real. During Charlemont's years of residence in Rome as part of his Grand Tour, he became the friend and patron of the Italian artist and antiquarian Giovanni Piranesi, who is best remembered for his fantastically complex and detailed vision of the ruins of ancient Rome. Although Charlemont and Piranesi subsequently fell out, and the dedication to Charlemont of one of Piranesi's sets of engravings was deleted by the artist to show his displeasure with his patron, the concepts of Piranesi's work must have had a profound influence on the earl's thinking when the Casino was discussed with Sir William Chambers, its designer. Ideas of scale and proportion which create illusion and deception, so obviously conveyed in the Veduta and Antichitá of Piranesi, have been incorporated into the design of the Casino, which both inside and out is rather more than it appears to be - either a decorative garden temple or a gentleman's seaside chalet. Charlemont's ambition when he returned from Rome was to live by and spread the ideas of a culmination of these ambitions - a three-dimensional statement of the interdependence of high ideals of life and intellect.

The opulence of detail on the Casino is quite ravishing, with walls, floors and ceilings richly enhanced in a neoclassical manner which attempts to emulate the quality of some of the antiquities Charlemont would have seen and studied in Rome. Based on the form of a Greek cross, with arms of equal length, the entrance from the northern arm brings one into the quite tiny yet stunningly beautiful lobby, and this leads directly through to the main salon from which the view stretches across the bay to the Great Sugarloaf Mountain in the distance. This room, the only one in the entire building which actually looks out on the bay, has a single enormous window which fills it with light and a sense of communing with the out-of-doors. This is the core of the Casino, with a library and a study both opening off it, and must have commanded a wonderful prospect of Dublin Bay before the building was encroached upon. Today, it is only from the roof terrace that some idea of the original view can be appreciated. Above the trees and between the chimneys of the Poolbeg Power Station, the southern shore can be seen as far as Dalkey Island. The obelisk on Killiney Hill, built in 1742, thirteen years before the Casino was begun, represents one of the few elements of Lord Charlemont's view which can still be seen, other than the line of the hills and small stretches of water. With the exception of the Great South Wall which had bisected the bay by 1767, the space between the Casino and the Killiney Obelisk was uninterrupted until the extensive reclamations of the nineteenth and twentieth centuries placed a body of land in between. From the Port Centre office building on Alexandra Road to the Poolbeg station, the view from the Casino is now an entirely industrial one and with future growth and building will probably totally obscure the bay, severing the relationship between Dublin's most magnificent Georgian

building and its *raison d'etre*, the bay.

Clontarf is principally famous as the location for two historical events. The first may or may not have taken place there, and the second did not take place at all. The Battle of Clontarf in 1014, was fought somewhere between the walled city of Dublin and the shores of Howth - the name Clontarf nowadays covers a much smaller area than implied by the word previously. The second event is the 'monster meeting' called by Daniel O'Connell in 1843 to agitate for repeal of the Union with Great Britain. The planned meeting was proscribed by the administration of the day, and O'Connell wisely decided to cancel it rather than risk a violent conflict. Later, changes of fortune enhanced the area as a recreational centre, with the development of Bull Island, the main seaward feature of the Clontarf shoreline, and the establishment of a great estate by the Guinness family in the middle years of the last century, later to become St Anne's Park, which, with two hundred hectares of land under trees and open parkland, is the second largest park in the Dublin area and by far the largest on the bay. Like Marino House, the mansion around which St Anne's Park was created has vanished and is survived only by various outbuildings and park furnishings. In recent years the Corporation has established a rose garden in the park for those to whom the wild natural wastes of the nearby Bull Island are not so appealing.

On a humid July afternoon the air in the rose garden has the scent and physical weight of candyfloss, pungent and sweet. The superabundance of the roses is almost overpowering, as the banked masses on display of reds, whites, pinks and yellows surround you. There is something

Top right: Yachts from Clontarf Yacht Club moored in the protected waters between the Port and the northern shore.

Right: Clontarf marina.

surreal or fantastical about the place. This is an ideal spot for wedding photographs and behind every mass of blossoms another wedding party is being arranged by harassed and equipment-laden photographers. The ladies' dresses are causing the trouble, or is it the roses? Balloon-like gowns of orange satin are clashing with the red beds. In the far corner a white wedding is in difficulty with the pink roses. Like magnificent wind-borne tea cosies, ladies glide over the lawns pursued by the importuning photographers. 'Try the pale yellow,' one calls hopefully, but by now the lime green cosies have crossed to the scarlet beds and encounter the whites approaching from the other side. This is just the moment for the Red Queen to enter and scream 'Off with their heads' at the offending cameramen. The wedding parties are content just to be decorative and have had enough organising already that day. Now, in the rose garden nothing can be more important than to be beautiful. The roses bloom and bloom. Such extravagance is away beyond the normal or the expected in a Dublin park. The temperate climate of the bay and the protection of the estate's mature planting as well as a south-facing aspect are stated as reasons.

Unlike St Anne's, where the park survives but the mansion is gone, the case with Clontarf Castle

is the reverse, and the building stands with only a carpark for its broad acres. The relationship of the castle with the Tudors has not been a happy one, although the connection and influence appear to be prevailing even into the present. From sequestration after the Reformation, the Tudor sense of style appears to have become mixed up in the bloodstream of the building, causing some ironic consequences. The nineteenth-century restoration was done in a Tudor revival manner after the entire earlier castle had been demolished,

The first stretch of open water on the north side of Dublin Bay, at Clontarf Road, with a very characteristic grouping of houses and small churches facing the water.

leaving a polite pastiche of the more vigorous period it wished to recreate. The final indignity has been perpetrated by the housing estate which now occupies the land between the castle and Castle Avenue. Under the very nostrils of the mock machicolations on the castle, these attractive *bijou* residences are in a new interpretation of the earlier idiom developed to a kind of cardboard Tudor, appropriate for a cutout from a breakfast cereal packet.

Stormy or calm, the sea remains without pretensions towards being another period or personality; it is essentially itself, and easier to cope with than the vagaries of architectural taste.

Before setting out to draw on the Clontarf shore, I had been reading in a newspaper of the decimation by poachers of the elephant population in Africa in the last twenty years, and was brooding on the fact that it would be an inglorious age in which to have lived which witnessed the extinction of the wild elephant. For the elephant to survive only in zoos seems a tragedy for such a noble creature, and this does indeed appear to be its fate. Such were my melancholy thoughts as I walked along the muddy bed of the bay at the base of the slipway of the Clontarf Yacht Club.

Two men were digging for ragworm at the edge of the water and I went over to see what they had dug up. Not being a fisherman, I had never seen a ragworm at close quarters, and a digger obligingly removed one from the bottom of the bucket which contained a slithering mass of light brown spiny creatures. He proceeded to display its points for me as though it were a pedigree, trained for the ragworm shows. The ragworm has fangs, but this specimen refused to display them. It was returned to the bucket and another produced, equally uncooperative. A third finally obliged on begin given a smart pinch by the fisherman, pouting its peculiar mouth and momentarily shooting out two dark arrows. There must have been fifty worms in the bucket, and one sees people engaged in digging for them all along the shores of the bay at low tide. Obviously one can hardly draw a parallel between the possible destruction of the elephant and there being any threat to the ragworm population, yet I came away feeling that even such humble creatures as these should hardly be caught in bucketfuls without some thought being given to the pointless killing of any species in excess of what is strictly necessary. The elephant is magnificent and the ragworm rather revolting, yet this is merely a value judgement, irrelevant to the survival of either species. I look forward to seeing signs on the various seafronts and drying-out strands, stating that the poaching of ragworm is prohibited!

Top: The foreshore at the boat slip of Clontarf Sailing Club, with the thin outline of Bull Island behind.

Above: Brian Boru's Well on Castle Avenue. The inscription reads 'Erected over Brian Boroimh's Well by subscription A.D. 1860.' This well is associated with legends of Brian Boru and the Battle of Clontarf. The cast-iron plaque is now brightly painted with shamrocks of an unlikely greenness.

Right: Dollymount seen from Bull Island at low tide.

Beyond the Clontarf slipway the slobland continues under the Bull Island bridge and all along the channel between the island and the road. This channel, which once ran the full length of the island before emerging into the bay at Sutton, is now blocked by the massive roadway which joins the island to the mainland. Unfortunately, this natural wintering place for vast numbers of Brent geese and other species may be diminished by the changes made to their habitat by the road, which, without a passageway for the tide to pass under it, has led to the silting up of the channel and changes in the growth there. Beyond this motorway the island thins to a narrow strip of sand dunes and gradually disappears.

The road beyond this point is of more fitful interest than previously, with the repetition of the same elements, concentrated in the later post-war period of bungalows rather like the gate lodges of country estates. In the midst of these bungalows is Kilbarrack Graveyard in which remain the ruins of a sixteenth-century church. Not much inspiration here for an elegy. The building has been so clumsily repaired with cement and so much of it appears to be in danger of imminent collapse that it presents a rather unromantic spectacle. To add to this sense of neglect the grass is kept at bay with weed-killer, surrounding the church with an area of scorched earth and yellowing soil. As in all old graveyards the tombstones totter and many lie on the ground or have been shattered by vandals. The siting of this little church must have been quite charming in its day, on the edge of the bay, perched on a knoll of ground, and even now the ruin commands an excellent view across towards the distant city and the mountains. Amongst the recumbent stones, one caught my attention as it carried a family name with which I was unfamiliar and which to me sounded rather improbable in contrast to the more conventional names of the other stones. Later I looked up the name, McGlue, in the phone directory and found it to be still represented in the area.

The journey along this shoreline begins with the circumference of Marino Crescent and ends at the complete circle of the Red Rock Martello tower. In between lies a French curve of low coastline until the more open waters of the bay appear below the rugged outline of Howth. Here, from the slender tower of Sutton church to the end of the coastal road, at the point where it rises inland over Shielmartin, the shore runs straight, with Bull Island diminished to a mere sandbank, and the far-distant mountains of Wicklow again taking a dominant role in the landscape. The widening out of the bay at this point restores the viewer to a feeling of the open sea, a sense which had become lost when the sand dunes of Bull Island intervened.

The sea traffic of yachts and shipping passes by and on the rocks off the shore cormorants perch, their wings outstretched like marine traffic-policemen, directing the passing vessels. Other than at high tide the mud flats form an interlude between land and water. On the dun-coloured ground, moisture glistens and the colour range is strictly one of the browns of seaweed, wet sand, mud and the occasional group of lighter-coloured stones along the water's edge. Suddenly a group of the little stones will all remove themselves to a different spot. Hallucina-

tions? No, the small stones are a group of dunlins, round and featureless with their heads tucked in, and a cocktail-stick leg hardly visible beneath them. They dart about playing 'follow my leader', then all come to rest somewhere else. Gulls, curlews, sandpipers and godwits are all busy along the muddy stretches of the bay, puncturing the smooth ooze of the ground for sustenance with their variously shaped beaks. The curlew seems best equipped for this task, probing in the mud with its long and delicate curve of a beak and striding authoritatively amongst the more comic and diminutive of the inhabitants of the shoreline.

On the slope above the western end of the Sutton shore, and overshadowed by trees, the Carricbrack Road skirts the old Sutton graveyard. Below the trees and barely visible even from close-up, is the church of St Fintan, an Early

Christian foundation, although the remains are principally medieval. This church is not just small, it is minute, and a glance at the sketch will immediately make this obvious. The two tombstones which are of conventional height and stand inside the railing of a family plot to the left of the church door are as high as the main walls of the building. This is an altogether exceptional piece of architecture, about which not a great deal is known, being overshadowed historically by the Abbey of St Mary in Howth, although both ceased to function ecclesiastically at roughly the same time, in the sixteenth century.

There is a sense of looking at a reliquary in a museum cabinet when confronted by St Fintan's

Typical early nineteenth-century houses on the Clontarf Road. The development of residential areas continued to spread along the shore of the bay throughout the nineteenth century.

Church, for like those over-decorated and somewhat clumsy containers for revered objects, this building has too many features for its small size. The west gable alone possesses an entrance door as well as a circular window above it, with a disproportionately large bell-cote topping the composition. The tiny interior has five windows, all of them of different size and design, as well as three niches related to the religious functions of the building. But this evident confusion does not detract from the singular charm of the church, built, as it were, from a previously assembled collection of architectural fragments. It forms, with the three other Early Christian churches around the bay (at Killiney, Dalkey and Dalkey Island), a stunning introduction to the inhabitants of the area as the country emerged into the historical epoch. The other example which survives, on Ireland's Eye, has been too mutilated to afford much insight into the period of their origins. It is really beyond understanding that any building such as St Fintan's should not be a national monument, and that it survives by goodwill rather than with state protection. The reverence and superstition which contributed to the safety of antiquities in the past no longer have any currency, and state care is a vital requirement for the continued survival of the treasures which have not fallen to corporate or freelance vandals.

At either end of the coastline which links them together, there is an unlikely parallel between the gorgeous architecture of Lord Charlemont's Casino and the virtually monastic seclusion of the church of St Fintan in Sutton. The guiding force for both lies in an intellectual preoccupation which is essentially solitary. The Casino, with its art and its library, provided all that a scholar might need to gain seclusion from the world, while at St Fintan's the stone church, which was originally contained by a surrounding rampart or wall which also possibly enclosed some timber dwellings, there are the elements of the ideal hermitage, overlooking the vast sweep of Dublin Bay.

The distinguished nineteenth-century tradition of purpose-built yacht clubs, so visible in Dun Laoghaire, does not appear to have had much following on the opposite shore. The oldest club on the northern side, the Clontarf Yacht Club, occupies a converted private residence which in its façade has something of the character of the Dun Laoghaire clubs, a long low building of Classical design with ornamental urns decorating the parapet. Between the club and the water is the public roadway, so the club building tends to be submerged in the ordinary structures that surround it. The other sailing clubs which are to be found between here and Howth appear to have been designed with the conviction that the practice of architecture is a dead art, and there is no evidence whatsoever of an awareness of any criteria other than convenience and cost. This is particularly sad as the sites of both the Kilbarrack Sailing Club and Sutton Dingy Club are on the foreshore and presented an untrammeled opportunity to produce something worthy of the long tradition of sailing on Dublin Bay.

Nowhere on the shores of the bay is there so much open land as is to be found between Fairview and Sutton, with, after the Phoenix Park, the largest cultivated public park in the Dublin area at St Anne's, as well as the most extensive wilderness at Bull Island. Both have arrived at their present state of being the 'lungs of the northern shore' by unexpected chances of fate and fortune, which were grasped at an opportune moment and with admirable foresight by the civic authorities of the day, upholding the often forgotten principle that cities should be pleasurable places in which to spend one's time.

Red Rock Martello Tower and the Howth cliff path with the crescent shape of Bull Island separated from the mainland by a thin channel of water.

Howth

The immense portal dolmen which stands in the demesne of Howth Castle was the inspiration for 'Aideen's Grave' by Sir Samuel Ferguson, an acute rendering of a late nineteenth-century understanding of the heroics of Bronze Age life on the Howth peninsula. This combination of the romantic and the scholarly fleshes out the sparse and enigmatic remains of the society which inhabited the massif of Howth when it was still an island, separated from the mainland by a channel similar to that which divides the Clontarf shore from Bull Island today. Looking out from the southern shores of the bay, the narrow isthmus is now visible only because it has been built upon, and it is easy to see how the great bulk of the peninsula would have appeared to early settlers, cut off and secure from mainland incursions.

The description which Ferguson gives of the surrounding landscape is of an area of great natural beauty and remoteness. Writing as he was in a period before the Sutton shoreline had been intensely developed, it would not have been difficult to conceive of the place as having changed little from the era of the dolmen builders.

> And all the sands that, left and right,
> The grassy isthmus-ridge confine,
> In yellow bars lie bare and bright
> Among the sparkling brine.
>
> The cliff behind stands clear and bare,
> And bare, above, the heathery steep
> Scales the clear heaven's expanse, to where
> The Dannan druids sleep.

This is Ferguson reacting to the Howth of his own time, sparsely populated and with few obstacles against communing with its remote past. Towards the end of this long poem the writer speculates on the future, and there is an ironic twist to his words in the light of subsequent

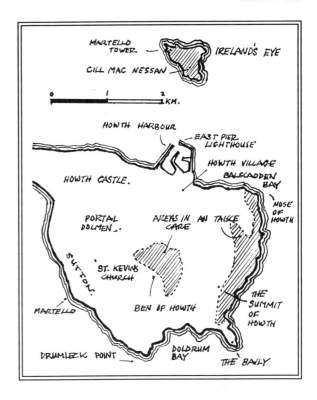

Left: The view down Abbey Street towards the east pier of the harbour. Fine Victorian houses line the street facing into the grounds of the abbey.

history. To anybody who has been immured in a traffic jam on the road which runs below the dolmen, the answer to Ferguson's question concerning the future is that he was not far off the mark. He expected invaders, though from further afield than merely other parts of County Dublin. He asks 'What change shall o'er the scene have crossed?', and continues

> And haply, where yon curlew calls
> Athwart the marsh, 'mid groves and bowers
> See rise some mighty chieftain's halls
> With unimagined towers.
>
> And baying hounds, and coursers bright,
> And burnished cars of dazzling sheen,
> With courtly train of dame and knight
> Where now the fern is green.

Left: 'Aideen's Grave', 'Finn Mac Cumhaill's Quoit' or the Cromlech of Howth. This portal dolmen in Howth Demesne, built around 2000 B.C., is a type of funerary monument common along the east coast, usually composed of three or more upright stones and a capstone placed on top. In this case the capstone, which has fallen, weighs about eighty tonnes, although heavier ones are known. The technology of earthen ramps, timber rollers and an abundance of manpower would have made the construction of this dolmen less formidable than it might appear.

Above: The isthmus of Sutton from the Ben of Howth. A midden was excavated on the eastern side of the isthmus which showed that Howth peninsula had a shoreline cutting it off from the mainland and running more or less directly across from the shore of Sutton Creek to the Baldoyle side. This would have been about 3500 B.C., fifteen hundred years before the building of the dolmen.

Right: The Martello at Red Rock which has been much altered since it ceased to be part of the defensive surroundings of the city. In the distance is Dalkey Island, on which the corresponding Martello can be seen.

We now know all about the 'burnished cars of dazzling sheen' and can legitimately wish for things to be as they were in some distant and more heroic time.

Howth when seen from the bay has a striking remoteness and impregnability. It is a rocky outcrop surrounded by defensive cliffs continually lashed by the sea. A more authentic voice than the romantic antiquarianism of Ferguson comes from the Early Christian period in a poem attributed to St Columba which presents a very identifiable image of Howth, no less true now than when it was written, over a thousand years ago.

Delightful to be on Ben Edar
Before going o'er the white sea
Delightful the dashing of the wave
    against its face
The bareness of its shore and border.

One can see the poet sailing in his currach under the cliffs of the southern face of Howth and composing these terse lines which still so graphically describe the coastline between Red Rock and Balscadden Bay. The physical aloofness of the cliff face is in marked contrast to the shoreline of the rest of the bay, all of which is now densely populated and its outlines softened by occupation and planting. Howth turns its blind side to the bay and maintains a separateness. Killiney and Dun Laoghaire are oriented towards the bay, and the latter with its wide embracing arms seems to unite land and sea with a dramatic gesture. Bull Island skirts the bay with a line of perpetual motion, and the Great South Wall sticks out an enquiring finger into the deeper waters. Yet Howth disdains to be involved. Everything of importance on the peninsula, with the exception of the Baily Lighthouse, faces to the north and is on the outer side, away from the interior of the bay. The physical form of the landscape demands that Howth be the perimeter of Dublin Bay, and yet it remains apart from it.

As with every other part of the bay, the capricious Master of the Hour, who dictated how people came and went and exerted an enormous influence on their lives, was the tide. The harbour of the peninsula, which predates Dun Laoghaire and was ultimately superseded by it as the principal embarkation port for passage across the Irish Sea, is the principal fishing port of the bay area, even though placed outside its confines. A failure virtually from its inception as a deepwater port, due to constant silting, it became in the late nineteenth century a major harbour for the herring fleets and even today, after considerable recent redevelopment, is base for a substantial modern fleet.

Perhaps the builders and designers of Howth Harbour were skeptical from the beginning as to its feasibility? The east and west piers of Dun Laoghaire Harbour end in terminal lighthouses, stone exclamation marks to emphasise something well done. In Howth the mouth of the harbour is sufficiently narrow so that one lighthouse is adequate, the beautiful cone of cut stone at the end of the east pier. But this is not the final statement of the builders. Behind the lighthouse the granite wall which divides the upper and lower levels of the pier continues and ends in a most eloquent stone question mark! This finial lacks only the circular stone dot of a bollard to complete the impression of a three-dimensional statement of enquiry. The question was answered in the negative from the interior of the harbour. The few years during which Howth Harbour was used as the port for the mailboat were fraught with

The southern façade of Howth Castle which manages to span five hundred years in its various additions, showing a variety of styles from the genuinely medieval gate tower behind the low range of buildings to the right, to the imitation medieval keep built by Sir Edwin Lutyens at the left end of the low range. Georgian and Victorian to the early twentieth century make up the remainder of the building's fragmentary design.

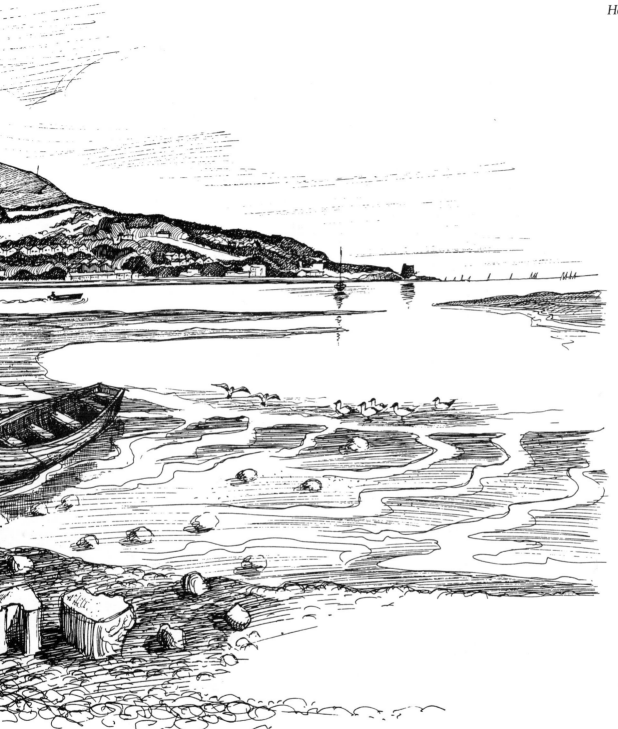

Poppies grow on the shore of Sutton Creek where the Hill of Howth shows the only continuous low-lying land on the peninsula. The demesne of Howth Castle is on the left with the obviously designed parkland rising up the hill to the barren slopes of Dung Hill and Black Linn. Between the saddle of the two hills and lower down is the Shielmartin graveyard where the minute Saint Fintan's Church is located, now totally hidden by trees but, like the dolmen, built in what was originally a commanding position. On the right-hand tip of the peninsula is Red Rock Martello Tower.

Above: Not quite Céad Míle Fáilte at Red Rock.

Right: Looking back towards the city from the Baily across Doldrum Bay, the rugged cliff face of Howth's southern side appears inaccessible and was a danger to shipping in previous centuries.

problems, and before long the vital service of communication had been lost to the larger harbour and its rival township.

Opposite Howth Harbour, and giving it an enclosed and protected feeling, is the highly improbable outline of Ireland's Eye, which suggests more a cardboard cutout of a pirate's island from a toy theatre than the refuge of an Early Christian settlement. The fabulous outline of the jagged rocks invites inquiry and the island is much visited by day trippers in the small boats which ply from the east pier during the summer. These rugged outlines appeal to my sense of the absurd, particularly after looking at the yacht marina which now occupies the eastern side of the har-

bour and possesses all the charm and grace of a carpark. Practical certainly, and efficient in the accommodating of the ever-increasing number of yachts, but the parallel with car parking is apposite and it begs a question, what next? Marinas, in the manner of all things concerned with either trade or leisure, tend to inexorably expand, and in this case the filling of the space available for expansion heralds the disappearance of the harbour as a place where one can take pleasure in the meeting of the elements of wind, sea and sky on an unencumbered breakwater. Few people find it satisfactory to take relaxation in a carpark, and a yachting marina occupying Howth Harbour is hardly more appealing.

The surrounding cliff face, which must have equally encouraged defenders and defeated developers, has left the peninsula with its sea coast substantially intact, and those in search of invigorating walks on the narrow paths which traverse much of the wild contours of the cliff line can find themselves on the only portion of the coastal area of Dublin Bay which shows no evidence of the improving or destructive hand of man.

However, on the Hill of Howth the improving hand can best be seen not in the now burgeoning trim parks of bland suburbia which appear to be infiltrating themselves into every crevice of the rolling hills, but in the sculptured landscape of the Howth Demesne. Here, many centuries of the St Lawrence family's preoccupation with landscaping has rendered hillsides originally barren into rich acres of mature trees and gardens both wild and ordered.

A painting by the mid-nineteenth-century artist, James Arthur O'Connor, shows the view looking down from the slopes of Muck Rock on the demesne, and out over the castle and Ireland's Eye. Prominently in the foreground is the dolmen, Aideen's Grave, isolated in the middle of an empty field, and further off the square bulk of the castle is surrounded by a bank of trees. Since this

painting was done, the entire foreground has been clothed in soil, physically carried up from below to support the rhododendron gardens which now envelop the rocky land and entirely surround the dolmen. The sense of massiveness of the dolmen, which made such a strong impact on Ferguson, has been diminished by the changed surroundings, although the immense weight of the fallen capstone remains impressive. It has been in its present tilted position for at least two hundred years.

If the St Anne's rose garden represents a civil servant's vision of the Garden of Eden, the Howth rhododendron garden in bloom, with around a thousand varieties of plant, represents an altogether more vigorous and primeval interpretation of the same concept. This remarkable hillside garden becomes a rolling carpet of mauves, pinks, reds, purples and whites when the flowers are in bloom and resembles the natural habitat of these hillside shrubs with their humid and sheltered setting. Around the peninsula, some of the spirit of this abundance had been emulated by contemporary gardeners, and a natural meeting of planting and landscape occur. More often it is the case of nature being enslaved to the lawnmower and the regular bungaloid windows look out upon a billiard table of daisyless lawn which appears as though it had been bought by the square metre in a department store.

The cliff walk, which begins on Shielmartin Road and traverses the peninsula, winds its way around the jagged line of the southern face of the peninsula, eventually surfacing at the summit of Howth from which an unbroken panoramic prospect of the bay may be seen. The hills across the bay on the southern side roll along the horizon, their gentle undulations interrupted by the peak of the Great Sugarloaf and the blunt nose of Bray Head. Otherwise it is all a modulated landscape. The lowlands of the coast rise abruptly into the still-farmed foothills of the Dublin Mountains, with some peaks, such as the Three

Left: Balscadden Bay was one of the alternative sites proposed for the building of Howth Harbour but was overruled in favour of the present location. There has been little change in the landscape here for a century.

Above: The medieval atmosphere of this corner of Howth makes this alley and the surrounding streets one of the most attractive and interesting sections of the peninsula.

Evening at the west pier of Howth. At the extreme right is the Harbour Master's Office and, at the opposite end, the Mariners' Hall.

Rock Mountain, suddenly breaking rank. From the summit of Howth, settlement along the opposite coast appears to be confined to the water's edge, and an exceptionally clear day is required to be able to pick out much detail on the shore. Despite a millennium of occupation, the strongest impression is that made by the natural landscape, and it is only when you look towards the city that the urban dominance can really be appreciated.

Abruptly below the summit is the Baily promontory, with its lighthouse perched on the edge of the cliff. Clearly a naturally ideal defensive site, it bears the remains of a fort, which can still be seen running across the rugged projection of cliff. From this point to the tip of Sorrento Point opposite, a line can be drawn inside which the waters of the bay are enclosed. This is the best position from which the entirety of the bay may be seen, along with the relationship between the port and the bay which it encloses.

From the protective converging fingers of the two Bull walls, minute toy-like ships emerge like drops released from a pippette, one at a time, and slowly the proportions grow as they move closer until suddenly they have assumed the proportions of real ships. For those heading north, their course lies below the Baily Light, and what had seemed fragile and minute becomes a massive container ship, sailing below the cliffs and disappearing towards the horizon.

From the summit a last glimpse of the city may be had - perhaps not the city so much as its identifying flagpoles, the twin stacks of the Poolbeg Power Station which clearly define the position of the city from any angle and for considerable distances. The cliff walk continues along the eastern coast, turning at the nose of Howth before the land slopes down into the pebbled shore of Balscadden Bay, the end of this rugged sequence of cliffs which terminate just before the harbour. Victorian photographs of Balscadden show a line of bathing boxes arranged like a collection of wheeled telephone kiosks in a row, set back from the water's edge. As one of the more bizarre relics of our grandsires' prudery, they have no place in contemporary bathing practices, as undressing in public has long ceased to be a breach of decorum.

The imaginative failures of the sailing clubs of the northern shore are more than redeemed by the new club building of the Howth Yacht Club, which contributes a sculpturally designed building to the harbour area and forms an interesting focal point to activity all along the Harbour Road. Contemporary architects, their minds strait-jacketed by designing office buildings, often appear to have lost the capacity to produce buildings which one can walk around without feeling a loss of interest. This yacht club is a series of changing faces, which show an awareness of the building's position, opening out over the harbour with extravagant canopies and a definite sense of occasion. Here the civic quality of the sailing club buildings of Dun Laoghaire has been both adequately emulated and interpreted in a fresh manner.

Howth harbour has fared badly from an aesthetic point of view, even if its functions and the demands upon its capacity have been well rationalised. The practice followed in the expansion of Dublin Port - of reclaiming land from the sea by rubble infill - may be acceptable in an industrial context, but here I feel it to be totally inappropriate and an abuse of the harbour as marine architecture. The sharp lines and detailed surfaces are qualities which contribute to the character of stone-built structures, and the juxtaposing of them with accumulations of rough stone and builders' rubble is to diminish the excellent workmanship of the past. Where important structures of stone exist, it should be implicit in their use that whatever the underlying material of new work, the surfaces should reflect the mode of the existing materials.

As an active fishing port, Howth possesses a very different atmosphere from Dun Laoghaire,

The 'College of Howth', a fifteenth-century residence for the priests of the abbey, which is more properly called a collegiate church as no abbots are recorded.

The prospect of Dublin Bay from Howth summit. The Isle of Man Steam Co. ship Lady of Man *steams out of the bay under the Baily Lighthouse, and further out the various container ships head into or out of the port. Bray Head on the southern side is almost directly above the Baily; the Muglins and Dalkey Islands lie between it and the beginning of Killiney Hill, capped by the obelisk. The major feature of the southern shore is Dun Laoghaire Harbour with a flurry of yachts at its mouth.*

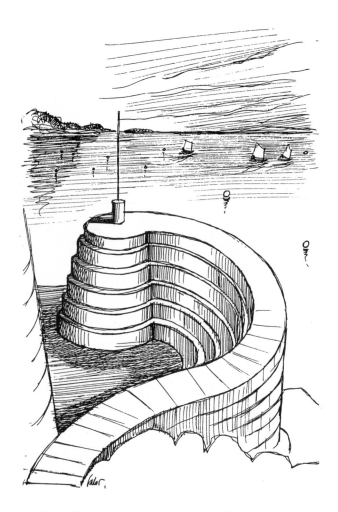

Above: The stone question mark at the lighthouse.

Right: The lighthouse at the end of the east pier in Howth with the keepers' little house attached on the right.

and the mass of trawlers moored along the west pier are probably closer in relationship to the traditional activities of a harbour than is to be found anywhere else in the bay, with the exception of the port. Old photographs of the harbour in the nineteenth century show a crowded scene which differs from the present only in the supremacy of sail, now to be seen only on some of the smaller boats. The naming of boats, like racehorses, is often whimsical, and the reasons behind a particular choice quite inscrutable. A sunken trawler which lies submerged along the east pier just inside the harbour mouth has a wraith-like aspect, the surface of the wooden hull concealed by a green membrane of fine seaweed. What prompted the owner to name it *Excalibur*? The assisting hand of the water nymph has yet to raise it above the waters.

Fishing ports habitually have their piers littered with the artifacts of the fishermen's calling. The modern trawler has added much to the bric-a-brac of nets and anchors to encumber the piers and slipways. On the piers of Howth Harbour, amongst the broken winches and sea-green plastic nets, lie piled otter boards from the trawlers. Constructed of timber and iron, they look like the shields of a race of heroes who might lately have constructed a great tomb on the hillside overlooking the harbour. The scale is just about right for the dolmen builders.

Above the harbour the land rises steeply towards the moorland which runs all along the top of the Hill of Howth. St Mary's Abbey stands on a plateau, buttressed by a defensive rampart and topped by the slender and empty bell-cote which can be seen from most of the harbour, although the abbey is concealed by a screen of trees. In the eighteenth century the strand and shoreline lay below the walls of the abbey, running straight along from here to the gates of Howth Castle. The streets which lie directly behind the abbey grounds, and run down the hill at either side to the harbour, enclose an area which has had little

intrusive development during the last hundred years, and has much potential, more so than anywhere else around Dublin Bay, towards being conserved as an historic enclave. It is not that there is much which is pre-nineteenth century except the buildings associated with the abbey, but that there is little which is later. The atmosphere of an old port town clings to these streets, and the 'College' building on Abbey Street might be rewardingly developed as a nucleus to enhance what already exists. This building, although roofless, has been occupied up to fairly recently, and if restored would form an exciting location for a local museum, as Rothe House does in Kilkenny. For bizarre contrasts it would be difficult to exceed the combination of this lovely building and the small shop which clings to its side, the exterior painted with an effect of multicoloured balloons! This represents an imaginative attempt to decorate an ugly modern addition, but I question the motif. Looking directly down the hill from the college, the harbour is at the bottom. Confined between the buildings at the end of the street, the sea rises to the horizon and gulls wheel in the air above, drawing one down to the bustle of the harbour, from here no more than suggested by protruding masts.

Behind the village the hill rises to the series of small peaks which run along above the tree line. This heathland, now under the control of An Taisce, so distinctive a feature of the Hill of Howth, is much bisected by the paths of walkers like a site of pilgrimage. The paths run between the bracken, contrasting the whiteness of pebbles with the dark surrounding growth. The soil here is too acid to support anything but the typical heather and gorse, and so close is the rock surface below the covering of soft turves that this mat of vegetation is easily eroded. Within the confines of those plants which are capable of surviving on so windswept a summit, a stunning range of colours is to be seen in bright contrast to the dun-coloured ground. Gold and purple assume an internal luminescence here on the dark hilltop and the fragments of rock which protrude everywhere have a bleached appearance, scoured by the wind and rain which sweep in from the Irish Sea to envelop the Hill of Howth in mist. From here the castle and harbour are diminutive and distant versions of their real selves. This is the point from which the well known eighteenth-century prospect of Howth Castle by an unknown painter has been taken, a semi-bird's-eye view of the gardens and demesne. The activity on the lawns

Right: : Howth Harbour was reorganised and deepened in the late 1970s, with the space being divided into a trawler harbour on the west side and a yacht marina between Howth Yacht Club and the east pier. Directly behind the club house is the mooring of the modern lifeboat. This is the view from the height of Castle Hill, and Baldoyle and Portmarnock appear in the background.

Below: 'The Steps', which join Church Street to the harbour front.

and parterre in the painting show ladies and gentlemen, elegantly clad and formally taking their leisure. With the parkland of Howth Castle now occupied by a golf course, the figures who pass before the house are vastly different, casually clad and carrying a few clubs with them.

Between the trees, houses are everywhere to be seen, overrunning the isthmus of Sutton, occupying the foreshore of Sutton Creek, rising to the boundaries of the demesne and threatening to surround it. Such change is more noticeable here in Howth than in any other area of the bay because one is dealing with a contained space. The more any section of the bay becomes available to vast numbers of people, the more under threat are those very qualities which recommend particular locations and make them attractive. The sanctuary of Bull Island is now accessible to double-decker buses and the throngs which they bring, as well to as the legion who come and park their cars on the beach. Howth is in the same predicament, with the unspoilt and fragile heathland which makes it unique in the perimeter of the bay, liable to destruction by being virtually trodden underfoot by the admiring mass of residents and visitors intent on relaxation and fresh air.

It is difficult to see a solution to the problem of what is precious in an environment being destroyed by the very people who have come to enjoy it. The houses on the lower reaches of the peninsula already stand shoulder to shoulder, and it can hardly be long before the residents are in the same uncomfortable position. It is a phenomenon common everywhere that those who come first look with positive disdain on those who come after them, and quietly, or more volubly wish that the newcomers would go somewhere else. Anyone to whom I talked on the peninsula was less than kind concerning the latest rash of house building, harbour developments, influx of new residents, or foreshore buildings, yet each complainant had come in from somewhere else not so long before, and at that time also represented change. The difference is that with the passage of time the problem of congestion becomes exacerbated until it reaches a crisis point. While the bog asphodel and heath orchid still bloom naturally on Howth, there is the possibility of adopting some plan to conserve and preserve the breathing space so necessary to a community. When, like the elephant, they live only in a walled enclosure as 'specimens', it will be too late.

Nothing demonstrates the actuality of urban sprawl around Dublin bay as effectively as the satellite photographs taken at a height of 832 kilometres above the earth. This is a case of distance lending enchantment to the view. From such a height, the curve of the land with all its details of roads and occupation looks fascinating, the deep blue of the water setting off the green of a million gardens. You might be looking down through the deep seas on the submerged city of Atlantis, the place looks so uninhabited and far away. Out of the welter of detail, Howth stands out as the last preserve of open land on the bay. The narrow white roads which curve and convolute all over the landscape of the bay diminish at the borders of Howth and leave a clear space like an acropolis to occupy the centre of this mass of land which hangs on the northern tip of the Dublin Bay.

While it is not really necessary to stand back eight hundred kilometres in order to appreciate the beauties of Dublin Bay, from this overview the importance of the bay as a breathing space and recreational facility, and its accumulated natural amenities, are instantly visible in a manner which becomes more fragmented the closer one gets.

The sunken trawler Excalibur *at the west pier. Two Galway hookers are moored behind, to the right.*

Gazetteer of Dublin Bay

Lord Carnarvon 'Can you see anything?'
Howard Carter 'Yes, wonderful things.'

THE CONTENTS OF THIS GAZETTEER are drawn from the great variety of familiar objects, buildings and things found around the circumference of the bay. Because of their repetitiveness some of these are closely associated with Dublin Bay. Martello towers and lighthouses are the most obvious but there are other things equally well represented though not generally linked with the bay; Early Christian churches, sculptures, castles are amongst these. Many of the buildings noted here are on the very shores of the bay and can easily be found. Others are not much farther inland, but the building of houses and the accompanying growth of trees has obscured their position. Some others are situated off the coast on the few islands which occur in the bay, and are accessible by boats for most of the year. I have not included those Martello towers which are now used as houses and stand in private grounds, unless their position appeared to warrant inclusion, such as the tower at Red Rock in Sutton. In categories such as sculpture, I have made no distinction between ancient and modern; an Early Christian stone cross has as much right as anything produced in more recent times to be seen as three-dimensional art. Interestingly, those qualities which are lasting as well as those which are transient are emphasised by this juxtaposing of works which span more than a thousand years.

Everyone who drives over the East Link Bridge must wonder what the sculptures there are called, and whom they are by. The gazetteer answers such questions. By grouping modern and ancient works together, it is inevitable that some comparisons arise. Differences of materials are the most immediate, and the enduring nature of stone contrasts sharply with the currently popular and infinitely more transient material of sheet steel. While the Early Christian stone crosses at Blackrock and Killiney may be, through time and erosion, a mere simulacrum of their former selves, they are still quite beautiful and sculpturally robust. Perhaps this is not an important consideration for a contemporary sculptor, but it is hard to imagine the works at the East Link being around for even a fraction of that time. Have the values of our throwaway society affected art also? It would appear so, for most of the steel sculptures which I looked at showed signs of corrosion. Not so those in bronze or stone, which look like they have greater powers of survival. My personal bias is towards the value of permanance, whether the subject is Martello towers, sailing clubs or sculptures. Works of art which are in the process of self-destructing seem to be rather deprived of their purpose.

Of the Martellos, churches and castles, very few have not been tampered with and there is practically nothing one can look at in the sure conviction that somebody in the past has not 'improved' it - as with the church on Ireland's Eye - or removed something of significance - as with the Casino. The Joyce Museum is a rare find amongst much interesting material in that it presents an opportunity to examine a Martello which is well cared for.

This gazetteer is neither comprehensive nor definitive, being based on a combination of two unscientific principles - location and access. It depends for its validity on the inherent interest of its contents. To divide the contents according to period would give a preponderance to the nineteenth century, with the medieval and modern eras about equal, but in distinctly second place. This dominance of the last century indicates the phenomenal building activity of that century, greatly surpassing its predecessor which generally receives all the credit for giving Dublin a memorable body of buildings. Another factor which is noticeable amongst these buildings is the variety and contrasting styles of stonework, giving principally to the nineteenth century the claim to have produced the best masonry to be found in Dublin, city or bay.

If some of my inclusions or omissions appear unwarranted, it must be attributed to the essentially arbitrary nature of such a compendium of objects. Harbours and swimming baths are other potential categories, and there may be many more. What is consistent is the existence of all manner of interesting things to be seen around Dublin Bay, and the more you look the wider the range becomes. The looking is the operative experience. Visit these places and see for yourself.

Martello Tower, Dalkey Island, 1904. Seen from the battery. These are two of the three buildings standing on the island and part of the defensive encircling of the bay which also included the Half Moon Battery on the South Wall. Both tower and battery are gradually falling apart through neglect. As an accessible complex they deserve to be repaired and conserved.

Rathdown-type Stone, St Begnet's Churchyard, Castle Street, Dalkey. Carved memorial or grave stone of approximately the tenth century, decorated with circles, cup marks and a cross.

Archbold's Castle, Castle Street, Dalkey. One of the two surviving sixteenth-century castles, this castle has not been restored, and lacks battlements. The castles of Dalkey were used by the merchants of Dublin as stronghouses for the safekeeping of goods, in connection with the nearby Bullock Harbour.

St. Begnet's Church, Dalkey Island, *c*. tenth century. A well-preserved building with some incongruous later additions. The flat-lintelled door and projecting sidewalls or 'ante' are characteristic of early churches. Used as living quarters during the construction of the Martello tower, a fireplace has been inserted in the east wall and a door and window in the south corner.

Muglins Beacon, off Dalkey Island. The waters around these rocks are a popular area for sea-angling. The automatic light replaced a beacon erected on the Muglins in the late nineteenth century.

St. Begnet's Church, Castle Street, Dalkey, fifteenth century. Possibly on the site of an earlier church, it replaced the church of the same dedication on Dalkey Island, which fell into disuse in the early medieval period.

Kish Bank Telescopic Lighthouse. This lighthouse was constructed in Dun Laoghaire harbour and then towed to its position on the Kish Bank, seven miles out from the harbour. The upper floors which contain the lantern, helicopter pad and residential accomodation were enclosed within the base and subsequently raised in a telescopic manner to their full height after the lower section had been secured on the sea bed.

Dublin Bay One Design 24', designed by Milne and built on the Clyde *c*. 1938, but not finished until 1946 due to the interruption of the war. Eight boats were built of which five still race in Dublin Bay. These are *Fenestra, Adastra, Arandora, Harmony* and *Euphanzel*.

Killiney Obelisk, Killiney Hill, 1742. The mutilated remains of a famine relief work organised by the local landowner, John Mapas of Killiney Castle. It was enclosed by a boundary wall and had a flight of steps to the first floor. Two inscriptions on the northern face state: 'Last year being hard with the poor, the Walls about these Hills and This etc. erected by John Mapas, Esq, June, 1742.' 'Repaired by Robert Warren, Esq., MDCCCXL'(1840).

Boucher's Obelisk, Killiney Hill Park. Located on the hill to the seaward side of the larger obelisk, and slightly down the slope. This hexagonal building contains a small room with a door and window and an inscription 'Mount Mapas' over the door. Perhaps the obelisk was constructed the wrong way round, as it faces into the rock, but if reoriented could look towards the sea and Dalkey Island.

'Thus Daedalus Flew', by Niall O'Neill, Killiney Hill Park, Victoria Gate, Killiney Hill Road, 1986. (Bronze.) Daedalus, the supreme artificer and inventor from Greek mythology, as well as the *alter ego* chosen by James Joyce. The bronze figure, excellently sited inside Victoria Gate, seems to derive more from Christian than from Classical imagery.

The Wishing Stone, Killiney Hill Park, 1852. Stone step pyramid adjacent to Boucher's Obelisk. A slab in the topmost stone is inscribed MDCCCLII. Popular legend states that 'if you walk around each level clockwise to the top and then face Dalkey Island, your wish will be granted'. Presumably erected by John Warren, then the local landowner, who repaired the obelisk in 1840.

Killiney Church, Marino Avenue West, Killiney Hill Road. Eleventh-century church with later annex. Dedicated to the seven saintly daughters of Lénine. Unlike many of the other early churches, this one has not been altered or 'improved' since it ceased to be used as a church in the seventeenth century. Contains many interesting details.

Granite Cross, Killiney Church, Marino Avenue West, Killiney Hill Road. Small eleventh-century cross, mounted on wall of sixteenth-century annex to earlier church. The central boss may represent a head, like that on the cross in Blackrock, but is much eroded.

Goat Castle, Castle Street, Dalkey, now Dalkey Town Hall. One of a number of sixteenth-century towers from the period of Dalkey's importance as a port for Dublin. Extensively restored in the nineteenth century.

Bullock Castle, Bullock Harbour, Breffni Road, Dalkey, twelfth century. Part of the harbour defenses built by the monks of St Mary's Abbey, a portion of whose foundation still remains off Capel Street in Dublin. There is a sculpted human face high up on the south-west angle of the west tower, nearest to the road.

'Goats', by Katy Goodhue, Dillon Park, Coliemore Road, Dalkey, 1986. A static version of the all too nimble live goats that inhabit Dalkey Island, directly opposite the park and across the sound. Constructed of reinforced concrete, it is not ageing too well, which is a pity as it suits the site quite admirably.

The Druid's Chair, Killiney Avenue, off Killiney Hill Road, eighteenth century. This arrangement of granite boulders represents a chair which once overlooked the bay, but an estate wall has been built right in front of it, making its position appear purposeless. The oak glade which surrounds it, and probably the 'antiquity', were planted sometime before 1778, to grace a gentleman's park.

The National Maritime Museum of Ireland, Haig Terrace, Dun Laoghaire, 1837. Formerly the Mariners' Church, built to serve the needs of the crews of visiting ships in the harbour, and acquired by the Maritime Institute of Ireland as a museum in 1976. It contains an important and fascinating collection of material relating to maritime history, both local and international.

Royal St George Yacht Club, Dun Laoghaire Harbour, 1842-45. Designed by John Skipton Mulvany, who is responsible also for the Royal Irish Yacht Club building to the west of it, as well as the nearby railway station. An Ionic collonade with projecting pavillions, it is based on extending the original building, by duplicating the pavillion and inserting a connecting collonade.

'Celebration', by Dick Joynt, Eden Park, Glasthule, 1986. (Kilkenny limestone.) People with prams constantly pass through this little park or sit on the grass nearby. The figure of a woman holding a child up in the air in a protective manner appears very much in harmony with these surroundings. The treatment of the woman's head is reminiscent of that on the early cross in Blackrock.

Royal Irish Yacht Club, Dun Laoghaire Harbour, 1850. Designed by John Skipton Mulvany. The façade of this building, an Ionic collonade flanked by pavillions, makes it the most distinguished yacht club on the bay. On its landward side it still has some open space between passing heavy traffic and the entrance to the ferry. It is one of the first purpose-built yacht clubs in the world.

National Yacht Club, off Crofton Road, Dun Laoghaire, 1870. A building showing Classical allusions rather than anything more definite in its design. The latest of a trio of nineteenth-century buildings which once dominated the shoreline of Dun Laoghaire Harbour, but have been rather diminished by the ferry facilities.

'Archer II', by Niall O'Neill, Newtownsmith, Sandycove, 1985. As enigmatic as an Easter Island figure, this strange personage aims his tiny bow out over the horizon. Constructed of reinforced concrete over a granite core.

George IV Testimonial, Crofton Road, Dun Laoghaire, 1821. Granite obelisk commemorating the laying of the first stone of the new harbour, and the granting of royal patronage by the king in the changing of the name from Dunleary to Kingstown. One of the balls which support the base was blown off some years ago and has not been replaced. Are the Corporation just waiting for the monument to fall down? There are several commemorative inscriptions on this monument. The principal one reads 'To commemorate the visit of the King to this part of his dominions and to record that on the third of September 1821 his majesty in person graciously named this asylum harbour the Royal Harbour of George IV and on the same day embarked from hence'.

James Joyce Museum, Martello Tower, Sandycove. Opened as a Joyce Museum in 1962, it contains a collection of memorabilia of the writer. A century after the tower was built (in 1804), it was the scene in August 1904 of an uncomfortable visit by Joyce to his friend Gogarty, who had rented the building. The opening pages of *Ulysses* takes place on the roof and in the round room of the tower.

Boyd Obelisk, East Pier, Dun Laoghaire Harbour, post 1861. Decorated with a rope motif and cockle shells, the inscription on the obelisk tells its story. 'Erected by members of the Royal St George Yacht Club to commemorate the heroism of Captn J. Mc Neil Boyd, RN, HMS *Ajax*, who perished near this spot with five of his ship's company, Thomas Murphy, John Curry, John Russell, James Johnson, Alexander Forsyth, in a noble attempt to rescue the crew of the brig *Neptune*, wrecked during the storm IX February MDCCCLXI (1861).

The Irish Lights Depot, Dun Laoghaire. The Commissioners of Irish Lights are the authority for the eighty-five lighthouses around the Irish coast and the depot is their principal workshop where buoys, beacons and other seamarks are repaired. The large buoy in the drawing is the LANBY or Large Automatic Navigational Buoy, two of which are permanently on station with one at the depot in reserve.

Castor and Pollux, De Vesci Terrace, Dun Laoghaire, *c.* 1840. Looking rather more like South Sea Islanders wielding clubs, these figures from Greek mythology had amongst their functions the protecting of sailors at sea, and from the parapet of De Vesci Terrace they gaze out over the bay, standing on either side of the De Vesci crest.

King Laoghaire's Chair, De Vesci Gardens, Dun Laoghaire. An enigma of impenetrable obscurity. Is this massive granite seat an eighteenth-century antiquity or the throne of the Iron Age King Laoghaire? The seat, which looks like the centrepiece of a three-piece-suite, came to light early in this century when roadworks unearthed it in the area of the king's *dún*. Surprisingly, it is quite comfortable and beautifully finished.

The East Pier Battery, Dun Laoghaire. Constructed in the mid-nineteenth century around the lighthouse, its external wall is a superb example of granite masonry. Within the battery are four gun emplacements for traversing cannon as well as four modern guns trained on the mouth of the bay. Like the Martello towers and other parts of the defensive network around the bay, it never saw action.

The Motor Yacht Club, West Pier, Dun Laoghaire. The most recent club building to be erected in the harbour, catering for motor boats and dinghy sailing. The architectural excellence of the buildings at the end of the west pier are in marked contrast to those, this club among them, at the Coal Harbour end, which might be anywhere and might serve any mundane purpose.

West Pier Lighthouse, Dun Laoghaire Harbour, *c.* 1850. This lighthouse, and the granite keeper's house nearby form a very interesting contrast to the treatment of the same elements on the east pier, where they are combined in one structure.

Dublin Bay One Design 21', designed by Milne. Seven of these boats were built between 1903 and 1907 and are based in Dun Laoghaire. Some years ago their rigging was modernised, but at present all seven are being restored to the original gaff-rigged form at Tyrrells boatyard, Arklow. They are an important class in the Dublin Bay Sailing Club racing calendar. The boats are *Innisfallen, Maureen, Estelle, Garavogue, Oola, Naneen* and *Geraldine.*

'Christ the King', by Andrew O'Connor, Haig Terrace, Dun Laoghaire, 1926. (Bronze) Lengthy inscriptions on the base, in French, German, Spanish, Irish and English, imply more than they state about the history of this work, the finest piece of sculpture to be found around the bay. Between 1949, when a local committee chose O'Connor's work for Dun Laoghaire, and 1978, almost thirty years later when the sculpture was erected, there is an interesting and unexplained hiatus.

East Pier Lighthouse, Dun Laoghaire. Within the battery at the end of the east pier is the lighthouse, only the top of which can normally be seen from the outside. The pier was begun in 1817 and completed twenty-five years later in 1842, when the light was turned on.

'Red Sails at Sunset' by Bernard Mortell, Brighton Vale, Seapoint, 1986. Situated on a little knoll of ground above the water, this sheet-steel sculpture instantly suggests a connection with the sea and the movement of sails. Off shore the sailboarders mirror the movement of the sculpture.

'The Water Wag', designed by J.E. and Mamie Doyle, 1887. This small wooden boat, which is still sailed in Dublin Bay, is the oldest and also the original one-design racing yacht, having been altered very little in design since around 1900. Water Wags are still being built, over a century after they were first raced in 1887 in Kingstown Harbour.

'The Black Rock', by Rowan Gillespie, Temple Road, Blackrock. Three slender figures, male and female, support a large neolithic-looking boulder with unconvincing ease. The Black Rock, from which the area derives its name, was quarried away during the building of the railway in 1834, and this work provides a new focus for legends to develop, and is an interesting variation on the dolmen theme.

Obelisk, Obelisk Park (St Augustine's School), Carysfort Avenue, Blackrock, *c.* 1732 or earlier. Unlike the Killiney Obelisk, which has been much repaired and altered, this one has survived in excellent condition and is a splendid example of a Georgian landscape ornament. The rock base contains a large domed space, and the doors in the obelisk lead into a similar small room. It was built as a mausoleum for the Allen family.

'Cut-out People', by Dan McCarthy, Blackrock Park, 1986. Steel plate on a concrete plinth. Whether one is driving past on the road or walking around them in the park, these figures appear to move and change constantly with an airy grace above the bay.

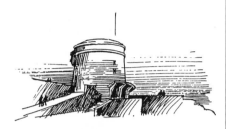

Martello Tower, Brighton Vale, Seapoint, 1804. The only one of the towers on the southern shore of the bay which has not been pushed inland by infill of land or by roadways.

Bathing House, Foreshore, Blackrock, eighteenth century. Ruins of a hexagonal brick building with Gothic windows, part of a small complex of bathing houses and enclosed sea-water pool.

Bathing House, Vance's Harbour, Blackrock, eighteenth century. Lord Cloncurry's estate of Maretimo was cut off from the shore by the building of the railway in the 1830s, and a handsome tower bridge was constructed by the company to allow access from the estate to the foreshore and its bathing facilities. Ironically the house is gone, but this little Doric temple remains, with a small stone-built boat harbour.

'Stele for Cecil King', by Colm Brennan, Tobernea Park, Temple Hill, Blackrock, 1986. (Mild steel plate.) The stele is a form of memorial common in ancient Egypt, well known in such examples as 'Cleopatra's Needle.' Here, a sculptor pays homage to the memory of an abstract painter in an interpretation of the traditional stele form which is reminiscent of industrial machinery.

Granite Cross, Main Street, Blackrock, Early Christian period. Nothing is known about the origin of this cross which has stood on the main street of Blackrock since the mid-eighteenth century. In 1865 the town commissioners decided to remove it as an 'obstruction', but after a public controversy this order was reprieved. Nineteenth-century photographs show it perched on the top of a stone structure resembling a large postbox about three metres high. Funeral processions used to make a circle in front of the cross before proceeding past it.

Martello Tower, Williamstown, Seafort Parade, off Rock Road, 1804. All the Martello towers are different in detail although similar in overall design. In the case of this tower, the wall surrounding the internal parapet projects out over the slightly inclined wall, a feature not found elsewhere. Due to landfill around the tower, it appears much shorter than it is.

W.B. Yeats, by Andrew O'Connor, Sandymount Green. Yeats was born nearby in No. 5 Sandymount Avenue, and appropriately is remembered with this bust, an excellent portrait of the poet in middle age. Sited in a secluded corner of the green, it seems to cast a bemused eye on life around it.

Monkstown Castle, Castle Park, Monkstown, fourteenth century. Established by the monks of St Mary's Abbey, and like Bullock Castle intended to protect the monastic lands and fisheries in the area. The present gate tower and tower house are mostly sixteenth century, the latter being much mutilated.

Martello Tower, Strand Road, Sandymount, 1804. One of a series of gun batteries built to withstand an expected Napoleonic invasion. The majority of the towers in Ireland are concentrated around Dublin Bay, and twenty-one are still standing between Balbriggan and Bray. The Strand Road tower is the closest one to the city on either shore.

Poolbeg Yacht and Boat Club, founded 1971. The sailing club closest to the city centre, with a considerable number of yachts moored in Trawlers Pond on the Liffey, and the only sailing club to actually be on the river. Nearby, the Ringsend Registered Fishermen and Private Boat Owners have foreshore space but no premises.

St Patrick's Rowing Club, Irishtown, founded in 1935. The slipway for this club is on the open water where the Dodder and the Grand Canal enter the Liffey.

'An Gallán Gréine do James Joyce', by Cliodna Cussen, Sandymount Beach Road Park, 1983, (Stone.) The differences between a genuine antiquity, an eighteenth-century pastiche and a modern interpretation are difficult to define, except that the former and the latter are concerned with meaning and the middle example is purely decorative. This neo-Iron Age monument, a granite pun, is a gift which might have amused Joyce.

'An Gallán Gréine do James Joyce', by Cliodna Cussen, Sandymount Beach Road Park, 1983. (Stone.) On the 21 December (the winter solstice) the rays of the setting sun fall on the axis of the sundial and on the centrepiece of the stone circle.

Monument to an Axe, by Niall O'Neill, East Link Bridge, 1983. (Steel.) O'Neill is also the sculptor of the figure of Daedalus inside the Victoria Gate at Killiney Hill. The best sited of the sculptures at the East Link Bridge, and also the one which needs the least explanation.

Ashford Obelisk, Irishtown Green. This strange monument, which obviously can't decide whether it wants to be an obelisk or not, was erected in 1894 to commemorate 'the valuable service rendered for a period of half a century to the poor of Irishtown parish'. It is a memorial to Dr William Ashford, son of the artist of the same name, who lived in Sandymount Park House nearby, which was designed by James Gandon.

Matt Talbot, by James Power, Talbot Memorial Bridge (City Quay end), 1988. (Limestone.) Talbot (1856-1925) was a docker, ascetic and religious extremist who has a considerable following in Dublin. He is buried in papal magnificence in the church of Our Lady of Lourdes on Sean Mac-Dermott St. There is an interesting contrast between the passivity of this figure and the strength of the Mariner on the opposite quay, the only sculpture concerned with the life of the port. Talbot Memorial Bridge is not, as the name would seem to imply, a memorial to Talbot, but a fine example of compromise. One faction in the Corporation wished to commemorate those merchant seamen killed during World War II, the other faction wished to commemorate Talbot and, unable to agree, they arrived at the ungrammatical and misleading title which the bridge now bears. Are the seamen on the north shore or do they have the right-hand lane? A conundrum certainly.

Stella Maris Rowing Club, Ringsend, founded in 1937. One of a number of clubs grouped around Trawlers' Pond on the southern approach to the East Link Bridge. There has been for centuries a thriving community of sailors and rowers in Irishtown and Ringsend, which were important areas in the ship-building and fishing traditions of the port.

'Release', by Jim Buckley, East Link Bridge, 1983. (Steel.) Standing on the narrow tarmac strip between two rows of cars hardly does much to enhance this work. Created in the Arklow Shipyard and now backed by moored yachts, the suspended horseshoe shape acquires a marine suggestion, intentionally or otherwise. The small piece on the ground which appears to be pecking at the foot of the larger sculpture is 'ACE', by Vivienne Roche, 1983.

North Bank Lighthouse, River Liffey Channel, 1940. A lighthouse has stood here since 1908, but was replaced by this automatic light. It stands in the river between the Poolbeg Power Station and the Half Moon Battery.

North Bull Lighthouse, North Bull Wall, Bull Island, 1880. This lighthouse, which marks the northern side of the river channel, is built at the end of the part of the wall which is submerged at high tide. The wall, which was completed in 1823, runs three thousand metres from the Dollymount shore. With the completion of the North Bull Wall, the force of the ebb tide deepened the channel and lowered the harbour bar.

North Wall Extension Lighthouse, Dublin Port, 1900. First lit in August 1904, contemporary with events at the Sandycove Martello. Architecturally the least interesting of all the lighthouses around the bay, it marks the western side of the entrance to Alexandra Basin.

'Dark Night', by Michael Warren, Port Centre, Alexandra Road, 1981. (Wood.) This sculpture, composed of heavy timber beams, occupies the centre of the terrace outside the Port Centre. In its weathered textures and abstract form it reflects both the more traditional materials of the early history of the port and the modern architecture of the building. These timbers might be the relics of bygone port structures as much as twentieth-century art objects.

Eastern Breakwater Lighthouse, Dublin Port *c.* 1900, first lit 1904. Built on what was then the easternmost extremity of the expanding port, it marked the conclusion of an encircling arm of break-waters which doubled the area of land reclaimed in the nineteenth century.

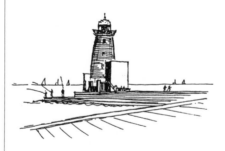

Poolbeg Lighthouse, Great South Wall. Built between 1761 and 1768 to mark the sandbanks at the entrance to the river channel, it replaced a lightship previously moored at the spot. Situated about three kilometres from Ringsend at the end of a granite causeway, the lighthouse was finished first and then the wall was built back towards the city, meeting the outgoing section at where the Pigeon House now stands.

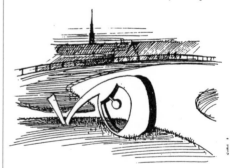

'Greenwells Glory', by Sean Adamson, East Link Bridge, 1983. (Painted steel.) Placed on the margin of grass between the road and the parapet of the bridge, the siting does not do much to enhance this brightly coloured work which needs space around it to balance the dramatic splash of orange which it introduces into this rather arid environment.

Lord Charlemont's Casino, Marino, Clontarf, 1762-73. Designed by Sir William Chambers. Now open to the public after years of neglect, this Georgian masterpiece has been meticulously restored. The exuberance of the external stone carving and internal plasterwork, combined with the intricacy of the plan, make this building difficult to absorb until it has been looked at many times.

Realt na Mara, North Bull Wall, 1961-72. At the end of the Bull Wall, where the half-tide section commences, this monument stands in a splendidly commanding position overlooking the channel. The design of a concrete tripod, surmounted by a globe, resolves into the conventional with the placing of a typical religious image of the period on the top. Bull Island is the only inhabited island in the bay.

Kilbarrack Sailing Club, Sutton Creek, Kilbarrack. Founded in 1943, the present club house and dinghy park is surrounded by a pallisade which would have deterred the Vikings.

'Wind Sculpture', by Eamonn O'Dogherty, Clontarf Promenade, 1988. (Painted steel.) O'Dogherty is also the sculptor of the figure of Anna Livia in the millennium fountain on O'Connell Street. This is the only piece of monumental sculpture amongst those placed around the bay in the last fifteen years. Excellently sited, it suggests movement and the activities of the bay.

Kilbarrack Church, Dublin Road, Kilbarrack. Shown as a ruin on John Roque's map of Dublin in 1756, this is a traditional place of burial for those who have lost their lives at sea. The church ruins display no features of any architectural distinction beyond the site itself, overlooking the bay.

Sutton Dinghy Club, Sutton Creek. Founded in the 1930s. This is one of the characteristic small clubs which exist for smaller boats all around the bay.

Clontarf Yacht and Boat Club on the Clontarf Road. Founded in 1875, the club has occupied this building, a former private house, since its inception.

Interpretive Centre, North Bull Island, 1985. A centre for the conservational, educational and recreational use of the island which forms a unique nature reserve within Dublin Bay as well as a 5km-long beach, Dollymount Strand. During the migratory period, the bird density on the island is the highest in the country. Bull Island has been recognised by UNESCO as a biosphere reserve.

Howth Yacht Club, Howth. The only modern yacht club of any visual distinction, it dominates the harbour area and is the focal point of the reclaimed land on the foreshore.

Howth 17-footer, designed by Sir Walter Boyd, 1898. The world's oldest surviving one-design class of keel boat racing yachts, which still sail out of Howth in their original rig. All sixteen yachts of this class are stationed in Howth. The last boat in this class was built in 1914. The boats are *Anita, Aura, Bobolink, Deilginis, Eileen, Echo, Gladys, Hera, Leila, Mimosa, Nautilus, Pauline, Rita, Rosemary, Silver Moon* and *Zaida*.

George the Fourth's Footprints, West Pier, Howth Harbour, 1821. The king landed on 12 August 1821, and placed his dainty feet on Irish land at this spot. The event was commemorated by carving the imprints of his feet into the granite slab of the pier. A plaque recording the visit was originally in the recess of the wall facing the pier.

Howth Castle, Howth, fifteenth century and later. The existing castle consists of a medieval tower, eighteenth-century remodelling of the central portion and later additions in this century by Lutyens, mirroring the fifteenth-century remains. The St Lawrence family have been lords of Howth for eight hundred years and still live in the castle, which is the oldest continuously inhabited building in Ireland.

East Pier Lighthouse, Howth Harbour, 1813. The lighthouse of the nineteenth-century harbour has been superseded by recent improvements, which include the construction of a breakwater at the harbour head on which the modern light stands.

Tomb of the St Lawrence family, Howth Abbey, 1542. On the top of the tomb is a double effigy of Sir Christopher St Lawrence and his wife, Anna Plunkett of Ratoath. Decorative panels run around the sides, with crests and Church dignitaries under Gothic arches. Here are shown St Thomas of Canterbury, St Katherine of Alexandria and St Peter, each with an identifying symbol of staff, wheel and key.

Portal Dolmen, Howth Demesne, *c*. 2000 B.C. Now surrounded by the rhododendron grove which diminishes the impression of its size, the dolmen would originally have stood on the open hillside and been visible for miles around.

Martello Tower, Ireland's Eye, 1804. There are three towers located around the Howth Peninsula, two on the mainland and this, the third, on the island directly opposite the harbour.

Martello Tower, Castle Hill, Howth Village, 1804. This tower occupies the position thought to have been the original location of the St Lawrence family's twelfth-century castle prior to the establishment of the present Howth Castle.

Cill Mac Nessan, Ireland's Eye, Howth, eleventh century. This little church stands on a bleak fern-covered hillside opposite Howth Harbour. It has been so heavily restored in the nineteenth century that it is difficult to establish its original form.

Martello Tower, Red Rock, Sutton, 1804. Unlike the majority of the towers this one was not built of excellent granite masonry, but of roughly coursed local red limestone which was plastered over. In other respects the tower corresponds to the overall form and details of the other towers around the bay.

The College, Abbey Street, Howth Village, fifteenth century. Situated on the edge of the abbey grounds, this building was the residence of the clergy who were connected with the abbey. Popularly known as The College, it is a building which recommends itself for restoration and appropriate re-use.

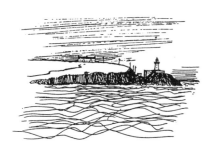

Baily Lighthouse, Howth, 1813. Designed by George Halpin. An earlier lighthouse was built in the eighteenth century on the summit of Howth, but it was too often obscured by fog, for which reason its successor was built down on the promontary close to the sea. Fragments of the earlier lighthouse can be seen built into a cottage to the east of the summit carpark.

Saint Fintan's Church, Carrickbrack Road, Shielmartin, Sutton, twelfth century. A very interesting and curious building, its diminutive size makes it the smallest ecclesiastical building on the shores of Dublin Bay and one of the smallest in the country. It has been much encroached upon by gravestones as can be seen when compared to nineteenth-century drawings of the church.

St Mary's Abbey, Howth Village, fourteenth and fifteenth centuries. The Norse king of Dublin, Sitric, founded a church here in the eleventh century, of which no evidence remains. The present medieval building is an amalgam of successive additions, the most recent of which is the sixteenth-century bell cote. The bells are to be seen on the terrace of Howth Castle.

Corr Castle, Deerpark, Howth Road, fifteenth century. Tower house attached to the demesne of Howth Castle, it acted as an outpost on the isthmus of Sutton.

Bibliography

MAPS

Brooking C., *The City of Dublin 1728* (Dublin 1988)
Clarke H.B., *Dublin 840 - 1540* (Dublin 1978)
Kissane N., *Historic Dublin Maps* (Dublin 1989)
National Library, *Ireland from Maps* (Dublin 1980)
O'Sullivan A.J., (text) *et al*, *Dublin Bay Map Guide* (Dublin 1988)
Roque J., *Two Maps of 18th C. Dublin* (Kent 1977)
Taylor J., *Environs of Dublin, 1816* (Dublin 1989)
Taylor J., *Dun Laoghaire 1843* (Dublin 1989)
Taylor J., *Dublin City 1849* (Dublin 1989)

DUBLIN BAY

Brunton M. *et al*, *Managing Dublin Bay* (Dublin 1987)
ERU, *Dublin Bay, Water Quality* (Dublin 1989)
O'Rafferty T., *A Future for Dublin Bay?* (Dublin 1984)
O'Sullivan D., *Dublin Bay, A Century of Sailing* (Dublin 1984)
Various authors, *Dublin Bay, An Outstanding Natural Resource at Risk* (Dublin 1989)

DUBLIN PORT

Brady, Shipman, Martin, *Landscape Development* (Dublin 1989)
Cahill G. *et al*, *Dublin City Quays* (Dublin 1986)
Gilligan H.A., *A History of Dublin Port* (Dublin 1988)
McCarthy *et al*, *Development Plan* (Dublin 1988)
McCarthy *et al*, *Environmental Impact Study* (Dublin 1989)
Various authors, *Custom House Docks Financial Services Centre* (Dublin 1989)

THE LIFFEY

De Courcy J., Conlin S., *Anna Liffey, The River of Dublin* (Dublin 1988)
Healy E., Moriarty C., O'Flaherty G., *The Book of the Liffey, From Source to Sea* (Dublin 1988)

GENERAL

Brady H. *et al*, *Dublin, A City in Crisis* (Dublin 1975)
Brennan C. *et al*, *Sculpture at East Link* (Dublin 1985)
Craig M., *The Architecture of Ireland* (London & Dublin 1982)
Craig M., *Dublin 1660-1860* (Dublin 1969)
Craig M., Glin Kt of, *Ireland Observed* (Cork 1970)
Dixon Hardy P., *The Dublin Penny Journal* (Dublin 1834-36)
Dunton J., *A Merry Ramble to the Wild Irish* (Dublin 1982)
Gaskin J.J., *Varieties of Irish History* (Dublin 1869)
Gerald of Wales, *The History and Topography of Ireland* (London 1982)
Hall A.M. & S.C., *Halls' Ireland* (London 1984)
Harbison P., *Guide to the National Monuments of Ireland* (Dublin 1975)
Joyce J., *Ulysses* (London 1955)
Joyce W. St J., *The Neighbourhood of Dublin* (Dublin 1988)
Leask H.G., *Irish Churches and Monastic Buildings* (Dundalk 1967)
Malins E. & Glin Kt of, *Lost Demesnes* (London 1976)
Maxwell C., *Dublin under the Georges* (Dublin 1979)
McBrierty V.J. *et al*, *The Howth Peninsula* (Dublin 1981)
McCoil L., *The Book of Blackrock* (Dublin 1977)
McDonald F., *The Destruction of Dublin* (Dublin 1985)
McIntyre D., *The Meadow and the Bull* (Dublin 1987)
McKenna D., *A History of Sandymount, Irishtown, Ringsend* (Dublin 1989)
O'Brien F., *The Dalkey Archive* (London 1986)
O'Neill A., *The Hill of Howth* (Dublin 1971)
O'Sullivan J. & Cannon S., *The Book of Dun Laoghaire* (Dublin 1987)
Pearson P., *Dun Laoghaire-Kingstown* (Dublin 1981)
Plunkett J., *Strumpet City* (London 1969)
Strong L.A.G., *Sea Wall* (London 1933)
Strong L.A.G., *The Garden* (London 1931)

Acknowledgements

I would like to thank the individuals and the staff of various institutions who were helpful to me in the course of working on this book.
The National Library of Ireland; Dun Laoghaire, Dalkey and the ILAC Centre Public Libraries; Niall Walsh and the Sculptors Society of Ireland; Robert Nicholson, Curator, the James Joyce Museum and Dublin and East Tourism; Terry Durney and the Custom House Dock Development Authority; Dudley Stewart, The Bolton Trust; Bill Taylor and Gerry Keily, Dublin Port; The National Maritime Museum of Ireland; Anne Grady, National Parks and Monuments Service of the Office of Public Works; Anna Logan, Chief Guide, the Casino, Marino; Freddie Kay, Commissioners of Irish Lights; Brendan Ebrill, secretary, Dublin Bay Sailing Club; Hal Sisk, Lawrence Thompson, Fionan de Barra, Eithne Kipper, Patricia Haugaard.
To all the many people who gave me advice, suggestions, impressions and encouragement I would like to convey my sincere thanks, in particular to Jack O'Sullivan for sharing his enthusiasm for Dublin Bay, and also to those who helped me unwittingly in the many casual encounters on beaches and breakwaters, as they contributed individual perspectives which enriched my own.